THE BRITISH FINANCIAL SYSTEM

The
British Financial
System

Jack Revell

MACMILLAN

First published 1973 by
THE MACMILLAN PRESS LTD
London and Basingstoke
Associated companies in New York Dublin
Melbourne Johannesburg and Madras

SBN 333 07702 4 (hard cover)
333 14925 4 (paper cover)

Printed in Great Britain by
HAZELL WATSON & VINEY LTD
Aylesbury, Bucks

To Pat

Contents

PART B.   THE BANKING SYSTEM

Chapter 5.   The Banking System and the Bank of England

Chapter 6.   Deposit Banks

Chapter 7.   The Banking Mechanism

Chapter 8.   The Discount Market

Chapter 9.   Secondary Banks

Chapter 10. Parallel Money Markets

Chapter 11. The International Money Market

PART C. OTHER DEPOSIT INSTITUTIONS

Chapter 12. Finance Houses

Chapter 13. Savings Banks

Chapter 14. Building Societies

PART D. OTHER FINANCIAL INSTITUTIONS

Chapter 15.   Insurance Companies and Pension Funds

Chapter 16.   Investment Trust Companies and Unit Trusts

Chapter 17.   Special Investment Agencies

Preface

For some years I have been struck by the fact that there is no book which deals with all types of British financial institution on a consistent basis within a single volume. To one who has a strong conviction that theoretical insight in monetary and financial matters depends greatly on knowledge of the institutions and markets which make up the financial system this has seemed a glaring gap. The present volume is a modest attempt to fill the gap. Most of the text is taken up with detailed analysis of the working of different types of financial institution and markets, but the first four chapters set this in context by considering the financial system as a whole and by providing some generalisations on what the different institutions and markets have in common. It is in this last sphere that further research is badly needed.

A work of this nature is bound to have a high factual content, but I have attempted, all too imperfectly in most places, to supplement this with an analysis of the significance of the facts. We are concerned with financial institutions as business organisations, and try to see what factors determine their operation and their development. Even this restricted object has resulted in a lengthy volume; it has been kept down to its present length by avoiding the discussion of the historical background, of monetary theory and of monetary policy except where these were immediately relevant.

I started to write this book some six years ago, but little progress was made until 1971 because of a variety of academic and administrative commitments. As it turned out this was a fortunate thing, because in the middle of September 1971 the Bank of England introduced sweeping changes into its regulation of banks and finance houses which had repercussions throughout the financial system. It has been said that the British financial system has changed more during the last twenty years than during the whole of the preceding century. An author who tries to be up-to-date in this field faces an impossible task: many further changes will have occurred before his work appears in print. This volume was corrected up to the middle of July 1972, and a very few additional corrections were made in the winter of that year. For changes since that date the reader must find his own way among the sources suggested in the General Notes. I hope that the background knowledge which he has gained from this book will make his task easy.

The writings of previous authors form a smaller part of the raw material on which this work is based than of most economic texts. This is not because of any lack of respect for what has been written by others but arises out of a belief that those who take part in the business of finance have a lot to teach academics. The factual basis thus came from a great deal of 'leg work' in the City of London and elsewhere, meeting and discussing with officers of the various associations of financial institutions and with executives of the institutions themselves. They are far too numerous to mention, but I owe them all a big debt for lengthy discussions, pleasant lunches and their kindness in commenting on my drafts. Many of them will doubtless recognise some of their own ideas in the pages that follow. A special word of thanks is due to my friends in the Bank of England, who spent many hours scanning successive drafts and trying to purge them of errors.

Among academic colleagues I am grateful to Professor Ronald Henderson, who first awakened my interest in this subject and asked me to take over his lectures in Cambridge while he was on sabbatical leave. Professor James Meade, Aubrey Silberston and Professor Richard Stone encouraged me to start writing this book. Professor Andrew Bain, Tony Cramp, Professor Max Gaskin, Stephanie Holmans, Jeffrey Owens, Alan Roe, Professor Brian Tew and Michael Wright made helpful comments on several chapters. My friend and colleague Frank Townson kept track of the drafts in the early stages and spotted many errors. Despite all this help from academic colleagues and friends in the financial world, doubtless some errors persist, and for these I alone am responsible.

The preparation of the final typescript, the typing of the tables and the drawing of the figures were done most competently by Lilian Lund. Lilian Silk, Jenny Bursey and Rosemary Mason typed some of the earlier drafts, and Meriel Jones, Paula Jones and Marian Waters helped in the final preparation. Angela Cooper provided considerable help in proof reading and in preparing the index.

More than convention dictates that the final word of acknowledgement should be to my wife. For years she has cheerfully accepted 'the book' as sufficient excuse for innumerable lapses on my part. As a slight recompense this book is dedicated to her.

Bangor, May 1973   JACK REVELL

General Notes

1. Suggestions for further reading will be found at the end of most chapters, but these are only books which deal with the topics of the chapter. For general background reading a study of the *Report*, *Memoranda of Evidence* and *Minutes of Evidence* of the Radcliffe Committee will be found a most useful source. They will serve to show how much the financial system of this country has changed over the period since 1959. For changes which have occurred since the writing of this book the reader should consult the current literature. Articles in the *Bank of England Quarterly Bulletin* will be found particularly useful, and a study of current issues of such journals as *Midland Bank Review*, *The Banker, The Bankers' Magazine, Building Societies' Gazette, Money Management and Unitholder* and *Euromoney* will fill in many gaps.

2. Because of the limitations on space a great deal of weight has been placed on the tables in this volume, and they should be studied carefully. It is always a useful exercise to go to current issues of the sources given at the foot of most tables and to fill in recent figures.

3. *Abbreviations and notation used in tables*

BV	book value
MV	market value
NV	nominal value
–	nil or negligible
...	not available or not applicable

4. Because of rounding totals often differ from the sum of constituent items.

5. References to tables in the *Bank of England Quarterly Bulletin* are to the Statistical Annex unless page numbers are given.

PART A

The Financial System as a Whole

1 Structure of the Financial System

1. THE BASIC STRUCTURE

A. *The national balance sheet*

A book that aims at describing and analysing the financial system of any country must devote a great deal of its space to the working of the various financial institutions and financial markets, but these are not the whole of the financial system, and they are not even an essential part of it. Of course, no financial system can develop very far without the aid of specialised financial institutions and financial markets, but there are still primitive economies in which they play little or no part. The essential feature of any financial system consists of a number of financial inter-relationships between the persons and bodies that make up an economy, and the basic structure of a financial system has three features: (1) the extent of these financial inter-relationships, (2) the forms of the financial claims in which the inter-relationships are expressed and (3) the pattern of relationships between persons and bodies of different kinds, between independent 'economic units' as we shall term them in future. The form of social accounting statement which exposes the basic structure of a financial system is a national balance sheet, a specimen of which for the United Kingdom is shown in Table 1.1.

While many readers will be familiar with the form and structure of the national income and expenditure accounts as given in the annual Blue Book, and may even have noticed that these have been extended in recent years to cover financial transactions, few of them will have seen a national balance sheet because it represents a relatively new development in social accounting. Before we can use the information in Table 1.1 to describe the basic structure of the British financial system, we must therefore explain the basic characteristics of a national balance sheet.

Conceptually a national balance sheet has exactly the same relationship to the national income and expenditure and financial transactions accounts as a company balance sheet has to the profit and loss account. Both forms of balance sheet present a snapshot at a particu-

Table 1.1   National balance sheet of the United Kingdom,
            31 December 1966

£ hundred million

	Personal sector	Financial institutions	Non-financial companies	Public sector	All national sectors	Rest of the world	Total
A. Physical assets	523	26	476	412	1,437	–	1,437
B. Financial assets							
1. Money	83	37	40	15	175	46	221
2. Near-money	148	41	5	–	194	16	210
3. Bonds	55	91	16	3	165	17	182
4. Shares & debentures	174	120	30	8	332	12	344
5. Overseas claims	19	25	74	2	120	44	164
6. Loans	14	190	7	172	383	34	417
7. Debtors	47	5	73	42	167	3	170
8. Life policies	206	–	–	–	206	–	206
Total	746	509	245	242	1,742	172	1,914
C. Liabilities							
1. Money	–	176	–	33	209	12	221
2. Near-money	–	95	13	102	210	1	210
3. Bonds	–	–	–	182	182	–	182
4. Shares & debentures	–	69	275	–	344	–	344
5. Overseas claims	–	2	42	–	44	120	164
6. Loans	116	4	58	188	366	51	417
7. Creditors	35	10	91	28	164	6	170
8. Life funds	–	148	–	58	206	–	206
Total	151	504	479	591	1,725	189	1,914
D. Net worth (A + B - C)	1,118	31	242	63	1,454	-17	1,437

lar point of time, and summarise the position which the organisation has reached as a result of all its past activity. Whereas all the other forms of account are concerned with changes during a particular period, the *flows* during the period, the balance sheet is concerned with the *stocks* of assets and liabilities, the amounts held and outstanding on the date to which the balance sheet refers. If we are concerned with the financial structure of a company—the extent of its liabilities outstanding, whether it has a large or small volume of cash and other liquid assets which can be used to tide over a period in which expenditure is greater than receipts and so on—we naturally look to the balance sheet to expose the situation at a glance; in exactly the same way we look to the national balance sheet to expose the basic structure of a financial system.

At first sight Table 1.1 looks quite different from the normal balance sheet to which most readers will be accustomed, but this is only because the items have been rearranged somewhat. The normal form of a company balance sheet can be summarised as follows:

Liabilities	*Assets*
Capital	Fixed assets
Reserves	Current assets
Long-term liabilities	
Current liabilities	

(American practice puts assets on the left-hand side and liabilities on the right-hand side.) Both sides of the balance sheet add up to the same total, and there is an item, usually found under the heading of 'reserves', which is a residual to ensure that the two sides balance. Leaving aside the differences in terminology, which are not very significant in this context, we can see that there would be very little difference in form and layout from a company balance sheet if we had set out the national balance sheet in the following form:

Liabilities	*Assets*
C. Liabilities	A. Physical assets
D. Net worth	B. Financial assets

In other words, there is no difference between a form which leads to the expression $D = A + B - C$ and one which leads to the expression $C + D = A + B$. We have adopted our particular form for a national balance sheet because it suits the purposes that we have in mind, but it will be found that company balance sheets are increasingly being set out in a form very close to this one.

While the difference in layout between a national balance sheet and a company balance sheet is thus one of form only, there are some important differences between the two types of balance sheet. These arise mainly because the purposes of business accounting and social accounting are quite different. The purpose of business accounting—and the same is true of the accounting of charities, clubs and public authorities —is to show what has happened to the money which has been put at the disposal of the directors and managers of the organisation. This leads naturally to the valuation of all the assets at what they cost when they were purchased. Less logically it leads to the valuation of all liabilities at the amount which will have to be paid out when the liabilities are redeemed, without taking any account of the varying dates on which they are due for redemption. Accountants do worry over the distortions which are produced in balance sheets as a result of inflation, but they have not succeeded in evolving a form of accounts which can cope with the problem of inflation while still showing the stewardship of the directors over the sums entrusted to them. When current values get badly out of line with those shown in the balance sheet, accountants often revalue certain items in the main balance sheet or give a note of the current value. We can thus say that conventional balance sheets of all types consist of items valued at original cost as amended by subsequent revaluations. These are the 'book values' to which we shall be referring throughout this work.

A national balance sheet, however, has quite a different purpose. It is designed to show the position which a whole economy and its constituent economic units have reached at a particular point of time and to show the basic structure of the economy, whereas a company balance sheet is concerned only with one economic unit. The purpose of a national balance sheet cannot be fulfilled if the items from different economic units are valued differently according to the price level at the time that items were acquired; the same item must be valued identically, no matter who happens to own or hold it. This leads naturally to the proposition that in a national balance sheet all items must be valued at current prices because there is no other price level which can be applied consistently across the board. We say that all items are valued at 'market values'; where there is no market on which items are traded or where the markets that exist are for obsolescent items or for bankrupt stock, we must construct a value that has the same conceptual basis as a true market value. Some economists would disagree strongly with applying the same basis of market valuation to liabilities because they hold that companies and other organisations make their decisions in the light of the value of a debt at redemption. However, we shall see later that the market value is an approximation to the *present* value of a debt that is due for redemption some time hence, and once again it is present or current values which should be used.

B. *Financial and real wealth*

We can now turn back to Table 1.1 and see what it tells us about the nature of the financial system. We have already defined the essential feature of any financial system as the set of financial inter-relationships between independent economic units. If we want to show relationships between units in the economy, we obviously cannot be content with one column of figures showing the balance sheet of the whole economy, but equally we must summarise drastically to produce a single table to show the structure rather than the details. This leads to the grouping of all the economic units into four broad sectors within the economy and to the addition of a fifth sector for the rest of the world. These five sectors are the same sectors as are used in the national income and expenditure accounts (the Blue Book).

Sectors are merely statistical abstractions; they do not have any real existence in the same way that the independent economic units do. It is the independent economic units which have financial links and not sectors, and so the national balance sheet shows links between economic units in the same sector as well as links between economic units in different sectors. In accounting terminology the sector balance sheets are *combined* balance sheets of all economic units in the sectors, and not *consolidated* sector balance sheets.

The first line in Table 1.1 consists of a set of figures for the value of physical assets, comprising land and the buildings erected thereon, the productive plant and equipment of industry, stocks and work in progress and consumer durables (motor cars, furniture, television sets, washing machines and other items of household equipment). The physical assets represent the real wealth of the community. There follow two blocks of figures, the first showing the financial assets held by each sector and the second the liabilities of each sector. The financial claims comprising financial assets and liabilities are split into the same eight groups. The table is completed by a row for 'net worth', which is merely the result of adding together physical and financial assets and subtracting liabilities.

The first point to be dealt with concerns only the 'total' column of Table 1.1. A glance at the two blocks of financial items in this column will verify that each of the figures under financial assets is repeated without change under liabilities. Since financial assets and liabilities cancel out in this column, it necessarily follows that total net worth is equal to the total value of physical assets.

The fact that each individual type of financial claim has the same total under assets and under liabilities and that financial assets in total are equal to liabilities in total has a clear implication: a financial claim must be at one and the same time an asset to one economic unit and a liability to another. A financial claim represents a link between two economic units, and each will record the claim in its balance sheet, one as an asset and the other as a liability. That this is so can be seen readily if we take some examples of financial claims. Bonds are issued by the central government and by local authorities (both in the public sector); they are liabilities of central government and local authorities. At the same time bonds are held as assets by economic units in every sector, and the total value of bonds should be the same whether we count up the bond holdings of individual economic units or whether we add together the liabilities of the central government and of local authorities. Like nearly all the measurements made in compiling a national balance sheet the two totals are never exactly the same when they are directly measured. In Table 1.1 we have removed all the statistical discrepancies, so that all totals which ought in principle to be equal are in fact equal.

A further and more homely example should clinch the point. If I lend you £100, I have an asset of £100 and you have a liability to me of £100. The same point can be made equally well for all the different types of financial claim included under the various sub-groups shown in the table. Each of them is at one and the same time an asset to one economic unit and a liability to another. We shall be considering the various types of financial claim that make up the sub-groups and the characteristics of financial claims in general in Chapter 2, and we do not need to go into them here. A word must be said, however, about the special position of company shares.

Shares are of two kinds, preference and ordinary shares, but neither sort is a debt owed by one economic unit to another. The shareholders of a company are in law the owners of the company, and they cannot owe themselves a debt. Quite naturally a shareholder would include the value of company shares which he owned among his assets when he was drawing up his balance sheet, but there is no sense in which the company owes the shareholder the market value of his share; the market value of the share serves only to inform the present shareholder what he could get for his share if he sold it to somebody else, and the company does not come into this transaction. However, the cancellation of financial claims would not work unless we showed an imputed debt equal to the value of shares held as assets. Normally we should separate the imputed debt from proper liabilities, but for our immediate purpose it is more useful to include share capital as a liability entry along with the other liabilities. A more general point arises here: the cancellation of financial claims in a national balance sheet would equally not work out if we gave different values to the same financial claim as an asset and as a liability. Some economists would contend that liabilities should be valued differently from assets. If this were done, the basic structure of the financial system would be obscured in the table, but the facts of the case would not be altered. These are that any financial claim involves two economic units, to one of which it is an asset and to the other a liability (or share capital).

Two essential features of any financial system can now be summarised. (1) A financial system consists of a network of financial links between economic units, a web of debts and shares. (2) The financial system is a superstructure erected on the basis of the real wealth of the community. In Table 1.1 the total of real wealth is £143,700 million. Erected on this basis is a superstructure of financial claims to a total value of £191,400 million, and the total value of financial claims is 1·3 times the value of real wealth. This particular ratio differs markedly between countries, even between highly developed countries with sophisticated financial systems, and the United Kingdom has the highest ratio of any country for which we can work out the figures. It is quite natural to inquire what determines the ratio of the value of financial claims to the value of real wealth and whether a high ratio is a sign of financial development. These questions are best answered later in this chapter after we have considered the circumstances in which financial claims are issued.

C. *Net worth and national wealth*

So far we have been concerned only with the total column of Table 1.1, and it is only for this column that the cancellation of financial assets and liabilities holds. This total column results from adding across the figures for the four sectors into which the national economy of the United Kingdom is divided, together with the figures for the rest of the world; it does not hold for individual sectors or for the sum of the four national sectors shown in the column headed 'all national sectors'. The financial system which we are examining is thus broader in scope than the nation; it includes also the financial links between U.K. residents and the residents of other countries.

Each of the columns of the table is completed with a figure for 'net worth', which is derived by adding together all the assets, both physical and financial, owned by economic units within the sector and then deducting their total liabilities. Net worth is thus a very simple concept. If you or I were asked to work out how much we were worth, we should naturally begin by listing the values of all our assets (a house, a motor car, money in the bank, building society deposits, company shares and so on) and adding them up. Then we should do the same for our liabilities (the mortgage on the house, hire purchase debt and perhaps a bank overdraft), and arrive at a net figure. This net figure would be our net worth. The extent to which financial assets were balanced by liabilities would differ for each economic unit, and there would be no necessary cancelling of financial claims.

As we should expect in a human society, the bulk of net worth is attributable to the personal sector. At first sight, indeed, it is somewhat surprising that there can be net worth in other sectors, but this arises because each balance sheet of individual economic units which is added together to form the sector balance sheets can contain only those items which that economic unit can appropriate to itself. Government offices, coal mines and local authority houses are owned collectively by the whole community, but no individual would think of claiming his share of them as part of his own wealth. A somewhat similar situation arises with companies. There is no reason why the total value found by valuing each item separately of the various physical and financial assets owned by companies *less* the liabilities to third parties should exactly equal the value which the stock exchange places on the shares of the company at any moment of time; the difference, whether it is positive or negative, has to be entered as the net worth of the company because no individual shareholder can appropriate it while the company is continuing in business.

The other point to which we must direct attention is the net worth of the financial institutions sector. This is relatively very small because the liabilities of financial institutions are very nearly equal to their financial assets. We shall see later in this chapter that the function of financial institutions is to come between lenders and borrowers; they issue claims of one sort to lenders and acquire claims of another sort issued by borrowers, and this necessarily involves a near equality in their financial assets and liabilities.

This concept of net worth can be applied to the nation as well as to individual economic units and to sectors. One measure of what the nation is worth, or 'national wealth' as it is called, comes from the net worth figure in the column headed 'all national sectors', but the same answer can be obtained by another route. The cancellation of financial claims within the four national sectors is incomplete only to the relatively small extent that financial claims issued by U.K. economic units are held by residents of the rest of the world and that financial claims issued by residents of the rest of the world are held by U.K. residents. The major part of national wealth is thus going to consist of physical assets located within the United Kingdom, but to this figure we must add the value of net claims of U.K. residents on the rest of the world, or the 'net foreign balance'. At the end of 1966 the net worth of the rest of the world sector was −£1700 million, and the net foreign balance was the same figure with its sign reversed. The reversal of sign is necessary because the figures in the rest of the world sector column view matters from the point of view of the rest of the world: its assets are claims on us, and its liabilities are our claims on overseas residents. The net foreign balance views the position from our point of view. National wealth at the end of 1966 was thus £145,400 million, whether we take the net worth of all national sectors or add together the value of physical assets and the net foreign balance (143,700 + 1700 = 145,400).

2. FINANCIAL TRANSACTIONS AND REVALUATIONS

A. *How financial claims arise*

While we were concerned with the basic structure of the financial system, we examined the national balance sheet, which showed the *stock* of assets and liabilities at a moment of time. When we come to consider how financial claims arise, we are concerned with the *flow* of financial activity over a period of time, and this is shown in another form of social account, a financial transactions table. This table has several different forms, each of which is given a different name— sources and uses of funds table, sector financing table or flow of funds table, for example—but all the forms are presenting basically the same information, and we need examine only one of them.

To understand a financial transactions table we must first explain the concepts of *financial surplus* and *financial deficit* as they apply both to individual economic units and to the groupings of economic units called sectors. Basically an economic unit or a sector is said to have a financial surplus in a given period, a year or a quarter usually, if the total of its receipts is greater than the total of its expenditure; it has a financial deficit if the total of its expenditure is greater than the total of its receipts. It goes without saying that the coverage of both receipts and expenditure must be complete, with receipts including income and transfers on current or capital account which have been received and expenditure including capital formation (the purchase of physical assets) and any transfers on capital or current account which have been made.

In practice the figures for the financial surpluses or deficits of sectors are arrived at by first striking a figure of saving for each sector. Saving is equal to total income (including current transfers received net of current transfers made) *less* consumption expenditure. The financial surplus or deficit is then equal to saving *less* all expenditure on capital account, which comprises gross fixed capital formation, the increase in the value of stocks and work in progress and capital taxes and transfers (death duties, for example).

We can express the concept of financial surpluses and deficits symbolically by adapting the familiar Keynesian notation. If we use Y for all income (including current transfers), C for all current expenditure and I for all capital expenditure, we can complete the system by adding a new symbol, F, for financial surplus or deficit. We can then write

$$Y_i - C_i = S_i$$
$$S_i - I_i = F_i.$$

At first sight this expression appears to be nonsense, because $S \equiv I$, but this identity holds only for the economy as a whole; it does not apply to the individual economic unit or sector denoted by the subscript i. Indeed, the problem of finance arises precisely because saving does not equal investment for individual economic units or for sectors.

Our real interest begins when the figures for the financial surpluses and deficits of sectors have been struck, because we are concerned to identify the financial transactions the total value of which will add up to the surplus or deficit. If an economic unit has a financial surplus it must on balance do either or both of two things: it must buy financial assets and/or pay off outstanding debt. If an economic unit has a financial deficit it can finance it in either or both of two ways: it must sell financial assets which it owns and/or incur new debt (borrowing). These four possibilities can be set out schematically as follows, with a plus sign indicating an increase and a minus sign a decrease:

	Surplus	*Deficit*
Assets	+	−
Liabilities	−	+

So far we have allowed for only one complication, the fact that an economic unit may follow both of the possibilities open at the same time. If it has a surplus, it may buy some new financial assets and pay off some outstanding liabilities, the net total of its two sets of transactions equalling its financial surplus. If it has a deficit, it may both sell some financial assets and incur new liabilities (borrowing). The real situation is rather more complicated in two directions. In the first place an enonomic unit with a financial surplus may buy financial assets to a value greater than its surplus, the difference being made up by borrowing, or it may sell some financial assets and buy fresh ones to a greater value than the previous ones. If it has a deficit, it may actually buy some additional financial assets and borrow to a greater amount than its deficit, or it may redeem some debt and incur new debt to a value equal to its deficit plus the redeemed debt. Any combination of plus and minus signs for assets and liabilities is possible, the only limitation being that the net total of plus and minus for assets and liabilities must equal the financial surplus or deficit. In the second place we must reckon with the fact that within any sector some economic units will have a financial surplus at the same time that others have a financial deficit. When we come to measure actual financial transactions and set them out in a table for the various sectors, we are almost certain to be netting off sales by some economic units against purchases by other economic units in the same sector.

A fresh financial claim arises whenever an act of borrowing or of issuing share capital takes place. The lending unit has an increase in its assets, and the borrowing unit has an increase in its liabilities. Correspondingly the redemption of debt leads to a reduction in the value of financial claims outstanding, implying a reduction in the assets of the lending unit and a reduction in the liabilities of the borrowing unit. Since all financial activity involves equal movements in both assets and liabilities and in the same direction, it can readily be seen that over the economy as a whole all financial surpluses and deficits must balance out. If we leave aside the fairly rare occasions on which surplus units add to their borrowing in order to finance the purchase of financial assets to a value greater than their surplus, the financial system can be seen as a means whereby the financial surpluses of some economic units are transferred to deficit units.

By itself this description of the way in which financial claims arise does not take us very far, and we must probe further into the process.

To simplify the exposition we shall assume that only economic units with a financial deficit incur fresh borrowing and that only units with a surplus are in a position to redeem outstanding debt, and we shall concentrate on the origin of financial deficits. Since we arrive at the figure for the financial surplus or deficit by first assessing saving (the difference between income and expenditure on current account) and deducting from it capital formation and net capital transfers made, it seems reasonable to say, as a first approximation, that an economic unit will have a financial deficit if the capital formation undertaken by it together with the net capital transfers which it has made add up to more than its saving over the same period. Since capital transfers are a small element in the situation, we can simplify further and say that a deficit arises when a unit's capital formation (or investment) is greater than its saving.

Although this statement is an over-simplification, it nevertheless expresses a most important part of the truth. It is quite obvious that the most important reason for which a company issues fresh financial claims, either by borrowing or by issuing new share capital, is to finance extensions to its capital equipment. Similarly the most important single reason for which households incur debt (not being incorporated they cannot issue share capital) is for the finance of capital formation in the form of house purchase.

The statement is an over-simplification in two main directions. (1) A deficit arises because expenditure in total, covering both current and capital expenditure, is greater than income in total. An economic unit may well engage in no capital formation and yet have a deficit because its consumption expenditure is greater than its income. (2) There is an important group of economic units, financial institutions, which have relatively very small financial surpluses or deficits and yet issue large volumes of financial claims.

The first point involves us in considering the boundary between consumption (current) expenditure and capital expenditure. The simple distinction is that capital expenditure is on goods which will last beyond the period during which the expenditure is being measured, whereas the goods and services purchased with consumption expenditure are consumed within the period and have no continuing physical existence. For the most part there can be no dispute about the sorts of goods the purchase of which involves capital expenditure and which are as a consequence included in the national balance sheet as physical assets. Land and buildings, plant and equipment and stocks of goods are all obvious cases. There is, however, one important class of goods expenditure on which is classed as consumption in the national income accounts, but which we have included among the physical assets of the national balance sheet. These are consumer durables, such as private motor cars, television sets, washing machines, furniture and similar household goods. We have included them in the national balance sheet because they are so often bought with borrowed funds; if the liabilities are shown, it seems reasonable to include the goods as assets.

The second point mentioned above brings us to the ways in which financial institutions (banks, insurance companies, building societies, investment trust companies and similar bodies) differ from other economic units. For the most part they do little saving and little capital formation, and their financial surpluses or deficits are very small relative to the volume of funds which they handle. Their *raison d'être* is the channelling of funds from surplus units to deficit units, and they do this by creating two financial claims where normally one would suffice; a surplus unit lends to a financial institution in a form that suits the lending unit's convenience, and the financial institution lends to a deficit unit in a form that suits the latter's convenience. Financial institutions borrow, not in order to finance their own deficits, but in order to finance the deficits of other units. That part of financing activity which goes through financial institutions thus results in double the value of financial claims compared with that part that goes direct from surplus unit to deficit unit. Indeed it may be more than double since often more than one financial institution is involved in the chain: surplus unit A lending to financial institution B, which lends to financial institution C, which passes the finance on to deficit unit D.

We can now see what determines the total value of financial claims (net of the value of claims redeemed) issued during a period. In the first place it depends on the extent to which some units are in financial surplus while other units are in financial deficit. The greater the reliance of economic units on their own saving, whether that of the current period or that of a past period held in the form of financial assets, the lower the value of financial claims issued during the period; the smaller the reliance on their own saving, the higher the value of financial claims issued. In the second place the net value of financial claims issued will be higher if a large proportion of funds is channelled through financial institutions, with their multiplier effect on the value of claims issued, rather than direct from surplus unit to deficit unit.

B. *Financial transactions*

So far our discussion of the issue of financial claims has been rather abstract, and we can make the process clearer by considering actual figures. At the same time we can deal with financial transactions as a whole, comprising transactions in existing claims as well as the issue of new claims. Table 1.2 shows identified financial transactions during 1966, the year leading up to the national balance sheet of Table 1.1. The titles of the rows and columns are identical to those of Table 1.1, except that physical assets are necessarily omitted from a table which

Table 1.2   Financial transactions table, 1966

£ hundred million

	Personal sector	Financial institutions	Non-financial companies	Public sector	All national sectors	Rest of the world	Total
A. Financial surplus (+)/ *deficit (−)*	20	−	−10	−12	−2	2	−
B. Financial assets							
1. Money	3	4	2	2	11	7	18
2. Near-money	8	1	−	−	9	1	10
3. Bonds	2	4	1	−	7	−	7
4. Shares & debentures	−4	14	3	2	15	−2	13
5. Overseas claims	−1	1	5	−3	2	9	11
6. Loans	1	18	1	17	37	1	38
7. Debtors	2	1	6	1	10	−	10
8. Life policies	17	−	−	−	17	−	17
Total	28	43	18	19	108	16	124
C. Liabilities							
1. Money	−	16	−	2	18	−	18
2. Near-money	−	11	−	−1	10	−	10
3. Bonds	−	−	−	7	7	−	7
4. Shares & debentures	−	2	11	−	13	−	13
5. Overseas claims	−	−	9	−	9	2	11
6. Loans	6	−	3	17	26	12	38
7. Creditors	2	1	5	2	10	−	10
8. Life funds	−	13	−	4	17	−	17
Total	8	43	28	31	110	14	124

deals only with financial transactions. Once again statistical discrepancies have been removed from the figures as derived from the original sources, and in this case the adjustment has had to be rather more arbitrary than with the national balance sheet. As a result many of the figures given in the table and quoted in the text will not agree with those shown in the relevant statistics of the Bank of England and the Central Statistical Office. They are to be regarded as illustrations of principles, although for the most part they are close to what actually happened in 1966.

Table 1.2 exhibits many of the features which our previous discussion would lead us to expect. In the first place the total column is once again completely symmetrical between financial assets and liabilities, not only overall but also for each individual row. This is a necessary reflection of the fact that each financial claim is simultaneously an asset to one economic unit and a liability to another. In the second place the net total of the financial surpluses and deficits of all sectors, arrived at by deducting the additional liabilities incurred during the year from the additional financial assets acquired during the year, comes to zero. Indeed on these figures the financial system is seen as a means of putting the financial surplus of the personal sector at the disposal of the other national sectors, aided in this year by the rest of the world. In the third place we find that financial institutions, which had by far the largest value of transactions, had neither surplus nor deficit, reflecting their essentially intermediary role.

There is one important respect in which the financial assets half of the table is not symmetrical wth the liabilities half: whereas existing liabilities are only rarely transferred from one economic unit to another, existing financial assets are constantly being traded between economic units. This statement can be true of nearly all kinds of financial asset, but the transfer between economic units takes place only rarely for the last three items shown (loans, debtors and life policies). The statement is particularly true of the third and fourth items, bonds and shares, which are mostly marketable securities, with a highly organised market in the stock exchange.

As we have already pointed out, there is a good deal of netting out of transactions between economic units in the same sector in the figures of Table 1.2, so that the extent of transfers of existing financial assets between economic units is obscured in the table. The row marked 'shares and debentures' does, however, show up this trading in existing assets. The total value of shares and debentures issued during the year was £1300 million, but financial institutions alone (largely insurance companies and pension funds in this instance) bought £1400 million, and purchases by non-financial companies and the public sector accounted between them for a further £500 million. The shares needed for this excess of purchases over new issues were supplied by the personal sector, which ran down its holding by £400 million, and the rest of the world.[1]

Although financial claims are split down into eight broad groups in Tables 1.1 and 1.2, very few of the headings suggest the familiar titles of financial claims which are included in the items. The different types of financial claim will be described in detail in Chapter 2 and there is no need to anticipate here, but we can clothe the figures of Table 1.2 with flesh and bone by splitting down some of the items into their constituent parts, and following those transactions involving financial institutions through to their ultimate destination.

We can usefully start with the personal sector. The increase of £300 million (in round figures) of money balances held was composed of an increase of about £40 million in holdings of notes and coin (although this figure is only a very rough estimate) and an increase of £250 million of bank deposits. Likewise the increase of £800 million in the holdings of near-money was composed of several parts: a net decrease of £100 million in holdings of national savings certificates, premium bonds and so on, a £725 million increase in deposits with building societies and an £85 million increase in deposits with savings banks. The increase of £200 million in holdings of bonds was the result of taking up that amount of local authority debt, most of it in the form of the generally unmarketable local authority mortgages. The largest single item is the increase of £1700 million in life policies, covering not only normal life and endowment assurance but also rights in all types of pension scheme. Among liabilities the increase of £600 million in loans consisted of £100 million in miscellaneous loans and £674 million of loans for house purchase, mainly from building societies but also from insurance companies and local authorities, partly offset by a drop of £90 million in hire purchase and similar debt and by a decrease of the same amount in borrowing from banks.

There is one of these sets of financial transactions which we can trace through. The £1700 million increase in personal sector holdings of life policies has its counterpart in the increase of £1300 million in

1. It must not be inferred that financial institutions bought up all the new issues of shares and then looked around for the balance of their needs. There is no means from these figures of telling which sectors bought new issues and which bought existing shares.

the liabilities of financial institutions (insurance companies and pension funds) and in the £400 million increase in public sector liabilities for certain pension schemes in the sector. The funds placed at the disposal of insurance companies and pension funds were used for the purchase of a wide variety of financial claims, especially bonds and shares—£36 million of government stocks, £20 million of local authority debt and £750 million of company shares and debentures.

From Table 1.2 we can thus see how the surplus of the personal sector has found its way towards financing the deficits of other sectors. A small part of the surplus has been laid out in claims which are a direct source of finance to deficit sectors, but over recent years the personal sector has also been divesting itself of many of the direct claims which it held previously, both government bonds and company shares. The greater part of the surplus has found its way to its destination through the various kinds of financial institution.

Table 1.2 presents the picture of the financial activity that took place during 1966 as it appears if we confine our attention to the identified financial transactions. The method that is followed in the official statistics is somewhat different, since the transactions table starts with a financial surplus or deficit derived from the national income and expenditure accounts. With this method saving for each sector is first estimated as the difference between income and expenditure on current account, and then net capital expenditure is deducted. Errors in estimating income, current expenditure and capital formation will thus affect the figure for financial surplus or deficit, and it can never fully be accounted for by identified financial transactions. Our own method of showing only identified financial transactions probably presents a truer picture of overall financial activity than does the other method.

C. *Revaluations*

The financial surplus or deficit shown in Table 1.2 is one element in the change of net worth of an economic unit or sector during a year, but it is not the only element. In the first place, economic units in all sectors undertook some capital formation, and the value of the physical assets which were acquired as a result is obviously part of the change in net worth during the year. In the second place, many of the assets and liabilities with which an economic unit started the year will have changed their values during the year. An increase in the value of an existing asset or a decrease in the value of an existing liability

add to wealth as surely as the acquisition of a new asset or the repayment of an existing liability, and revaluations during the year must be
taken into account before we can strike the closing balance sheet for
the year.

A revaluation table on its own would have exactly the same format
as Table 1.1, showing the revaluations of physical assets and financial
assets and liabilities. It would cover the revaluation of assets and
liabilities held at the beginning of the year and also the revaluation by
the end of the year of assets acquired and liabilities incurred during the
course of the year. It would have a number of zeros because many types
of financial claim are not subject to revaluation. In fact it is only those
financial claims which are marketable—bonds, shares and debentures
and those claims issued by the rest of the world which are of the same
types—which are revalued as their market prices change. The other
claims, like money, near-money, loans, debtors, creditors and life
policies are entered in the national balance sheet at their face (nominal)
values, and cannot be revalued. Revaluations are thus equivalent to
unrealised capital gains or losses.

Instead of showing a separate revaluation table for 1966, we have
presented an integrated picture of the financial accounts for that year
in Table 1.3. Only two sectors are included—the personal sector and
the total column—so as not to make the table too cumbersome. For
each sector the first column gives the balance sheet at the beginning
of 1966 (which is, of course, the same as that at the end of 1965). The
second column takes the relevant transactions figures from Table 1.2,
with the addition of transactions in physical assets (equal to gross capital formation). After a third column for revaluations, the final column
shows the closing balance sheet, consisting of the relevant figures from
Table 1.1.

Three relationships are immediately apparent in this table. (1) For
all sectors the four columns have the following relationship:

opening balance sheet + transactions + revaluations =
closing balance sheet.

This shows that transactions and revaluations between them fully
account for differences between successive balance sheets. (2) Within
every column of the table the following relationship holds:

physical assets + financial assets − liabilities = net worth.

In other words the change in net worth arises from changes in transactions and in revaluations. (3) For the sector labelled 'total' (consist-

Table 1.3   Integrated financial accounts, 1966

£ hundred million

	Personal sector				Total			
	Opening balance sheet	Transactions	Revaluations	Closing balance sheet	Opening balance sheet	Transactions	Revaluations	Closing balance sheet
A. Physical assets	491	29	3	523	1,345	92	–	1,437
B. Financial assets								
1. Money	80	3	–	83	203	18	–	221
2. Near-money	140	8	–	148	200	10	1	210
3. Bonds	53	2	–	55	176	7	– 1	182
4. Shares & debentures	186	– 4	– 8	174	359	13	– 28	344
5. Overseas claims	19	– 1	1	19	155	11	– 2	164
6. Loans	13	1	–	14	379	38	–	417
7. Debtors	45	2	–	47	160	10	1	170
8. Life policies	189	17	–	206	189	17	–	206
Total	725	28	– 7	746	1,821	124	– 31	1,914
C. Liabilities								
1. Money	–	–	–	–	203	18	–	221
2. Near-money	–	–	–	–	200	10	1	210
3. Bonds	–	–	–	–	176	7	– 1	182
4. Shares & debentures	–	–	–	–	359	13	– 28	344
5. Overseas claims	–	–	–	–	155	11	– 2	164
6. Loans	110	6	–	116	379	38	–	417
7. Creditors	33	2	–	35	160	10	1	170
8. Life funds	–	–	–	–	189	17	–	206
Total	143	8	–	151	1,821	124	– 31	1,914
D. Net worth (A + B – C)	1,073	49	– 4	1,118	1,345	92	–	1,437

ing of the sum of the four national sectors and the rest of the world)
the entries under financial assets are repeated exactly under liabilities.
This arises yet again from the fact that each financial claim appears
twice, once as an asset and once as a liability. Under transactions new
claims are entered immediately as assets of the acquiring sector and as
liabilities of the issuing sector; existing claims may be traded between
economic units, whether in the same or a different sector, while remaining the liability of the issuing sector. Under revaluations it is the
same claim which is being revalued as an asset and as a liability.

Integrated accounts of this type have not yet been produced for any
country by the official statistical bodies, although the figures quoted
here come from the continuation of the work on national balance
sheets which the author did while he was at the Department of
Applied Economics, University of Cambridge. However, plans are in
hand for the Bank of England and the Central Statistical Office to take
over this work from the Department of Applied Economics, and to
produce official statistics on these lines. The United Nations has recently revised its recommendations on the form of national accounts
produced by member countries, and the new recommendations include
integrated accounts like those in Table 1.3.

3. THE FINANCIAL SUPERSTRUCTURE

A. *The size of the superstructure*

Now that we have considered the forms of financial activity over a
period in their entirety, we can revert to the question which we touched
on earlier—the factors determining the size of the financial superstructure relative to the base of physical assets. This is measured
quite simply from the national balance sheet by the ratio

$$\frac{\text{value of financial claims}}{\text{national wealth}}$$

with all values expressed in current prices.[2] In the literature this is
referred to as the *financial inter-relations ratio* (F.I.R. for short). On
the figures of Table 1.1 the F.I.R. for the United Kingdom in 1966 was
1·32. Because of the probable errors in estimation of figures in national

2. On p. 9 above we used a simpler expression, relating the value of financial
claims to the value of physical assets. For Britain there is not much difference
between the two expressions because the net foreign balance, which is added to
the value of physical assets to give national wealth, is relatively small.

balance sheets, it is difficult to give a precise figure for the F.I.R. of any country at one point of time, and the ratio varies considerably over time because of the price changes of the items entering into both numerator and denominator.

In order to provide some international comparisons we must go back to the period 1958–61. At that time the F.I.R. for the United Kingdom was between 1·65 and 1·75, and this was by far the highest ratio of any country for which it was possible to make the calculation. The next highest ratio was 1·40 for Japan. The U.S.A. had a ratio of 1·17 and Italy one of 1·06, but most of the other developed countries had ratios between about 0·60 and 0·75. Less developed countries like India and the socialist countries had ratios between 0·30 and 0·40.[3]

Since a national balance sheet shows the position which an economy has reached as a result of all its past activity, it can be regarded as the sum of all past transactions as amended by revaluations. Abstracting for the moment from the problem of revaluations, we can easily identify from our past discussion a number of factors which will determine the volume of financial claims created in relation to a given volume of capital formation. (1) The greater the extent to which economic units depend on funds from outside to finance their capital formation, the larger the volume of claims issued, and conversely the greater the extent to which they rely on their own saving, current or accumulated, the lower the volume of claims issued. (2) Since financial institutions have a multiplier effect on the volume of claims issued, the larger the proportion of financial activity which involves financial institutions the larger the volume of claims issued, and conversely. This factor is reinforced if the nature of the financial system is such that a high proportion of funds goes through two or more financial institutions before reaching its ultimate destination. (3) Because military expenditure and other forms of consumption do not result in the addition of physical assets in the balance sheet, the ratio is increased to the extent that the government and other economic units issue claims to finance deficits resulting to some extent from consumption expenditure. The trends in these three factors over the fairly recent past will determine whether the financial inter-relations ratio is high or low at the present, taking financial claims at the prices at which they were issued.

Revaluations complicate the issue considerably. In the numerator of the ratio only ordinary shares have values which rise with inflation,

3. Raymond Goldsmith, 'The uses of national balance sheets', *Review of Income and Wealth*, Series 12, Number 2 (June 1966) p. 131.

and the values of other financial claims are either unaffected or, like the value of bonds, tend to fall during a period of inflation. The values of the physical assets in the denominator, on the other hand, fully reflect changes in the general price level. Inflation thus has a very strong influence on the F.I.R. In several countries runaway inflation has resulted in monetary reforms which have effectively wiped out many previously existing financial claims.

B. *The development of a financial system*[4]

So far we have been concerned with the structure of a financial system in the highly complex form which it has reached in Britain and other developed countries. In order to appreciate the significance of the various elements in financial structure—the financial inter-relationships between economic units, the types of financial claim, the markets on which claims are traded and the financial institutions—it is probably better to approach the question of financial structure historically, and to show the different stages of development through which these complex financial systems have passed. In order to do this we shall divide the economy notionally into two sectors—surplus units (households) and deficit units (business and government). We shall distinguish four main stages of development of a financial system, but the process of development is, of course, discussed in a highly schematic way. No financial system has ever gone through these four stages in exactly the order postulated; sometimes the stages overlap; sometimes the system doubles back on itself for a while and sometimes stages are missed out. We are not considering the development of any specific system, but rather the 'logical-historical' order of development. Our main concern will be to show the tremendous influence which the financial system has had at all stages of its development on the rate of growth and development of the economy on the 'real' side.

The process of development can be thought of as starting with the general use of *commodity money*, whether it be in the form of metals such as gold and silver, of cowrie shells or of animals such as cattle and sheep. Barter had reached quite sophisticated forms among the ancients, but with the development of commodity money man was able to separate the acts of sale and purchase; even with the most highly-developed forms of barter there was no means of storing purchasing

4. The following treatment is based largely on B. J. Moore, *An Introduction to the Theory of Finance* (New York: The Free Press; London: Collier–Macmillan, 1968) pp. 91–5.

power. In this rudimentary financial system no deficit financing was possible. Because it was not possible to borrow (except in kind), expenditure was limited by the share of income accruing to each economic unit. Each economic unit could save only in the form of money balances, and hence its current expenditure could exceed its current income only if it had accumulated money balances from past saving. The only other possibility for 'business' enterprise arose from the possibility of selling one form of physical asset (surplus land, for example) in order to purchase another form (a plough or oxen, perhaps). With such a rudimentary financial system there were constraints on economic development.

Before the next major stage of financial development occurred, various expedients were devised to overcome the constraints on economic development. Among 'business' units partnerships were formed in order to pool accumulated savings. However, it was governments which led the way most often. Taxation was perhaps the most primitive form of accumulation, but governments devised various other methods of obtaining their share of accruing income. The issue of legal tender money ('fiat money', as it is sometimes called) was such a device because it could be obtained only by surrendering commodity money. Lotteries, organised either directly by the government or by private individuals under government licence, served the same purpose as long as the total prize money was less than the total of contributions.

The various expedients listed in the last paragraph were not sufficient for long, and the next major stage in the development of finance can be said to begin with the development of *borrowing*. For the first time economic units were not limited in their expenditure by the share of income accruing to them; deficit financing became possible. Deficit units issued interest-bearing financial claims direct to surplus units in the form of bonds, mortgages and loans; these are known as *primary securities*. Those economic units which had the desire to run business risks for profit were able to have under their control physical assets to a greater total value than their net worth. Surplus units were able to hold wealth in a form that was far less risky than the ownership of physical assets, although it was less liquid than money balances. Both enterprise and saving were encouraged by the relaxation of restraints.

Almost contemporaneously with the issue of primary securities came the development of *markets*, on which these securities could be traded after they had been issued. Once again it was governments which led the way; they were often the first to issue primary claims, and their claims were often the first to have organised markets. Such a development greatly enhanced the desirability of primary securities to surplus units because it increased the liquidity of the claims. Left to themselves surplus units would generally want to hold a large proportion of short-term claims because they were not certain when they would have need of money balances. The development of these markets encouraged surplus units to lend for a longer period more in accord with the needs of deficit units, because surplus units could turn these longer-term securities into money balances at any time by selling them on the market to other surplus units.

The second stage of evolution, marked by the development of borrowing, still left the ownership of physical assets used for business in the hands of the deficit units. The next stage of evolution came when the administration of businesses could be divorced from their ownership through the development of *equity securities*. Surplus units could obtain title to a share of the profits of a business without having the trouble of managing it. By the device of incorporation of the business the shareholders (the holders of the equity claims) became owners of the business, with their liability limited to the amount of money which they had subscribed. Because of limited liability equity claims were considerably less risky than direct ownership of businesses, and the risk to surplus units could be still further reduced by holding a portfolio of equity claims in several different companies. They also offered a hedge against a rise in the general price level. As with the bonds issued as primary securities, the development of a market on which equity claims could be traded between surplus units further enhanced liquidity and reduced the risk of a holder being unable to obtain a money balance when it was needed.

The process so far has consisted of deficit units issuing claims which are less risky and more convenient to surplus units than outright ownership and management of business assets. The need of businesses for the use of financial resources over a relatively long period set a constraint on these methods of financing. Each surplus unit needed a large part of its portfolio of financial assets in a form that ensured ready access to money balances in case of need, and even the development of markets could not entirely obviate the need for large money balances. Wealthy surplus units could have relatively high proportions of their assets in non-money form, but less wealthy ones could not venture beyond money balances. In order to increase the total amount of deficit financing it was necessary to meet the needs of the less wealthy surplus units for liquidity while providing the longer-term finance that business needed. These divergent needs could be reconciled only by the growth of specialised bodies, which issued relatively risk-free, convenient and liquid claims to surplus units, and acquired primary securities from deficit units. These specialised bodies are financial institutions, or *financial intermediaries*, as it is more useful to call them in this context. The securities which they issue are termed *indirect claims* or *secondary claims*.

Financial intermediaries can be split into two groups, monetary and non-monetary. Monetary financial intermediaries issue claims which are generally acceptable as money; they are banks and they issue both bank-notes and deposits. In most financial systems they were the first to develop, and they often, in fact, became important even before primary securities were issued. Their significance is obvious: there is no loss of liquidity in holding the claims that they issue once these claims have become generally acceptable as a complete substitute for commodity or legal-tender money. Many of the non-monetary intermediaries, savings banks and building societies in particular, concentrated on providing close substitutes for bank money in the form of deposits withdrawable on demand or short notice at their face value; we may call these near-banks. The others issued claims which suited the convenience of surplus units in other ways—giving them shares in a large diversified portfolio of primary claims (investment trust companies and unit trusts) or pro-viding income or capital on retirement or death (insurance companies and pension funds). The primary claims which financial intermediaries acquire are either direct loans and mortgages to deficit units or normal primary securities, obtained either at issue or on the open market. Financial intermediaries thus interpose themselves between surplus and deficit units, issuing claims that are tailored to suit the needs of the surplus units and acquiring the claims issued by deficit units.

The last development which we may note is of what Professor Tew has called *asset-switchers* and *liability-switchers*.[5] This is a refinement of the functions of existing institutions rather than the development of new institutions, but it is a refinement which is very important to the smooth running of a complex financial system. Asset-switchers are those units which always ready to change the composition of their port-folios by selling some claims and buying others with the proceeds. Their willingness to switch in this way for relatively small differentials in expected reward smooths out the whole process of distribution of funds in the system. Financial intermediaries are the main asset-switchers, although any economic unit with a diversified portfolio may play this role. The government is the major liability-switcher. The government issues a wide variety of financial claims—bonds, treasury

5. Brian Tew, *Monetary Theory* (London: Routledge & Kegan Paul, 1969) p. 14.
    *

bills, national savings and money; it is willing to switch between these various forms of liability, largely at the holder's behest, but often in pursuance of its own policy aims.

The evolution of financial systems which we have been describing was a very uneven one, with the earlier stages lasting for centuries and the later stages succeeding one another in quick succession. In Britain for example the eighteenth century saw the issue of primary securities by both government and companies authorised by the Crown or by Parliament, and there was a banking system in existence. The real growth of equity claims did not come until after the first Companies Act was passed in the 1860s, and many sorts of financial institution are of even more recent growth. Certainly a period of 200 years would encompass the growth of the financial system as we know it today, and evolution and innovation have been particularly rapid in the recent past. This financial system is one incorporating in a highly developed form traces of all the main stages of evolution except that of commodity money.

The one thread which has run through the evolution of the financial system is the prompting of financial innovation by the needs of deficit units. Different sorts of financial claim and eventually different sorts of institution have appeared with the sole purpose of enticing surplus units to economise on the money balances that they hold and to hold a larger stock of financial claims in total. The development of the financial system has therefore been accompanied by a growth in the financial wealth of surplus units relative to their incomes without the need to pay a higher reward to surplus units for parting with purchasing power. This is the position as it is reflected in the balance sheet—the stock position. In the flow of income, saving and expenditure the development of the financial system has resulted in the ever greater separation between surplus and deficit units and between ownership and control of businesses.

It would be a mistake to imagine, however, that this process has been without disturbances, an automatic response of the financial system to the needs of deficit units. In most countries at some time there have been long periods when the financial system has failed to adapt itself to the needs of deficit units. While it is legitimate partly to abstract from the problem of finance when we are looking at the basic working of a macro-economy and to concentrate on the fact that saving and investment are always identically equal, we should never forget that the levels of saving, investment and income which are realisable depend on the development of the financial system.

FURTHER READING

J. Revell, *The Wealth of the Nation: the National Balance Sheet of the United Kingdom, 1957–1961* (Cambridge: Cambridge University Press, 1967).

J. Revell & A. Roe, 'National balance sheets and national accounting— a progress report', *Economic Trends* (May 1971).

A. Roe, *The Financial Interdependence of the Economy 1957–1966* (London: Chapman & Hall, 1971) (No. 11 in *A Programme for Growth*).

R. Goldsmith, 'The uses of national balance sheets', *Review of Income and Wealth,* Series 12, Number 2 (June 1966).

B. J. Moore, *An Introduction to the Theory of Finance* (New York: The Free Press; London: Collier–Macmillan, 1968).

A study of the article entitled 'Analysis of financial statistics' in recent issues of the *Bank of England Quarterly Bulletin* will be very useful in obtaining an idea of the pattern of financing flows and their magnitude.

2 Financial Claims

In Chapter 1 we looked at the different kinds of financial claim under a number of broad headings, very few of which contained familiar names. In this chapter we shall begin to consider the types of claim which make up these broad headings and to describe their characteristics. Because this is not a textbook on monetary theory, we shall not attempt to cover a wide range of theoretical points, but shall limit ourselves to those parts of theory which are essential for understanding future chapters.

1. TYPES OF CLAIM

A. *Characteristics*

We can usefully begin by giving a formal definition of a financial claim as a claim to the payment of a future sum of money and/or a periodic payment of money. The 'and/or' in this definition implies that either one of the payments will be a sufficient condition, but that both may be promised. In many cases there is no periodic payment: treasury bills and commercial bills, which are issued at a discount and repaid at par, and national savings certificates, on which accrued interest is paid in full when they are cashed, are cases in point. Similarly there may be no promise to repay a definite sum in the future: perpetual bonds are promises to pay an annual rate of interest without providing for future redemption, and ordinary shares (equities) carry no promise of redemption. Typically, however, a financial claim carries an obligation on the issuer to pay interest periodically and to redeem the claim at a stated value in one of three ways: (1) on demand, (2) after the giving of a stated period of notice or (3) on a definite date or within a range of dates.

The future payments of periodic interest and on redemption may or may not be fixed. With a bond the rate of interest is fixed for the life of the bond, and the redemption value is stated in advance. With an ordinary share neither payment is fixed; the periodic payment fluctuates according to the proportion of available profits which the directors decide to distribute to shareholders, and the holder receives the current market value at the time of his sale to another holder or his share of the amount received by realising the assets of the company when it is wound up. With a bank deposit account or a building society deposit the issuer promises to repay the face value on withdrawal but has the right to vary the rate of interest at will.

For a contractual right to receive a future payment, either of a lump sum on redemption or of periodic interest, to rank as a financial claim the promise to pay must be unconditional. A life assurance policy is a financial claim because it promises to pay a given sum either on the holder's death or on his prior attainment of a stated age; one or other of these two events is bound to occur. By contrast a policy for motor insurance or fire insurance is not a financial claim because payment is conditional on the holder's suffering insurable damage, an event which may not occur to him. There are many contractual obligations to make future payments which are not financial claims because they are peculiar to the holder and cannot be assigned to another person; the payment of a salary under a contract of service comes into this category.

Each financial claim has a number of different characteristics, and claims are normally classified according to these characteristics. All schemes of classification have their difficult cases, and that of financial claims is conceptually very difficult because not all the characteristics remain unchanged over the life of the claim and because many of them can vary according to circumstances; others again are essentially subjective in nature.

One of the most important characteristics is that of *reversibility*, the ease with which the holder of a claim can recover the money balance which he has surrendered to the issuer of the claim. Reversibility can be achieved in two ways, either by providing for recourse to the issuer, as with a bank deposit or a building society deposit, or by the existence of a secondary market, on which the holder can sell the claim to somebody else. The easy reversibility of a financial transaction greatly increases the willingness of surplus units to undertake the transaction. In practice most claims are reversible in some degree, but the ease differs considerably. The least reversible of financial claims are loans for a fixed period for which there is no secondary market and the ordinary shares of small private companies, which may be sold only to persons of whom the directors of the company approve.

Every financial claim has some degree of *risk* attached to it. Risk is essentially a subjective phenomenon because there is no objective way of measuring it, and it can change considerably over the life of a claim. The risk that the promises to pay embodied in the financial claim may not be met exists at three levels: (1) the general level of economic activity, (2) the particular industry or segment of the market to which the issuer belongs and (3) the circumstances of the particular issuer.

There are many other characteristics of financial claims, but those which we have examined so far can all be subsumed under the heading of *liquidity*. Liquidity can be defined quite briefly as the ease of converting a financial claim into cash without loss of capital value, but this serves only to mask the nature of a very complex concept. The liquidity of a particular claim can change over time and can differ from one holder to another.

The ease of reversibility is obviously closely connected with liquidity, but this is not a unique characteristic which can be measured. To begin with it depends on the time available, either because notice is required or because the secondary market may not be broad enough to accept sudden sales without a sharp drop of price. It also depends on the holder and the size of his holding in relation to the amount of the claim in issue. Very large financial institutions like the Prudential Assurance Company and small bodies which happen to hold a high proportion of a particular claim must both move very slowly and carefully if their sales are not 'to turn the market against them'.

An important part of the definition of liquidity is the proviso that there shall be no capital loss, but this also hides a peculiar difficulty. At times of price stability capital certainty, the ease with which future capital value can be predicted, can be interpreted quite happily to mean *money-value certainty*, the ability to recover the full sum of money which was advanced. When inflation has been proceeding for some time, holders are no longer content to receive back the same number of depreciated pounds which they advanced several years previously. They must, at the least, be compensated by a higher rate of interest, but increasingly they will begin to think in terms of *real-value certainty*. This will lead them to regard ordinary shares, the value of which adjusts itself spasmodically to inflation, as actually more liquid for long-term precautionary purposes than short-term claims with absolute money value certainty.

For all these reasons it is impossible to order financial claims in a unique hierarchy according to their relative liquidity. For practical purposes, however, we can make out a rough list in descending order of liquidity, from money through near-money, bills and bonds to shares, long-term loans and life policies. Life policies are ranked at the bottom of the list because they are generally held to maturity; under certain circumstances they can, of course, become relatively liquid because they can be used easily as collateral for a loan and can generally be surrendered for cash. Nevertheless, this list is realistic enough to serve as the basis for a general classification of financial claims.

B. *Different kinds of financial claim*

Table 2.1 sets out the different kinds of sterling financial claim, and shows the amounts in issue in December 1966 and 1970; the 1966 figures are given because many of the estimates are dependent on the completion of a full national balance sheet, which has not yet gone beyond that year. The figures differ in several respects from those shown in the national balance sheet for 1966 (Table 1.1): (1) only sterling claims are shown; (2) the definition of money is more restrictive, with a corresponding widening of the definition of near-money; (3) company debentures are classified under bonds instead of being coupled with company shares.

This table is to be regarded as indicating the orders of magnitude of the different amounts in issue. Those figures which are known exactly are shown to the full accuracy, but many estimates are rounded off and the more dubious estimates enclosed in brackets. The figures are taken from a variety of sources, but for our purposes it is not necessary to go into details of these or of the exact definitions used in estimation.

The definition of money used here corresponds to the measure of the money stock known as M1. It covers only those items which form means of payment, and treats all kinds of bank deposit other than current accounts as near-money. Much ink has been spilt on controversies over the most useful definition of money. Our use of the restrictive definition will be justified shortly.

Near-money has been split into two parts: (1) wholesale, referring to the large-unit items which are of interest to companies and financial institutions, and (2) retail, items used almost exclusively by persons. The items included in both groups are mostly those which can be redeemed, usually on demand or short notice, at face value by recourse

Table 2.1 Amounts in issue of sterling financial claims, December 1966 and 1970

£ million

		1966		1970	
1. Money (M1)					
Notes and coin		2,695		3,320	
Bank current accounts		5,149	7,844	6,315	9,635
2. Wholesale near-money					
Secondary bank time deposits		2,565		4,772	
Certificates of deposit		—		1,089	
Local authority deposits		1,671		1,820	
Finance house deposits		648	5,212	688	8,962
3. Retail near-money					
Deposit bank deposit accounts		4,140		5,277	
Building society deposits		5,883		10,142	
Savings bank deposits		4,052		4,400	
Other national savings		4,208	18,283	4,067	23,870
4. Bills					
Treasury bills		2,642		2,244	
Commercial bills		800	3,450	1,100	3,350
5. Bonds					
British government	MV	12,040		15,415	
Local authority: quoted	MV	1,278		1,732	
unquoted	NV	3,538		5,822	
Company debentures	MV	3,800	20,650	5,100	28,100
6. Shares					
Preference	MV	1,400		800	
Ordinary: quoted	MV	24,500		35,000	
unquoted	MV	(4,000)		(4,000)	
Unit trust units	MV	582	30,500	1,398	41,000
7. Loans					
Bank advances		6,350		7,650	
Instalment credit		1,450		1,500	
House purchase		8,000		12,020	
Other		23,250	39,050	(30,000)	(51,000)
8. Life policies			20,700		(29,000)
9. Debtors/creditors			17,000		(20,000)

to the issuer. Deposit bank deposit accounts are included under retail because it is known that persons hold 80% of the total amount at the present time. All of these items except 'other national savings' will be described in detail in the chapters on banks and other deposit institutions, and we do not need to consider them further here. Other national savings consist of four items of unmarketable government debt. (1) Defence bonds, national development bonds and British savings bonds have one characteristic in common: interest is subject to full rates of tax, but the bonds are redeemed at a price above the nominal value (typically 103 after five or seven years), the capital gain being free of capital gains tax. (2) Premium savings bonds bear no interest, but prizes are drawn monthly. They are a form of national lottery. (3) National savings certificates are issued in small denominations, and the rate of interest accrues over the life of the certificate in such a way that early withdrawal is penalised by a low rate of interest. Interest is completely free of all tax. (4) SAYE ('save-as-you-earn') schemes are contractual savings schemes, operated through the National Savings Department, trustee savings banks and building societies. They have the same basic characteristics as national savings certificates. Because of the tax advantages all items of national savings have limitations on the total amount which an individual may hold.

The characteristic feature of bills is that they are short-term claims, issued at a discount and redeemed at par. They will be described in Chapter 8. Bonds, shares and debtors/creditors will figure in later sections of this chapter, and the only point to be made here concerns the nature of the unquoted local authority bonds. Of the amount outstanding in 1970 about £350 million consisted of negotiable bonds, and the rest of local authority mortgages. The mortgages (representing a mortgaging of the authority's rate revenue and not of buildings) cover a wide range of claims. They are issued in large denominations to financial institutions and in small denominations (often down to a few hundred pounds) to individuals. For the large-unit mortgages there is a secondary market (described in Chapter 10); the small denomination mortgages are extremely illiquid because there is no secondary market and the authority will rarely repay them before time unless interest rates have fallen since issue.

One of the largest items in the table is 'other loans'. These consist of many different types of loan, including loans between persons, but by far the greatest part consists of government loans to local authorities, public corporations, overseas governments and industrial companies. The item called 'life policies' suggests policies issued by life assurance companies, but rights in pension schemes, both funded and unfunded (like that of the Civil Service), are also included.

C. *Money and other claims*

We have defined financial claims in terms of claims to future payments. The promise to make these future payments is invariably given in return for the immediate surrender of a money balance. A financial claim is created when a surplus unit surrenders the command over resources represented by a money balance in favour of a deficit unit and receives in return a promise to make certain future payments. In Chapter 1 we saw that financial claims were created because certain economic units needed to make expenditures in excess of their receipts; it is the surrendered money balance which enables deficit units to make this expenditure.

While we are looking at matters from this point of view, it is natural to restrict our definition of money to those items which are generally accepted as a means of payment. The controversy about the definition of money and the appropriate measurement of the money stock arises in another context, that of the relationship, whatever it may be, between the stock of money and the level of economic activity. For this purpose it may be sensible to consider a wider definition of money since economic units may regard certain near-money claims as so close to money that their behaviour is related, not to their immediate command over means of payment, but to their stock of assets which are either money or can be converted into money at very short notice.

This approach serves to single out money as somehow different from the other types of financial claim listed in Table 2.1, but there is also another claim, the last in the list, debtors/creditors, which differs in kind from the intervening claims. In the ordinary business of life money is not the first financial claim to enter into the picture. Although the many occasions on which a transaction is settled immediately by payment of money serve to obscure the fact, all transactions can be divided into two stages. In the first stage legal ownership of a good or entitlement to a service is transferred and in the second stage payment is made; the gap between these two stages is bridged by a debt, which is an asset, debtors, to the economic unit which will receive the payment and a liability, creditors, to the economic unit which will make the payment.

The most obvious form of debtors/creditors consists of trade credit. Even the least sophisticated household pays the milkman and the newsagent at the end of the week, and most economic units run accounts for public utilities like the telephone, gas and electricity and with a wide range of tradesmen. This trade credit is only a part of debtors/creditors, however; the remainder consists of items called 'accruals'. Whenever a service is provided continuously, payment is invariably made at intervals. Wages and salaries are always paid in arrears at the end of a week or a month; students' grants are a rare example of an income paid in advance. Rent, insurance, rates and season tickets are examples of items which are paid for in advance. Whenever an accountant draws up a set of accounts for an organisation, he has to apportion payments made in advance and arrears. The easiest way to see how this is done is to assume that all payments are made one year in advance or for one year in arrears, and that the accounts are being drawn up on a date exactly halfway through the year. For payments made in advance one-half will be charged to expenses and the other half booked to debtors. No payment due in arrears will have been made, but one-half of the sum eventually due is booked to creditors. If the organisation went out of business on the day of the accounts, it would receive a refund for the debtors items and would have to settle the creditors items.

So far we have spoken loosely of two forms of transaction: those forming part of the 'ordinary business of life' and those in which a money balance is surrendered to a deficit unit in return for a financial claim. We must now refine this distinction, and we shall do so in terms of two circulations of money, which Keynes called the *industrial circulation* and the *financial circulation*.[1] The industrial circulation consists of all those transactions concerned with the circulation of income— payments for factors of production, payments to firms for consumption and capital goods and all transfers between firms, government and households. The financial circulation comprises all other transactions, which are those of lending and borrowing and the purchase and sale of existing financial assets. Because the industrial circulation of money includes a whole number of inter-firm and inter-household transactions and transfer payments, all of which are excluded from the computation of G.N.P., the total value of transactions in this circulation is many times larger than G.N.P.: a recent calculation gave the total value as five times G.N.P. in 1957.[2] The total value of transactions in the financial

1. J. M. Keynes, *A Treatise on Money: the Pure Theory of Money* (Vol. V of *The Collected Writings of John Maynard Keynes*) (London: Macmillan, 1971) p. 42.

2. P. J. Welham, *Monetary Circulation in the United Kingdom* (Oxford: Basil Blackwell, 1969).

circulation is yet larger; the same calculation estimated that it was fourteen times G.N.P. in 1957.

Figure 2.1 shows the relationship between the two circulations of money in terms of the familiar 'circular flow of income' diagram; this covers only those transactions included in G.N.P., but it will serve our purpose as an illustration. The diagram is in two halves, (a) and (b). In

Figure 2.1   The industrial and financial circulations

(a) Purchase of a direct security

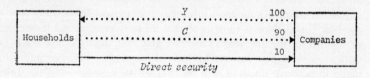

(b) Financial intermediation

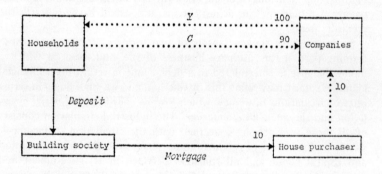

Key: ...... Industrial circulation   ———— Financial circulation

both cases firms distribute 100 of income to households, who purchase 90 of consumption goods from firms and save 10. In (a) this 10 is used for the purchase of a newly-issued direct security issued by firms; in (b) it is deposited with a building society, which makes a loan to a house purchaser. In both cases the 10 passes back immediately into the industrial circulation; in the first case the firms use the money balance for the purchase of capital goods from other firms, and in the second case the house purchaser pays the builder for his house. Money leaks out of the industrial circulation into the financial circulation, but it soon returns into the industrial circulation. Its passage through the financial circulation is clearly marked, however, because it leaves behind it one or more financial claims—one in (a), where a direct security is purchased, and two in (b), the direct claim issued by the house purchaser to the building society and the indirect claim issued by the building society to the surplus unit. In the diagram the financial claims which remain after the passage of the money balance through the financial circulation are indicated by the heavy black lines.

Once a money balance has passed through the financial circulation and gone back into the industrial circulation, it ceases to be distinguishable from any other money balance. If we could somehow tag it for identification, we should see that it might pass several times through the industrial circulation and then be drawn once more through the financial circulation, leaving behind it again one or more financial claims. It is because the whole stock of money is continually circulating in this way, some of it passing through the financial circulation at different times, that the total value of financial claims generated by the passage of money balances through the financial circulation (items 2 to 8 in Table 2.1) is so much larger than the stock of money—just under twenty times as large in 1970.

The second of these financial transactions is also illustrated in Figure 2.2 in a slightly different way. The circulation is seen at two levels, as

Figure 2.2   Financial intermediation

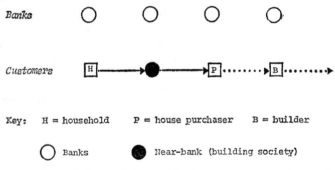

Key: H = household   P = house purchaser   B = builder

   ○ Banks   ● Near-bank (building society)

a movement of balances from one bank account to another and as a series of transactions between non-bank economic units. Once again the transactions which leave behind financial claims are indicated by heavy black lines, and the transactions in the industrial circulation are shown in dotted lines. This diagram does not add anything to our understanding of the financial circulation, but we have a definite purpose in introducing this way of looking at financial transactions. As we shall see in Chapters 7 and 11, when we are looking at some theoretical points on the banking system and on the euro-dollar market respectively, a clear understanding of the distinction between the industrial and financial circulations is essential; we shall develop this diagram to illustrate the points.

Of the claims listed in Table 2.1 only money and debtors/creditors enter into the industrial circulation. The remaining types of financial claim are all generated when money balances move through the financial circulation, and they have no place in the industrial circulation. Debtors/creditors can arise, however, in the financial circulation as well as in the industrial circulation as there are many lagged payments for the purchase of financial claims, especially where brokers are used as agents. The balance sheets of financial institutions like insurance companies, pension funds and investment trust companies contain large items of creditors for amounts due to stockbrokers for securities purchased and of debtors for amounts due from stockbrokers for securities sold. In the field of insurance it is common practice for insurance brokers effectively to receive part of their remuneration by delaying the passing to insurance companies and Lloyd's syndicates of premiums received.

2. BONDS

The remainder of this chapter will be taken up with the explanation of a few elementary points about the characteristics of the two major classes of marketable security, bonds and equities; these points are ones necessary for the understanding of the investment policies of financial institutions of the insurance and provident and portfolio types.

Bonds consist of those fixed-interest marketable securities issued by the central government (including those issued by nationalised industries and guaranteed by the central government), local authorities and companies of all kinds. Those issued by central government and local authorities are usually called 'stocks', while those issued by companies are called 'debentures' or sometimes 'loan stocks'. The characteristics of all bonds are virtually the same, and we shall use government stocks to illustrate the principles involved.

Bonds can be split into two main classes—perpetual bonds and redeemable bonds. Among government stocks there are no examples of perpetual bonds, stocks which will never be redeemed, but there are a few local authority securities of this type. The nearest approach to a perpetual bond among government stocks consists of undated stocks, which have no final date by which they must be redeemed. Thus, $2\frac{1}{2}\%$ Consols, which were issued in 1888, are dated 'on or after 5 April 1923'. Obviously the government will not redeem them unless it can issue replacement stocks with a lower *coupon* (bearing a lower rate of interest) than $2\frac{1}{2}\%$; even when the general level of interest rates was as low as 2% immediately after the last war, the government did not redeem Consols. The remainder of the stocks are all dated, that is they carry a date (more usually a range of dates) of redemption.

There are two basic points which determine the prices and yields of bonds. (1) Once a fixed-interest security has been bought, the interest received by the purchaser is fixed and immutable. Unless he buys the bond at par, the income yield (or 'running yield') to the holder will not be the same as the coupon, but this yield is fixed for him from the moment of purchase. (2) Investors seek the same rate of return (income *plus* capital gain) from all investments after allowing for the risks involved in each security.

We can begin with the very elementary propositions about the relationship between the ruling rate of interest and the price of an undated bond, say $2\frac{1}{2}\%$ Consols. What we have to determine is the amount which investors would pay for the right to receive an annuity (annual payment of income) of £2.50 for ever. This we can work out from the formula

$$P = \frac{100 \times 2 \cdot 5}{i},$$

where i is the ruling rate of interest on riskfree securities. By inserting various values of i we can easily establish three propositions: (1) when i is above the coupon ($2 \cdot 5\%$), the price is below 100; (2) when i is equal to the coupon the price is 100; (3) when i is below the coupon, the price is above 100. For example, when $i = 5 \cdot 0$, the price is 50 (meaning that for every £100 *nominal* we are willing to pay £50); when $i = 2 \cdot 0$, the price is 125. The important feature is that the price and the yield on a perpetual bond move in opposite directions to exactly the same extent: if the price doubles, the yield is halved, and *vice versa*.

Redeemable bonds usually have a range of dates within which they may be redeemed; the borrower may not redeem them before the first date, and he must redeem them on or before the last date. Examples of redeemable British government stocks are 3% Savings Bonds 1965–75, 4% Funding 1960–90 and $5\frac{1}{2}\%$ Treasury 2008–12. From what we have said before, it is obvious that the borrower will not redeem the bond before the last possible date if i is above the coupon of the stock. It naturally suits the borrower to have as wide a range of redemption dates as possible, so that he can select a relatively cheap moment at which to redeem the stock and to replace it with another stock; conversely, the lender prefers a narrow range of redemption dates.

The calculation of the price of a redeemable stock at different levels of i involves quite complicated arithmetic, and we can content ourselves with the basic principles. In purchasing a redeemable bond the investor is concerned with the two sets of future payments: (1) an annuity (annual payment) over the remaining life of the bond and (2) a lump sum at a stated time in the future. Each of these elements has to be valued separately in terms of its present value. In the price calculation for redeemable bonds the value at which the bond will be redeemed (usually 100) begins to dominate the price as maturity approaches. This is because the capital sum is being discounted for a short period, so that its present value rises, while the present value of the annuity declines because it will be paid for a small number of years. Conversely, the present value of the annuity dominates the price when maturity is far off. Thus, as bonds approach maturity, their prices become anchored to the eventual payment of 100, and do not fluctuate much when i changes; long-dated bonds, on the other hand, behave more like perpetual bonds, with far more volatile prices. Short-dated securities in general thus have good capital certainty but poor income certainty (because the proceeds of redemption have to be reinvested at the ruling rate of interest), whereas long-dated securities have poor capital certainty but good income certainty.

There are special characteristics of individual issues of bonds which have an influence on their prices. (1) There are different degrees of risk associated with classes of issuer. Thus, local authority stocks are conventionally regarded as more risky than government stocks although no U.K. local authority has ever defaulted on its debt; company debentures are looked on as more risky than either government or local authority stocks. There are thus price differentials between these three classes. (2) A special type of risk is associated with the size of the particular issue. A large issue of government stock is traded daily on the stock exchange, and a seller can always find a purchaser; small issues of local authority or company bonds are traded far less frequently, and the market is 'narrow'. (3) Because many investors are taxed less severely on capital gains than on income, low-coupon stocks usually command a premium over high-coupon stocks. At any given level of i, a low-coupon stock will have a lower price than a high-coupon stock, and the total return on the former will contain a higher proportion of capital gain. (4) Various other characteristics attract special classes of investor. 2½% Consols have a quarterly payment of interest, whereas most government stocks have a half-yearly payment; Consols are thus attractive to widows and pensioners. Other stocks are tax-free to overseas residents.

So far we have concentrated our attention on the way in which the prices of bonds change with movements in the general level of interest rates; now we must look briefly at the relation between the yields on short-term and long-term bonds—the short-term and long-term rates of interest, in other words. The term structure of interest rates, as it is called, is a most complex phenomenon, and we can do no more than state a couple of simple principles. The complexity arises from the fact that the present level of interest rates is largely determined by expectations about the future level of interest rates.

As a first principle we can state that when interest rates are expected to rise lenders will try to go short (so as to have the use of their money when interest rates have risen) and borrowers will try to go long (to secure present relatively low rates for as long as possible); if interest rates are expected to fall, the converse will happen: lenders will try to go long (to secure present high rates for as long as possible), and borrowers will try to go short (so as to be able to re-negotiate their loans when rates have fallen). Changes in expectations about the level of interest rates in the future thus change the balance of supply and demand in the markets for long-dated and short-dated bonds.

The second principle is that the short-term market is normally dominated by lenders, while the long-term market is normally dominated by borrowers. From this it follows that borrowers normally have to pay higher rates in the long-term market than they do in the short-term market: long-term rates are normally above short-term rates, and the yield curve rises from short to long. From the first principle above, though, it is clear that this 'normal' relationship will tend to be changed when interest rates are expected to fall, because lenders will then be trying to lend long rather than short.

3. EQUITIES

Equities differ from all other financial claims in being certificates of part ownership of an enterprise instead of being evidence of debts. They are of two main kinds—preference shares and ordinary shares.

Preference shares bear a fixed rate of interest, and some of them ('participating preference shares') also receive a fluctuating amount out of the profits of the enterprise. As the name indicates, the shares have a preference over the ordinary shares in that the fixed interest on them must be met by the company before it distributes any dividend to its ordinary shareholders. For some purposes it is convenient to group debentures and preference shares together as 'prior charges'. They are both fixed-interest securities, and the interest on both of them must be met before any dividend can be paid on ordinary shares. There is one important difference, however. The interest on debentures can be deducted from trading profits before arriving at the figure of profit on which corporation tax is payable, but the interest on preference shares is not so deductible. This difference is of importance to many classes of financial institution subject to corporation tax. To avoid double-taxation of profits the interest received from a holding of preference shares does not enter into the total of investment income *less* expenses on which the institution pays tax; it is said to be 'franked income'. Debenture interest is not franked.

The main feature of ordinary shares is that the income to be received from them is not fixed in any way. Ordinary shareholders are entitled to whatever share of profits after tax the directors of the company think appropriate. In a time of inflation the trend of profits in money terms is likely to be upwards, and so there is a presumption that the dividends on ordinary shares will also move upwards. Because the expected annuity represented by dividends is on a rising trend during a period of inflation, the price which investors are willing to pay for the annuity rises similarly. Ordinary shares, in other words, are a hedge against inflation. Over the past twenty-five years, as inflation has continued, there has been a swing towards the holding of ordinary shares on the part of many investors including financial institutions; the movement has been termed the 'cult of the equity'. The traumatic experience of the Wall Street crash and the long depression of the 1930s has gradually faded from memory, and attention has been directed towards the rise in capital value and in income to be expected from a holding of ordinary shares.

Against this background it is worth pausing to examine how good a hedge against inflation equities have proved to be in recent years. Some useful figures are those computed regularly by a firm of stockbrokers, de Zoete & Bevan (formerly de Zoete & Gorton).[3] They com-

3. de Zoete & Bevan, *Equity and Fixed Interest Investment 1919–1972* (privately circulated).

pare the value of a fund of 30 high-class ordinary shares with the value of a fund invested in 2½% Consols. Both funds start off with £1000 invested on 1 January 1919; all income is reinvested, and no allowance is made for tax or commission. By 1 January 1972 the equity fund would have grown in value to £177,201, whereas the Consols fund would have reached only £5500. Over the same period the overall yield (annual rate of compound interest earned) would have been 10·2% on the equity fund and only 3·3% on the Consols fund.

The results just quoted are most impressive, but we need to probe a little further. Table 2.2, taken from the same source, gets close to the question of hedging against inflation by showing real indexes (price

Table 2.2. The real value of equity prices and dividends

Indexes (1919 = 100) divided by cost of living indexes

Year (1 January)	Equity price index	Equity dividend index	Consols price index
1919	100	100	100
1929	303	235.	125
1939	296	239	160
1949	228	158	105
1959	275.	228	45
1960	407	272	43
1969	470	277	19
1970	362	265	16
1971	287	220	13

Source: de Zoete & Bevan, *Equity and Fixed Interest Investment 1919-1972*, p. 24.

and dividend indexes of the same two funds divided by the cost of living index). Once again the results overwhelmingly favour the equity fund, and the performance of Consols seems abysmal. We have only to re-base the index on 1929 or 1939 instead of 1919, however, to get a rather different picture; equity prices and dividends in real terms did not exceed their 1929 or 1939 levels until 1960. The figures for the years from 1969 onwards show the effect of large price fluctuations in ordinary shares from year to year. It is obvious that anybody who buys his ordinary shares at the top of the market may have to wait a long while before they provide an adequate hedge against inflation, while somebody who buys at the bottom of the market may well be protected all the way. Timing is thus of considerable importance.

Because there is nothing fixed about either the price or dividends of ordinary shares, they are to be regarded as more risky than bonds. Up to 1959 this extra element of risk was reflected in a yield on ordinary shares which was higher than that on bonds. After 1959 the average yield on ordinary shares fell below that on government bonds; this phenomenon is known as a 'reverse yield gap', and it is illustrated in Table 2.3. One can advance many special reasons for the reverse yield

Table 2.3   The reverse yield gap

Annual averages of percentage yields

Year	2½% Consols Gross flat yield	FT index of industrial ordinary shares Dividend yield	Reverse yield gap
1958	4.98	6.27	− 1.29
1959	4.82	4.86	− 0.04
1960	5.42	4.26	1.16
1961	6.20	4.87	1.33
1962	5.98	5.49	0.49
1963	5.58	4.93	0.65
1964	6.03	4.96	1.07
1965	6.42	5.74	0.68
1966	6.80	5.98	0.82
1967	6.69	5.36	1.33
1968	7.39	4.05	3.34
1969	8.88	4.43	4.45
1970	9.16	4.75	4.41
1971	9.05	4.16	4.89

Source: *Financial Statistics* (e.g. March 1972, Tables 107 & 109).

gap, but basically it has been caused by a great increase in the demand for equities resulting from the beliefs (1) that inflation was likely to continue, (2) that equities were a good hedge against inflation and (3) that slumps like that of the 1930s were unlikely to recur. One implication of the gap is, of course, that a switch from bonds to equities entailed an immediate drop in income.

In recent years the reverse yield gap has become very large, and it is worth inquiring what the figure representing the reverse yield gap implies. When we were looking at bonds, we were able to indicate rational ways of valuing the fixed stream of income and the fixed future redemption value. Since there is nothing fixed about the stream of income from equities, it would seem that there is no rational way of valuing it. In fact, however, investors are implicitly comparing the *expected* dividends from equities against the *fixed* interest obtainable on bonds; the reverse yield gap tells us what assumptions investors are making about the future growth of dividends. It can be shown that the rate at which the market values future dividends is the ratio of the last reported dividend to the current price of the shares *plus* the expected annual rate of growth in dividends.[4] The reverse yield gap is thus equal to the expected annual rate of growth in dividends. The table tells us that in 1969, for instance, the market was implicitly assuming that dividends would in future grow at the rate of 4.45% per annum; in fact, investors were assuming a faster rate of growth in dividends because most of them were probably comparing yields, not on Consols as in the table, but on debentures, with a reverse yield gap in that year of around 5·9%.

It is worth mentioning investment in real property (interests in land and buildings) in the context of hedges against inflation. As we shall see when we look at building societies in Chapter 14, the prices of land and buildings have risen even faster than those of ordinary shares during recent years, and financial institutions like insurance companies, pension funds and specialised unit trusts have invested increasing amounts in properties. Properties are not, of course, financial claims, although the leases on land and buildings have many of the features of financial claims, but for financial institutions properties are an alternative form of asset to hold in their portofolios.

4. Let D be the annual dividend on an ordinary share, and let i be the true rate of interest at which to value future dividends. Suppose that the rate of growth in dividends which is expected is g per annum, so that successive dividends will be D, $D(1 + g)$, $D(1 + g)^2$ . . . Then the price P of the share will be given by

$$P = \frac{D}{1 + i} + \frac{D(1 + g)}{(1 + i)^2} + \frac{D(1 + g)^2}{(1 + i)^3} + \cdots$$

$$= \frac{D}{i - g}$$

or $\quad i = \frac{D}{P} + g.$

FURTHER READING

B. Tew, *Monetary Theory* (London: Routledge & Kegan Paul, 1969).

W. T. Newlyn, *Theory of Money* (Oxford: Oxford University Press, 2nd ed., 1971).

A. J. Merrett & A. Sykes, 'Return on equities and fixed interest securities: 1919–1966', *District Bank Review* (June 1966).

H. Rose, 'Reflections on the equity boom, 1966–69', *Three Banks Review* (June 1969).

3 Markets

We have already seen the important part which the development of markets for financial claims plays in the evolution of a financial system, and in this chapter we look at the functions and organisation of certain markets. Because our main concern is with financial institutions we can be brief. Money markets are so intimately concerned with the banking system that we shall look at them in detail in the chapters devoted to banks of various kinds. After some introductory remarks we go on to look at the domestic capital market in all its various aspects and briefly at the international capital market.

1. TYPES AND ORGANISATION

We can usefully begin by making two distinctions. The first relates to types of market and the second to the types of participant in markets of all kinds. (1) *A primary market* is one on which new financial claims are issued, whereas a *secondary market* is one on which previously issued financial claims are traded. (2) *Brokers* are intermediaries whose function it is to bring together buyers and sellers, whereas *dealers* act as principals, buying and selling financial claims which they themselves hold in their portfolios and making a profit out of the margin between buying and selling prices.

The distinction between primary and secondary markets is quite clear conceptually, but there are many cases in which it becomes blurred in practice. One good example of this is the market for British government stocks. In formal terms these are issued in large amounts offered for public subscription, but in most cases the bulk of the new issues is taken up by organs of the central government ('the Departments'), and the actual issue to the public is made as they are fed out 'on tap' by the Government Broker in the secondary market. As we shall see, secondary markets and their requirements have a very strong influence on the forms and procedures on certain markets. When the requirements of the secondary markets or the intervention of the authorities begin to stifle trading in markets, either primary or secondary, 'parallel' markets are often formed in much the same way as new types of financial intermediary grow up when banks and older intermediaries are subject to close regulation or 'cartel' agreements.

Similarly the distinction between brokers and dealers is hard and fast in conceptual terms, but sometimes blurred in practice. Many of the older markets enforce a rigid separation between the two functions, but in many others a particular firm may be acting on occasion as both broker and dealer. A good example is the operation of issuing houses in the new issue market for company securities: often their functions are those of lending their names, giving advice and organising the mechanics of the issue, but on many occasions they assume the risk by buying securities outright from companies and selling them to the public. Brokers and dealers are often limited companies, but in some of the older markets unincorporated businesses or unlimited companies are the only firms permitted to operate.

The word 'market' is used somewhat loosely in discussions of the financial system, and the normal operations of financial intermediaries are sometimes brought within the term. Thus, one hears talk of the market for deposits with banks or building societies or for house mortgages. We shall limit ourselves to cases in which there is an organised apparatus of dealers or brokers acting as intermediary between buyer and seller. This definition does not necessarily cut out entirely the cases mentioned above; it merely limits the concept of the market to those parts of the operations of banks and building societies in which brokers are employed to find the best terms or the availability of funds and leaves out those cases (by far the majority) in which borrowers or lenders approach the financial institutions direct.

The degree of organisation varies considerably between markets. We shall be dealing here only with the more highly organised markets, and we shall mention the others in the various chapters. These 'fringe' markets exist in practically all spheres, since it is nearly always possible to find a buyer for any negotiable financial claim as long as one is prepared to take trouble and to wait. Many of these markets on which financial claims are traded are informal, consisting of solicitors or accountants finding purchasers among their clients or of informal contacts on social occasions.

The organised markets which come within the scope of this chapter can be divided into three classes: (1) the foreign exchange market, (2) money markets and (3) the capital market. Of these three the foreign exchange market sticks out as differing in kind from the other two: it is entirely international and there is no change in the form of the financial claim (a bank balance) but only in its location. The remaining two classes differ mainly in the maturity of the claims traded. Money markets are those on which the claims are very short-term, and the capital market consists of those separate markets on which long-term claims are issued and traded. Once again the distinction has become partly blurred in recent years. Up to twenty years ago it would have been safe to say that money market claims ranged from overnight money to bills or deposits with less than one year to maturity, but we shall see later that the parallel money markets in both sterling and other currencies now deal in deposits and loans with maturities of up to seven years.

The foreign exchange markets are peripheral to our main concern, but they are worth describing because their method of organisation has been taken over by many other markets. There are two markets for foreign exchange—the wholesale market, in which banks in different centres deal with each other through brokers, and the retail market, in which customers approach their banks for foreign exchange in the form of bank-notes and travellers' cheques; we are concerned only with the wholesale market. The market is exclusively a telephone and teleprinter market, with direct telephone lines between the brokers and the main banks in London and telephone and teleprinter links with smaller banks in London and banks in overseas centres. Deals are concluded usually within a matter of seconds and confirmed by the exchange of written notes.[1] This form of organisation has been taken over by the various money markets, largely because the foreign exchange brokers were among the first to operate in the new parallel money markets. Even though it preserves the ritual of personal contact between representatives of the discount houses and the various banks, the discount market is effectively a telephone market organised on similar lines to the foreign exchange market.

At the other end of the scale the stock exchange remains entirely a market with a trading floor, on which all deals are conducted between brokers and jobbers (dealers) in London and between pairs of brokers in the provincial exchanges. This is the original form of organisation of

1. An excellent description will be found in P. Einzig, *A Textbook on Foreign Exchange* (London: Macmillan, 1966) Chaps. 2 & 3.

a market, and in Continental centres it persists in many spheres outside the stock exchange.

In looking at the organisation and working of markets there are
several points to consider. The first of these is the extent to which the
formal market is by-passed by deals conducted outside the organisation, whether these are just occasional deals or amount to a separate
'parallel' market. Apart from the new money markets, London is remarkably free of parallel markets as compared with other centres. We have
seen that stifling regulation by the exchange authorities can be one
reason for the establishment of a parallel market. Other reasons are
limitations on the minimum size of transactions or of amounts of each
type of security and excessive commissions charged by brokers on the
original market. The second point to be looked at is the extent to
which the central bank intervenes on the market in furtherance of
monetary policy or of its general function of supporting the financial
system.

2. NEW ISSUE MARKET

It is logical to start our more detailed consideration of the capital
market with the primary market, the market on which new issues of
securities are floated. We shall look at British government securities
separately in a later section, so that we are concerned with U.K. local
authority, overseas public authority and U.K. and overseas company
securities, with emphasis on the procedures for the issue of new securities by U.K. companies. We shall concentrate on issues by which new
money is raised, thus neglecting bonus and exchange issues and stock
exchange introductions. Bonus issues are mere book-keeping entries
in the company's balance sheet, by which amounts are transferred from
the heading of 'reserves' to that of 'share capital'; in this process the
nominal value of the shares is increased, so that the dividends as declared represent a smaller percentage of the nominal value of each
share. Exchange issues arise when other companies are acquired, not
for cash, but by the issue of shares in the acquiring company. Stock
exchange introductions are the seeking of a quotation for already
existing shares. The figures of new issues on the U.K. capital market,
both gross and for U.K. companies net of redemptions of existing
securities, are analysed in Table 3.1. The 'international issues' mentioned in the middle of the table are dealt with in the last main section
of this chapter.

Two types of body are active in the new issue market—issuing houses and stockbrokers. The main issuing houses, fifty-eight of them in mid-1972, are members of the Issuing Houses Association. The members comprise the banks active in this field (the seventeen accepting houses and several other 'merchant' or 'investment' banks, classified under 'other U.K. banks' in Table 5.1) and many non-bank issuing houses.

Table 3.1   Capital issues on the U.K. market, 1970 and 1971

£ million

		1970	1971
Gross capital issues			
U.K. local authorities			
Stocks		120.0	101.7
Negotiable bonds		339.0	520.4
U.K. quoted public companies		361.4	598.6
Overseas public authorities		64.1	79.8
Overseas companies		96.9	186.8
	Total	981.6	1,487.3
International issues			
U.K. borrowers		*20.2*	*28.4*
Overseas borrowers		*152.4*	*224.5*
Domestic issues		*809.0*	*1,234.4*
Net domestic issues by U.K. quoted public companies			
Debentures & loan stocks		82.4	209.6
Convertibles		105.0	63.5
Preference shares		12.4	11.4
Ordinary shares		76.0	224.7
		275.8	509.2

Source: *Bank of England Quarterly Bulletin*, March 1972, Table 15.

There are also some thirty houses, which are not members of the Association; they include several South African mining finance houses and the largest of the finance houses in the instalment credit field (United Dominions Trust). Apart from the very occasional incursion into the field the main deposit banks have avoided new issue activity. Stockbrokers are concerned in every issue, because it is they alone who can carry out the requirements of the stock exchange authorities; the addition of an issuing house is not obligatory, but issuing houses are concerned with something like two-thirds of all the issues in which new money is raised.

The functions of an issuing house (including stockbrokers in that term when they are acting without an issuing house) can best be seen when we have examined the various methods by which new securities can be issued. These are five in number. (1) With *public issues* subscriptions are invited from the public for the issue at a stated price. The advertisement for the issue consists of a detailed prospectus, which usually covers 1½–2 pages of a newspaper. (2) In the *offer for sale* subscriptions are also solicited from the public on the basis of a prospectus, but in this case it is the issuing house and not the company raising new money which is making the offer. In nearly every case the issuing house buys the securities from the company and offers them for sale at a price higher than that which it has paid to the company; very occasionally the issuing house acts on a fee basis. (3) Offers by *tender* are also addressed to the public at large, but the public is invited to state the price (above a certain minimum) and the amount for which it is tendering. Nearly all tenders are settled at a single price which just disposes of the issue, sometimes after large tenders have been scaled down to ensure a wide holding of the security, but in some tenders the stock exchange permits the sale at the prices offered by each tenderer. (4) With *placings* we pass on to a form of issue in which the securities are offered to a select group known to the issuing house; these are usually financial institutions such as investment trust companies, insurance companies, pension funds and unit trusts. When a stock exchange quotation is sought for the securities, these are known as stock exchange or public placings, but unquoted securities can be dealt with in the same way (private placings). (5) With *issues to shareholders* (usually known as *rights issues*) it is the existing shareholders who are allotted new securities in proportion to their existing shareholdings, and this is invariably done at a privileged price. A company might, for example, have 1 million shares in issue standing at a price of £2 each; if it issued a further 1 million shares at £1.50 each, the value of each of the 2 million shares after the issue would be £1.75. The shareholder can renounce his allotment and sell it to others; in this case the value of the rights would be 25p (1.75 − 1.50).

In all cases one of the main functions of the issuing house and/or stockbroker is lending their names to the issue; they are known to have examined the issuing body in detail, and their reputations are at stake. Offers for sale differ from the other methods because the issuing house is generally acting as a principal and not as an agent, having bought the securities from the issuing body before issue and selling them at its own risk. Even when it is acting as agent, however, the issuing house is at risk because it guarantees that the money will be raised. To cover itself it arranges for *underwriting* of the issue by a number of financial institutions on its list. These institutions are paid a fee (usually about 1½% of the value of the issue), which is payable whether or not the body is required to take up unsold securities. Underwriting commission is a useful source of additional income to financial institutions like insurance companies, pension funds and investment trust companies. In all cases the issuing house provides advice, expertise and administration; the last of these can be considerable in issues which are offered to the general public by one of the first three methods.

Table 3.2 analyses gross capital issues (including international issues to the extent that U.K. institutions are involved) in three separate

Table 3.2   Gross capital issues on the U.K. market by method of issue, 1965–71

Percentages

	1965	1968	1971
Public issues & offers for sale	27.8	8.2	11.8
Tenders	.4	3.7	5.6
Placings	59.2	53.4	68.6
Issues to shareholders	12.6	34.6	14.0
Total	100.0	100.0	100.0
£ *million*	*818*	*1,328*	*1,487*

Source: *Bank of England Quarterly Bulletin* (e.g. March 1972, Table 15).
Note: International issues are included.

years over the period 1965–71 according to the methods of issue. Although the proportions are considerably different in the three years, there are two trends. The first is the steady growth in the proportion offered by tender; this is largely because U.K. local authorities are increasingly favouring this method rather than public issue. The second trend is the increased proportion of placings (1965 was an exceptionally high figure for the early years of the period). This is caused not so much by a switch of method as by an increase in the proportion of those types of security which are always issued by placings—local authority negotiable bonds and international issues.

Our discussion of the methods of issue has largely concentrated on the issue of company securities, and it is worth digressing for a moment to see how important the capital market is as a source of funds to U.K. quoted public companies. Table 3.1 shows that the securities of these companies account for rather less than one-half of all domestic issues. Table 3.3 shows that the capital market is of relatively small importance as a source of funds to non-financial companies as compared with their internal sources (mainly undistributed profit). The figures in this table are compiled from the published accounts of just over

Table 3.3   Sources of funds of U.K. industrial and commercial
companies, 1969 and 1970

	1966	1970
Undistributed income	69.3	48.7
Capital transfers	.7	9.4
Bank lending	4.8	20.2
Other loans and mortgages	2.7	4.6
U.K. capital issues by quoted companies	14.8	3.5
Overseas sources	7.6	13.5
Total	100.0	100.0
£ *million*	*3,884*	*5,559*

Source: *Financial Statistics*, March 1972, Table 81.

1000 of the largest quoted non-financial companies, and they necessarily cover the world-wide activities of these companies. An alternative way of looking at the importance of the capital market to companies is to examine the sources of funds for capital formation in the U.K. of all companies, using official statistics rather than company accounts.[2] On this basis rough estimates for the period 1966–70 suggest that internal sources accounted for 65%, capital issues for 10%, bank borrowing for 13% and other sources (including government grants and direct investment by overseas companies) for 12%.

The costs of raising funds on the capital market are quite heavy; as with all other financial operations, many of the costs are fixed irrespective of the size of issue, and large issues are relatively cheaper than small issues. One study of the costs of issue found that the mean costs of issue as a percentage of the size of issue varied for offers for

2. See 'Company finance: 1952–65', *Bank of England Quarterly Bulletin* (March 1967).

sale from 25·6% for issues of up to £100,000 down to 6·2% for issues over £1 million; for placings the equivalent figures were 24·8% and 3·6%. The authors pointed to another large source of cost—the fact that in all types of issue except tenders the price is fixed in advance of issue on the advice of the issuing houses; if trading takes place immediately after issue at a higher price, it can be said that the difference is really part of the cost of issue. If this additional cost is added in, the figures quoted above for offers for sale become 34·4% for issues up to £100,000 and 14·1% for issues over £1 million; for placings the respective figures are 58·7% and 16·3%[3]

Any company which needs to raise a large volume of outside funds must be concerned about securing a quotation for its securities on a stock exchange, and the requirements which the stock exchange imposes for quotation therefore have a strong influence on the forms and procedures of the new issue market. The main concerns of the secondary market authorities are that there should be a wide market in any securities quoted on the exchange and that shareholders should have as much relevant information about the issuing body as is reasonable. Their regulations therefore affect the primary market in the following main ways. (1) The exchange fixes a minimum size for quotation. The Federation of Stock Exchanges requires that the total market value of a company's securities should be not less than £250,000, with each individual security having a minimum market value of £100,000; in addition not less than 35% of the ordinary shares and not less than 30% of preference shares and debentures must be held by the public. (2) The exchange must approve the details of the issue, and gives permission for placings, in which the holders are restricted largely to institutions and a few individuals, only when the size of the issue would make it too expensive to adopt any other method. (3) Whenever a security is granted a quotation for the first time, the issuing bodies must ensure that a minimum proportion is supplied to jobbers in the market so that realistic prices may be set. (4) The exchange has very rigorous standards for the amount of information to be given in the prospectus whenever securities are to be offered to the public by one of the first three methods.

Both the London Stock Exchange and the issuing houses have been greatly concerned in recent attempts to regulate the process of acquisition of one company by another—mergers and takeovers. As the merger movement has gathered force during the past decade, regula-

3. A. J. Merrett, M. Howe & G. D. Newbould, *Equity Issues and the London Capital Market* (London: Longmans, 1967) pp. 114 and 184

tions have been issued to cover such actions as the dealing in shares of a company subject to a takeover bid and the conditions under which a given bid price must be offered to all shareholders of the acquired company. Both the Stock Exchange Council and the Issuing Houses Association have taken a prominent part in the establishment of the City Takeover Panel, which attempts to regulate these matters in order to forestall official intervention.

3. THE STOCK EXCHANGE

A. *Quoted securities and transactions*

Table 3.4 shows the numbers and the aggregate market value as at 31 March 1971 of all the securities quoted on the London Stock Exchange. The table is divided into two main categories—(1) gilt-edged and foreign stocks and (2) company securities. Although the Radcliffe Committee preferred to restrict the use of the term 'gilt-edged' to securities issued by or guaranteed by the British government, the more usual practice is to include U.K. local authority securities, Commonwealth public authority securities and securities issued by international organisations like the World Bank; among public authority securities only those issued by authorities in countries outside the British Commonwealth are thus excluded.

By far the greater part of the aggregate market value and of the total number of securities is accounted for by company securities—83% of the total market value as against 17% for the gilt-edged and foreign stocks. Rather surprisingly it is the securities of overseas companies (including a very small part of securities of U.K. companies in currencies other than sterling) which form the larger part of the company securities market in terms of total market value—48% of the overall total as against 35% for the securities of U.K. companies (including a very small part of sterling securities issued by overseas companies). From the fact that the number of securities of overseas companies is so much smaller than the number of securities of U.K. companies it is easy to see that most of these overseas companies are the large multinational corporations.

Table 3.5 looks at the activity of the London Stock Exchange in terms of the value of turnover and the numbers of transactions. Because of the rigid separation between brokers and jobbers to which we shall refer in the next section the value of turnover is measured by the sum of sales and purchases, thus duplicating the value of securities transferred as against other stock exchanges on which the sale of a security by the client of one broker to the client of another broker is recorded once only.

The total value of turnover of gilt-edged and foreign stocks is far

Table 3.4   Securities quoted on the London Stock Exchange, 31 March 1971

	Securities Nos.	Market value £ million
Gilt-edged and foreign stocks		
British government & guaranteed	66	17,161
U.K. local authority	696	1,814
Overseas public authorities	489	1,889
Total	1,251	20,864
Sterling	*1,092*	*19,562*
Other currencies	*159*	*1,302*
Company securities		
Debentures & loan stocks	2,247	3,650
Convertibles	303	1,023
Preference shares	1,771	· 862
Ordinary shares	3,452	94,104
Total	7,773	99,640
U.K. companies & overseas companies in sterling	*7,243*	*41,909*
Overseas companies & U.K. companies in other currencies	*530*	*57,730*
Grand total	9,024	120,504

Source: London Stock Exchange, *Statistics relating to Quoted Securities, 31st March 1971.*

greater than that of company securities—77% of the total (74% for British government securities alone) as against 23%. On the other hand company securities accounted for 79% of the total number of transactions. The remaining columns spell out the consequences of this disparity between the gilt-edged market and the market for company securities in terms of the average size of bargain and (in the last column) the ratio of turnover to total market value. The high degree
    *

of activity in the market for British government securities is one of the factors which make those securities attractive to a wide range of holders, outweighing the fact that the yields on them are normally lower than on other fixed interest securities.

Table 3.5　Transactions on the London Stock Exchange, 1971

	Transactions		Average bargain £'000	Average MV in issue £m.	$\frac{(1)}{(4)}$
	Value £m.	Number '000			
	(1)	(2)	(3)	(4)	(5)
British government					
Up to 5 years	22,062	144	153.2	6,600	3.34
Over 5 years & undated	25,394	386	65.8	11,830	2.15
U.K. local authority	1,521	93	16.4	2,456	.62
Commonwealth & foreign	218	38	5.7	1,061	.21
Debentures & preference	1,679	˙704	2.4	5,806	.29
Ordinary shares	13,377	5,258	2.5	42,983	.31
Total	64,252	6,623	9.7	70,735	.91

Sources:　(1) *Financial Statistics*, March 1972, Table 101; (2) London Stock Exchange;　(3) Bank of England.

When we examine the working of the stock exchange, we shall refer to the influence of the financial institutions, and we can usefully try to see how important they are as holders of quoted securities and what proportion of stock exchange turnover is accounted for by these bodies. The available information is summarised in Table 3.6. For nearly every type of security the proportion held by financial institutions has risen over the period from 1964 to 1970 (the exception is a switch from debentures to preferences shares in order to secure franked income), and in most cases the proportion of total turnover accounted for by the institutions has also risen. In all cases the financial institutions represent a large and sometimes dominant proportion of the market. Insurance companies, pension funds, investment trust companies and unit trusts are the only financial institutions concerned with U.K. company securities; for British government and local authority securities discount houses, building societies and savings banks are included among institutional bodies. In the case of British government securities with up to five years to maturity 28% of total nominal value was held by banks in 1970, and discount houses accounted for 61% of total turnover.

The counterpart of the growing market share of financial institutions is a continuing process of sales by persons, who are divesting themselves of direct holdings of securities in favour of investment through financial intermediaries. Studies of the holders of U.K. quoted ordinary shares undertaken at Cambridge have shown that persons held 65·8% of total market value in 1957, 54·0% in 1963 and 47·4% in 1969.[4]

Table 3.6   The share of financial institutions in total market holdings and turnover of quoted securities

Percentages

	Holdings at 31 March		Turnover	
	1964	1970	1966	1970
British government				
Up to 5 years	43	46	67	76
Over 5 years & undated	43	51	50	52
U.K. local authority	41	44	24	22
U.K. debentures	69	57	57	58
U.K. preference shares	41	64		
U.K. ordinary shares	25	31	30	37

Source: The financial institutions: Part 3, *Bank of England Quarterly Bulletin*, June 1971.

Notes: Holdings of British government and U.K. local authority are percentages of total *nominal value*; holdings of U.K. company securities are percentages of total *market value*.

The official statistics of sector financial transactions show continuing personal sales of British government securities as well as of company securities.

B. *Organisation and trading*

Until 1973 London was not the only stock exchange in the United Kingdom, although it was by far the largest. About ten years ago there were as many as twenty-two separate provincial exchanges in centres such as Liverpool, Manchester, Bradford, Glasgow, Cardiff and Belfast; two of them were in the Irish Republic. The greater part of the securities quoted on the provincial exchanges also had a London quotation, but

4. J. Moyle *The Pattern of Ordinary Share Ownership 1957–1970* (Cambridge: Cambridge University Press, 1971) Table 4.2.

there were some securities, mainly of local companies, which were quoted only outside London. A study which the author carried out showed that at 31 December 1962 securities quoted only on one or more provincial exchanges represented 0·6% of the total market value of debentures quoted in London, 8·3% of preference shares and 1·4% of ordinary shares; there were also some harbour board mortgages and bonds. The overall market value of the securities with no London quotation was £565 million as against a total London market value of all securities on the same date of £43,998 million.[5] From about 1965 onwards the provincial exchanges were merged into three regional stock exchanges, and on 25 March 1973 these combined with London to form a national stock exchange, under the title of The Stock Exchange. It has trading floors in several of the former provincial centres.

The London Stock Exchange differed from all other stock exchanges in the world in one main feature of organisation—the jobber system. The jobber is a dealer, who acts as principal in all transactions. Most exchanges admit members who act on occasion as dealers, but London was unique in enforcing a rigid functional separation between jobbers and brokers and in prohibiting direct dealings between brokers. The provincial exchanges, which used not to have specialist jobbers, began to develop jobbing firms during the process of federation, and the new national stock exchange will operate on the jobber system. These days many of the larger deals between financial institutions are negotiated outside the stock exchange, but the letter of the law requires that the deals should then be 'put through' the stock exchange, attracting brokers' commission and the 'turn', or profit, of the jobber, although the latter is usually narrowed in such cases. The jobbing system is both the strength and weakness of the London Stock Exchange. Its justification is that it can provide a highly competitive market when it is working properly, and one in which jobbers, acting as principals in all dealings, can even out violent fluctuations in price. However, it has been the main difficulty in the lengthy negotiations for the formation of a national stock exchange, and the results of the system are under attack from several quarters. It is in the context of these problems that we must examine the trading system of the London Stock Exchange.

As in most other fields of financial life there has been a concentration of stock exchange firms over the past fifty years. In 1920 there were 475 firms of brokers with 1513 partners; by 1971 there were

5. J. Revell, *The Wealth of the Nation* (Cambridge: Cambridge University Press, 1967) Table 16.1.

only 176 firms with a slightly larger number of partners, 1773. The decline in the number of jobbers is much more serious as a threat to the efficient working of the system. In 1920 there were nearly as many jobbing firms as firms of brokers, 411, and they had 1465 partners; by 1971 the number of firms was down to 27, and these firms had only 268 partners. Each jobbing firm specialises in a section of the market, and the number of firms in several sections is now down to the irreducible minimum of two. The two largest firms of jobbers, both formed by recent mergers, account for something like three-quarters of total turnover in the market.

Until very recently the only permitted form of organisation of both brokers and jobbers was the partnership; some partnerships had only one partner, and twenty was the legal maximum for the number of partners. Because they were unincorporated, stock exchange partnerships could accumulate reserves only with considerable difficulty since all profits were subject to full rates of income tax and surtax in the hands of the partners. Before the war most stock exchange members were wealthy individuals who were able to face the unlimited liability for all debts of the firm, but of recent years professional expertise has become of considerably greater importance, and partners are chosen from a different and far less wealthy group. As we shall see, the need for capital has grown, and all these factors have combined to make the unincorporated form of organisation a barrier to the smooth working of the stock exchange. Progressively the Stock Exchange Council has eased the situation, and the Inland Revenue has been prepared to allow the accumulation of reserves in forms that escape the full rigours of personal tax. The first easing was provided by a rule that partnerships could include limited partners, who provided capital but took no active part in the affairs of the partnership, and this was followed by permission for partnerships to assume the form of unlimited liability companies. Partnerships were also allowed to form service companies, which carried out all the trading of the partnership, hiring staff, renting premises and paying dividends to the partnership; the Inland Revenue permitted the accumulation of some reserves in these companies. Finally, in 1969, the Stock Exchange Council permitted brokers and jobbers to form limited companies. Because it was concerned that the London Stock Exchange should not become like most Continental exchanges, on which the dominant members are the large banks of the country, the Council made a proviso that none of the outside shareholders of these limited companies should hold more than 10% of the share capital. In the short time since it was introduced this new rule has enabled many firms to obtain additional capital from merchant banks and insurance companies.

The need for this new form of organisation can best be understood if we consider the financial pressures on firms of brokers and jobbers. The first problem which has faced brokers has been a great increase in the volume of paperwork in a form which requires highly trained staff. Although bargains in the gilt-edged market are settled immediately, all other bargains are settled at the end of the fortnightly account, and this imposes peaks of clerical work. Computers have eased the situation marginally, but a reduction in costs will not be achieved until the system of centralised settlement and accounting on stock exchange computers which has been under discussion for some time is finally introduced. The fortnightly accounting system also imposes pressures for financing clients. A particular case of difficulty occurred during the boom in Australian mining shares recently. The vast amount of paperwork in Australia caused delays of several months in the registration of transfers by the companies concerned, but customers who had sold Australian shares and switched into other securities were not willing to pay interest while the paperwork was being sorted out. Stockbrokers are able to borrow from banks (under 'money at call' within the fortnightly account and under 'advances' for longer periods), but customers who do not settle promptly impose a considerable burden on the firms. With the growing importance of institutional clients stockbrokers have invested heavily in research departments, which have turned out to be very expensive parts of their organisations. The larger firms of stockbrokers have also formed branches in provincial towns (they are not permitted to do so within twenty-five miles of a provincial stock exchange) and overseas.

Jobbers face the same pressures of paperwork and research departments, but the overwhelming problem is that of financing the 'book' of securities in which they trade. Ideally a jobber should hold lines of all the stocks in which he deals, but this has long ceased to be possible. In the gilt-edged market jobbers can borrow stocks through money brokers,[6] and the authorities have encouraged the discount houses to become, as it were, second-tier jobbers in short-dated government stocks. The borrowing of equities is not permitted. Jobbers are able to finance part of their book of securities by borrowing from banks, but the need for capital remains because the loans are not for the full value of the securities pledged as collateral. The shortage of capital means that jobbers can hold only a restricted book, and this leads to

6. See pp. 221–3.

the situation in which many large deals of the institutions have to be arranged outside the stock exchange and then to be 'put through'. The institutions increasingly resent the payment of commission and jobber's turn for bargains which the exchange has really played no part in arranging, and recently the Accepting Houses Committee began discussions with the Stock Exchange Council about a proposal for a computer dealing system outside the exchange for bargains of over about £50,000. If all large dealing of institutions were removed from the exchange in this way, the stock exchange would become only a market for pricing marginal transactions as some of the commodity markets are.

One of the main points in this situation is the rate structure of brokers' commission. The Stock Exchange Council lays down minimum rates of commission which must be charged. The rates of commission for a number of different values of bargain ('consideration') in the main types of security are shown in Table 3.7. Commission on bargains

Table 3.7   Minimum rates of commission on the London Stock Exchange

Percentages of value of bargain

	Value of bargain					
	£50	£1,000	£10,000	£50,000	£100,000	£1 million
Gilt-edged						
5-10 years	2.00	.50	.15	.07	.07	.06
Over 10 years	2.00	.50	.26	.14	.14	.13
Debentures	4.00	.75	.56	.38	.35	.26
Ordinary & preference	4.00	1.25	.94	.63	.56	.32

Source: London Stock Exchange (author's calculations).

in gilt-edged stocks with five years or less to final redemption is at the discretion of the brokers. Table 3.7 takes into account the volume discounts on transactions in company securities exceeding £50,000 and in gilt-edged securities exceeding £250,000 which became effective in January 1973. There is indeed some tapering of rates for larger bargains, but the basic problem is caused by the fact that the commission rates do not fully reflect the levels of cost incurred for bargains of different size. Because many costs are fixed irrespective of the size of transaction, the rates are completely uneconomic for small bargains, and many stockbrokers discourage clients whose transactions are small; at the other end of the scale the *absolute* level of costs incurred for a bargain of £1 million is probably no greater than for a bargain of £50,000. The institutions are not only subsidising the small personal clients of the brokers but also bearing all the costs of the large research departments. One large accepting house revealed recently that its annual payment of stock exchange commission was in excess of £1 million.

Some of the problems which we have examined are likely to be overcome, in part at least, by the turning of many stock exchange firms into limited companies, by the formation of a national stock exchange, by centralised settlement and accounting and by other measures being contemplated. An efficient dealing mechanism is of such importance for the working of financial institutions and of the financial system as a whole that arrangements outside the stock exchange will grow up unless the stock exchange solves its problems.

4. THE GILT-EDGED MARKET

The gilt-edged market, and particularly that part of it concerned with stocks issued by the British government, differs in many ways from the market for company securities. (1) Britain has the largest national debt in relation to G.N.P. of any developed country. (2) Government bonds are held by all types of organisation, and they play a special role in the asset management of financial institutions. (3) As we saw in Table 3.5, transactions in quoted British government securities account for just under three-quarters of the total value of turnover on the London Stock Exchange, and bargains in them have an exceptionally high average value. It is a highly active market, and it is the possibility of easy sale which ensures their attractiveness to financial institutions and other holders. (4) Because the market is so broad and active, large holders can obtain dealing profits by an active policy of 'switching' from one stock to another as temporary price anomalies become apparent. (5) The authorities intervene actively in the market for their own securities, partly to further monetary policy and partly to support the market.

The gilt-edged market has certain special forms of organisation. Dealing is 'for cash' (settlement on the next business day), instead of on the basis of a fortnightly account. Jobbers in the market and discount houses, which have a special function in the market for 'shorts' (stocks with five years or less redemption), are given facilities for quick registration of sales and purchases—the 'Z Accounts', to which we refer in Chapter 8. Gilt-edged jobbers and money brokers are able to borrow large sums of money at call from the banks.

The intervention in the market by the authorities is conducted by the Government Broker (the senior partner in a firm of stockbrokers, with another partner as his deputy) on the instructions of the Chief Cashier of the Bank of England. The authorities buy and sell stocks according to the needs of the time, and they are generally prepared to facilitate switches of stocks by the financial institutions if these accord with current policy. For their selling operations the authorities have command over a large volume of government stocks held by the Issue Department of the Bank of England (as 'backing' for the note issue), by the National Debt Commissioners[7] and by other government funds. These holdings are fed as new stocks are issued and taken up by 'the Departments' (as described above) or as stock is purchased on the market. While the authorities hold a wide range of their own debt in this way, the newly-issued stocks, which are being fed out to the market 'on tap', play the major role in enabling the Bank of England to influence interest rates for short, medium and long securities. Government stocks fulfil such an important function in the portfolios of financial institutions and other holders that movements in the yields on government bonds affect the whole structure of interest rates in the economy.

Consideration of the policy of the authorities in debt management over recent years would take us well into questions of monetary theory and policy and thus beyond the scope of this book. All that we can do is to give a very quick sketch of the basic issues involved and to refer the reader to the articles listed at the end of the chapter.

The authorities have three main policy interests in the market for government stocks: (1) to influence the level of interest rates and the money supply, (2) to support the markets so that firm holders can be found for as much as possible of government debt and (3) to minimise the cost of servicing the debt. The third interest is ever present, but it has had to take a back seat over recent years. The dilemma facing the authorities in their debt management is that the first two policy interests so often conflict.

Over the ten to twelve years up to the summer of 1971 the support function of the authorities dominated the conduct of debt management. This was based on the belief that institutions and others would

7. Their full and correct title is, somewhat amusingly, the Commissioners for the Reduction of the National Debt.

not remain willing holders of government stocks in large quantities if they felt that the market was being manipulated for monetary policy reasons. The policy of the authorities has been described as that of 'leaning into the wind'; they would not take the initiative in setting any particular level of interest rates, but they would intervene to moderate fluctuations in price and yield. On occasion this meant that they would sell large amounts of stock in one period (sometimes as much as £1000 million during a quarter), and be forced to buy back as much or more during the next period. The conflict between the support function and the monetary policy function of the authorities showed itself acutely at times of credit squeeze, when the extension of credit by banks and other financial institutions was being strictly controlled but when the authorities were sometimes buying government stocks from the general public at the same time. As we shall see when we look at the banking mechanism in Chapter 7, government sales of bonds reduce the money supply and government purchases increase the money supply. The authorities were thus on occasion nullifying the effects of their own credit squeeze by pumping money into the economy.

Along with the announcement of the new arrangements for the control of banks, discount houses and finance houses which we shall examine in the next few chapters the authorities declared a change of policy in debt management, and this new policy is in many ways the most important feature of the arrangements for credit control. Under the new market policy the authorities have declared themselves as willing to tolerate much wider fluctuations in interest rates; they will no longer respond to offers for the sale of stock by the public unless it suits their policy to do so. On the face of it this change of policy means subordinating the support function to the monetary policy function. The hope of the authorities is that the banks and other financial institutions will themselves begin to act in a supporting role. Up to the time that this chapter is being written the resolve of the authorities has not been put to any real test, and it remains an open question whether they will keep their nerve in a severe market crisis. The conflict between the need to support the market in order to secure and maintain firm holdings of government debt and the need of the new policy for wider fluctuations in interest rates remains, and only time can tell in which direction it will be resolved under crisis conditions.

5. INTERNATIONAL ASPECTS

We have already seen that the aggregate market value of the securities of overseas companies quoted on the London Stock Exchange exceeds that of the securities of U.K. companies. Over recent years very many investment banks and stock exchange firms from the U.S.A., Canada, Japan and other countries have established offices in London, and the total number is probably not far short of 100.[8] These firms provide an alternative channel to the London Stock Exchange for investment in the securities of companies in their own countries. Several of the investment firms play a special role in the market for foreign and international bonds (which we are going to examine below), and some of the U.S. and Canadian firms are part of the market for dollar certificates of deposit.

Over the past decade or so there has come into being a large international capital market of a form different from those that obtained before. For long periods in the past it had been customary for nationals of one country to raise long-term funds on the capital markets of Britain, the U.S.A. and other countries, but the new market is one in which long-term capital is raised on a number of capital markets simultaneously and in a currency which may not be that of any of the capital markets concerned. It is the long-term counterpart to the euro-currency markets at which we shall be looking in Chapter 11. Like them it originated from the initiative of certain accepting houses in London, although once again their participation is now dwarfed by that of American banks and by other banks of many countries. Like the euro-dollar market its growth owed a lot to measures taken by the U.S. authorities to counter their balance of payments deficit. The securities issued and traded on this market are usually called 'euro-bonds'.[9]

The rapid growth of the euro-bond market dates from 1963, when the U.S. authorities took steps to hinder the raising of capital in New York by foreign nationals. Table 3.8 shows the volume of issues over the four years to 1970. Foreign issues are those raised on one capital market by foreign nationals; between 40% and 50% of the amounts under this heading consists of bonds issued in New York by nationals

8. See M. Campbell, 'Foreign securities houses in London', *The Banker* (March 1972).

9. The following short description of the market is largely based on 'The international capital markets of Europe', *Bank of England Quarterly Bulletin* (September 1970).

of Canada, which was exempted from the measures of the U.S. authorities. The international issues are those in which several capital markets are involved; they are the euro-bonds. The figures at the bottom of the table are the conversion into U.S. dollars of Bank of England estimates of the amounts of euro-bonds for which U.K. banks

Table 3.8   Foreign and international bond issues, 1967–70

U.S.$ million

	1967	1968	1969	1970
Total issues				
Foreign issues	2,333	2,991	2,174	1,926
International issues	1,889	3,368	3,110	2,836
Total issues abroad	4,222	6,359	5,284	4,762
Borrowing countries or areas				
Western Europe	1,019	1,009	1,517	1,594
Canada	1,172	1,255	1,412	1,046
United States	598	2,232	1,257	840
Japan	15	193	255	120
Rest of the world	675	698	551	478
International institutions	744	971	291	684
Total	4,222	6,359	5,284	4,762
Participation of U.K. institutions in international issues				
U.K. borrowers	52	50	2	48
Overseas borrowers	291	666	498	366
Total	343	716	500	414

Sources: (1) Bank for International Settlements, *Annual Report 1970–71*, p.53;   (2) *Bank of England Quarterly Bulletin*, Table 15.

arranged subscriptions; British participation varied between 15% and 21% of the total value of euro-bonds issued in the four years.

The method of issue of euro-bonds is based on that of the U.S. bond market. A small number of banks in each country organise a syndicate of other banks in their respective countries, and the various banks place the bonds with their customers. Once the issue has been successfully placed, an advertisement is made in various newspapers announcing the issue; because this advertisement merely describes the issue and lists the names of the participating banks, it is known familiarly as a 'tombstone' advertisement.

Euro-bonds are issued in a variety of currencies, of which the U.S. dollar is the most important. In 1969 the U.S. dollar accounted for 44% of all foreign and international issues, and the Deutschemark for 43%. The only other currencies of note were the Swiss franc (8%) and sterling (2%). A small number of issues is made in European units of account, the value of which is fixed in relation to the gold values of the seventeen members of the European Payments Union; the device is designed to protect borrowers and lenders from unilateral changes of parity of the constituent currencies other than their own. Some issues are made which give a currency option.

Although straight bonds are the most important form of security, many issues are made in other forms. Of these the convertibles, carrying the option to convert into the equity of the issuing company at a stated price, are the most popular. Some issues have warrants attached, which give the holder the right to subscribe for the equity of the issuing company at a stated price; the difference between convertibles and warrants is that the latter entail the providing of further money. A beginning has been made with international issues of equities, for which there should be a big demand when conditions are right.

A secondary market is as essential for the development of international issues as it is for the success of domestic issues, but the international character of the primary market imposes some difficulties. Most euro-bonds issues are quoted on various national stock exchanges, but the trading banks have had to play a large part in the organisation of the secondary market. In the early days they acted as jobbers, but the large losses incurred in 1969 led many banks to do no more than arrange transactions by bringing buyers and sellers together. There are some small issues of euro-bonds which are unquoted. The physical separation of the many markets has also caused delivery delays, but these are being overcome by the organisation of clearing systems and the issue of depositary receipts, which can be transferred in place of the actual bonds.

FURTHER READING

J. D. Hamilton, *Stockbroking Today* (London: Macmillan, 1968).
R. J. Briston, *The Stock Exchange and Investment Analysis* (London: George Allen & Unwin, 1970).

A. J. Merrett, M. Howe & G. D. Newbould, *Equity Issues and the London Capital Market* (London: Longmans, 1967).

K. Midgley & R. G. Burns, *Business Finance and the Capital Market* (London: Macmillan, 1969).

P. Einzig, *The Euro-Bond Market* (London: Macmillan, 1969).

J. Chown & R. Valentine, *The International Bond Market in the 1960s* (London: Pall Mall, 1969).

On the debt management policy of the authorities over recent years the best short source is 'Official transactions in the gilt-edged market', *Bank of England Quarterly Bulletin* (June 1966). A more thorough survey of the topic would need to take in the written and oral evidence of the Bank of England and H.M. Treasury to the Radcliffe Committee. The change in policy associated with the new arrangements for credit control is referred to in the various documents and speeches in the June, September and December 1971 issues of the *Bank of England Quarterly Bulletin*.

4 Financial Institutions

We saw in Chapter 1 that the growth of specialised financial institutions—or financial intermediaries—was the last stage in the long process of development of a modern financial system. They are called financial intermediaries because they greatly improve the efficiency of the financial system by coming between surplus units and deficit units, taking up the direct claims issued by the deficit units and issuing secondary or indirect claims which, in one way or another, are better suited than direct claims to the needs of surplus units. In this chapter we shall examine the working of financial intermediaries. Because the remainder of this book is devoted to a detailed examination of the working of each type of financial institution in turn, we shall be concerned here only with the points which financial institutions of all kinds have in common and with the contrasts between the different types of intermediary.

1. CLASSIFICATION

A. *Main types*

Discussions of problems of classification are usually rather boring, but in this case we can use such a discussion as a peg on which to hang the consideration of the different functions and methods of operation of various types of financial institution. We shall be concerned mainly with the development of a workable classification system, which we can use in the remainder of the book, but a consideration of various other characteristics by which financial institutions could be classified brings out a number of useful points about their different methods of operation.

To begin with we must point out that there is nothing sacrosanct

about the definition of any particular body as a financial intermediary.
Most economic units, at one time or another, fulfil an intermediary role.
A homely example would be if I were to use my superior creditworthiness to obtain a bank overdraft, which I then passed on to my son so
that he could buy a motor car. (Just in case he reads this, I had better
add that I have no intention of doing so!) I should be acting in that
case as a financial intermediary. Another example, which occurs far
more often than the first, is an industrial company with access to
borrowing facilities which finds that willy-nilly it is passing on this
credit to its customers because they delay in paying their bills. During
the recent credit squeeze industrial companies have gone even further
than this by making specific loans to other companies which could not
borrow the funds they needed from the banks. This example points to
an ever-present feature of the financial system—the fact that deficit
units are always able to choose between obtaining direct or indirect
finance according to the terms and availability of credit from the two
sources. At times when financial intermediaries are unable to offer
competitive terms to attract the funds for lending or when they are
prevented by quantitative controls from fulfilling the demand for
loans, their erstwhile customers will obtain direct finance if it is available. This process is known by the rather clumsy term disintermedi-
ation.

Obviously in this book we are going to deal only with bodies whose
main function is that of acting as a financial intermediary, but the
point made above is strongly emphasised when we add that the largest
financial intermediary in our economy is not classified as such because
its other functions far outweigh its financial role. This is the central
government, which acts as a financial intermediary mainly by raising
through its own borrowing nearly all the external finance required by
public corporations and a large part of that needed by local authorities
and then making loans to these bodies.

The easiest way in which to classify financial institutions is according
to the nature of the claims which they issue, by their liabilities. This
is because financial institutions tend to be more specialised on the
liabilities side of their balance sheet than on the assets side. A workable classification system on this basis would be as follows:

1. Deposit institutions
2. Insurance and provident institutions
3. Portfolio institutions
4. Special investment agencies

The structure of this book is built around this scheme of classification. The chapters dealing with the operation of different types of intermediary are grouped into three major sections, which deal with the banking system, other deposit institutions and other financial institutions. It is a measure of the wide variety of bodies included under the heading of deposit institutions that it should take two major sections of the book to deal with them, whereas the remaining three headings can be covered in a chapter apiece.

Deposit institutions can be split into banks and other deposit institutions, or 'near-banks', as they are sometimes called. We shall see later, however, that there is not just one banking system in this country. There are two systems, each working in different ways and performing largely different functions. Thus we shall further split the banking system into the deposit banking system and the secondary banking system. The deposit banking system is concerned with the operation of the payments mechanism; apart from the deposit banks proper (the London clearing banks, Scottish banks, Northern Ireland banks and a few others) it also includes the Banking Department of the Bank of England, the National Giro and discount houses. The secondary banking system has very little to do with payments, and the banks in it are more concerned with the financial intermediary side of banking, the accepting of deposits which cannot be transferred by cheque and the making of loans. The banks which make up this secondary system are called 'accepting houses, overseas banks and other banks' in the official statistics, but we shall refer to them simply as secondary banks.

The other deposit institutions consist of finance houses, savings banks and building societies. Like banks they are included under deposit institutions because the claims which they issue are sight (withdrawable on demand) or short-term deposits. Most writers would probably classify finance houses in a group of their own, stressing the hire-purchase side of their business. It is true that they issue some claims which are not deposits, but the real case for including them here is that they perform much the same functions as secondary banks; the major difference is that they deal in much smaller accounts than secondary banks do. We shall regard them as 'retail secondary banks'.

The remaining three groups of financial institutions are again distinguished by the nature of the secondary claims which they issue. The characteristic feature of the bodies included under 'insurance and provident institutions' is that the claims which they issue have their values determined by actuarial calculations based on mortality statistics and expected future interest rates; they may be called 'life policies' for short, although independent pension funds in fact rarely issue policy documents. However, many insurance companies also do insurance business other than that concerned with the laws of mortality, such as fire and motor insurance.

The next group, here called 'portfolio institutions', has the characteristic that the secondary claims which it issues are essentially of the same sort as the direct claims which it holds. Investment trust companies and unit trusts hold diversified portfolios of stock exchange securities, mainly ordinary shares, and they themselves issue ordinary shares and debentures in the case of investment trust companies and units in the case of unit trusts, which have the same characteristics as the assets. The reason for their existence as financial intermediaries is that they give holders of their claims the benefits of professional management and of proportionate shares in far larger portfolios than they could own individually, thus reducing risks.

The last group, 'special investment agencies', is very small in Britain. It consists of bodies which raise money on the capital market and make loans to or purchase the shares of other companies. They are 'special' in the sense that each specialises in lending to a particular sector of industry—the Industrial and Commercial Finance Corporation to small and medium-sized industrial firms, the Finance Corporation for Industry to larger firms, the Agricultural Mortgage Corporation to farmers and so on. We shall give a complete list of them in Chapter 17. In less developed financial systems than our own such bodies, often public or semi-public, play a large part in the finance of industry because only the few largest industrial concerns have direct access to the capital market.

Our list of the main types of financial institution under each heading now reads as follows:

1. *Deposit institutions*

    (a) *Deposit banking system*

    > Bank of England Banking Department
    > Deposit banks
    > National Giro
    > Discount houses

    (b) *Secondary banking system*

    > Secondary banks

(c) *Other deposit institutions*

>Finance houses
>Savings banks
>Building societies

2. *Insurance and provident institutions*

>Insurance companies
>Lloyd's underwriters
>Pension funds

3. *Portfolio institutions*

>Investment trust companies
>Unit trusts

4. *Special investment agencies*

This is as far as we need to go in classifying institutions for the time being. In the chapters describing the working of each main type we can introduce the various sub-types which exist in almost every field.

B. *Assets of financial institutions*

Our classification system has been based on the types of claims issued by each kind of institution; in other words it has been based largely on the nature of their liabilities. The picture of the broad functions which financial intermediaries perform in the financial system would be incomplete without a consideration of the nature of the different types of direct claim which they hold as assets.

Table 4.1 analyses the assets of deposit institutions into a number of headings which are designed to show the functions performed by the different institutions. All the five types except finance houses hold public sector debt, but the reasons for holding it are different. Deposit banks and building societies hold public sector debt largely as liquid assets, whereas savings banks automatically pass on all the deposits which they receive either to the central government or to local authorities. Secondary banks hold short-term loans to local authorities as part of their general asset structure. The main business of all types of deposit institution except savings banks consists of loans of different kinds, and it is here that the differences in function show up. The deposit banks lend almost entirely to U.K. residents for a variety of purposes, with businesses predominating. Secondary banks do most of their lending to overseas residents, and most of this business is in currencies other than sterling and matched by deposits in these other currencies. Building societies lend for house purchase to persons and housing associations, although they finance the building of houses to a very small extent. Somewhat surprisingly finance houses lend more for

Table 4.1   Assets of deposit institutions, end-1970

Percentages

	Deposit banks	Secondary banks	Savings banks	Building societies	Finance houses
Public sector debt	29.1	11.0	96.6	15.7	–
Loans					
House purchase	3.0	.4	–	80.5	–
Other personal	4.7	.5	–	–	33.1
Business	37.5	12.2	–	–	47.3
Other U.K.	8.9	–	–	–	–
Overseas	4.2	71.9	–	–	13.9
Other	12.6	4.0	3.4	3.8	5.7
Total	100.0	100.0	100.0	100.0	100.0

Sources: (1) *Financial Statistics;*   (2) *Consumer Credit: Report of the Committee,* Vol. 1, Table 2.19.

Notes: (1) The figures for deposit and secondary banks exclude inter-bank items.
         (2) The figures for finance houses refer to end-1969.

business purposes than for consumer finance, although part of this business lending will be to unincorporated businesses in the personal sector.

The assets of the remaining types of financial institution are analysed in Table 4.2. These consist largely of stock exchange securities, the only differences between the types of institution being in the proportions under the different headings. For them the public sector debt is held as an earning asset, and consists largely of the quoted stocks of the British government and local authorities. These institutions thus differ considerably from the deposit institutions: instead of lending directly to the deficit units, they buy the direct claims of deficit units on the stock exchange, more often than not some time after the claims have been issued.

Now that we have dealt with the nature of both liabilities and assets of the different types of intermediary, we can go on to look

briefly at their functions from another point of view—the sectors of
the economy from which they draw their funds and to which they lend.
Most types of institution are concerned with a number of sectors on
both sides of their balance sheets. The two outstanding exceptions are
savings banks and building societies, and these form special channels
of finance. In both cases the deposits which they issue are held almost
exclusively by households, but the sectors to which they lend are

Table 4.2   Assets of other financial institutions, end-1970

Percentages

	Insurance companies.	Pension funds	Investment trust companies	Unit trusts
Public sector debt	17.0	20.0	1.2	2.0
U.K. debentures & preference	12.6	14.4	3.8	3.8
U.K. ordinary shares	31.1	51.6	56.9	78.6
Overseas company securities	4.4	1.0	33.1	10.3
House purchase loans	7.7	–	–	–
Other	27.1	13.1	5.0	5.3
Total	100.0	100.0	100.0	100.0

Sources: (1) Table 15.9; (2) *Bank of England Quarterly Bulletin*,
March 1972, Tables 17 and 18.

Note: The figures for insurance companies refer only to U.K.
business.

different—the public sector exclusively in the case of savings banks
and the personal sector for 80% of their assets in the case of building
societies, the remaining 20% being cash balances and public sector
debt held as liquid assets. There are several other types of institution
which draw their funds overwhelmingly from the personal sector, but in
each case they acquire direct claims issued by several other sectors;
pension funds, unit trusts and the life assurance business of insurance
companies all come into this category. Among banks there is some
degree of sector specialisation on one side or the other of the balance
sheet, but in only two cases is it marked. Discount houses obtain all
but a small part of their funds from other banks, while they acquire
direct securities issued by the public sector, by non-financial companies and by the rest of the world. Secondary banks represent almost
a closed financial circuit in sector terms; about 80% of their de-

posits come from and 80% of their loans go to the rest of the world,
and the remainder of their business is mainly with very large non-
financial companies, apart from their holdings of local authority debt.

It remains only to consider the relative importance as channels of
funds to deficit units of the different types of institution and their
relative rates of growth over recent years. This is done in Table 4.3, in

Table 4.3   Total assets of financial institutions

£ million

		End-year		Ratio
		1960	1970	*1970/1960*
Deposit institutions				
Deposit banks		9,900	14,000	*1.4*
Discount houses		1,100	2,350	*2.1*
Secondary banks		2,750	28,400	*10.3*
Savings banks		3,150	4,400	*1.4*
Building societies		3,200	11,000	*3.4*
Finance houses		900	1,400	*1.6*
	Total	21,000	61,550	*2.9*
Other institutions				
Insurance companies		8,800	16,000	*1.8*
Pension funds		3,300	7,300	*2.2*
Investment trust companies		2,000	4,470	*2.2*
Unit trusts		190	1,345	*7.1*
Special investment agencies		350	530	*1.5*
	Total	14,640	29,645	*2.0*

which the 1960 figures are careful estimates based on considerable research, whereas the 1970 figures are much rougher estimates in several
cases. The figures shown are estimates of the total market value of
all kinds of asset, including their premises.

C. *Other characteristics*

So far we have limited our classification of financial institutions to
one based on the nature of the secondary claims which they issue,
with some consideration of their functions as shown by the assets
which they hold. There are many other ways in which financial institu-

tions can be classified, and a brief consideration of these will bring out important points about the operations of financial institutions.

The first distinction is that between *public* and *private* institutions. There are, of course, several government departments and funds whose function is entirely financial—the National Loans Fund, the National Debt Commissioners and several others; we are treating these as part of central government and not as separate financial institutions. The official financial statistics treat the ordinary departments of the National Savings Bank and the trustee savings banks and the Issue Department of the Bank of England as part of central government; we do not need to be so particular about sector classification, and we can deal with both the ordinary and investment departments of savings banks together and largely ignore the artificial division of the Bank of England into two departments. The only other public financial institutions in Britain are certain special investment agencies—the Film Finance Corporation and the Commonwealth Development Corporation, for example.

Among the private financial institutions there are two further distinctions which are important. The first is between *unincorporated* and *incorporated* bodies, and the second between *mutual* and *proprietary* bodies. Unincorporated businesses in any sphere are those owned by a single individual or consisting of a group of partners. Incorporated businesses are those which have achieved corporate status, usually by registration under the Companies Acts, and all proprietary bodies are incorporated. Mutual bodies may be either incorporated or unincorporated; as their name implies, they consist solely of their members, who have joined together to provide a financial service for their mutual benefit. As there are no outside shareholders, all profits are either retained as reserves or distributed to the members as bonuses.

In the nineteeth century it was generally thought improper for banks and discount houses to have the protection for folly and imprudent action which is provided by limited liability. The name 'joint-stock banks', which is still occasionally used for the main deposit banks, shows that unincorporated business was the general rule. Nowadays, however, there are only two or three unincorporated banks and three 'discount brokers' operating on the fringe of the discount market. Unincorporated businesses are still the rule, however, among stockbrokers, jobbers and Lloyd's underwriters; it is only a matter of a year or so before incorporation becomes general in these spheres. Examples of unincorporated mutual bodies are trustee savings banks and pension funds. Among incorporated bodies the mutual form of organisation is quite common in life assurance; the bodies are usually called 'societies' to distinguish them from the proprietary 'companies'. Building societies are incorporated under the Building Societies Acts, but operate as mutual bodies.

The main economic importance of these legal distinctions is the relative ease of access to external finance of the different kinds of body. An unincorporated business is in no better position than an individual person to raise outside finance; it can borrow from a bank or an individual or it can admit a 'sleeping partner', but it cannot appeal for outside shareholders to subscribe to its funds. The tax laws, moreover, make it very difficult for reserves to be accumulated in the business without suffering the full rigours of income tax and surtax. Mutual bodies are equally prevented from seeking outside finance except in the form of loans, but they are not subject to the same tax laws as individuals and thus they can accumulate reserves. Proprietary companies do not differ in their operation from companies in industry and commerce, having bodies of shareholders distinct from the persons benefiting from the services of the institution. There is one further feature of the mutual bodies which affects their operation: they were generally formed to benefit the poorer sections of the community, and there is still a strong element of 'social service' in the way in which they conduct their business.

The next distinction is usually referred to in terms of 'wholesale' and 'retail' institutions. The wholesale institutions are those which operate only in large amounts, whereas the retail institutions are geared to collecting together small amounts. The terminology is unfortunate because the normal use of the term 'wholesale' implies an element of 'breaking bulk', receiving large amounts and giving them out in small portions, and this side of wholesale business is entirely absent. Indeed, it is the retail business which involves breaking bulk by transforming large holdings of direct claims into small-unit secondary claims.

This distinction between wholesale and retail can hardly serve as a basis for classification of institutions since many institutions operate in both markets. However, over the past few years both aspects of financial business have grown fast. The retail business has grown through increasing affluence and the introduction of persons to financial matters who previously were not concerned at all, and wholesale business has grown through the increasing sophistication which companies and other large bodies are bringing to the handling of their financial affairs.

The last distinction which we shall mention is that between *first degree* and *second degree* financial intermediaries. Second degree intermediaries are those which receive all their funds from other financial intermediaries. It is difficult to think of any institutions which perform only second degree functions: perhaps insurance companies which specialise exclusively in the reinsurance market are the only example. Many institutions, however, act partly as second degree intermediaries. Examples are the discount houses, whose main function is to act as specialised banks enabling other banks to adjust their liquidity, and secondary banks in their activities on the inter-bank markets in sterling and other currencies.

2. OPERATION

A. *Economies of scale*

As we have seen financial intermediaries operate by acquiring the direct claims of deficit units and issuing in turn their own secondary claims in a form more attractive to surplus units than the direct claims. There are costs involved in this process of intermediation, and these costs must be met out of a margin between the borrowing and lending rates of interest of the intermediaries. The margin must cover the actual expenses of operation, the earning of a surplus to build up reserves, taxation and (for all except mutual bodies) the profits distributed to the owners of the business. In this main section we examine the ways in which intermediaries are able to pay less for borrowing than they receive from their direct claims, concentrating particularly on the costs of operation. In the next main section we shall look at the income side and at the determinants of the margin between borrowing and lending rates, as well as at reserves and taxation.

The basic reason for the ability of financial intermediaries to impose a margin is that they exploit the *economies of scale*.[1]

The economies of scale take several forms; some apply only to the assets side of the balance sheet, some only to the liabilities side and some to both sides.

On the assets side we start with the fact that the actual costs incurred in carrying out a transaction are largely independent of the value of the transaction. A transaction involving the purchase of securities to the value of £1 has to go through exactly the same process and to be

1. The following treatment is based to a great extent on B. J. Moore, *An Introduction to the Theory of Finance* (New York: The Free Press; London: Collier–Macmillan, 1968) pp. 98–100.

recorded in exactly the same way as a transaction involving the purchase of securities to the value of £1 million. For this reason the commissions payable on dealing in securities are a lower percentage of high-value transactions than of small-value ones. The first economy is thus one of *dealing costs* or trading costs.

This economy leads straight to the second one. Because dealing costs in the form of commissions are relatively high proportions of small transactions, it is much easier to secure *diversification* in a large portfolio of securities than in a small one. Unit trusts are a perfect example of this. If a unit trust portfolio consisted of fifty different securities, it would cost a person with £500 to invest at least as much and probably more than the unit trusts manager's margin to have his individual portfolio of equal spread. If we were to cost his time in handling fifty separate securities, recording the dividends for tax purposes and dealing with such matters as rights issues, we should find that it was much cheaper to buy unit trust units to the value of £500. A diversified portfolio spreads the risks in holding financial assets, and financial institutions exploit the economies of scale to enable holders to achieve this spread of risks cheaply.

Lastly financial intermediaries offer the advantages of *specialised management*. Not only can they handle the administration of the portfolio more cheaply because of the scale of their operation, but they are in a better position than an individual to achieve a well balanced portfolio. In Professor Tew's happy phrase, financial claims are 'branded goods',[2] each issuing body differing in standing and creditworthiness. It takes considerable expertise, often backed by large research departments, to assess the prospects for individual issuing bodies and the section of industry or commerce to which they belong. Thus financial intermediaries further reduce risk for surplus units by being better able to select an optimum portfolio.

The next use of the economies of scale applies to both assets and liabilities, and is in many ways the most important. Financial intermediaries operate largely by pooling independent risks in such a way that fluctuations are evened out: they take advantage of the *law of large numbers*. The whole operation of the liabilities side of life assurance depends on the fact that, while individual mortality cannot be predicted, that of a large population can be reduced to a predictable form. Banks rely on the fact that the transactions of a large number of customers will be partly self-cancelling; if the banks have forewarning of the actions of their larger customers and some experience of seasonal

2. Brian Tew, *Monetary Theory* (London: Routledge & Kegan Paul, 1969) p. 44.

fluctuations affecting large numbers of customers, they can roughly predict the level of their deposits and act accordingly. On the assets side the same pooling of risks applies, whether in the form of reducing the impact of individual failures to repay loans or in the lessening of the effect of an individual company failure on a portfolio.

By utilising the law of large numbers financial intermediaries are able to offer secondary claims which are in many cases considerably more *liquid* than the direct claims held as assets: bank deposits are more liquid than bank loans and building society shares and deposits are more liquid than house mortgages. Many writers commonly treat it as axiomatic that the distinguishing feature of financial intermediaries is that their liabilities are more liquid than their assets, and that the function of intermediaries is to borrow short and lend long—the so-called 'transformation function'. This is undoubtedly true of many deposit institutions, but it is stretching the common meaning of the word liquidity to apply the same doctrine to life policies or even units of unit trusts. Life policies and units are less risky than the direct claims held against them, but their maturity is no shorter. Because interest rates commonly follow a progression from low levels for the shortest maturities to higher levels for longer maturities, it is common for financial intermediaries to have assets of somewhat longer maturity than liabilities. However, it is only in a less developed financial system that the major function of intermediaries is the transformation of long-term direct claims into liquid secondary claims. In our own financial system contractual saving in the form of life assurance and pension funds largely provides the counterpart of long-term direct securities, and the average period of turnover of assets in deposit institutions such as building societies is very little longer than the average period of turnover of the liabilities.

Another use of the economies of scale by financial intermediaries lies in the provision of access to sources of credit which the deficit units would not enjoy on their own. The function of the intermediary here may be no more than the provision of a *name* that is known to the market and a guarantee that the borrower will repay. Although the intermediary may not be directly involved in the actual financial transaction, the giving of the guarantee implies that the act is that of a financial intermediary because the guaranteeing body has a contingent liability to repay the debt if the borrower defaults to the body from which it has borrowed. The classic case here is that of the accepting houses, which made their main business the lending of their names to the transactions of others, both by accepting bills of exchange and by sponsoring the issues of direct securities by companies and by foreign governments (in the latter case usually without entering into a guarantee).

Lastly financial intermediaries are able to benefit from the scale of their operations by providing numerous *non-financial services* which enhance the attractiveness of their secondary claims. We shall look at the nature of these later when we deal with competition between intermediaries, but we must mention that they are often sufficiently important to transform the nature of the secondary claim. A good example lies in the attraction of holding a bank account. In their advertising the banks are always reminding us of the convenience of using a bank account rather than notes and coin; they stress the greater safety, the convenience of standing orders for regular bills, the financial advice which is available from bank managers and the access to borrowing which a bank account offers. Bank deposits are no more liquid than legal tender money; the attraction lies solely in convenience and reduction of the risks of loss or theft.

We may summarise the effects of the economies of scale on the secondary claims of financial institutions by saying that these secondary claims are (1) less risky, (2) more convenient and (3) often more liquid than direct claims. By exploiting the economies of scale financial intermediaries can offer these facilities at far less cost than the surplus unit could achieve on its own—if indeed it could achieve them **at all.**

B. *Administrative costs*

In looking at the costs of dealing in securities we saw that the costs were largely fixed irrespective of the size of transaction, and that this led to dealing commission being a smaller percentage of large transactions than of small ones. The same relationship between costs and the size of transaction or account holds throughout the field of finance. A deposit of £1 million costs no more to process and probably less to attract than a deposit of £1. The administrative costs may usefully be divided into the initial costs in opening an account of any kind and the running costs.

In many financial operations the initial costs hinge around the drawing up of a policy or agreement. In retail business this is usually in standard form, and there are no specific legal costs, but with wholesale business many deals are tailor-made for each customer. In business involving direct lending one of the major elements in the initial cost is likely to be the establishment of creditworthiness. This presents few problems in wholesale business because the customers are well-known. In retail business the verifying of creditworthiness is easy for a deposit bank because it handles the customer's bank account, but it can be difficult and time-consuming for such lenders as finance houses, to whom borrowers may be going for the first time. Once the agreement has been signed, the remainder of the initial cost arises from the entry of the new account on the records. (We treat commission to agents for the introduction of business as a selling cost.)

The running costs involved in any account are usually straight-forward. In most cases they consist of recording changes in the account, of paying interest quarterly or half-yearly and of informing the holder periodically of the level of his account. With life assurance and lending by bodies other than banks there is also the collection of premiums or repayment instalments. These operations are not very costly in whole-sale business, and for a large part of retail business the use of banker's order ensures regular payment without reminders. The costs of collection rise to high levels, however, when the customer has no bank account. Sometimes he can be prevailed upon to call in at a branch to make his payment weekly or monthly, but some collections are made door-to-door. It is considerations such as this which determine the wide margins in financial business for the poorer classes of the community.

Because a large part of the administration of a financial institution consists of maintaining records and processing transactions, finance is a labour-intensive industry. The official statistics of employment[3] show that the numbers employed in insurance, banking and finance rose from 538,000 in mid-1959 to 638,000 in 1964 and 711,000 in 1969. This represented 2·4% of the total number of employees in 1959 and 3·0% in 1969. Starting in 1969 figures are available on a different basis (the 1968 Standard Industrial Classification as opposed to the 1958 S.I.C.), and these give more detail, but for a narrower definition of insurance, banking and finance. The relevant figures for 1969 in thousands of employees are:

	U.K. total	Males	Females
Insurance	308	177	131
Banking and bill discounting	264	129	135
Other financial institutions	73	37	36
Total	645	343	302

3. *Annual Abstract of Statistics* (e.g. 1970, Tables 134 & 135).

We can also provide rough estimates of the numbers employed in 1969 or 1970 in certain specific types of financial institution:

		Thousands
Deposit banks		200
Trustee savings banks		13
Building societies		23
Finance houses		16
Insurance companies		200
	Total	452

We have very little knowledge of the breakdown of the operating expenses of the different types of financial institution, but it is clear that labour costs account for a very large proportion, particularly for institutions in the retail market. For deposit banks and trustee savings banks, for both of which we have some indication of the proportion, labour costs are over 70% of total operating expenses. In addition to wages and salaries these labour costs include the contribution of employers to pension schemes for the staff. During recent years financial institutions have had a further burden of costs directly attributable to the employment of labour in the form of selective employment tax.

The sort of routine record-keeping tasks which are characteristic of finance are ideal for computers. Financial institutions were thus one of the first general fields of application of computers. Teething troubles were frequent, but by the time of writing the bulk of deposit bank, building society and insurance company accounts are maintained on computers. This has not yet resulted in a reduction in numbers employed, but the fall in the rate of increase shown in the statistics quoted above is probably a result of the introduction of computers. Eventually computers will leave the bulk of the staff free for less routine tasks, particularly contact with customers.

Even though computers may not yet have begun to reduce administrative costs, there have already been other effects. The most important of these is an increase in the standardisation in the services offered at the retail end of financial business, coupled with the provision of 'packages' of services, out of which the customer chooses a certain number of units. This process is particularly evident in insurance.

C. *Selling costs*

In one respect financial institutions are like any other commercial concern: they have a product to sell, and they must adopt a strategy for selling it. For certain types of institution—unit trusts and life assurance are good examples—the current methods of operation largely depend on a steady growth in business, and here the selling function is of particular importance. Although only advertising, the maintenance of a field sales force and the paying of commission for the introduction of business would normally be counted as selling costs, we are going to examine in this section certain administrative costs which have significance for selling. The most important of these are the costs involved in providing a branch network and door-to-door representatives.

An important part of the selling function is the maintenance of contact with existing customers so that opportunities for new business from them may be exploited. For certain types of business this contact is maintained through a branch network. Local branches are also part of the convenience associated with secondary claims, and they form the focal point for the provision of the various non-financial services which add to the attractiveness of secondary claims. For deposit banking they are the *sine qua non* of a nationwide banking system, but they are also important for building societies and trustee savings banks. Insurance companies and finance houses also have branches, but here the functions are somewhat different. We can make rough estimates of the total number of branches of different types of financial institution:

Deposit banks	14,000
Trustee savings banks	1,500
Building societies	1,850
Finance houses	800

A network of agents can be a substitute for or a supplement to a branch network. Typically financial institutions pay commission for the introduction of new business, and they enrol as agents professional and other people who are able to steer business in their direction. Many of these agents are accountants and solicitors (for insurance, unit trusts and building societies), estate agents (for building societies), stockbrokers (for unit trusts) and garage proprietors and retailers (for finance houses). Insurance brokers, who play such a large part in insurance business and often act as brokers for mortgages from building societies and other sources, are in a somewhat anomalous position since they act in the interests of their clients but receive their remuneration as commission from the body to which they introduce business. Often these agents perform a large or small part of the administrative function. Insurance brokers in particular service the policies which they have introduced to the companies, and building society agents receive and pay out shares and deposits for the society.

It is thus typical of the British financial system that it is partly held together by a series of agency relationships. These often extend to links between financial intermediaries of different types. Thus building societies have close links with one or two insurance companies because of their insistence on overseeing the fire insurance of mortgaged houses, and banks receive commission for introductions to unit trusts, building societies and insurance companies.

Several types of financial institution maintain forces of door-to-door representatives. In industrial (home service) life assurance and finance houses their main function is to collect regular premiums or instalments, but they are also a source of new business. Unit trusts are not permitted by regulation to canvass for sales on the doorstep, but the linking of life assurance with unit trusts has enabled them to get round this prohibition. So far only two or three of the larger management groups have built up field sales forces.

Advertising is one field in which selling is the only motive, and financial institutions have become more aggressive over the past decade or so. One has only to contrast the typical deposit bank advertisement of ten years ago—a discreet listing of the bank's name, address, the name of the chairman and its total assets—with the witty cartoon films of recent years. (It is still unwise to refer to the bank manager's cupboard when asking for an overdraft!) Table 4.4 shows statistics of the amounts spent on advertising in the press and on television by five types of financial institution over selected years from 1958.[4] The total expenditure has grown about sixfold over this period, representing a growth of something like four times in real terms. A comparison of the columns for 1969 and 1970 shows that, in recent years at least, the growth has not been steady; the expenditure on advertising has been assessed according to the circumstances of the particular type of business each year. Of the totals shown only 5–6% consists of expenditure on television advertising, but this is partly because the Independent Television Authority has maintained restrictions on financial advertising. In addition to the sums shown in Table 4.4 financial institutions

4. The figures were supplied by Legion Publishing Co. Ltd., to whom the author is grateful for permission to use them.

spend on advertising by the production of leaflets, window displays and by taking stands at exhibitions. Some measure of total advertising expenditure is given by the fact that the figures shown for building societies are only around 60% of the totals returned to the Chief Registrar of Friendly Societies under the heading of 'advertising'.

Table 4.4   Expenditure on press and television advertising by financial Institutions

£ thousand

		1958	1963	1966	1969	1970
Banks		542	1,582	2,643	3,984	3,401
Building societies		790	824	1,310	1,566	2,313
Finance houses		...	531	469	1,136	1,216
Insurance		611	1,227	1,652	3,036	2,863
Unit trusts		...	.718	1,420	3,150	1,883
	Total	1,943	4,882	7,494	12,872	11,676

Source: *Statistical Review of Press and Television Advertising.*

Note: The figures include collective advertising by associations such as the British Insurance Association and the Building Societies Association.

The points which we have made so far about selling apply almost entirely to retail business. For institutions in the wholesale market the problems are rather different. They normally do some discreet advertising, a lot of it consisting of prestige advertisements in the financial press, and some of them are beginning to open branches in the larger provincial centres. A great deal of their selling effort, however, consists of circulars to institutional clients, giving the results of research or general comments on the state of the market which they serve. Another part consists of the personal entertainment of officials of these institutional and other clients.

D. *Size and specialisation*

Because distances in the United Kingdom are so small, most of the larger institutions in the retail side of the business operate throughout the country. The only exceptions are trustee savings banks, which operate only in their own areas. Deposit banks in Scotland and Northern Ireland are formally separate from the London clearing banks, but there are many links of common ownership. Building societies comprise
*

twenty or so large societies operating throughout the country and a multitude of tiny societies operating only in their own towns. There is very little local element in insurance business, but there are small specialised companies. In the wholesale side of finance the institutions are located in London and Edinburgh, with occasional branches in such towns as Birmingham, Liverpool, Manchester and Leeds.

The result of the nationwide operations of the larger institutions in nearly all spheres of financial business is that within each type of financial institution a handful of institutions typically accounts for more than 50% of total assets. Among the deposit banks the main groups (five in England and Wales and three in Scotland) account for all but a tiny fraction of total business. The six largest building societies have more than 50% of total assets, while the twenty largest have 75% of total assets; the total number of building societies is around 500. In insurance forty large 'composite companies' (those doing both life and non-life business) accounted for 65% of total life funds and 85% of general funds.

Over the past ten to fifteen years mergers have been common in most spheres of finance. These have taken two forms, the taking over of small bodies by their larger brethren, and the merging of pairs of large or medium-sized bodies; in the latter case the business of the two bodies has often been complementary in type or geographically. The pressures towards merger have been mainly rising costs. The cost of labour services and of premises has generally risen faster than other prices, and financial institutions have had to face the high capital costs of installing computer systems. In certain fields, notably banking, the increase in size of large industrial customers has forced institutions to merge in order to be able to mobilize the large funds which these customers require.

This cursory description of the merger movement seems to imply that Mammon is on the side of the big battalions, and that the days of the small institution are numbered. This is certainly not true in many fields. A high proportion of the more important financial innovations of recent years has come from relatively small institutions. The classic example is probably the euro-dollar market, which was developed for several years through the initiative of accepting houses and British overseas banks before the London clearing banks came in through subsidiaries and before the American banks had overcome their initial mistrust. In most fields of finance there is still a place for the nimbleness and innovation of the smaller institution.

Although all our emphasis so far has been on the economies of scale, these economies can be 'bought in'. No financial system can develop far without a complicated infrastructure. It needs well-qualified lawyers and accountants, a fair and speedy system of courts and a high level of honesty in commercial dealings. In addition it needs the support of numerous specialist services. Whenever an institution is below the optimum size for a particular function, it can usually obtain the necessary service from outside. Administration is one of the features making for size in financial institutions, but there are many companies which perform the administrative function for numbers of small financial institutions. Among investment trust companies, for example, many consist of nothing more than a brass plate to indicate their registered office and a board of part-time directors; the keeping of the register of shareholders, the management of the portfolio and all other necessary services can be contracted for outside the company. Even the size of their customers need not be a determining factor; the accepting houses, lacking their own large resources, habitually arrange loans of many millions of pounds by organising consortia of other banks.

In the early days computers were often a factor forcing mergers of institutions, but now that computer service bureaux have become highly developed, even the smallest institutions can have access to the most sophisticated computer services. This development may indeed give a new lease of life to the smaller institutions in many spheres.

Another factor leading to the faster expansion of the larger institutions has been the need to open new branches. Institutions which have committed themselves in this direction have faced rising expenses, but some of the smaller institutions have realised that it was possible to obtain the advantages of a branch network on the backs of those institutions which already owned one. These smaller institutions have formed links with deposit banks, savings banks and building societies, and many of them have tried, so far with only limited success, to persuade the authorities to allow the sale of their units or policies over the counters of sub-post offices.

E. *Competition*

Competition in the financial system takes two main forms, interest rate competition and competition in the provision of services, and it takes place both between institutions of the same type and between institutions of different type. Despite many agreements on rates of interest, insurance tariffs and on rates of commission payable to agents, the financial system is highly competitive; where one form of competition is inhibited, it is replaced by competition in another form.

What we have called 'interest rate competition' is really something much wider—the competition for funds to lend and customers to lend them to. Financial intermediaries thus usually compete on both sides of their balance sheets. There are some exceptions. The 'other financial institutions' whose assets consist mainly of stock exchange securities compete mainly in their choice of already-issued claims, although they do some direct lending and they often obtain especially advantageous securities direct from the issuing body because of special connexions. There is also one class of intermediary for which competition takes a rather special form: pension funds have a source of funds which is largely captive since employees who are eligible usually join a pension scheme without question, and it is only if the performance of the fund fell markedly below that of comparable institutions or of insured schemes that members would begin to put pressure on the trustees and investment manager.

Table 4.5 shows under 'assets' the main areas of competition for lending and under 'liabilities' the main areas of competition for funds. An asterisk indicates the areas in which various types of institution are active, but the table needs care in interpretation. An example is the case of insurance companies, which are shown as making house purchase and personal loans (loans on policies); in neither case do insurance companies actively seek business, but regard these loans as facilities which will assist in the sale of life policies. Similarly, investment trust companies do indeed, as shown, provide finance for small businesses, but it is only a very small part of their function, and they are not particularly important in the market. In the areas of competition indicated in the table financial intermediaries compete with others of the same type and with intermediaries of different types.

The areas of competition indicated in Table 4.5 are widely drawn, but in practice most of the markets are fragmented in different ways. In the first place many financial intermediaries of all types specialise in different parts of their markets, and they will meet competition from the intermediaries of other types which operate in that particular market; some secondary banks, some unit trusts and all special investment agencies are specialised in this way. In the second place, there is in most spheres of activity a differentiation between wholesale and retail institutions. This fragments the market for competition both between institutions of the same type and between institutions of different types. A good example is the case of secondary banks and

Table 4.5 Areas of competition between financial institutions

| | Deposit institutions | | | | | | Other institutions | | | | | Other competitors |
	Deposit banks	National Giro	Secondary banks	Savings banks	Building societies	Finance houses	Insurance	Pension funds	Investment trust companies	Unit trusts	Special investment agencies	
Assets												
Overdrafts	*											
Term loans to industry	*		*			*					*	
Small business finance	*					*			*		*	Local authorities
House purchase loans	*	*			*	*	*					
Personal loans	*					*	*					
Diversified portfolios							*		*	*		
Liabilities												
Current accounts	*	*	*	*								
Other deposits: wholesale	*		*			*						
retail	*			*	*	*						Local authorities
Life policies							*	*				
Non-financial services												
Executor and trustee	*		*				*					Public Trustee, solicitors
Portfolio management	*		*				*	*				Stockbrokers, accountants
Unit trust management	*		*							*		
Nominee companies	*		*									
Credit cards	*		*									
Company registrar	*		*									Accountants
Financial advice: wholesale	*											Accountants
retail												Accountants
Issue of company securities	*										*	Stockbrokers
Computer services	*											

finance houses, which both make term loans to industry; secondary banks operate very much in the wholesale market, limiting themselves to a few score of the best-known non-financial companies, whereas finance houses lend to smaller concerns. The two types of institution compete in this market only at the margin.

In most of the areas of competition interest rates (in the sense of terms offered for the holding of secondary claims and the terms charged for lending) are uniform as between competing institutions, and this uniformity may be the result of unfettered competition or of agreement as to the rates to be paid and charged in that particular market. Often it is difficult to compare rates between institutions. It is easiest to do so in markets where all institutions offer almost identical claims— deposits of deposit banks, savings banks and building societies are good examples; in some cases, however, as with life assurance policies, the claims have a complicated set of characteristics, and only experts in the market can reduce the terms to a comparable basis. The different tax privileges accorded to such claims as savings bank deposits (in the ordinary departments), building society shares and deposits and life assurance also make it difficult to achieve straight comparisons of terms; a grossing-up of the yield at the marginal rate of tax paid by the individual is necessary before comparison can be made.

Not all the competition to attract funds and customers for loans takes the form of varying the yields offered and the charges levied, and in many cases the offering of exceptionally generous terms will lead to suspicion that there is something shady about an institution which has to offer much more than the market rate. The competition consists also of offering a number of ancillary facilities, which make one claim more attractive than another offering the same interest rate terms. For deposits competition often consists of providing easier and quicker withdrawal facilities or of providing the extra convenience of a wide-spread branch network. Sometimes claims are made more attractive by linking them to life assurance policies, with their tax advantages, or by providing guaranteed loan facilities in case of need. For institutions most of whose business is introduced by agents competition often takes the form of higher commission rates.

Alongside all the competition for funds and customers on the lending side there is competition, as we have already indicated, with direct claims. The saver always has the possibility of acquiring direct securities, and he will be comparing the terms offered on these with those of secondary claims. For deposit institutions most of this competition comes from the public sector; national savings securities of all types compete with claims offered by deposit institutions in the retail market, and short-term loans to local authorities are important competitors for wholesale deposits.

Financial institutions also offer a wide range of ancillary services. The most important of these are shown in Table 4.5 under the heading of 'non-financial services'. The services are mostly closely connected with finance, but we have used this term to indicate that no financial claim is involved between the institution and its customer. In most of these 'non-financial' services there is competition with bodies other than financial institutions; in addition to those shown in the last column there are in many cases specialist companies which offer nothing but the service in question.

F. *Groups and associations*

All the discussion about financial institutions which we have had so far has treated each type of institution as an independent entity. We shall have to continue with this treatment throughout the book because we are concerned with the methods of operation of the different types, and each type has its special characteristics. The reality of the financial system is far more complex. It consists of numbers of groups under common ownership comprising institutions of different types and of close links between independent institutions of different types. The only institutions which are completely or largely outside these group-ings are the National Giro, savings banks, building societies and pension funds.

Not surprisingly the deposit banks form the centre of many groups. Among the deposit banks themselves several banks are under common ownership, and the geographical groupings of London clearing banks, Scottish banks and Northern Ireland banks have many links of common ownership. Deposit banks have subsidiaries, or 'affiliates', operating in the secondary banking system, many of them have a subsidiary or associated bank operating overseas, most of them have a subsidiary or associated finance house and several have departments or subsidi-aries managing a unit trust. The tendency is towards what has been called 'department store banking', the situation in which most if not all financial services can be obtained by visiting a single branch.

Unit trust management groups are beginning to expand into adjoin-ing spheres, and many of them are beginning to talk of their being at the centre of the 'money industry', implying that they wish to offer all types of saving outlet for their customers. They have formed their own life assurance companies in some cases, and one management group has actually formed its own building society to cater for the liquid asset element in its customers' savings.

There are also many other groups operating in the financial sphere. Many of these are the financial groups which are often mentioned in the press in connexion with company take-overs; often they have their own merchant bank (which usually does little deposit business and hence escapes inclusion in official statistics), unit trust management company or insurance company. The only other commonly-found grouping is between merchant banks and investment trust companies; this arose because many investment trust companies were founded by merchant banks, often for the investments of their customers, and the banks still act as managers now that the investment trust company's securities have become available to a wider public.

Alongside the links of common ownership or of shareholdings in other companies there are several informal links formed for specific purposes. We have already mentioned the insurance agencies of building societies, which arose out of the need for fire insurance of mortgaged houses. These links between individual building societies and individual insurance companies have been strengthened recently as many building societies have begun to offer assurance-linked bonds. Those unit trust management groups which have not formed their own life assurance companies to operate assurance-linked unit trust schemes have linked up with insurance companies for this purpose.

The financial system thus consists of numbers of links between financial institutions of different types. As we saw earlier, many of these links are purely agency services, but there are also groupings of various types, ranging from common ownership to informal links involving one particular aspect of an institution's business. We shall be referring to these links throughout the chapters which deal with the working of different types of intermediary.

Another characteristic of our financial system to which we shall be referring constantly is the presence of collective associations in nearly all fields. These associations have very important functions, although they are not equally important in all fields. Their two most important functions are the drafting and enforcing of collective agreements about the regulation of business and the negotiation with the authorities over that matter and over monetary policy measures. They also carry out collective advertising and act as the channel for the collection of statistics, official and unofficial.

3. MARGIN AND RESERVES

As we have seen, the functioning of financial intermediaries depends on there being a gap or 'margin' between the rate of interest paid out on secondary claims and the rate of interest received on holdings of direct claims. Out of this margin the intermediary has to meet the expenses of operation, pay taxation and achieve a surplus. We have already looked at the expenses of operation in some detail, and in this main section we are going to consider the margin and the role of the surplus in feeding reserves.

A. *Margin and surplus*

In practical terms it does no great violence to the true state of affairs to concentrate attention on the interest yield of the assets held by financial intermediaries and largely to ignore any other earnings which they may have. In nearly every case these additional earnings are the gilt on the gingerbread, and they often bear no greater relationship to total revenue than do, say, the catering profits of British Rail to its total revenue. These sidelines and additional earnings are quite important, however, in the context of the structure of the financial system. They can be divided into two main types: (1) those arising from payments for services, whether these are connected with the main business of the intermediaries or whether they come from ancillary non-financial services and (2) the earnings additional to the receipt of interest or dividends which come from the holding of a portfolio of direct claims. Examples of the first type are the charges made by deposit banks for operating current accounts and the receipt of commission for the passing on of business to financial institutions of a different type. Among the second type are dealing profits arising from the switching of portfolios and the commission received for acting as underwriters in the new issue markets for company and local authority securities.

The last source of additional earnings which we shall mention is that of rent from the leasing out of spare office and shop accommodation. Many financial institutions deliberately build or purchase branch premises larger than they need in order to be able to let out the spare space to professional firms or to shops. Throughout the country firms of solicitors, accountants and estate agents occupy offices over or adjacent to bank or building society branches.

The major source of revenue for financial intermediaries is the margin between their lending and borrowing rates of interest (including the premiums of life assurance and the payments on the secondary claims issued by investment trust companies and unit trusts within this term). Some years ago *Punch* had a supplement on the City of London, in which it described the function of financial institutions as shovelling capital from one place to another; it added that the institutions live on 'what sticks to their shovels'. The margin can thus be said to measure the *cost of intermediation*. This cost consists of four main elements: (1) operating expenses, (2) taxation, (3) additions to net worth (reserves) and, in the case of proprietary institutions, (4) distribution to the proprietors.

The relationship between the various elements in the margin can be set out schematically as follows:

(1) lending rate — borrowing rate   =   margin
(2) margin — operating expenses   =   gross surplus
(3) gross surplus — taxation   =   net surplus.

It is the net surplus to which we have been referring for short as 'the surplus'. Out of it have to come the additions to net worth and the distribution to proprietors.

We have already examined in some detail the various items of operating expenses which affect financial institutions. All that we need to do here is to reiterate the distinction between retail and wholesale operations. Institutions operating in the retail market have two major sources of expenses, staff costs (including employers' pension contributions) and the costs of either a branch network or a field force of agents. For the wholesale market the staff costs are much lower, and there is often little need for either branches or a field force. It is mainly for this reason that the margins are very much smaller in the wholesale market than in retail operations.

So far we have not examined the impact of taxation. There are peculiarities of tax position affecting most types of institutions, and we shall deal with them in later chapters. We can summarise the position by saying that the general case is that financial institutions are subject to the same rules of corporation tax as other incorporated bodies or to the same rules of income tax and surtax as other unincorporated trading bodies.

Although the surplus, net of taxation, is usually only a small part of the total margin, it plays a key role in the operation of financial intermediaries. Financial intermediaries differ from enterprises in other parts of the economy in that they do not obtain the major part of their resources from equity capital, whether it is subscribed by shareholders or retained from the flow of net revenue; instead their liabilities are nearly as large as their assets. Nevertheless, as we shall see in the next section, there are many pressures for the maintenance of a minimum ratio of net worth to total assets, and surplus, as the source for additions to net worth, is correspondingly important. Financial institutions cannot continue their operations for long unless the margin is wide enough to yield a surplus.

There are two particular factors which affect the size of surplus which intermediaries of different types need to earn: (1) the reserve ratio which they must maintain and (2) their rate of expansion. The first of these is particularly important to proprietary institutions, since the shareholders are concerned with the rate of return on their shares and not the proportion of the margin which represents surplus. Another way of looking at the reserve ratio is to regard it as the opposite of the borrowing ratio, the ratio which the stock market or surplus units regard as suitable between borrowed funds and the net worth of the enterprise. The less risky a particular type of business or a particular institution is generally thought to be the higher the borrowing ratio which the market will tolerate; the higher the borrowing ratio the lower the rate of surplus which the institution needs to earn on its assets in order to achieve a given rate of return on shareholders' funds.[5]

The earning of a surplus is a particular constraint on institutions which are expanding fast since they must earn correspondingly large surpluses to maintain their minimum net worth (reserve) ratios. There is a simple formula which expresses the relationship between a reserve ratio, the rate of surplus and the rate of growth. If we express the reserve ratio r, the rate of surplus s and the rate of growth g as percentages of *total assets*, the formula is

$$\Delta r = s - \frac{rg}{100 + g}.$$

We can see the effect of this relationship most simply by considering the case in which an intermediary wishes to maintain its reserve ratio unchanged. In that case $\Delta r = 0$, and we can bring s over to the other side of the equation and write

$$s = \frac{rg}{100 + g}.$$

5. An example of this effect of 'gearing' on the rate of surplus is given in Chapter 12 (see pp. 332–3 and Table 12.11).

Two examples will be sufficient to show the effect of the rate of growth on the surplus needed to maintain a given reserve ratio, say 4%, unchanged. If $g = 2\%$, $s = 8/102 = 0.078$. If, on the other hand, $g = 10\%$, s rises to $40/110 = 0.364$. This is a constraint which does not apply with nearly so much force to proprietary institutions as to mutual bodies, because the former always have the possibility of raising fresh equity capital from outside.

There can obviously be many situations in which a financial institution needs to widen its margin, either because it is growing fast or because operating expenses or taxation have risen. Different types of institution vary markedly in the extent to which they can control their margins and in the speed at which they can change their margins.

Financial intermediaries fall into three main classes according to the degree of control which they have over their margins. (1) Certain institutions operate with completely fixed margins. The best examples are the ordinary departments of both the National Savings Bank and the trustee savings banks, which receive a fixed service charge from the Treasury. (2) Other institutions operate in competitive markets on both sides of their balance sheet. Finance houses, unit trusts, investment trust companies and insurance companies are examples. When intermediaries are competing freely both for funds and for lending, the extent of the margin will be determined by the costs of the different institutions. The most efficient institutions—those with lowest costs—can expand, with the need to maintain their reserve ratios or to raise fresh outside capital acting as a brake on continued expansion through narrower margins. (3) Building societies are the best example of the third class, which have a competitive borrowing rate but fix their lending rate by a cost-plus calculation. For them the margin is something to be calculated before arriving at the lending rate. Because they charge less than the market will bear for their lending, they usually have to ration their loans to match the funds available.

The most important factor in determining the speed with which institutions can move to adjust their margins is the degree to which they can alter the terms on existing contracts. At one extreme there are bodies like deposit banks and building societies, which can alter the terms of existing contracts at any time and at the other there are bodies like life assurance companies (often called life offices), which can alter only the terms of new contracts. In practice the contrast between these two extremes is not so great as would appear. While they were operating their 'cartel' agreement on interest rates, deposit banks were dependent on a change in Bank rate for a change in their own rates. Building societies provide an example of the costs and resultant lags in adjusting to a changed general level of interest rates. Lenders and borrowers have to be notified of the changed terms, and before the days of computers the complicated calculations necessary on each account made the societies reluctant to change their terms for what might be only a temporary change in the general level of interest rates. Moreover, it is usually a lengthier process to make changed terms effective for their loans than for their deposits, so that they face a temporary narrowing of the margin every time they alter their terms. Those institutions at the other extreme, which cannot alter the terms of contracts once they have been negotiated, usually have some sort of cushion. The effect of their fixed contracts is that marginal earnings can depart quite markedly from average earnings for a period. Insurance companies can compensate for this to some extent on that part of their business which is with profits since the declaring of bonuses is under their control.

B. *Reserves*

In our discussion of the relation between surplus and reserves we have been careful to make it clear that reserves are the equivalent of net worth. This is particularly necessary because there is a tendency, originating in the U.S.A., to use the term 'reserves' to cover holdings of cash and liquid assets. The same term can hardly be used for items on opposite sides of the balance sheet—net worth on the liabilities side and liquid assets on the assets side—without causing considerable confusion. Throughout this book we shall draw the reader's attention specifically to those cases in which the word means anything other than 'net worth'.

As we mentioned above, financial institutions differ from enterprises in other spheres in not obtaining their main resources from equity capital. Instead they exist by issuing secondary claims and holding direct claims to a nearly equal amount. The small difference in amount, the amount by which total assets exceed total liabilities, plays a most important part in their operation. The position of this net worth can be seen from the schematic balance sheet (see p. 104) typical of a financial intermediary.

'Net worth', in any context, refers to the excess of total assets over total liabilities. We are, however, departing slightly from the use of the term in Chapter 1. There we found it convenient to treat share capital as a definite liability, but here we are using the term 'net worth'

to mean the excess of total assets over the total of liabilities to depositors of the intermediary—to outside parties, in other words. 'Net
worth', as we are using it here, includes share capital, and is equivalent to 'capital and reserves'. It represents what would be left in the
business if all the depositors withdrew their funds.

Liabilities		*Assets*	
Deposits	95	Liquid assets	15
Net worth	5	Loans	83
		Fixed assets	2
	100		100

In the example above the total of assets of all kinds (100) exceeds
the total of liabilities to outside parties (deposits 95) by 5. The counterpart on the assets side of this 5 of net worth (capital and reserves) is
not any specific assets, but a general excess of total assets over total
liabilities to outside parties of 5. Another way of saying the same thing
is to refer to this excess as equivalent to 'free assets' of 5. There is
certainly no connexion between the 5 of capital and reserves and any
part of the liquid assets held.

We have described the capital and reserves as what would be left in
the business if all the outside parties withdrew their funds, and we
must now see what functions the reserves of mutual bodies and the
capital and reserves of proprietary institutions perform. Basically this
cushion of free assets is present to meet the contingency that the
realisable values of the assets should not be sufficient to meet withdrawals of funds. The proportion of reserves or capital and reserves
(we shall talk of them as 'reserves' for short) should in theory be related to the proportion of assets the realisable values of which are
particularly at risk. Assets of this type fall into three categories: (1)
fixed assets such as premises and computers, the full value of which
can never be realised in a quick sale, (2) marketable securities, the
market value of which may well fall below the book value at which
they are carried in the balance sheet, and (3) loans, on which some of
the borrowers may default. In practice most financial institutions make
separate and specific provision for the second and third categories. It
makes no difference to the reality, although it may complicate the
reading of balance sheets, whether they so do by making a specific reserve on the liabilities side ('investment reserve' and 'provision for
bad and doubtful debts') or by deducting such a reserve or provision

from the values on the assets side. A further function which reserves perform is to act as an insurance against the possibility of large and unforeseen expenses; large damages awarded against the institution in a law suit would be a case in point. Many financial institutions are at risk because adding their name to a transaction carries a contingent liability if the immediate debtor defaults, and reserves are the insurance cushion for this risk.

Reserves are thus an insurance against a number of contingencies, and all financial institutions adhere to certain minimum reserve ratios. In many cases these are the ratios customary in that line of business, and the institutions do not depart from them for fear of losing public confidence in their stability. In several cases minimum reserve ratios are laid down by law or by official regulation and thus play a part in the control of financial intermediaries by the authorities. Insurance companies are required by law to adhere to minimum ratios of capital and reserves. For building societies minimum reserve ratios, varying somewhat with the size of society, are laid down by the Chief Registrar of Friendly Societies if shares and deposits with the society are to be permitted investments for trustees, and the same minimum ratios are required to qualify for membership of the Building Societies Association. The Bank of England keeps a close watch on the reserve ratios of the bodies under its direct surveillance in the banking system— deposit banks, accepting houses, other secondary banks and discount houses. In all cases it works to certain minimum ratios, although nobody outside the Bank knows what these ratios are.

If reserves are a cushion maintained for insurance purposes, it follows that surplus, which feeds these reserves, has the nature of an insurance premium. We have already seen the extent to which the earning of surplus affects the margin necessary and hence the cost of intermediation. It is thus sensible to ask whether the keeping of reserves is the best and cheapest way of securing the necessary insurance. There are at least three alternatives to be considered: (1) the provision of central bank or government guarantees, (2) the specific insuring of liabilities and (3) the spreading of risks on to the shoulders of other intermediaries. Although the knowledge that the Bank of England is not likely to stand by and permit the failure of an important financial institution contributes greatly to the stability of the financial system, institutions would not welcome more specific guarantees because of the probability that these would entail closer regulation. The specific insuring of liabilities is practised very little in Britain, although it is an important feature of the U.S. financial system. The spreading of risks on to other intermediaries in the form of reinsurance is an important part of the market for insurance.

C. *Balance sheet management*

By introducing reserves and their functions into the discussion we have paved the way for a consideration of the structure of the balance sheet as a whole, in particular the relationship between certain types of asset and liability. In this section we shall be concerned only with broad principles, and we shall begin by looking at theoretical norms for the balance sheet structure of different types of institution. No actual institution will ever adhere exactly to these norms; rather are they a point of reference for considering the prudence and profitability with which actual institutions are conducted. Later in the discussion we shall relax some of our insistence on these theoretical norms, but the detailed balance sheet behaviour of different types of intermediary will not be discussed until we reach the chapters which deal with the operation of each kind of institution in turn.

We used the terms 'prudence' and 'profitability' above, and it can be said that the basic problem of balance sheet management for financial institutions is the reconciliation of these two objectives. Since financial intermediaries depend for their very existence on the confidence of the general public in their safety as repositories for personal and corporate wealth, prudence is essential to the successful operation of intermediaries. Not only must financial institutions be conducted with prudence, but they must be seen to be conducted with prudence. As we shall see, this need to appear prudent is often an additional constraint on their management over and above the actual needs of prudent behaviour.

Nearly all discussion of prudent behaviour in financial institutions is confined to the role of liquid assets. It is natural that this should be so because banks were historically the first financial institutions in all countries, and because the nature of the cash flow of banks is such that the holding of liquid assets is a necessity. We shall argue, however, that this emphasis on liquid assets is misplaced. Many types of financial intermediary have assets and liabilities producing a cash flow for which the holding of liquid assets is irrelevant, and we must probe further before we can frame a generalisation applicable to all types of intermediary.

To begin with we must distinguish two features of liquid assets. The term implies that they are assets which can be 'sold' at a moment's notice with little risk of loss, and for this reason they are nearly always very short-term assets. The main reason for holding them is obviously to guard against unexpected or unpredictable contingencies which require immediate access to cash. Because they are short-term, however, they are also held to meet entirely predictable expenditures occurring only a short time into the future. A financial institution thus normally holds liquid assets for two distinct reasons: (1) to meet unpredictable withdrawals of liabilities or unpredictable expenditures on operating account and (2) to cover predictable withdrawals of liabilities or predictable expenditures on operating account (payments of taxes, rent, interest and so on) in the near future. All financial institutions need to hold liquid assets for the second reason, but not all of them have unpredictable outflows which must be met at short notice. It should never be forgotten that a theoretical alternative to the holding of liquid assets is the availability of borrowing facilities, a line of credit, from another institution. On the whole surprisingly little use is made of this alternative.

If we want to frame a generalisation applicable to all types of institution, we must go further back into their operation and consider the nature of the various cash flows. The general financial problem facing financial institutions is no different from that facing any other kind of economic unit, from the humblest household to the largest corporation or the government; it is to marry the flows of income and expenditure. The nature of these flows and their timing and predictability determine the financial dispositions which are necessary to achieve the marriage.

We may begin by considering the simplest possible situation, that in which the claims issued by an intermediary are all of fixed maturity. As we shall see, this is the situation facing a secondary bank for the greater part of its business. Prudence demands that each fixed-term deposit should be exactly matched by a fixed-term asset maturing on the same day as the deposit. Such a balance sheet is perfectly safe apart from the danger of default on the loans held as assets; this danger is met by the net worth (reserves) of the institution. Such an institution will hold assets which would normally be classified as liquid for two purposes: (1) to 'match' its short-term liabilities and (2) to meet short-term predictable expenditures such as the payment of interest and taxes. Any holding of liquid assets beyond what is necessary for these two purposes does not improve the safety of the position and is nearly always detrimental to profitability. As an example we may consider the somewhat extreme case of a secondary bank all of whose deposits mature within a period of six months to one year hence. If it matches, say, three-quarters of these deposits with assets of equal maturity and holds liquid assets, ranging in maturity between sight and one month, against the remaining quarter of its deposits, it must replace these liquid assets several times before the deposits mature. Its safety is not increased because it will not allow its depositors to withdraw before maturity, but it has reduced its chances of making a profit. In the first place the liquid assets will almost certainly yield less than assets of longer maturity; in the second place the institution faces the risk of a general fall in interest rates, which would reduce the yield on the replacement liquid assets and narrow its margin still further. Equally, if it holds assets which are generally of longer term than its deposits, a sprinkling of liquid assets will do little to help. Its problem is that of replacing deposits when the original ones mature, and the disposal of the liquid assets will cover only a small part of the maturing deposits. The most that liquid assets can do is to provide a breathing space during which new deposits can be obtained on the most attractive terms available.

The case of a deposit bank provides a complete contrast with that of a secondary bank. Nearly all the deposits are withdrawable on demand or on very short notice. The actual times at which depositors will exercise their rights of withdrawal are unpredictable, although large banks can be sure that net outflows will be fairly small or else predictable on a seasonal basis. This is the situation for which liquid assets are the answer—the unpredictability of outflows. The liquid assets are also of use to cope with unpredictable elements on the assets side—the actual drawing by customers on their overdraft facilities, for example.

The examples chosen from the banking field are simple ones in the sense that the liabilities are all discrete deposits, maturing on a single date or withdrawable on demand or short notice. The situation facing other types of intermediary is complicated to the extent that the inflow of liabilities or the proceeds from assets are by instalments. Instalments are nearly always predictable, and the dictates of prudence can be followed by the same principle of matching maturities as long as we consider each instalment as a separate liability or asset. A finance house specialising in instalment credit advances the full amount of a loan immediately, and has to secure the funds necessary by issuing a deposit or other liability of the full amount. It can match the instalments on the loan if it has deposits of different maturities, each of the amount of the instalment and maturing on the date that the instalment is received. A life office receives its premiums by instalments over a very long period, and the total liability will mature on the death of the policyholder or on a fixed date. It can match by acquiring assets with each instalment which have maturities equal to the remaining term of the liability.

It is with these cases of instalments, however, that the conflict between prudence and profitability is at its most acute, and the extent of the conflict depends on the power of the intermediary to vary its interest rates during the currency of the claim. A building society is relatively fortunate because it can vary the interest rates on both its liabilities and its assets. A life office, on the other hand, has a fixed instalment which may be payable over a period as long as sixty or more years. The life office is at considerable risk because the premium rate is calculated on the basis of rates of interest ruling when the policy is issued whereas each premium has to be invested at the rate of interest current on its receipt. The maximum protection is given by matching long-term liabilities with long-term assets.

It would seem from this analysis that the general principles of balance sheet management by financial institutions depend greatly on the concept of matching, both by maturity and by currency whenever business is undertaken in foreign currencies. It is only when the cash flow is unpredictable that liquid assets are needed for balance sheet management, although some short-term assets may be needed to meet predictable operational expenses.

These general principles are the theoretical norms to which we referred at the beginning of the section. No institution will ever follow them slavishly; rather are they the standard against which the actual position will be judged. We can list a number of reasons for which institutions will deviate from these norms. (1) Because interest rates are normally higher for longer maturities than for short maturities, an institution will usually widen its margin by having assets somewhat longer than maturities. (2) Most institutions will 'take a view' on the likely changes in interest rates during the immediate future and adjust their balance sheets accordingly. (3) The examples which we gave assumed that each institution had only one kind of business, whereas the opposite is nearly always true. Thus, most secondary banks have some deposit banking business and many make loans which are repayable by instalments rather than in one lump on maturity. (4) Most financial institutions have some other elements in the situation which can be varied. A life office, for example, is not committed to bonuses until they have been declared, and it can often vary its inflow of new business by quoting favourable rates for policies which involve only a single premium. (5) At times when the cash inflow is larger than the outflow institutions can meet withdrawals of liabilities by reducing their acquisition of new assets rather than by disposing of liquid assets.

FURTHER READING

R. W. Goldsmith, *Financial Institutions* (New York: Random House, 1968).
B. J. Moore. *An Introduction to the Theory of Finance* (New York: The Free Press; London: Collier–Macmillan, 1968).

PART B

The Banking System

5 The Banking System and the Bank of England

Modern thinking tends to deny that banks are unique among financial institutions, but on any showing they form a most important part of the financial system. The banking system is responsible for the main part of the payments mechanism in the economy, and its influence reaches into all corners. The other services which it performs are numerous, and the whole banking mechanism is complex. For these reasons we shall need to devote seven chapters in all to the banking system, including the domestic and international money markets which are so closely tied to it. The present chapter outlines the system as a whole, describing the different kinds of bank and their functions, and then goes on to deal with the Bank of England.

The present is a particularly difficult time at which to analyse the working of the British banking system. In September 1971 new arrangements for the control of banks and for fostering competition between them were put into operation by the Bank of England. As a result of this a number of the agreements and conventions which bound parts of the system together were dropped, and the distinctions between different kinds of bank have already become blurred. We shall describe in some detail the way in which the banking system was working up to September 1971, and indicate the changes which were then introduced. As far as we are able at this early stage we shall chart the likely direction of future changes in the structure of the system. This book is being written at the end of an epoch. The one thing which is certain is that the banking system and indeed other parts of the financial system will never again be as they were before September 1971.

1. TYPES OF BANK

A. *Classification*

There is no satisfactory all-embracing definition of a bank, rather a series of definitions of the types of body that can be considered as banks for certain purposes. Equally there is no single list from which we can obtain the titles of all banks, but again a number of lists compiled for different purposes. Fortunately there is little dispute about the great majority of bodies which we consider as banks in this book; any doubts that there are concern the borderline for the smaller institutions. For practical purposes we shall adopt the list of banks used for official statistics. This will give us a coherent and consistent population of banks to study, although it leaves out entirely some of the smaller 'merchant banks'.

Table 5.1 sets out the classification of banks which we shall adopt, and shows for each type of bank the numbers and total deposits as at December 1970 and 1971. This classification is based partly on function and partly on ownership, separating U.K.-owned banks from foreign-owned banks. It is not a classification which we shall be able to continue into other tables, because the official statistics use a different classification. This dates from the statistics prepared for the Radcliffe Committee, and was originally based on the membership of various banking associations; over time it has been expanded to include several categories of banks which are not members of any association. Fortunately our classification of deposit banks is identical to that of the Bank of England, and our category of secondary banks covers exactly what the Bank of England terms 'accepting houses, overseas banks and other banks in the United Kingdom'.

The main classification of banks consists of four groups. At the top, in lonely eminence, stands the Bank of England. As the central bank it acts as banker for the government, for overseas central banks, for the London clearing banks and for some other banks. It is also responsible for controlling, supervising and supporting the whole banking system and certain other parts of the financial system. The deposit banks are banks with branch networks which operate the main payments mechanism, and are bodies which normally spring to mind when banks are being talked about. The secondary banks perform many of the same functions as deposit banks, but they do not compete actively in the payments mechanism, at least within this country. They have few branches in the U.K., and most of these are in the City

Table 5.1 Banks operating in the United Kingdom, December 1970 and 1971

	Numbers		Total deposits £ million	
	1970	1971	1970	1971
Bank of England	1	1	726	525
Deposit banks				
London clearing banks	6	6	10,606	12,557
Scottish clearing banks	4	3	1,119	1,211
Northern Ireland banks	7	7	333	325
National Giro	1	1	58	75
Other	7	7	335	412
Total	25	· 24	12,451	14,580
Secondary banks				
U.K. banks				
Accepting houses	24	24	3,006	3,355
Subsidiaries of deposit banks	20	21	3,478	4,567
Other	8	11	397	500
British overseas banks	12	11	2,235	1,967
Consortium banks	10	18	1,296	1,922
Foreign banks				
Australia and New Zealand	7	7	123	191
Canada	5	5	1,323	1,541
U.S.A.	32	34	11,567	13,010
France	8	8	536	801
Japan	11	11	731	907
Other countries	57	61	2,834	3,873
Total	194	211	27,526	32,634
Discount houses	11	11	2,260	2,977

Source: Bank of England. The deposit figures for those categories which are not distinguished in the *Bank of England Quarterly Bulletin* were supplied with the authority of the banks concerned. The deposits for foreign banks from other countries are a residual figure.

Note: The numbers of banks in both years include subsidiaries operating in the Channel Islands (accepting houses 7, subsidiaries of deposit banks 8, British overseas banks 2).

of London. Nearly all of them have fairly strong connexions with overseas countries. Finally, discount houses are specialised banks, which exist mainly to perform money market services for other banks.

The banking system consists of all four classes of bank, but two of the classes have highly specialised functions—the Bank of England and the discount houses. We shall often have occasion to refer to deposit banks and secondary banks together, and we shall give them the collective name of 'commercial banks'. At this stage there is nothing more that need be said about the Bank of England and the discount houses, but we must look at the subsidiary classifications of the commercial banks.

Between them the deposit banks have branch networks covering the whole of the United Kingdom, the Isle of Man and the Channel Islands. The main distinction between the different types of deposit banks is geographical. The London clearing banks provide the main facilities in England and Wales, the Isle of Man and the Channel Islands, while Scotland and Northern Ireland have their own separate banking networks. The seven banks shown as 'other deposit banks' fall into three groups. (1) The Yorkshire Bank and the Isle of Man Bank (both owned by clearing banks) provide banking facilities in restricted areas. (2) Both the English and Scottish co-operative wholesale societies have banking departments, which provide the full range of banking facilities. They have relatively few bank branches, but their facilities are available at any co-operative retail shop. (3) The remaining group consists of one small private bank (C. Hoare & Co.), a small deposit bank owned by a London clearing bank (Lewis's Bank) and the English office of the Royal Bank of Ireland (which has no branches in Northern Ireland).

The types of secondary bank are much more numerous, but we can distinguish four main classes—U.K. banks, British overseas banks, consortium banks and foreign banks.

Of the U.K. secondary banks, the accepting houses are the seventeen members of the Accepting Houses Committee (twenty-four including their Channel Islands subsidiaries). These are the well-known merchant banks, one of whose main functions has always been the lending of their names by accepting bills of exchange. In the course of time they have acquired many other functions, notably in the provision of financial advice to companies and in the issuing of company securities. The subsidiaries of the deposit banks were formed since 1964 and 1965 to compete with accepting houses, British overseas banks and foreign banks in the market for 'wholesale' deposits and lending. The other U.K. secondary banks are also often called merchant banks, and their functions are similar to those of accepting houses. The small number of such banks which are included in the official statistics shows the restrictive nature of the classification of banks; there are many bodies which figure on lists of banks drawn up for other purposes (such as exemption from the Moneylenders Acts or the provisions of legislation for the protection of depositors) and which lie in the limbo between banks and finance houses.

Two of the three remaining classes of secondary banks can be considered together—British overseas banks and foreign banks. Like the U.K. secondary banks they have few branches in this country, but they differ from them in mostly conducting considerable deposit banking business overseas. The distinction between British overseas banks and foreign banks is one of ownership: British overseas banks are U.K.-owned and have their head offices in London, whereas foreign banks have only a branch office in London. Especially for countries with little or no money market of their own, London branches are very important, but their function and balance sheets are bound to be considerably different from those of a head office situated in London, which holds a large part of the general liquidity reserve of the bank, acts as 'lender of last resort' to its branches and performs many centralised services.

The ten British overseas banks (twelve with their Channel Island subsidiaries) operate deposit banking business mainly in present or former countries of the British Commonwealth, but some have branch networks in non-Commonwealth countries of Latin America and the Far East. Among the foreign banks the Canadian, Australian and New Zealand banks represent a kind of reverse traffic from Commonwealth countries, and there is also a bank with its head office in Hong Kong among the other foreign banks. Of the banks from countries other than those specifically listed Switzerland, Spain, Belgium, India, Pakistan and countries in the Middle East, Far East and Africa are well represented. The Netherlands, West Germany and Italy are countries whose banks still rely on correspondent relationships with British banks and have few or no branches in London. It is, of course, the American banks which dominate the picture, with well over 60% of the deposits of all foreign banks and a deposit total (including deposits in foreign currencies) which is larger than that of the London clearing banks.

The consortium banks are a new form of bank, representing partnerships between banks of a number of different countries. The first consortium bank was formed in 1964, but nearly all the banks shown in the table were founded from 1969 onwards. For such a short period of existence their deposit total, rivalling that of British overseas banks by December 1971, is indeed remarkable.

B. *Growth*

Table 5.1 presents a snapshot of the banking system as it was in the recent past, but it tells us nothing of the rates of deposit growth of the different kinds of bank. Because of the different classification of banks used in official statistics we cannot take the detail of Table 5.1 back in time, but in Table 5.2 we show the rate of growth in total

Table 5.2   Growth of U.K. bank deposits by type of bank, 1963–70

	£ million			*Ratio 1970/1963*
	1963	1967	1970	
Deposit banks				
London clearing banks	8,337	10,262	10,606	*1.27*
Scottish clearing banks	879	1,070	1,119	*1.27*
Northern Ireland banks	182	253	333	*1.83*
National Giro	...	...	58	...
Other	(300)	(360)	335	*1.12*
Total	(9,706)	(11,950)	12,451	*1.28*
Secondary banks				
Accepting houses	844	1,464	3,006	*3.56*
American banks	671	3,283	11,567	*17.24*
Subsidiaries of deposit banks	–	(800)	3,478	–
Other	2,219	4,050	9,475	*4.27*
Total	3,734	9,597	27,526	*7.37*

Sources: (1) *Bank of England Statistical Abstract*, No.1;   (2) *Bank of England Quarterly Bulletin*, June 1971;   (3) Table 5.1; (4)   author's estimates.

deposits of the different types of deposit banks and of four categories of secondary banks for the period from 1963 to 1970. The main impression from this table is the tremendous rate of growth in total deposits of the secondary banks. We shall see, however, that a large part of this growth was in foreign currency deposits at a time when sterling lending by all banks was rigidly restricted. Among the secondary banks the American banks and the subsidiaries of deposit banks had exceptionally fast rates of growth: between 1967 and 1970 the total deposits of American banks grew 3·5 times and those of the subsidiaries of deposit banks 4·3 times. Overall the secondary banks moved from a position in 1963 in which their total deposits were under 40% of those of deposit banks to one in which their total deposits were 2·2 times those of deposit banks. Taking the comparison farther back in time, we can estimate that deposit bank deposits in 1951 were more than £7500 million, against only about £875 million for secondary banks. This tremendous growth in secondary bank deposits came from two sources: (1) the growth in deposits of banks which had been established in London for decades and (2) the influx of new foreign banks to London and the founding of entirely new banks, like the subsidiaries of deposit banks and the consortium banks.

So far we have looked only at total deposits without examining their composition. During the period which we are considering, deposit banks were confined almost exclusively to sterling domestic business, whereas secondary banks, with their strong overseas connexions, had large deposits from overseas residents, the greater part of them not in sterling but in foreign currencies (overwhelmingly euro-dollars). Deposit banks accepted deposits from each other only in special circumstances, whereas secondary banks lent each other deposits on a large scale. Table 5.3 breaks the deposit totals down into sterling and other currencies and according to type of depositor. In terms of direct competition with deposit banks we should consider only sterling deposits coming from outside the banking system; on this basis the deposits of secondary banks rose from £1863 million in 1963 to £3899 million in 1970. (£861 million of the negotiable certificates of deposit were held within the banking system.) This total represents only 31% of the total deposits of deposit banks in 1970, but nevertheless the ratio of 1970 to 1963 at 2·09 is considerably higher than for deposit banks.

C. *Banking groups*

Although it is natural and convenient to divide banks into neat classes according to their main function or to the area in which they operate, not all banks are independent of each other, and links of cross-ownership occur, both between banks of the same class and between banks of different classes. The reality of the banking system is a number of groups of different types of bank, cutting across the boundaries that we have laid down and in recent years extending their membership into various types of non-bank financial intermediary. These groups are the result of two trends—for merger between banks of the same type and for the agglomeration of different kinds of financial institution into multi-purpose groups.

Table 5.3   Analysis of secondary bank deposits, 1963–70

	£ million			Ratio 1970/1963
	1963	1967	1970	
Sterling				
U.K. banks	229	736	1,694	7.39
Other U.K. residents	656	1,571	2,375	3.62
Overseas residents	1,207	1,186	1,296	1.07
Negotiable certificates of deposit	–	–	1,089	–
Total	2,092	3,493	6,454	3.09
Other currencies				
U.K. banks	394	1,575	5,357	13.60
Other U.K. residents	83	219	446	5.37
Overseas residents	1,166	4,061	13,620	11.68
Negotiable certificates of deposit	–	249	1,649	–
Total	1,643	6,104	21,072	12.83

Sources: (1) *Bank of England Statistical Abstract*, No.1;
            (2) *Bank of England Quarterly Bulletin*, June 1971.

There have been several stages in the formation of the present bank groups. Up to about 1958 the formation of groups was confined to the forging of links between different deposit banks and between overseas banks and deposit banks. Between 1959 and 1965 there were two main movements. The first was the rush of nearly all deposit banks to acquire a stake in hire purchase. Within the short space of a few months most of the independent London and Scottish clearing banks either bought an existing finance house outright or else acquired a substantial minority stake in one. The second movement was one of mergers between merchant banks, based on the complementarity of the kinds of business that they undertook—often an accepting house with a bank whose main line of business lay in the new issue field and company finance.

From about 1965 onwards the movement of agglomeration of different kinds of bank and financial institution acquired a fresh momentum. London and Scottish clearing banks formed new subsidi-aries to enter into competition with merchant and foreign banks in the business that has become typical of secondary banking—the taking of term deposits and the making of term loans. Separate subsidiaries were necessary because deposit banks themselves were obliged to hold high proportions of liquid assets, which made the business unprofitable for them.

Up to 1968 there were eleven London clearing banks, which split into the 'big five' (Barclays, Lloyds, Midland, National Provincial and Westminster) and the 'little six', of which three were subsidiaries of Scottish clearing banks and one was a subsidiary of another London clearing bank. In that year a move began to merge the London clearing banks into fewer and stronger units. Westminster began to merge with National Provincial and its subsidiary, District, a move which eventu-ally created the National Westminster Group. At the same time Bar-clays, Lloyds and Martins (a clearing bank with its head office in Liverpool) announced their intention of merging. The proposed merger was referred to the Monopolies Commission, which declared it to be against the public interest. As a result, Barclays and Martins joined together but Lloyds remained independent. There was also a merger between two Scottish clearing banks, and all three of the London clear-ing banks which were subsidiaries of Scottish banks came under a single ownership and were merged. As a result of these mergers the number of London clearing banks was reduced from eleven to six (of which one is a subsidiary of another London clearing bank), and the number of Scottish clearing banks was reduced from five to four (and to three by March 1971).

At around the same time the London clearing banks began to forge informal links with deposit banks in Europe; these links remain and are likely to be strengthened as a result of Britain's entry into E.E.C. The final chapter of the story came in 1970, when most of the major deposit banks entered into partnership with European and American banks and accepting houses to form consortium banks. There are strong forces driving deposit banks to forge international links and to estab-lish consortium banks. The greatest of these is the growing size and multinational character of industrial and commercial companies. Com-panies increasingly want a full range of financial services from their banks, and it needs a large bank to accommodate the borrowing and other requirements of one of today's giant companies.

The present position is summarised in Table 5.4, which shows the composition of the five major banking groups, the first four of which

Table 5.4   The major banking groups, mid-1971

Type of bank	Banking group				
	National Westminster	Midland	Barclays	Lloyds	National & Commercial
London clearing	National Westminster Coutts	Midland	Barclays	Lloyds	Williams & Glyn's
Scottish clearing		Clydesdale	B. of Scotland (35%)		Royal Bank of Scotland
Northern Ireland	Ulster	Northern			
Other deposit	Yorkshire (40%) Isle of Man		Yorkshire (32%) Lewis's	Yorkshire (20%)	Yorkshire (8%)
British overseas	Standard & Chartered (9.2%)	Standard & Chartered (4.6%)	Barclays International	Lloyds & BOLSA International (54.6%) National B. of New Zealand National & Grindlays (41.2%)	
Consortium	Orion (32%) Orion Termbank (25%) International Commercial (20%)	Midland & International (45%) European American Banking Corp. (29%)	Intercontinental Banking Services (14.3%)	Intercontinental Banking Services (14.3%)	United International (12.5%)
Secondary	Westminster Foreign County Coutts Finance	Midland B.Finance Corp.	Barclays (London & International)	Lloyds Associated Banking	National Commercial & Glyns Williams, Glyn & Co.
Finance house	Lombard Banking Portland Group Factors	Forward Trust	United Dominions Trust (28.3%)	Lloyds & Scottish (50%)	Lloyds & Scottish (50%)

are headed by a London clearing bank and the fifth of which, National & Commercial, is based in Scotland. (Italics are used to indicate a minority interest.) This table is complex enough, but it does not do full justice to the multiplicity of links which exist between banks of different types and between British and foreign banks. In particular the links between deposit banks and finance houses are more complex than is shown here. It will be noticed that the table shows only two of the Northern Ireland banks (the remaining five were owned by two banking groups in the Irish Republic, into which they merged in 1972, and were therefore strictly foreign banks) and only three of the other deposit banks.

The reality behind the banking system is thus a number of powerful banking groups, each comprising British banks of different types and various non-bank financial intermediaries and having links of many kinds with banks in other countries. To some extent we shall find the same problem of cross-ownership in other parts of the financial system, with various types of financial intermediary being owned by other types and by companies which are not financial intermediaries at all. Although this is a most important facet of the organisation of the financial system, we must continue to analyse the working of each type of bank and financial institution separately, because each type has its own methods of operation, based partly on the logic of its kind of business, partly on legislation or government regulation and partly on convention.

2. DEPOSIT BANKS AND SECONDARY BANKS

A. *Two banking systems*

So far we have divided banks into a number of different categories according to their functions, ownership and geographical areas of operation. It is now time to retrace our steps and to consider the two major divisions of banks—deposit banks and secondary banks. We have already looked at the tremendous growth in the total deposits of the secondary banks over the nineteen-sixties, but the significance of this was not altogether clear. The fact is that during the past decade a secondary banking system was formed alongside the main banking system of the deposit banks. This new banking system consisted partly of banks which had existed for many years and which went on performing their traditional functions and partly of newly-founded banks. These banks were welded into a separate banking system by certain

*

new types of business which they developed in common and by the growth of 'parallel' money markets, both in sterling and in other currencies. The main driving force in this development was undoubtedly the growth of the international money market, which is usually referred to as the euro-dollar market because most of the deposits and loans are denominated in U.S. dollars.

The result was that by the end of the decade Britain had two distinct banking systems, each with its own money market. This country was unique in the extent to which its banks were thus specialised, but it may turn out to have been only a short-lived phenomenon. It is, however, a fact of great importance, and we shall point out the differences briefly before we consider the details in later chapters. We shall be deliberately over-simplifying, but this will be corrected later.

The deposit banks, as we have seen, are the banks which operate the main payments mechanism in the country, and for this purpose they have extensive branch networks. This function dominated their behaviour to an extent greater than for deposit banks in any other country, and their other function, that of acting as financial intermediaries in chanelling funds from surplus to deficit units, was allowed to occupy a subordinate position. Competition between them was inhibited by a number of agreements and conventions. In particular they agreed on the rates of interest which they offered on interest-bearing deposits and on the general level of interest payable on advances. Since there was no direct competition between them on interest rates, they competed only in the provision of services, particularly by a constant expansion of their branch networks. They offered only two main types of deposit—current accounts, operated on by cheque and bearing no interest, and deposit accounts, interest-bearing and withdrawable on seven days' notice. Because their deposits were all short term, they had inhibitions about the types of asset which they should hold. They preferred the self-liquidating overdraft, although in practice they made some advances fixed for a period (term loans) in special circumstances and were content to see many overdrafts continuing for years at a time. They adjusted their liquidity through the discount market and here again they had a number of agreements and conventions to regulate their behaviour. In their services they avoided those in which the accepting houses and other merchant banks specialised—new issues for companies and the role of financial advisers to companies—although a few deposit banks made tentative inroads into these markets.

The attitude of the deposit banks towards interest-rate competition, both with each other and with non-bank financial intermediaries, was coloured by a theory, prevalent in both banking and academic circles, that the result of such competition would be the paying of more interest for roughly the same volume of deposits. The argument proceeded from the fact that the authorities were in a position to control the supply of money and that private sector non-bank financial intermediaries kept their working balances with deposit banks. On this view deposit banks did not lose deposits when a building society or finance house persuaded deposit bank customers to transfer deposits from the bank to a building society or finance house; equally they could not gain deposits by competing with building societies or finance houses. When we come to examine the banking mechanism in Chapter 7, we shall see that this argument largely falls to the ground if the authorities take account of the demand for money when they decide on the supply of money, but the theory played a considerable part in preventing direct competition on interest rates by deposit banks.

Secondary banks have had none of the inhibitions, agreements and conventions which dominated deposit banking, and they have competed vigorously. They had some current account business, but they did not seriously compete with deposit banks in operating the payments mechanism. Instead they concentrated on the financial intermediary role of banks. Both their deposits and advances were typically fixed for a definite period (term deposits and term loans), ranging from overnight to several years. Their operations were limited to the 'wholesale' end of banking.

There are, of course, links between the two banking systems. Deposit banks, as commercial organisations, have been far from the passive creatures that we have painted above, but they have conducted their competition with each other and with secondary banks through the specially-formed subsidiary banks in order to escape from the obligatory cash and liquid assets ratios. The deposit banks also had links with other banks in the secondary system, British overseas banks and consortium banks. There were links too between the different money markets, the discount houses increasingly operating in the parallel money markets, both as brokers and as principals.

The main differences between the deposit banks and secondary banks can best be seen by analysing their deposits and advances according to types of customers, currency and size. Table 5.5 gives the sector analysis of the deposits and advances of both deposit banks and secondary banks as at December 1970. It can be seen that the business of deposit banks is overwhelmingly domestic (only 4·4% of deposits and 7·2% of advances concerned overseas residents) and in sterling.

Deposit banks drew nearly 73% of their deposits from the personal sector, but only 27% of their advances went to the personal sector and 58% to companies. (This was partly, of course, because the controls on bank advances then in operation discriminated against the personal sector.) Secondary banks, on the other hand, were concerned with overseas residents for around 80% of both deposits and advances,

Table 5.5   Sector analysis of bank deposits and advances, December 1970

£ million

Sector	Deposit banks		Secondary banks	
	Deposits	Advances	Deposits	Advances
U.K. residents				
Government	225	1	3	-
Local authorities	142	97	18	1,727
Public corporations	89	224	24	28
Financial institutions	403	209	694	376
Companies	2,061	3,918	1,419	1,982
Other (mainly personal)	9,338	1,847	664	164
Negotiable sterling certificates of deposit	-	-	228	-
Overseas residents	568	491	16,170	14,101
Total	12,826	6,787	19,220	18,378
Percentages of total				
Overseas residents	*4.4*	*7.2*	*84.1*	*76.7*
Non-sterling	*.5*	*...*	*81.8*	*81.7*

Source: *Bank of England Quarterly Bulletin,* June 1971, Tables 8(2), 8(3), 10(1) and 12.

Notes: (1) All inter-bank deposits and advances are excluded.
         (2) Deposit banks include Banking Department of Bank of England and National Giro.

and a similar proportion of their deposits and advances was in currencies other than sterling. All but a tiny fraction of the lending by secondary banks to local authorities consisted of deposits placed through the parallel money market, and of their true advances in sterling nearly 70% went to non-financial companies, which also contributed about 50% of the deposits from domestic sectors.

The same sharp distinction between the types of business conducted by the two banking systems is seen when we look at the units in which they operate. The only size distribution of the deposits and advances of deposit banks is the one submitted to the Radcliffe Committee, and Table 5.6 reproduces the size distribution of deposits and advances of the London clearing banks at June 1958. This is very out of date, but the only major difference from figures for the present day would probably be a slight decline in the proportion of really large accounts among the deposits. The London clearing banks had 24·5 million accounts in 1970, and it is clear from Table 5.6 that the overwhelming

Table 5.6   Size distribution of London clearing bank deposits and advances, June 1958

Size of account	Deposits		Advances	
	% of depositors	% of deposits	% of borrowers	% of advances
Less than £10,000	99.510	60.1	98.073	33.2
£10,000–£99,999	.460	21.7	1.747	22.9
£100,000–£999,999	.029	12.9	.165	23.0
£1 million and over	.001	5.3	.015	20.8
Total	100.000	100.0	100.000	100.0

Source: Committee on the Working of the Monetary System, *Memoranda of Evidence*, Vol. 2, Statistical Appendix, Tables 13 and 18.

majority of these are quite small. We have no statistical information about the size of secondary bank deposits and advances, but we know that the minimum size of a deposit is generally £25–50,000 and that advances are commonly upwards of £500,000. Deposit banking business is 'retail', with a predominance of small accounts, while secondary banking business is 'wholesale', each bank having a small number of very large accounts.

B. *The future shape of the banking system*

In September 1971 the Bank of England introduced new measures for the control of banks which, together with the consequent changes, transformed the spirit of the banking system almost overnight. (1) The cash and liquid assets ratios, which had done so much to split the banking system into two parts because they had applied only to deposit banks, were replaced by a uniform reserve assets ratio applying to all kinds of bank. (2) The London and Scottish clearing banks renounced most of the agreements among themselves and with the discount houses which had blunted competition in the banking system. (3) Deposit banks dropped many of their inhibitions about the type of business which they could legitimately undertake.

In the three months which have elapsed between September 1971 and the time of writing, competition between the deposit banks has already begun, although so far it has been limited largely to 'wholesale' deposits and personal loans. The deposit banks have entered the domain of secondary banking apart from their subsidiaries, and they have begun to participate in the parallel money markets, which were hitherto the preserve of secondary banks. They have announced their willingness to base term lending on the term deposits which they have secured. They are even talking of equity participations in companies to which they lend. At the other end of the scale they have begun to make efforts to attract savings deposits and to lend to households in forms which they previously largely rejected as unsuitable—first and second mortgages of houses, for example. The concept of 'department store banking' is being used to describe the situation in which both large and small customers can find all the financial services they need under one roof—that of the deposit bank.

There is one useful analogy to what might happen in Britain. In 1967 the Canadian banking system was reformed on roughly similar lines to those now adopted in Britain. The major deposit banks there, the chartered banks, rapidly became most successful competitors in the provision of many new kinds of financial service—so successful that the authorities had to restrain them. Canada differs from Britain in not permitting free entry to foreign banks, and Canadian chartered banks did not have to face the formidable competition of American banks. In Britain the deposit banks could undoubtedly be most success-ful competitors with a whole range of non-bank financial intermedi-aries and secondary banks, but the big question mark is how far the authorities will let them go in swallowing up competitors—the accept-ing houses for example. The extent of competition from the powerful American banks has yet to be seen, but for some time they have been opening branches outside London.

If we compare the December 1971 columns of Table 5.1 with those for December 1970, there appears to have been little change. There are additional numbers and deposits under consortium and foreign banks, and the total deposits of deposit banks have grown. The sub-sidiaries of the deposit banks are still in existence, although two banks have merged the international operations of their subsidiaries with British overseas banks under their control, forming new subsidiaries for domestic banking. The deposit banks seem as yet to be undecided what to do with their subsidiaries, although they can now decide the question solely on the grounds of organisational efficiency.

This apparent lack of change obscures one important fact, however: we can no longer talk of two distinct banking systems and two distinct money markets. By competing openly for wholesale deposits and term loans, the deposit banks have taken important steps towards merging the two banking systems. Their participation in the parallel money markets and the increased participation of secondary banks in the discount market because of the new obligation to hold reserve assets have similarly brought the two money markets close together.

3. THE BANK OF ENGLAND

A. *The operation of monetary policy*

Since its nationalisation in 1946, the Bank of England has become one of the public corporations, but for many years before that it directed its operations towards the control and oversight of the banking system rather than to the profit of its shareholders. As the banker to the government, the clearing banks and overseas central banks it has always had many important levers under its control, and its main function is that of acting as agent to the government in carrying out many aspects of monetary policy. Its balance sheet is very similar in essence to that of any commercial bank, but before we examine that we must look at the way in which the Bank of England exercises its influence in the furtherance of monetary policy.

Its formal interventions are dealt with in other chapters, and can be catalogued easily enough. As banker to the London clearing banks and as 'lender of last resort' to the discount houses it intervenes in the discount market with the object of influencing short-term interest rates. Through the agency of the Government Broker it intervenes in the gilt-edged market to further monetary policy, to meet government needs for borrowing and to attempt to place government debt in the hands of those who will hold it for as long as possible. As the government's agent in managing the Exchange Equalisation Account the Bank of England intervenes in the foreign exchange market to maintain the exchange rate of sterling within the parity margins agreed with the International Monetary Fund. Under the statute of nationalisation the Bank was given power to issue directives to bankers. It has never exercised this power, but it has issued many 'requests' to bankers, covering such items as the ratio of liquid assets to deposits, the extent of their lending in the form of advances and bill finance and the sectors to be given preference when lending is to be restricted. In addition, it may require banks to deposit with it on occasion a stated proportion of their total deposits—the so-called 'special deposits'.

These are all points that will be dealt with in their context. What we are more concerned with in this section is the spirit in which the Bank of England's powers are exercised. To an overseas student the British banking system must appear rather queer because very few of the 'ground rules' of the banking game are enshrined in statutes or regulations; all is done by convention and understanding. Even the latest measures for the control of banks, although they have been codified to an extent greater than before, still lack legislative sanction.

The Bank of England obviously works in a way that is different from that of other central banks, and this is largely a question of history. For centuries before the art of central banking was developed the Bank of England was only one bank among many in the City of London; all the bankers knew each other personally and all did their business within a stone's throw of each other. Even today the Governor of the Bank of England regards himself primarily as a banker, and it is still true that all the important figures in the banking world meet frequently in the normal course of business and that they all work within a few hundred yards of each other. It is the fact that the British banking system consists partly of large banks with extensive branch networks and partly of specialised banks within the City of London that enables the system to work without many written rules.

In his relationship with other bankers the Governor of the Bank of England behaves somewhat like the senior partner of a respected firm of solicitors or accountants towards the junior partners. Much of the necessary business is conducted through informal and friendly conversations, and a frown or raised eyebrow adequately conveys surprise or displeasure. Much has been changed by the growth of the banking system and by the great increase in the number of people concerned, but this is still the spirit that informs the relationship between the banking community and the Bank of England. The spirit is epitomised admirably in a statement which the Governor made to the Radcliffe Committee[1]: 'I have left the banks in no doubt, during the recent phase of credit restriction, of my view that they should not allow their liquidity to fall significantly below 30 per cent; and I have made it clear that I reserved the right to make observations if there were any

1. Committee on the Working of the Monetary System, *Minutes of Evidence*, Qn. 1754.

considerable divergence'. This relationship still works reasonably well within the banking system proper for three reasons. The first is that the Bank of England has ultimate sanctions which it can employ in case of dire necessity. Discount houses know that the right of access to the Bank of England as 'lender of last resort' can be withdrawn, and accepting houses know that the Bank of England can refuse any longer to treat their acceptances as first-class paper. Everybody is aware too that the Bank of England has the legal right to issue directives to any bank. The second reason is that it is the duty of the Bank of England to convey the views of the banking community to the government. The Bank of England is consulted by the government on monetary policy, and very often the views stated by the Governor find agreement among the banking community; he is the channel through which banks make representations to the government. The third reason is that many major types of bank are represented by powerful associations (the Committee of London Clearing Bankers, the Accepting Houses Committee, the London Discount Market Association and so on); the Bank of England deals with these associations, and the associations could if necessary enforce a common front by the threat of expulsion.

In recent years monetary policy has been forced to take notice of many new banks and of financial institutions other than banks, and it is in dealings with them that the mechanism of Bank of England control and influence has begun to creak and groan a bit. Very often it is the 'fringe' institutions that are most in need of control, and they are the least susceptible to this paternal treatment. The story is told of the chairman of one of them who received an invitation to visit the Bank to be given some gentle advice on good behaviour. He is reported to have said on leaving that he had enjoyed the visit and hoped to be invited again!

With the growing ramifications of the financial system and the consequent need for monetary policy to be concerned with many more institutions, the system is moving towards codification of the rules. The traditional British dislike of written constitutions may be an anachronism in modern society, but within the banking system the conventions have worked well while the circumstances allowed; they produced a flexible control that could cover special cases without fuss or bother.

Coupled with the function of operating monetary policy goes another function of the Bank of England which is rarely mentioned, although it is in many ways the most important of all. It is that of supporting the financial system, helping it to overcome crises and ensuring that no panic develops. The Bank exercises this function unobtrusively for the most part, arranging for banks, other financial institutions and even non-financial bodies to be given help when they are in difficulties so that no 'crash' of a powerful institution shall seriously disturb confidence. In carrying out monetary policy the Bank of England must always be wary of pressing measures too far, and in all its actions it shows an awareness of the importance of its 'support' function.

Incidental to these main functions of the Bank of England are several others. It acts as registrar for all British government stocks and also for the stocks of some local authorities and Commonwealth governments. It prints banknotes in its own printing works. It acts as the government's agent in working the system of exchange controls. In recent years it has begun to publish regular financial statistics in its *Quarterly Bulletin*, the articles in which have come to be a standard source for students of the financial system.

B. *Balance sheet*

The balance sheet of the Bank of England shown in Table 5.7 differs from that of an ordinary commercial bank in only two respects: (1) it is divided into two departments and (2) the cash held consists only of notes and coin. The second of these two distinctions arises because there is no 'superior' bank with which it could hold working balances.

The division of the Bank into two departments dates from the Bank Charter Act of 1844, and it had its origin in the famous Currency Controversy that preceded the Act. It has lost nearly all its significance in modern times, but the distinction is strictly preserved in Bank of England accounting and operations. In national income statistics the Issue Department forms part of the central government sector, while the Banking Department alone is treated as a public corporation. In banking statistics the figures for the Banking Department are merged with those of other 'deposit' banks to avoid disclosing its individual position.

The balance sheet of the Issue Department is simplicity itself: its liabilities are the note issue, including notes held in the Banking Department, and its assets are very largely government securities. The mechanism of note issue is that they are supplied to the public by banks, which obtain them from the Banking Department, direct in the case of London clearing banks or through a clearing bank in the case of other banks. The real significance of the Issue Department's balance sheet, however, lies in the government securities held to match the notes issued. This is twofold. (1) The Issue Department takes up government securities when it issues notes. Because the Issue Department pays all its profits into the Exchequer, the note issue becomes an interest-free loan to the government. (2) The mass of government

Table 5.7   Balance sheet of Bank of England, 28 February 1971

£ million

Liabilities		Assets	
Issue Department			
Notes in circulation	3,662	Government debt	11
Notes in Banking Department	38	British government securities	3,450
		Other securities	239
	3,700		3,700
Banking Department			
Capital	15	Liquid assets	
Reserves	101	Notes and coin	40
Provision for retirement benefits	16	Treasury and other bills	540
		Investments *(BV)*	
Current liabilities		British government securities	161
Public deposits	18	Other securities	12
Special deposits	398	Advances and other accounts	74
Bankers' deposits	195	Premises and equipment	32
Other accounts	113		
Payable to H.M. Treasury	1		
	858		858

Source: Bank of England, *Report and Accounts,* 1971.

securities is one of the main holdings used by the Bank of England in its intervention in the gilt-edged market. The £11 million of 'government debt' is of historical interest only, since it represents the original loan made to the government by the founders of the Bank in 1694 and some later loans.

The balance sheet of the Banking Department has all the elements of a normal banking balance sheet. On the liabilities side are capital and reserves and deposits, which are those of the various customers of the Bank. Public deposits are those of the Exchequer, Paymaster General and certain other government accounts; the largest part of bankers' deposits is held by the London clearing banks; special deposits are the funds which banks are on occasion required to leave with the Bank of England. Discount houses and banks other than the London clearing banks usually have only nominal balances with the Bank of England. The 'other accounts' are mainly those of overseas central banks and the few remaining private customers, of whom the Bank's own staff form an important part.

The method of setting out the Bank's balance sheet was changed at the date of this table, and the items included under the various assets now need no further comment. The only notable thing about the assets is that the Bank fulfils its functions by standing ready at all times to change their composition as it intervenes in the various markets, particularly the discount market. We shall see later that the working of the system requires that at least one bank shall not be bound by rigid ratios between the various kinds of asset.

FURTHER READING

R. S. Sayers, *Modern Banking*, 7th ed. (Oxford: Oxford University Press, 1967).

E. Nevin & E. W. Davis, *The London Clearing Banks* (London: Elek Books, 1970).

Monopolies Commission, *Barclays Bank Limited, Lloyds Bank Limited and Martins Bank Limited: A Report on the Proposed Merger* (H.M.S.O., 1968).

First Report from the Select Committee on Nationalised Industries: Bank of England (H.M.S.O., 1970).

6 Deposit Banks

We have already described in the preceding chapter the nature of deposit banking business, stressing its dependence on the transmission of payments. In this chapter we are concerned, firstly, with certain general points about the operation of deposit banks and, secondly, with the details of the balance sheets of particular types of deposit bank.

1. DEPOSIT BANKING

A. *Operation*

The essential requirement for the key role which deposit banks play in the payments mechanism is that their deposits (or, at least, that part of them which is transferable by cheque—the current accounts) should be accepted without question as money. This requirement imposes on deposit banks the need to operate—and to be seen to operate—with extreme prudence. What is prudent in the view of public opinion may well change over time, but at any one time there is a consensus of opinion on the type of balance sheet which is acceptable. This consensus applies to each group of deposit banks separately, but within each group it imposes pressures for uniformity. The balance sheets of London clearing banks may well differ in details and in some substantial points from those of Scottish clearing banks, but all London clearing banks will have very similar balance sheets, and so will all Scottish clearing banks. This uniformity is expressed in adherence to certain customary ratios between types of asset and total deposits; since the Second World War these customary ratios, to which the banks adhered voluntarily in the first place, have been taken over by the authorities as a means of controlling the banks, at least until September 1971.

Until September 1971 the two main groups of deposit banks in Britain, the London and Scottish clearing banks, issued only two types of deposit: (1) current accounts, which could be transferred by cheque or credit transfer instrument and on which, by agreement among the banks, no interest was payable, and (2) deposit accounts, interest-bearing and withdrawable generally on seven days' notice. Within deposit accounts there were some small sub-groups. Both sets of banks had savings accounts, no separate statistics for which have ever been given, and the Sottish clearing banks had deposit receipts, which are withdrawable on demand but on which no interest is payable until they have been held for thirty days. Even the interest-bearing deposit accounts have, in practice, been withdrawable on demand, with the sacrifice of seven days' interest, or usable without notice to offset over-drawing on current account. All these forms of deposit are still in existence, and represent the staple fare offered by deposit banks; since September 1971, however, the deposit banks have begun to pay market rates of interest for large sums of money, either in the form of straight deposits or by the issue of negotiable certificates of deposit, and many of the larger deposits have had a fixed term of much longer than seven days. These larger fixed-term deposits can be regarded as something grafted on to deposit banking business; even today they are far more typical of the secondary banking system.

The deposit banker, as we saw in Chapter 5, has a large number of accounts, most of which are quite small, and they are nearly all with-drawable on demand or at very short notice. It is these facts which dictate the assets structure of deposit banks. Because they operate nationwide branch networks and are few in number, the deposit banks can regard their deposits as largely a revolving fund. In any one day the customers of the deposit banks make thousands of transactions, but most of these transactions are from one customer of the deposit banking system to another and have no effect on the total of deposits within the system. Of course, individual banks are more at risk that outgoings in any one day will exceed incomings, but even for the in-dividual bank the fluctuations in deposit totals from day to day are generally small. The exception for the individual bank is certain trans-actions by their large industrial and commercial customers, the paying of a dividend to shareholders, for example. For deposit banks as a whole there are certain seasonal drains on their deposits, particularly as corporate customers make their tax payments in the first three months of the calendar year.

In order to meet the likely fluctuations in their deposit totals deposit banks need to hold a certain proportion of liquid assets, which can be realised to meet withdrawals. To demonstrate that their business is being conducted with extreme prudence, they need to hold further liquid assets beyond what is strictly necessary. As we have seen, the proportion which these liquid assets should bear to deposit totals was fixed first by custom and finally by regulation. However, as soon as the proportion of a certain type of asset to deposits has been fixed as a requirement, this type of asset is no longer able to fulfil freely its original function. Specifically, once a fixed ratio of liquid assets to deposits has been laid down, the assets are no longer liquid and no longer available to meet normal fluctuations in deposits, although banks would undoubtedly be allowed to use them for their original purpose in a crisis. Deposit banks meet this situation in two ways: (1) they hold a certain proportion of liquid assets above the required minimum, and they do this particularly to meet the seasonal pressures; (2) they hold certain other assets, which do not count as liquid assets but which can be sold readily to replenish their liquid assets.

These points can be demonstrated clearly if we set out a schematic balance sheet of a deposit bank in abbreviated form.

Liabilities Deposits
Assets Cash
        Notes and coin
        Working balances with other banks
    Other liquid assets
        Money at call and short notice
        Bills discounted
    Investments
    Advances

The assets are set out in descending order of liquidity, from cash, the most liquid of all assets, to advances, and in ascending order of yield, from cash, which yields no interest, to advances, which are the banks' most profitable assets.

Deposit banks need to keep two forms of cash. The first is a stock of notes and coin to meet the needs of their customers, and the second is a working balance which can be used to settle their indebtedness to other banks, both within their own group and outside it. The bank with which they hold working balances is invariably outside their own group; for London clearing banks it is the Bank of England, and for all other banks it is usually a London clearing bank. Of the other liquid assets, the money at call and short notice, the greater part of which is lent to discount houses, is used to adjust day-to-day and unpredictable fluctuations, whereas the bills discounted are held to maturity and used to meet predictable fluctuations. The investments consist largely of British government stocks, and they are used as a cushion between liquid assets and advances. Because they are marketable, they can be sold to replenish the liquid assets or to meet the demands of customers for advances. This latter aspect is particularly necessary because so much of bank lending in this country takes the form of overdrafts, on which it is impossible to predict exactly when and to what extent the borrower will use the overdraft facility which has been granted to him. Overdraft limits are normally re-negotiated every six or twelve months.

To match their potentially volatile deposits the deposit banks adopted until September 1971 a very restrictive attitude towards the kinds of lending undertaken. The ideal was seen to be the 'self-liquidating' transaction—lending to farmers from seed time to harvest or lending on foreign trade while goods were in transit. In practice deposit banks went far beyond these ideal kinds of lending. Within the lending on overdraft which represented the bulk of their advances they were often prepared to see overdrafts continuing from year to year; such continuous overdraft lending was little different in principle from a loan for a number of years and often as difficult to cut back when the banks were under pressure to reduce lending. The great advantage in borrowing on overdraft is that interest is payable only on the actual amount borrowed day by day. Of recent years the deposit banks have also ventured into term loans, although these have never represented more than a small proportion of total advances. Term loans were first introduced as a form of lending to persons (the so-called 'personal loans'), but several banks extended their use to the finance of capital investment by small firms in agriculture and industry. In addition, the banks were persuaded by the government to make term loans for export trade and to finance ship-building; we shall be looking at these later. Since September 1971 the deposit banks have further extended term loans in line with the term deposits which they have begun to attract direct instead of through secondary banking subsidiaries.

B. *Competition*

Until September 1971 deposit banking was a form of business which depended very much on agreements between the banks as to the rates which they should pay on deposits and the rates which they should charge on advances, and it was also governed by a number of conventions to which all the deposit banks of a particular group adhered. (In nearly all respects the other deposit banks went their own way, but we shall not deal especially with their position.) Both the London clearing banks and the Scottish banks had the same basic rate structure by the end of the nineteen-sixties, with only slight modifications.

The only agreement which applied to all current accounts (and presumably still does so) was that no interest should be paid. The banks were free to set their own rates of commission for operating the account, and each bank had its own system, often leaving a wide range of discretion to the individual bank manager, thus permitting considerable discrimination between customers. Basically the systems had the common elements of levying a charge in proportion either to the number of transactions or to the value of turnover on the account, and then allowing an offset of a low rate of interest on the average balance in the account; because of the agreement that interest should not be paid, customers could on no account receive any payment even if the offsetting interest exceeded the charge calculated. There were, however some agreements in this field. The Northern Ireland banks had a uniform tariff of charges, and the Scottish clearing banks had one until 1965. There were also collective agreements between the London clearing banks for certain types of business—transactions of government departments and nationalised industries, the handling of trustee savings bank cheques and the so-called 'I.C.I.' terms extended to employees of large bodies in the public and private sectors whose wages and salaries were paid direct into a bank account.

For deposit accounts both the London clearing banks and the Scottish clearing banks paid a standard 2% below Bank rate. On savings accounts there is a split rate, with $4\frac{1}{2}$% paid on the first £250 and deposit rate thereafter; the $4\frac{1}{2}$% has remained unchanged since July 1966. Since September 1971 the London and Scottish clearing banks have renounced the agreements on deposit rates of interest, and each bank is free to set its own interest rates. The rates are now set in relation to a base rate, which can depart from Bank rate and can differ from bank to bank. Although base rate has been changed on a few occasions, most banks are maintaining the old differentials for smaller accounts, while offering a fluctuating market rate for larger deposits, which are usually fixed for a term. Some of the banks have fixed higher rates for deposits over about £10,000 or £25,000 but below the size on which market rate is payable. The London clearing banks have also begun to issue negotiable certificates of deposit.

Both the London clearing banks and the Scottish clearing banks had a common tariff for rates to be charged on advances, but this was much looser than the tariff on deposit accounts, fixing only the lower rates of charge and allowing complete discretion in lending to customers outside certain privileged categories. This tariff can be set out as follows:

Differential over

Bank rate	*Minimum*	*Types of customer*
$\frac{1}{2}$%	$4\frac{1}{2}$%	Nationalised industries (with Treasury guarantee)
1%	5%	Local authorities, building societies, insurance companies and first-class industrial and commercial companies
$1\frac{1}{2}$%	$6\frac{1}{2}$%	Finance houses

All types of borrower other than those listed were charged at the discretion of the bank, but the rates were invariably above the rate charged to first-class industrial and commercial companies (the 'blue chip' rate). Before October 1969 the whole schedule had been $\frac{1}{2}$% lower, with nationalised industries receiving advances at Bank rate. Under the tariff listed above it was rare for customers to be charged more than 3% over Bank rate, so that bank borrowing was cheap in this country, the banks preferring to restrict their advances to the more creditworthy customers.

With the prices of items on both sides of their balance sheets so closely fixed by agreement, competition between deposit banks was limited to a number of spheres. In the first place all the banks had one or more subsidiaries operating in secondary banking and in instalment credit, and they were able to compete in terms of price for large deposits through the side door of these subsidiaries. The Scottish clearing banks have important branches in London, and the rate agreements did not apply to them. Nevertheless the opportunities for price competition were limited until the agreements were dissolved in September 1971, and most of the competition was in the form of increasing the convenience of holding bank accounts by providing extra services. The most important service was that of a widespread branch network.

Table 6.1 shows an analysis of bank branches in 1966. It includes the branches of three of the other deposit banks (C. Hoare & Co., Yorkshire Bank and Isle of Man Bank). In the decade before 1966 and

for some years afterwards the deposit banks were aggressively expanding their branch networks, and some of the larger banks had expanded
their numbers of branches by as much as 25% during the decade. Not
all of the offices are full branches, providing a full banking service during normal banking hours; in 1966 as many as 3958 were sub-branches,
ranging from offices open on several days of the week to those open
on only one day or even for only a few hours during the week.

Table 6.1 Deposit bank branches, 1966

Region	Branches	Sub-branches	All offices
Number of offices			
England	8,005	3,090	11,095
Wales	592	427	1,019
Scotland	1,455	239	1,694
Northern .Ireland	260	177	437
Isle of Man and Channel Islands	49	25	74
Total	10,361	3,958	14,319
Adult population per office			
England	3,826	...	2,760
Wales	3,091	...	1,428
Scotland·	2,315	...	1,989
Northern Ireland	3,412	...	2,030
Isle of Man and Channel Islands	2,265	...	1,500
Average	3,554	...	2,571

Sources: (1) *List of Sorting Code Numbers Allocated to Bank Branches,*
1966;
(2) *Annual Abstract of Statistics,* 1966.

There has been considerable discussion about the problem of 'over-
banking', and two government committees, one in Great Britain and
the other in Northern Ireland, have examined the branch networks of
the deposit banks.[1] Discussion of this problem is complicated by the
fact that there are two separate issues. The first arises because deposit
banks have something of a 'public utility' character; while most of
their branch network is built up on criteria of profitability, banks have

1. See National Board for Prices and Incomes, Report No. 34, *Bank Charges,*
Cmnd. 3292, 1967, and Government of Northern Ireland, Ministry of Finance,
Report of the Committee of Inquiry into Bank Interest Rates, 1965–1966, Cmd. 499
(Northern Ireland), 1966.

some obligation to provide a service to customers in outlying districts, which are bound to be 'over-banked' in terms of any statistical measure. The second is that the number of bank branches and sub-branches in any given area depends partly on the number of competing deposit banks. We cannot go into the question in any detail, but Table 6.1 shows, as we should expect, that the adult population per banking office is lowest where the population is most widely dispersed. On this criterion Wales is the most heavily 'over-banked' part of the United Kingdom. However, there is no objective criterion by which we can decide whether the number of bank branches in a particular area is excessive.

During the past few years the banks have begun to close some branches, while continuing to open new branches in some areas. The recent mergers have been the cause of the closure of many overlapping branches, but the process is bound to be slow because an overlapping branch can be closed only when the other branch can handle all the business of both branches; in many cases closure must wait on re-building or extensive alteration. There are many signs that the deposit banks are now beginning a rationalisation of their branch networks. One of the forms which this is likely to take is a differentiation between the services provided at different branches in the same town. This is likely to result in the smaller branches on the outskirts offering only facilities for simple money transfers and encashing of cheques, while lending and the more sophisticated services will be concentrated on a central branch. The banks have invested heavily in automatic cash dispensers, which enable customers to obtain £10 in notes at any time.

C. *Margins*

The income of deposit banks comes from many different sources, but it is possible to isolate the main 'trading' activities, consisting of the offering of current and deposit accounts and the lending of money, and to set the bulk of the expenditure against the income from these sources. This concept of 'trading' income and expenditure leaves out of account investment income and dividends received from subsidiary and associated companies. Income from miscellaneous services is such a small part of the total that it makes little difference to the overall picture. Table 6.2 is an estimate of the trading income and expenditure of the London and Scottish clearing banks kindly made available by Mr. R. J. Barrett of stockbrokers Hoare & Co., Govett.

The general picture presented by Table 6.2 is very similar to that which we shall find with other types of financial intermediary. In particular the predominance of labour costs in total expenditure is typical of intermediaries operating in the retail side of financial intermediation. On these figures wages, salaries and other labour costs (mostly amounts set aside for pensions) accounted for 63·6% in 1969 and 67·9% in 1970 of total administrative expenses. This is in line with the report

Table 6.2   Estimated trading income and expenditure of London and Scottish clearing banks, 1969 and 1970

Percentages

	1969	1970
Income		
Interest on advances	**87.7**	86.0
Commission	**12.3**	14.0
Total	100.0	100.0
Expenditure		
Interest on deposits	34.6	30.8
Wages and salaries	26.7	29.3
Other labour costs	6.3	6.9
Other costs (including bad debt provisions, rent, etc.)	18.9	17.1
Total	86.5	84.1
Trading surplus	13.5	15.9

Source: Hoare & Co., Govett.

of the National Board for Prices and Incomes, which stated[2] that up to 1965 direct and indirect labour costs accounted for over 70% of total operating costs, but that the proportion had shown a declining trend over the decade up to 1965.

On these estimates total income was only about 2% higher in 1970 than in 1969, and in round figures was about £660 million for the London clearing banks and £60 million for the Scottish clearing banks. In 1970 it can be estimated from the published accounts that the total investment income (excluding dividends from subsidiaries and associated companies) of the London clearing banks was about £65 million.

2. *Bank Charges*, pp. 48–9.

Had this figure been added to income in Table 6.2, the surplus would have been around 23·5%.

There is one feature of the margin of deposit banks to which the P.I.B. report drew special attention, and this is the tendency of the margin to widen when interest rates are high and to narrow when interest rates are low. The agreements which existed up to September 1971 ensured a constant absolute margin between the rate of interest paid on deposit accounts and the rates charged on advances, since both were adjusted by the same amount when Bank rate changed. However, the London clearing banks had just over half of their deposits in the form of current accounts and the Scottish clearing banks had just under half. No interest is payable on current accounts, and even the notional rate of interest which is allowed as an offset to commission charges does not vary with Bank rate. On the assets side it is only the holdings of investments of which the yields are not immediately sensitive to changes in Bank rate, whereas the yields of bills, money at call and advances adjust themselves quickly. The proportion of assets whose yields are geared to Bank rate is greater than the proportion of deposits whose rates change with Bank rate. Thus, when Bank rate is raised, income increases by more than expenditure and the margin widens. The P.I.B. report referred to this phenomenon as an 'endowment' element in bank profits. It will still apply to the situation since September 1971.

2. LONDON CLEARING BANKS

A. *Balance sheet*

Since 1951 the London clearing banks have been required by the authorities to observe both a primary and a secondary ratio. Up to September 1971 the primary ratio was the cash ratio of 8%, and the secondary ratio was the liquid assets ratio of 28% (30% from 1957 to 1963). The primary ratio did not apply to any other type of bank. The denominator for both these ratios was gross deposits, and the liquid assets covered by the secondary ratio included the cash of the primary ratio. There was, however, an important difference between the two ratios. Both ratios were minima, below which the banks must not fall at any time, but they took care not to exceed the 8% cash ratio because cash earned no interest. The liquid assets ratio, on the other hand, was built up to a peak in January so that tax payments by their customers from January to March should not reduce the ratio below 28%. The

December 1970 figures in Table 6.3 are thus near the seasonal peak. Similar seasonal considerations apply to the reserve assets ratio under the new arrangements.

The item shown immediately below total liquid assets in Table 6.3 is special deposits with the Bank of England. These are deposits which banks are called upon to make with the Bank of England and which do not count as liquid assets; they receive a rate of interest equal to the yield on treasury bills. Effectively special deposits are a means of varying the liquid assets ratio, because they represent a further tranche of assets outside the liquid assets which must be held in a form dictated by the authorities.

The figures shown in Table 6.3 are a combination of the regular statistics published by the Bank of England and the monthly return of the Committee of London Clearing Bankers. By comparison with the published accounts of the individual banks it is clear that there are many omissions from the Committee's monthly return, and we shall draw attention to these as we go through the table.

On the liabilities sides there are several omissions, mostly of odd items like taxation, sundry creditors and future dividends. The most interesting omission is that of the loan capital issued by two of the banks, totalling £90 million in 1970. This is a very recent departure for deposit banks, but it provides a means of matching longer term lending with a non-deposit source of finance of comparable or longer maturity. Contingent liabilities of £1349 million arising out of acceptances, endorsements and guarantees for customers are not shown.

There are many points to be made about the exact definitions of the items included under liquid assets, but we shall defer these until we come to the new arrangements introduced in September 1971. The last figures for the maturity of the investments in British government stocks held by the London clearing banks were those presented to the Radcliffe Committee for 1958, which showed 49·4% with a maturity of up to five years. The regular statistics for all deposit banks give a figure of 59·7% for December 1970; since the London clearing banks form such a large part of the category of all deposit banks, it seems safe to assume that the London clearing banks have shortened the average maturity of their investments over this period.[3] Nearly all the stocks have a final maturity of less than ten years.

We have already described the nature of advances, but we must now give the details of the term lending of the London clearing banks and

3. *Bank of England Quarterly Bulletin* (December 1971) Statistical Annex, Table 8(1).

Table 6.3   Balance sheet of London clearing banks, 9 December 1970

	£ million	Percentages of gross deposits
Liabilities		
Deposits		
Current accounts	5,678	53.5
Deposit accounts	4,619	43.6
Other accounts	309	2.9
Gross deposits	10,606	100.0
Capital and reserves	1,200	11.3
Provisions	85	.8
Total	11,891	112.1
Assets		
Cash		
Notes and coin	669	6.3
Balances with Bank of England	162	1.5
Total cash	830	7.8
Money at call and short notice		
Discount houses	1,225	11.6
Other	365	3.4
Bills discounted		
British government treasury bills	406	3.8
U.K. commercial bills	305	2.9
Other	459	4.3
Total liquid assets	3,590	33.8
Special deposits with Bank of England	369	3.5
Investments (BV)		
British government stocks	873	8.2
Other	189	1.8
Advances and other accounts	5,597	52.8
Cheques in course of collection, etc.	397	3.7
Items in transit	212	2.0
Investments in subsidiaries	192	1.8
Premises	472	4.5
Total	11,891	112.1

Sources: (1) *Bank of England Quarterly Bulletin*, June 1971, Table 9(1);
(2) Committee of London Clearing Bankers.

Scottish clearing banks in the form of fixed-rate finance for exports and for shipbuilding for U.K. owners. The arrangements are complicated and have changed in detail several times. There are two separate schemes. (1) Short-term credit (up to two years) for export was provided at $\frac{1}{2}\%$ over Bank rate (minimum $4\frac{1}{2}\%$; up to September 1970 lending was at Bank rate) and bills with a tenor (life) of six months or less were counted as liquid assets. (2) Credit in excess of two years for both shipbuilding and exports guaranteed either by the government or by the Export Credits Guarantee Department is also at a fixed rate. In the case of shipbuilding credit 30% of the facility was refinanceable on the original terms with the Bank of England if the bank needed the cash to meet withdrawals of deposits; the same provision applied to export credit, but in this case refinancing was possible for that portion which was repayable within 18 months if this was larger than 30%. The most important point was that the refinanceable portion of these credits counted among liquid assets; these are the refinanceable export and shipbuilding credits shown under 'bills discounted' in later tables. (From April 1972 the refinanceable portion is under advances.) The total amount outstanding under the second scheme at mid-June 1969 was about £650 million of which rather over £250 million was refinanceable. Because lending under these schemes was unrestricted even when total lending was under a quantitative ceiling, the total outstanding grew quite fast, and might have reached nearly £1000 million in mid-1971.[4]

The next two items, 'cheques in course of collection, etc.' (the 'etc.' refers to small balances with other banks in the United Kingdom) and 'items in transit', are both suspense accounts designed to allow for the lag in recording transactions at two different bank branches. They balance the additional liability of the bank arising from the fact that the payee's account is credited immediately when he pays a cheque into his account, whereas the drawer's account will not be debited for several days. Collectively they are known as debit 'transit items'; 'cheques in course of collection' refer to cheques drawn on another bank, and 'items in transit' to cheques drawn on another branch of the same bank. The suspense item for credit transfer is shown under

4. Details of these schemes will be found in the following articles in the *Bank of England Quarterly Bulletin*: 'Finance for exports' (December 1969); 'Finance for shipbuilding' (June 1967); 'New refinance facilities for export and shipbuilding credits' (September 1969); 'Commentary' (December 1970) pp. 395–6; 'Commentary' (December 1971) p. 445; 'The finance of medium and long-term export and shipbuilding credits' (June 1972).

'deposits: other accounts'. In their own accounting the London clearing banks assume that 40% of debit items in transit (but not cheques in course of collection) will go to overdrawn accounts, and add this amount on to advances, deducting the remaining 60% from deposits. The items in transit in Table 6.3 consist of the 40% included under advances but here shown separately.

The item 'investments in subsidiaries' arises because we are looking at the balance sheets of the banks alone and not the consolidated accounts of the groups. Omitted from the returns of the Committee of London Clearing Bankers is £160 million of trade investments, holdings of shares in other companies which are less than a controlling interest. Also omitted after the item for 'premises' is the value of equipment. In the published accounts this had an original cost of £144 million, against which depreciation of £60 million had been charged. The major item here is undoubtedly computers, but these are not shown separately.

B. *Recent history*

Now that we have completed a survey of the items appearing in the balance sheet for one date, it is useful to glance back over the past twenty years to see how the proportions of the items have changed. This is done in Table 6.4.

Before we look at the actual figures, we must draw attention to certain changes in accounting methods which affect the comparability of the figures for 1970 with those for earlier years. Under British company law banking, insurance and shipping companies are allowed certain exemptions from the disclosure which is obligatory for the general run of companies. The two most important of these are (1) that profits may be stated after charging taxation and after transferring undisclosed sums to 'inner reserves' and (2) that the market value of investments need not be shown. The inner (or 'hidden') reserves were included, along with certain suspense accounts, under 'deposits: other accounts'. At the end of 1969 the London clearing banks, the Scottish clearing banks and U.K.-owned Northern Ireland banks decided to make full disclosure of their profits, and at the same time they agreed to certain uniform revisions of accounting procedures. Many secondary banks still take advantage of the exemptions.

The most important of the revised accounting procedures were four in number. (1) Inner reserves and sundry provisions for pensions, taxation and dividends were transferred from 'deposits: other accounts' to

Table 6.4   Balance sheet of London clearing banks, 1951–70

Percentages of gross deposits

	December				
	1951	1958	1963	1966	1970
Liabilities					
Deposits					
Current accounts	66.7	58.7	57.5	51.6	53.5
Deposit accounts	29.0	34.5	33.8	38.2˙	43.6
Other accounts	4.3	6.8	8.7	10.2	2.9
Gross deposits	100.0	100.0	100.0	100.0	100.0
Assets					
Cash					
Notes and coin	3.5	5.2	5.6	5.9	6.3
Balances with Bank of England	4.9	3.0	2.7	2.5	1.5
Money at call and short notice					
Discount houses	9.4	8.2	{ 6.9	9.0	11.6
Other			{ 2.5	3.4	3.4
Bills discounted					
British government treasury bills	12.5	16.5	11.3	7.2	3.8
U.K. commercial bills	2.9	1.9	2.8	3.7	2.9
Other	-	-	.9	1.3	4.3
Total liquid assets	33.2	34.6	32.7	32.9	33.8
Special deposits with Bank of England	-	-	-	2.0	3.5
Investments					
British government stocks	31.4	27.7	13.9	10.9	8.2
Other	1.2	1.5	1.4	1.5	1.8
Advances and other accounts	29.4	29.5	47.5	47.3	52.8

Sources: (1) *Bank of England Statistical Abstract*, Vol.1, Table 9(2);
           (2) *Bank of England Quarterly Bulletin*, September 1971,
               Table 9(2).
Note: Figures for 1951 and 1958 are at 31 December; other years on
      second Wednesday.

disclosed reserves. (2) Investments which had previously been shown
at cost *less* some undisclosed writing down were shown at 'amortised
value', with the difference between cost and redemption value added
on or deducted evenly over the remaining life of the investments. Market
values are now disclosed in the published accounts. (3) Provisions for
bad and doubtful debts (deducted from the value of advances) were

based on the average experience of the past five years. (4) An allocation of items in transit between current accounts and advances was made, and (for London clearing banks only) credits in course of transmission were netted against cheques in course of collection. The net effect of these changes was to reduce the gross deposits of the London clearing banks by about £850 million at the end of 1969 and to increase the balance sheet value of their investments by £75 million. Because the denominator of the liquid assets ratio had been reduced, the change had the effect of lowering the amount of liquid assets required to fulfil the 28% minimum.

The effect of these accounting changes is clearly shown in Table 6.4 by the sharp drop in 'deposits: other accounts' for 1970. During the period from 1951 the banks had been building up their inner reserves to cope with the depreciation of investments to be expected from the general rise in interest rates and the more vigorous use of monetary policy. The only way in which we can show the trend in the proportions of current accounts and deposit accounts is to leave other accounts out of the picture; we then get the following picture:

	1951	*1958*	*1963*	*1966*	*1970*
Current accounts	69·7	63·0	63·0	57·5	55·0
Deposit accounts	30·3	37·0	37·0	42·5	45·0
Total	100·0	100·0	100·0	100·0	100·0

The marked swing towards deposit accounts, largely as a result of higher interest rates, is unmistakable. It is often said that deposit accounts are used by the holders as an extension to their current accounts and not for the purpose of holding savings. A recent survey of the deposit accounts by one bank produced some interesting facts that disprove this view:[5] (1) personal customers accounted for 83% of all balances on deposit account; (2) only 44% of deposit account customers also had current accounts; (3) only about 20% of all deposit account customers had more than two debit entries in a period of six months.

The trends in the proportions of different types of asset are equally noteworthy. (1) The increased holdings of notes and coin were made within the 8% cash ratio by a reduction of balances at the Bank of England. (2) Money at call and short notice increased in importance

5. P. Wood & J. Rhys, 'The definition of money and the possibilities for monetary control', *The Bankers' Magazine* (April 1971).

as against bills discounted, and this was particularly at the expense of treasury bills. (3) The introduction of the schemes for fixed rate lending for exports and shipbuilding led to a large increase of the refinanceable part under 'other bills'. (4) Holdings of British government stocks were progressively run down to accommodate an increase of advances despite the quantitative controls on bank lending, which were in force for most of the period and which were continuous and particularly stringent from May 1965 to mid-1971.

The stability of the December liquid assets ratio over the entire period is remarkable. The secondary ratio was first made a requirement in 1951, and the minimum ratio was reduced from 30% to 28% in 1963. Although certain factors reduced the burden of this ratio on the banks during the period, it was higher by the end of the period than they would have kept voluntarily. These factors were: (1) a codification of the assets which could be counted as liquid added several items, shown under money at call other than to the discount houses; (2) the increase in commercial bill finance provided a source of liquid assets the supply of which was under the control of the banks (until bills were included in the total lending ceiling); (3) the inclusion of the refinanceable part of export and shipbuilding credits provided further relief; (4) the accounting changes of 1969 reduced the denominator of the ratio, raising the ratio attained at the end of 1969 from about 32% on the old basis to nearly 35% on the new.

C. *Changes from September 1971*

In September 1971, after nearly six months of discussion with the bodies concerned, the Bank of England instituted new arrangements for the control of credit to replace the ratio controls on London and Scottish clearing banks and the quantitative controls on lending by all banks and finance houses.[6] The new arrangements apply to all banks and (with some modification) to finance houses above a certain size; different arrangements apply to discount houses and certain other bodies operating in the discount market. In this chapter we are concerned with the basic concepts of the new scheme as it applies to deposit banks and with the detailed definitions. In Chapter 7 we shall look at the new arrangements as a weapon of control over banks, and we shall refer to the impact of the new measures on discount houses, secondary banks, the parallel money markets and finance houses in

6. The documents giving details of the new arrangements are listed under 'Further reading' at the end of this chapter.

appropriate chapters. The new scheme has not yet been applied to the
Northern Ireland banks, and it does not include the National Giro.

The new arrangements retain a primary ratio for the London clearing banks, which are required to keep a day-to-day total of 1½%
of eligible liabilities as at the last make-up day in the form of balances
with the head office of the Bank of England. This primary ratio is helpful in the daily management of the discount market, but it also enables the Bank of England to maintain its profits by having balances
on which it pays no interest. The secondary ratio under the new
arrangements is considerably different from the old liquid assets ratio.
Gross deposits are replaced by eligible liabilities as the denominator,
and liquid assets are replaced by reserve assets as the numerator. All
banks are required to maintain day by day a minimum ratio of reserve
assets to eligible liabilities of 12½%. The secondary ratio is made
variable by the retention of special deposits, and there is little doubt
that the Bank of England will use these more vigorously than it has in
the past. The last feature of the scheme is outside the banking system,
but it may well turn out to be the most important of all: the Bank of
England has stated that it is prepared to see much larger swings in
both short-term and long-term interest rates than it has allowed in
the past, and it has modified its tactics in both the gilt-edged and the
discount markets accordingly.

The definition of eligible liabilities is as follows:

(1) Sterling deposits with an original term of two years or less from
    (a) U.K. residents other than banks
    (b) overseas residents other than overseas offices
(2) Sterling deposits of whatever term from U.K. banks *less* any
    sterling claims on such banks
(3) The bank's net deposit liability, if any, in sterling to its overseas
    offices
(4) Sterling certificates of deposits issued of whatever term *less* any
    holdings of such certificates
(5) Net liability, if any, in currencies other than sterling
(6) 60% of credits in course of transmission *less* 60% of debit
    transit items
(7) All funds due to customers and third parties which are tem-
    porarily held on suspense accounts.

The basic principle behind these detailed definitions is that deposits
shall be liable to the holding of reserve assets once only in the hands
of the bank which is employing the funds outside the banking system.

Thus, if a minus figure results from items (2), (4) and (6), this is deducted from eligible liabilities; with items (3) and (5) minus figures are not deducted from eligible liabilities. Item (6) represents a splitting of transit items between those that affect current accounts and those that affect advances. A credit item moving to a current account increases deposits, while a debit item reduces deposits. However, if a credit item is moving to an overdrawn account, it reduces advances and a debit item increases advances. In their own accounting the clearing banks use the rule of thumb that 60% of items in transit affect current accounts and 40% affect advances, and these proportions have been taken over in the definition of eligible liabilities for all banks.

The definitions of reserve assets are equally complicated. They are set out in Table 6.5, alongside the definitions of items included under the old grouping of liquid assets. The main points can be summarised. (1) Balances with branches of the Bank of England count as reserve assets, but are not included in the London clearing banks' 1½% primary ratio. (2) Holdings of notes and coin are excluded from reserve assets. (3) An upper limit of 2% of eligible liabilities has been set on holdings of commercial bills which can count as reserve assets. As we shall see in Chapter 7, one of the main requirements of a ratio control is that the supply of the reserve assets shall be under the influence if not the control of the authorities; the same result could have been achieved by omitting commercial bills from reserve assets and setting the ratio at 10½%. The background to this limitation is undoubtedly the revival of commercial bills during the nineteen-sixties and the consequent weakening of the authorities' grip on the total of liquid assets. (4) Refinanceable export and shipbuilding credits do not count as reserve assets. (5) British government stocks with one year or less to final maturity, which did not count as liquid assets, are brought within the definition of reserve assets.

Although the London clearing banks have probably not completed their balance sheet adjustments at the time of writing, it is useful to set out the balance sheet on the old and the new bases side by side. This is done for the second reporting date, 20 October 1971, in Table 6.6. The bracketed figures are only rough estimates of the composition of reserve assets, figures for which have been given officially for all deposit banks but not for each type of bank. All the evidence points to the predominance of money at call in the reserve assets of the London clearing banks, but the other items are little better than guesses. Special deposits were repaid when the new arrangements came into force, and

Table 6.5 Definitions of liquid assets and reserve assets

	Liquid assets	Reserve assets
1. Cash		
(a) Balances at Bank of England (other than special deposits)	*	*
(b) Notes and coin	*	
2. Money at call or short notice		
(a) Money at call or callable (*secured*) to		
(1) discount houses	*	*
(2) discount brokers	*	*
(3) money trading banks	*	*
(4) money brokers	*	*
(5) stock exchange jobbers (*secured on British government stocks*)	*	*
(6) other U.K. banks (up to 1 month)	*	
(7) stockbrokers (up to 1 month, including from one account to another)	*	
(8) bullion brokers (up to 1 month)	*	
(b) Foreign currency balances	*	
(c) Foreign banknotes and coin	*	
(d) Company tax reserve certificates	*	*
3. Bills discounted		
(a) British & N. Ireland government treasury bills	*	*
(b) U.K. commercial bills (*eligible for re-discount at Bank of England; up to 2% of eligible liabilities*)	*	*
(c) Other bills		
(1) U.K. local authority bills (*eligible for re-discount at Bank of England*)	*	*
(2) treasury bills of overseas governments	*	
(3) commercial bills drawn on overseas residents	*	
(4) refinanceable export and shipbuilding credits	*	
4. British government stocks with 1 year or less to final maturity		*

Source: Reserve ratios: further definitions, *Bank of England Quarterly Bulletin*, December 1971.

Notes:
(1) British government stocks include stocks of nationalized industries guaranteed by H.M. government.
(2) Descriptions in italics apply only to the definition of the item as a reserve asset.
(3) Some banks included foreign banknotes and coin under notes and coin.
(4) Item 2(a)(6), money at call to other U.K. banks, would be deducted from eligible liabilities.

the London clearing banks subscribed to three new gilt-edged stocks so that they should not begin with excessive holdings of reserve assets.

In Table 6.6 eligible liabilities are a shade over 90% of gross deposits; the minimum reserve assets ratio is thus only 11¼% of gross deposits. The gap between the two magnitudes is likely to widen as the banks begin to attract deposits with an original maturity of over two years and in foreign currencies and as they acquire assets which are

Table 6.6   Balance sheet of London clearing banks, 20 October 1971

	Old basis		New basis	
	£ million	%	£ million	%
Liabilities				
Gross deposits	11,888	100.0		
Eligible liabilities			10,752	100.0
Assets				
Balances at Bank of England	216	1.8	216	2.0
Notes and coin	627	5.3		
Cash	843	7.1	216	2.0
Money at call and short notice	1,527	12.8	(1,150)	(10.7)
Bills discounted	1,120	9.4	(260)	(2.4)
Liquid assets	3,490	29.4		
Investments	1,991	16.7	(150)	(1.4)
Reserve assets			1,777	16.5
Advances	6,206	52.2	6,206	57.7

Sources: (1) *Bank of England Quarterly Bulletin*, December 1971, Table 9(1) and pp. 486-7; (2) author's estimates.
Note: The bracketed figures are rough estimates of the distribution of reserve assets.

deducted from eligible liabilities. The seasonal element in bank deposits applies under the new system as well as under the old, and it seems certain that the banks will build up excess reserve assets during the period from about April to January so that they shall not fall below the minimum during the tax-gathering season from January to March.

Of even greater interest is the evidence, which does not show up in the balance sheet, of the tremendous change in the attitude of the London clearing banks towards permissible types of business. From the start of the new arrangements to 17 November 1971 they issued around £155 million of sterling certificates of deposit, received sterling inter-bank deposits of £100 million and increased foreign currency deposits by about £140 million; on the assets side they bought £140 million of sterling certificates of deposits, placed £240 million in the sterling inter-bank market, acquired £160 million of foreign currency assets and placed £25 million in temporary loans to local authorities.[7] The types of lending have also been extended. During the same period they greatly expanded their lending to the personal sector, and some of it was in the form of first and second mortgage lending on house property. We do not know what proportion of their additional sterling deposits was for a fixed term, but they certainly stood ready to pay market rates of interest for deposits of about £25,000 or over, and some banks were willing to pay a higher rate for deposits of £10,000 or over. Most of the banks seem to have split their deposit taking activities into two levels: the normal bread-and-butter deposit business is still conducted at branches according to a fixed tariff related to a new base rate, which can and does depart from Bank rate, while the wholesale business is conducted by a money market division at head office or by the secondary bank subsidiaries.

By making use of the wholesale markets on both sides of their balance sheets the deposit banks have blurred the distinctions that formerly existed between deposit banks and secondary banks. Like secondary banks they can now make large loans and seek the supporting deposits afterwards on the parallel money market. This has made their method of operation more like that of U.S. commercial banks, which since about 1960 have found a large part of their liquidity on the liabilities side of their balance sheets.

The greatest change which has come over the deposit banking system is undoubtedly the ending of the agreements on rates of interest and the superseding of the old conventions limiting the types of business. A new and aggressive competitive spirit now reigns in deposit banking. It is too early to say exactly how the system will develop, but it is clear that deposit bankers do not regard any type of financial activity as outside their scope.

7. *Bank of England Quarterly Bulletin* (December 1971) p. 446.

3. SCOTTISH CLEARING AND NORTHERN IRELAND BANKS

In this main section we shall be concerned almost exclusively with the Scottish clearing banks; the Northern Ireland banks will be mentioned when their methods of working are known to differ. The term 'Scottish clearing banks' was not adopted until the middle of 1971. Up to that time they were known simply as 'Scottish banks', but the establishment of branches in Edinburgh and Glasgow by certain secondary banks made it necessary to introduce the qualification.

The deposit banking systems of Scotland and Northern Ireland both retain a considerable degree of independence from the English banking system despite the extent of common ownership between all three sets of banks. Many of the differences in banking practice between the London clearing banks and the two groups of regional banks have disappeared, and in most ways their method of conducting business is very similar to that of English deposit banks. Three basic differences persist, however, and these considerably affect the interpretation of their balance sheets. (1) Both the Scottish and the Northern Ireland banks retain the right of note issue. (2) They both keep the bulk of their working balances with London clearing banks and only small balances with the Bank of England, so that they are almost (but not quite) a second tier of deposit banks for whom the London clearing banks act as bankers. (3) They operate without the rigid cash and liquid asset ratios of the English banks. When special deposits were introduced for the London clearing banks in 1958, the Scottish clearing banks were made liable at only one-half of the rate for London clearing banks, but the Bank of England found it necessary to reach an understanding with the Scottish clearing banks about their normal liquidity ratios. This understanding was nowhere near so formal as the 30% (later 28%) requirement imposed on the London clearing banks. Special deposits have never been called from the Northern Ireland banks.

For Scottish clearing banks the right of note issue remains of considerable importance. The system governing the issue of notes is very simple, but a knowledge of its requirements is essential for understanding the balance sheets of Scottish clearing banks. Each bank has an 'authorised' circulation of notes; in aggregate these authorised circulations now amount to only £2·7 million. Beyond these tiny amounts any issue of notes by a Scottish clearing bank must be 'covered' by the holding of an equivalent value of Bank of England notes. Most of the required cover is held on deposit at the Bank of

England in the form of notes of a denomination of over £1000. Since the authorised circulations are so small, it is virtually true to say that a Scottish clearing bank must 'buy' a Bank of England note every time it issues one of its own. But for one important factor it would seem that the Scottish clearing banks might just as well use Bank of England notes and give up their own circulations; this factor is that cover is not required until notes have actually passed over the counter into circulation, and so the banks can hold a high proportion of their till money in the form of unissued notes of their own. The remainder of the till money consists of Bank of England notes, which Scottish clearing banks issue to customers on demand. No Scottish clearing bank re-issues the notes of another bank which come to it; these are exchanged regularly, and are, in effect, cleared as if they were cheques. In Northern Ireland the note issue system is the same in all essentials.

The assessment of the advantages which the Scottish clearing banks derive from the right of note issue is a complicated question. Two facts are fairly clear. (1) If the note issue were abolished, the banks would have to hold larger amounts of till money for their deposit banking business than the difference between their present total of notes and coin and the 'cover' cash. In December 1970 the 'non-cover' notes and coin amounted to 2·8% of gross deposits as compared with the equivalent figure of till money for the London clearing banks of 6·3%. The extra till money which the Scottish clearing banks would have to hold if they conducted only deposit banking would be at the expense of earning assets, and the advantage of note issue could notionally be measured by the earnings on these relinquished assets. (2) One feature of the ability to hold unissued notes as till money is that the cost of holding a stock of notes is not attributable to individual branches as is the holding of till money in the English banks; the cost is centralised and can be regarded as a fixed cost of the bank as a whole. This is one of the reasons why Scottish clearing banks are reputedly more lavish in the provision of branch offices than their English counterparts.[8]

The interpretation of the balance sheet of the Scottish clearing banks in Table 6.7 is considerably complicated by the note issue and by the working balances which they keep with the London clearing banks. The same is true to a large extent of the Northern Ireland banks, although we shall not comment on their position separately.

To begin with the figure for notes and coin consists of three dis-

8. On this question see M. Gaskin, *The Scottish Banks: a Modern Survey* (London: George Allen & Unwin, 1965) Chapter 7.

tinct elements: (1) 'cover' cash of £154 million (157—2.7); (2) notes
of other Scottish clearing banks amounting to perhaps £15–20 million
which are awaiting exchange and which for each bank will be counter-
balanced by roughly equivalent holdings by other Scottish clearing

Table 6.7   Balance sheet of Scottish clearing and Northern Ireland
            banks, December 1970

	Scottish clearing banks		N. Ireland banks	
	£ million	%	£ million	%
Liabilities				
Deposits				
Current accounts	470	36.8	185	52.6
Deposit accounts	545	42.7	113	32.1
Other accounts	104	8.2	35	9.9
Gross deposits	1,119	87.7	333	94.6
Notes outstanding	157	12.3	19	5.4
Gross deposits + notes outstanding	1,276	100.0	352	100.0
Assets				
Cash				
Notes and coin	185	14.5	16	4.5
Balances with Bank of England	1	.1	5	1.4
Total cash	186	14.6	21	6.0
Balances with other banks, etc.	95	7.4	38	10.8
Money at call and short notice	152	11.9	4	1.1
Bills discounted				
British government treasury bills	5	.4	–	–
Other	33	2.6	8	2.3
Total liquid assets	472	37.0	71	20.2
Special deposits with Bank of England	20	1.6	–	–
Investments (BV)	266	20.9	73	20.7
Advances and other accounts	585	45.9	195	55.4

Source: *Bank of England Quarterly Bulletin*, June 1971, Tables 9(2) and
        9(3).

banks; (3) 'free' cash which is truly available for the needs of deposit
banking customers—the residue amounting to between £11 million and
£16 million. The remainder of the 'cash' item is equally difficult to
compute. The balances with the Bank of England are tiny, and are used
for settling clearing differences between one Scottish clearing bank

and another; the working balances used for settling differences with other banks are held with London clearing banks. These working balances with London clearing banks are shown under 'balances with other banks, etc.', but unfortunaely the 'etc.' covers cheques in course of collection on other banks, which will be counter-balanced by roughly equivalent amounts of Scottish clearing bank cheques being collected by other banks. Professor Gaskin estimates that the total of working balances in London, both with the Bank of England and with London clearing banks, is kept to a conventional level of slightly over 1% of total deposits. On this basis the total working balances are around £12 million, and the Scottish clearing banks are seen to be conducting their deposit banking business on a cash ratio of around 2% or 2·5% and a liquid assets ratio well below 20%, while their ratios as published look reassuringly high.

Professor Gaskin sums up the significance of these facts as follows:[9]

'... the lowness of the *operative* cash ratio of the Scottish banks is a consequence of their possession of the right of note issue. On the one hand the till-money arrangement has reduced the practical need to hold legal tender; and, on the other, the very existence of the note cover fund and its integration in the asset structure for balance sheet purposes has created a similarity with English practice which has obviated any pressure on the Scottish banks, whether internal or external, to make their reserve practices uniform in substance with those of the English banks.'

There is one further factor which affects the liquid asset requirements of both Scottish clearing and Northern Ireland banks: they both hold higher proportions of investments than London clearing banks, and they treat a portion of these as additional liquid assets, a practice which the English banks had to abandon when the composition of liquid assets was codified as part of the imposition of a liquid assets ratio.

Whatever may have been the justification in the past for treating the deposit banking business as separate from the note issue, as we have done above, this will be the result of the new arrangements as they apply to the Scottish clearing banks. The definitions of eligible liabilities and reserve assets are exactly the same for Scottish clearing banks as for London clearing banks, so that the note issue is omitted from eligible liabilities and no part of notes and coin counts towards

9. Gaskin, *ibid.*, p. 99.

reserve assets. In the event the Scottish clearing banks seem to have been quite comfortably placed, and to have achieved reserve assets ratios of around 15% without any noticeable changes in their balance sheet structure.

Both Scottish clearing banks and Northern Ireland banks face competition from London clearing banks for the business of their larger customers, and this fact has tended to align their rates and practices with those of the English deposit banking system. Both of them, however, were able to maintain slightly wider margins for parts of their business. The Scottish clearing banks did this by offering 2½% under Bank rate for their deposit receipts instead of the standard 2% under Bank rate of the London clearing banks. In meeting competition for large accounts they had the useful loophole of their London branches, which were outside the rate agreements and which do a disproportionately large share of the total business of the Scottish banking system. The Northern Ireland banks discriminated in favour of large deposits by offering 2% under Bank rate only for deposits of £25,000 and over, and for smaller deposits they paid 2½% under Bank rate (3% under Bank rate when Bank rate was 6% or over).

4. NATIONAL GIRO

For many years most Continental countries and Japan have had a postal giro system alongside a fairly developed deposit banking system, and the Radcliffe Committee in its Report (paragraphs 960–4) recommended that the establishment of a giro system should be considered in this country. In 1965 the Labour government announced that it proposed to follow this recommendation, and the National Giro began business late in 1968. There are two essential features in a giro system: (1) centralised accounting and (2) use of the branch network provided by post offices. The National Giro in Britain has one additional feature which is not present in some other systems, that of permitting payments to and from the deposit banking system, although they are not encouraged.

The aim of a giro system is to provide a cheap and secure means of payment for the majority of the population who do not have a bank account. Even in Britain, with its highly developed banking system, only about 30% of the adult population have bank accounts, and there is considerable scope in reducing the dependence on notes and coin and in providing a speedy system of money transmission for business. Although it started well, the National Giro has made losses since its establishment, and as a result the Conservative government considered either closing it or selling it off to private enterprise. Instead they commissioned a firm of chartered accountants to make a report on the prospects for future profitability; in November 1971 the government announced that the National Giro would stay in operation, with some changes in management and with higher charges from July 1972. It has been given five years within which to become profitable.

The National Giro provides four basic servies: (1) transfer from one Giro account to another; (2) for personal customers withdrawal of cash up to £20 every other working day at either of two nominated post offices; (3) payments into Giro accounts by persons without an account; (4) payments by account-holders in Giro to persons who do not have a Giro account, either by cheque payable into a bank account or by a cheque cashable at a post office after authentication at Giro headquarters. We shall be looking at the types of money transfer in Chapter 7; in terms of the descriptions of bank transfer systems given there we can say that the National Giro offers credit transfer, debit transfer and direct debit. It is prepared to receive payment instructions from large customers in the form of magnetic tape for feeding directly into the Giro computer. All the accounting is carried out at the Giro Centre at Bootle near Liverpool by means of computer.

Of the four services listed above there is a charge from July 1972 of 10p or under for the last three services, while direct transfer between Giro accounts is performed without charge (5p if the balance is below £30). Postage between the account-holder and the Giro Centre is free, but there is a charge for stationery. For account-holders who have access to a bank account the charges are competitive with those made by banks, which are now costing each transaction at up to 10p; it must be remembered, however, that banks offer some notional interest offset, and that some 40% of current account customers pay no charges at all. For a person without a bank account the charges are certainly less than the poundage on postal orders or money orders and the postage involved.

For persons there are advantages other than cheapness, of which the most important is the wider coverage of post offices (22,000 open six days a week during normal business hours). This is largely nullified unfortunately by the fact that cash can be withdrawn only at two nominated post offices; the Giro badly needs a system of guaranteed cheque cards such as the deposit banks provide for their customers. The National Giro is a money transmission system pure and simple, and provides few of the incidental services which add to the attraction of a bank account. In particular, an account cannot be overdrawn under any circumstances, but the National Giro has entered into an agreement with one of the largest finance houses, Mercantile Credit, whereby Giro customers are given access to personal loans on favourable terms. In the first year of this scheme 60,000 loans totalling £13 million were made. No financial advice is given by Giro, and virtually the only incidental service is that of providing travellers' cheques. For persons who do not have a bank account the National Giro probably provides just what they need and nothing more—a cheap and convenient money transmission service.

For business the National Giro offers two particular services: (1) the cheap collection of payments from customers without bank accounts and (2) a much more speedy transfer of funds than the banking system can provide. There are two ways in which the first service is of importance. For such bodies as public utilities (gas, water, electricity and telephone) and local authorities a cheap and easy way of enabling their customers to pay bills is to incorporate a Giro form into the bill; those with Giro accounts add their Giro account number, sign the form and send it to Giro, while those without Giro accounts can pay cash over a post office counter. A variant of this method applies to mail order houses, which can print Giro forms in their catalogues; persons ordering goods fill in the Giro form and use the back of the form for giving details of their order. This first service is also of considerable importance for financial institutions like finance houses, building societies and insurance companies, which have to collect fixed payments at intervals. Giro provides a normal standing order service and (with the prior agreement of the debtor) a direct debit facility, both of which considerably reduce the cost of collecting small amounts from persons without bank accounts.

When payment is made through the banking system, the fact that the two bank accounts involved are likely to be at different bank branches means that up to four or five days can elapse before a transaction is completed and the company receives its funds. Because Giro accounting is centralised, it can ensure that companies receive the benefit of funds the day after they have been paid in. This aspect of the service is particularly attractive to companies with a widespread network of collecting points—chains of retail shops, bakers and dairies with many roundsmen and so on. Their local employees can pay takings into a post office during normal business hours on six days a week, and the company receives its funds the following day instead of several days later.

From the point of view of the economy as a whole the great advantage which the National Giro offers is the prospect of sharply reducing the use of notes and coin. The circulation, transport and sorting of notes and coin are costly services, and because they are performed by the banking system, they are paid for by the very people who make least use of notes and coin, the bank customers. An incidental advantage which the Radcliffe Committee noted was that persons who opened Giro accounts were unlikely to reduce their holdings of notes and coin proportionately; this would increase that part of the national debt which was without interest cost to the government.

Table 6.8   Balance sheet of National Giro, 9 December 1970

	£ million	Percentages of gross deposits
Liabilities		
Gross deposits	44.6	100.0
Assets		
Notes and coin and balances with Bank of England	2.3	5.2
Money at call and short notice to discount market and local authorities	8.9	20.0
Bills discounted		
British government treasury bills	.5	1.1
Other	.8	1.8
Investments *(BV)*		
British government securities	4.8	10.8
Other securities	20.2	45.3
Advances (loans to local authorities up to one year)	7.1	15.9
Total	44.6	100.0

Source: *Financial Statistics*, June 1971, Table 43.

The extent to which the National Giro invests its funds in the public sector is clearly shown in Table 6.8. Since the money at call to the discount market was only about £3 million on that date, and since 'other bills discounted' are largely local authority bills and 'other securities' are largely local authority negotiable bonds, virtually all the funds are lent to the public sector. Local authorities received around

75% of the funds under one heading or another. The National Giro makes its own investments, but there is a list of permitted investments in the statute setting up the Giro, and this can be extended only by permission of the Treasury. One particularly striking feature is the short-term nature of nearly all the assets, little more than £5 million having a maturity of over one year. Since investment income is such an important feature of the operation of the National Giro, providing the basis on which it can offer free transfer between Giro accounts, one would have thought that some longer-dated assets, with their higher yields, would have been permitted.

To date the National Giro has fewer than 500,000 accounts, and Table 6.9 shows that nearly 50% of the balances come from the public

Table 6.9   Sector analysis of National Giro deposits, 31 December
             1970

Sector	£ million
Government	15
Local authority	9
Public corporations	13
Financial institutions	1
Companies	4
Other (mainly personal)	16
Total	58

Source: *Bank of England Quarterly Bulletin*, June 1971, Table 8(2).

sector. Now that its continued existence depends on reaching the break-even point as quickly as possible, the National Giro is driven to develop those kinds of business which offer quick prospects of profit. These are generally services which the deposit banks already provide, and Giro is using its centralised operations to undercut the deposit banks. The best example is their undercutting of the 'I.C.I.' terms offered by deposit banks for the direct payment of wages and salaries into accounts. It is a pity that the National Giro is being driven in this direction, because the greatest service to the economy can be gained by providing a cheap and simple money transmission service for persons without bank accounts—business which the deposit banks are not particularly anxious to attract because of its high transactions/balances ratio. Unfortunately there is something of a vicious circle operating in the attraction of large numbers of personal accounts:

persons will not think it worthwhile until companies print Giro forms on their bills and companies hesitate to switch their methods until more persons have accounts with the Giro. As it is, perhaps the greatest service which Giro has rendered so far is to act as a prod to the deposit banks for the modernisation of their money transmission services. The deposit banks certainly opened their credit transfer services to non-customers and introduced their direct debit system earlier than they would have done had there been no prospect of a cheap and competitive Giro system.

FURTHER READING

The reading suggested for Chapter 5 also applies to this chapter.

The following items are suggested as additional reading:

National Board for Prices and Incomes, *Bank Charges*, Report No. 34, Cmnd. 3292 (H.M.S.O., 1967).

M. Gaskin, *The Scottish Banks: a Modern Survey* (London: George Allen & Unwin, 1965).

G. Davies, 'Giro's two year hard slog,' *The Banker* (October 1970) p. 1069.

The following articles from the *Bank of England Quarterly Bulletin*:

'Competition and credit control' (June 1971).

'Competition and credit control: extracts from a lecture by the Chief Cashier of the Bank of England' (December 1971).

'Reserve ratios: further definitions' (December 1971).

7 The Banking Mechanism

So far we have examined the balance sheets and methods of operation of the various kinds of deposit bank. In this chapter we go on to consider the working of the deposit banking system as a whole. We shall have to look at many of the points treated in conventional banking theory, although we shall not be approaching them in an altogether conventional way.

1. TRANSMISSION OF PAYMENTS

A. The payments mechanism

The money stock consists of two main elements: (1) legal tender, consisting of notes and coin, and (2) bank money, consisting of deposits recorded in the ledgers of the bank. In present-day Britain bank money is by far the larger of the two elements. In December 1971 notes and coin represented only 32% of the measure of the money stock referred to as M1,[1] which is defined as notes and coin *plus* sterling current accounts of U.K. private sector residents *less* 60% of transit items.

We have already stressed the function of deposit banks in operating the payments mechanism and the way in which this function often comes into conflict with their other function, that of acting as financial intermediaries. Deposit banks (and to a far lesser extent those other banks which also provide current account facilities) are intimately concerned with the circulation of both elements of the money stock.

Although notes and coin circulate from hand to hand without a record being kept of their movements, they have to be put into circulation and withdrawn from circulation according to the needs of

1. *Bank of England Quarterly Bulletin*, Statistical annex, Table 12.

the public, and both processes are conducted through banks. Thus deposit banks give out notes and coin over the counter in exchange for a cheque drawn on an existing bank deposit. Even those notes and coins which find their way into the pockets of the public through post offices are supplied to the local post offices through the deposit banks. The notes and coin which are drawn from banks by firms for wage payments find their way back to the banks a few days later as shops and places of entertainment pay in their takings. The processes of counting and parcelling notes and coin, sorting clean from dirty notes and moving notes and coin around the country to meet public demand represent quite large elements in the cost of operating current accounts. The first function of deposit banks in operating the payments mechanism is thus that of converting notes and coin into bank money and bank money into notes and coin on demand.

Bank money exists only in the form of figures recorded in ledgers—or in more recent times recorded on the magnetic tape of computers. The transmission of bank money thus consists entirely of recording changes in accounts on the receipt of transfer instructions. The most familiar of the forms of transfer instruction is the cheque, but the government, local authorities and companies use warrants to pay interest and dividends, and the government uses warrants for some of its other disbursements. Credit transfers can be initiated by a number of different forms of instruction—credit transfer slips, standing orders and typed lists of payees with the amounts and details of their bank accounts. None of these transfer instructions is itself money. Bank money consists of the deposits recorded in the ledgers or computers of the bank, and cheques and other instruments are only instructions for operating on the deposits.

The transfer instructions circulate within the banking system to inform the banks concerned that they should credit one account and debit another. In most cases they also circulate outside the banking system to enable the transactors to make appropriate entries in their accounts. Transfer instructions can follow one of three different routes, all of which are illustrated in Figure 7.1. In this diagram Mr Smith is assumed to be paying his gas bill; he banks with Barclays and the Gas Board banks with the Midland. Thick lines indicate circulation of the transfer instruction within the banking system, and dashed lines indicate circulation by post between the two transactors and by post or by hand between each transactor and his bank.

Perhaps the commonest way of all of paying a gas bill is to go into the Gas Board's local office with this bill and to pay cash over the

Figure 7.1 Systems of bank transfer

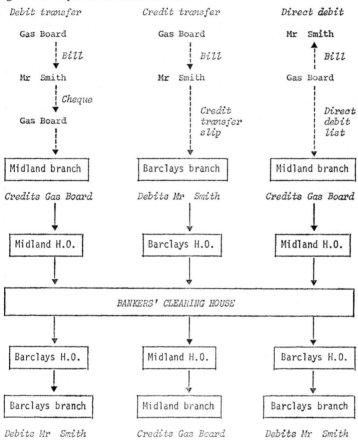

Debit transfer   *Credit transfer*   *Direct debit*

counter. This particular case does not concern us here because all that enters the banking system is some notes and coin indistinguishably mixed up with all the other takings of the day.

The next most common method is to pay by cheque, and this is illustrated in the left-hand column of Figure 7.1 under the heading of 'debit transfer'. The Gas Board sends a bill to Mr Smith by post, and he either returns it to the Board's accounting office by post with his cheque for the amount due or takes his cheque into the local office of the Gas Board. The Gas Board then pays the cheque into its local branch of the Midland Bank, whence it goes by post the same evening to head office in London. The following morning Midland presents the cheque to Barclays in the general clearing at the Bankers' Clearing House, the procedure of which will be described in the next section. The same day Barclays head office posts the cheque to the local branch at which Mr Smith has his account. This system of transfer is known as 'debit transfer' because the Gas Board was credited immediately it paid the cheque into its branch of Midland and the cheque then circulates within the banking system as an instruction to debit Mr Smith's account.

Of recent years most public utilities have printed credit transfer slips on their bills, and the sequence of events if Mr Smith had used one of these is illustrated in the centre column of Figure 7.1. As before the Gas Board sends the bill to Mr Smith, but this time he does not return it to the Gas Board with his payment but takes it himself to his bank, after completing the credit transfer slip. The order of events is the exact reverse of that in the debit transfer. Mr Smith is immediately debited, and the slip circulates within the banking system as an instruction to credit the Gas Board's account.

An even more recent innovation is the direct debit, which is illustrated in the last column of Figure 7.1. Once the instruction is within the banking system, the sequence of events is exactly the same as for a debit transfer; the difference lies in what happens before the instruction reaches the banking system. Before it could use this method the Gas Board would have to obtain Mr Smith's written agreement that his branch of Barclays should debit his account on instructions not from him but from the Gas Board. The Gas Board could then send Mr Smith his bill in the normal way, but it would add a note that his account would be debited with the amount shown on the bill unless he queried its accuracy within a period of two or three weeks. At the end of this period the Gas Board would send a list of direct debits due to its branch of the Midland Bank. This list would probably be on magnetic tape in a form directly usable by the bank's computer. Midland Bank would then initiate a series of instructions to the banks of the Board's debtors and would credit the Gas Board immediately with the total amount of the debits to be collected.

There are advantages and disadvantages attached to each of the three methods of bank transfer. Debit transfer has the great advantage of long familiarity, and the use of guaranteed cheque cards, under which the bank guarantees payment of cheques up to £30 (not to be confused with credit cards of the Barclaycard type), removes the difficulty of using cheques when the payer is not known. For collecting payments of fluctuating amounts, like public utility bills or amounts owed to shops, the credit transfer has the advantage of being open to persons without a bank account, but direct debit, provided that the payer's permission has been obtained in advance, removes the possibility of delayed payments, whether deliberate or arising from forgetfulness. For regular payments of instalments such as hire purchase or mortgage repayments or life assurance premiums both credit transfer, with its standing order or 'banker's order' procedure under which the bank is given instructions to make regular payment on certain dates, and direct debit considerably reduce collection costs.

The National Giro provides all three methods of transfer, although the greater part of the items passed through it are credit transfers. The credit transfer slip can be used as a cheque if it is sent to the payee instead of direct to the Giro Centre, and direct debits can be arranged. The great advantage of the Giro comes from the centralisation of its accounting in one computer centre; all transfers are completed on the day that the instructions are received at the Centre, normally the day after posting or paying in at a post office. For some large organisations, particularly retail shop chains, this brings about a great economy, because it reduces by a factor of two or three the amount of money circulating within the banking system and not yet credited to the organisation's account.

Looking into the future we can already envisage the day when all these methods of money transfer will be outdated. For a large part of its payments the society of the future will be able to dispense with notes and coin and with transfer instructions such as cheques and credit transfer slips. For shopping bank customers will be provided with embossed cards, which will be inserted in terminals connected directly to the bank computers to make instantaneous payment. For other payments households will obtain direct access to the bank computer by telephone line for instantaneous payment of their bills, and the accounting computers of companies will be connected to the bank computers. When this day arrives, the advantages of treating money transfer as a public utility like water, electricity or telephones rather than as an uncomfortable adjunct to the services of a financial intermediary will surely be apparent.

B. *Clearing arrangements*

The money transfer system involves the movement of bank deposits from one account to another at three different levels: (1) within the same branch, (2) between branches of the same bank and (3) between banks. As computers increasingly maintain the accounts for groups of branches, the proportion of movements which could be said to be within the same 'branch' goes up, and as banks merge to form larger units, the proportion of movements that are internal to the banks rises. The mechanism for clearing debit and credit transfer items between banks is the same as that between branches of the same bank: all the items affecting the other bank or the other branch are collected together and exchanged for items affecting the same two banks or branches but in the other direction. For example cheques drawn by customers of Lloyds in favour of customers of National Westminster are exchanged at a clearing for cheques drawn by customers of National Westminster in favour of customers of Lloyds. The essence of a clearing system is that only the net difference between the two sets of items exchanged is settled. For transfers between branches of the same bank settlement is made through the account which each branch maintains with its head office, while between different banks the settlement is made through the working balance which each bank maintains with some bank outside its own system—with the Bank of England in the case of the London clearing banks.

The centre of the clearing mechanism for deposit and other banks is the Bankers' Clearing House in London. Only the six London clearing banks and the Bank of England have access to this clearing house, but virtually all bank transfers go through it, either directly or indirectly in the form of settlement slips for cheques which have been presented outside the clearing house. The only transfers which do not go through the Bankers' Clearing House are those between pairs of Scottish banks, for which they maintain their own clearing, settling the net differences by cheques drawn on their balances at the Bank of England. Many of the other deposit banks, such as the Co-operative Bank, use one of the clearing banks as their agents in the Clearing House. There are special arrangements for dealing with cheques drawn on secondary banks and Irish banks; since secondary banks maintain their working balances with the London clearing banks, net differences on items exchanged in this way go through the Bankers' Clearing House.[2]

2. See Appendix 1 of R. S. Sayers, *Modern Banking* (Oxford: Oxford University Press, 7th edition, 1967). The reader is warned that there have been some changes since that account was written. In particular the provincial clearings have all been merged into the general clearing with the exception of the afternoon clearing at Liverpool.

The Bankers' Clearing House has two clearings, debit and credit, and the debit clearing is divided into two divisions, town clearing and general clearing. As Table 7.1 shows, the debit clearing is many times larger than the credit clearing; even the general clearing alone is $2\frac{1}{2}$ times as large. The town clearing dominates the picture in terms of the value of items cleared. The town clearing consists of items exchanged between about ninety clearing bank branches in the City of London, and the main object of this clearing, which takes places twice

Table 7.1   Bank clearings in England and Wales, January–June 1971 banks (old arrangements)

Monthly averages

Clearing		No. of items *Thousands*	Value *£ million*
London			
Credit clearing	Inter-bank	16,067	1,476
	Branch	9,880	3,344
Debit clearing			
Town	Inter-bank	265	61,556
	Branch	58	10,918
General	Inter-bank	57,948	8,387
	Branch	24,148	4,268
Liverpool		4	59
	Total	108,370	90,008

Sources: (1) Bankers' Clearing House;   (2) Bank of England.

a day, is to provide settlement the same day for the large items connected with London financial markets. The average size of item passed through this clearing during the first six months of 1971 was over £230,000; the growth of the parallel money markets over recent years is reflected in the rise in the monthly average value of items passed through the town clearing from about £15,000 million in 1960 to over £60,000 million in the first six months of 1971.

In terms of numbers of transactions the bulk of the payments go through either the credit clearing or the general clearing. Both take place during the morning, and settlement is the following day. Here the average value of the items is much smaller—£92 for the credit clearing and £145 for the general clearing in the first six months of 1971. The solitary clearing outside London, the afternoon clearing at

Liverpool, is the remnant of provincial clearings in twelve centres and of informal arrangements to exchange cheques in each town between local branches of the different banks. This centralisation is the inevitable result of the growth of computer accounting, which makes the exchange of cheques other than after process through the computer system an awkward anomaly.

Table 7.1 shows not only the inter-bank items passing through the Bankers' Clearing House but also, under the heading of 'branch', the items dealt with internally in each bank. The mergers among the London clearing banks which came into effect at the end of 1969 and during 1970 had the effect of increasing the proportion of items internal to each bank, and the official estimate is that the total effect was to transfer the following percentages of the various clearings from inter-bank to branch: town 8%, general 10% and credit 11%.[3]

From the figures of Table 7.1 we can obtain some idea of the rate of turnover of current account balances. Because only a part of the transactions affecting Scottish and secondary banks is reflected in the clearing figures, we cannot state an unambiguous total for current account balances concerned, but the total of current account balances in the London clearing banks and secondary banks, £6500 million on average during the first six months of 1971, would be a fair estimate. As against the total value of the clearings shown in Table 7.1 this suggests that current account balances are turned over on average about fourteen times a month. Just over 80% of the value of the clearings is in the town clearing and consists of largely financial items affecting very few accounts; if we ignore this part of the clearing the total value of ordinary transactions is £17,534 million a month, and we can say that current account balances are turned over about 2½ times a month.

We have already pointed out that the figures in Table 7.1 are a fairly complete record of money transfers through the banking system. Table 7.2 contrasts the total value of bank transfers (as in Table 7.1 but excluding the purely financial transactions of the town clearing) with the value of payments effected by all other means of money transmission except hand-to-hand payment by notes and coin. The table shows clearly the extent to which transfers by the banking system dominate the field of money transfer.

3. *Financial Statistics* (August 1971) note to Table 54.

Table 7.2   Value of payments by various means, 1970

Monthly averages

	£ million
Banking system	15,750
National Giro	342
Trustee savings banks	18
Money orders	17
Postal orders	47
Total	16,174

Sources: (1) Bankers' Clearing House;   (2) National Giro;   (3) Trustee
           Savings Banks Association;   (4) Post Office.

Notes: (1) The banking system figure excludes town clearing and
               includes an estimated allowance for branch clearings.
           (2) Money orders and postal orders include Irish and overseas
               items paid in U.K.

C. *Settlement of clearing*

We have dealt rather summarily with the mechanism of the clearing
because this is not of great importance for the working of the banking system. What we are far more concerned with is the settlement
of the net differences arising out of the clearing because this lies at
the root of the banking mechanism. In this section we shall describe the
principles of settlement, and in the next main section we shall go on
to consider the effects of the settlements for different kinds of transaction on the balance sheets of the banks.

The general principle of settlement for differences arising at the
clearing is quite simple: if Bank A and Bank B are two banks of the
same group (London clearing banks or Scottish banks, for example),
Bank A will not accept settlement by means of a cheque drawn by Bank
B on itself, but requires settlement by means of a cheque drawn on a
third bank outside the group. All banks therefore need to maintain
working balances with a bank or banks outside their own group for
the purposes of settlement. These working balances form part of the
cash of the bank, and we can summarise the principle of settlement
for clearing by saying that settlement is always 'in cash'.

The British banking system divides itself into two layers according
to the outside banks with which other banks maintain working balances. The London clearing banks have their working balances with

the Bank of England, and these constitute the greater part of the so-called 'bankers' deposits'. All other banks have working balances with London clearing banks. The only exception is that the Scottish banks, as we have seen, use working balances at the Bank of England for settling differences on clearing within the group of Scottish banks. This system of working balances is summarised in Figure 7.2, and it is in

Figure 7.2   Working balances of different kinds of bank

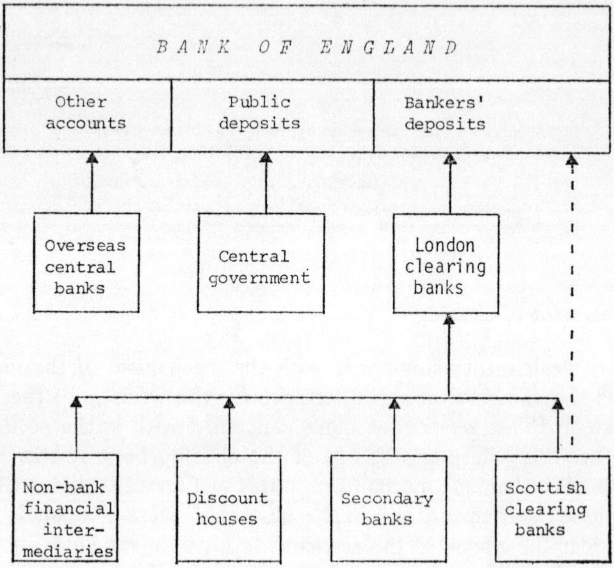

essence a very simple system. The position is complicated slightly by the fact that many banks other than London clearing banks have accounts at the Bank of England, but these are nominal balances not used for settlement of clearing differences; examples are the discount houses and accepting houses.

The main result of this double-layer system of working balances is that we can regard the customers of banks which maintain their working balances with the London clearing banks as if they were direct customers of the London clearing banks. Let us asume that two secondary banks, Barings and Rothschilds, maintain working balances with National Westminster and Lloyds respectively. Then, if a customer of Barings makes a payment by cheque to a customer of Rothschilds, the effect on the balance sheets of National Westminster and Lloyds will be identical with the effect produced by a cheque payment made by a customer of National Westminster to a customer of Lloyds. This fact enables us to simplify our account by confining the analysis to the London clearing banks.

Figure 7.2 shows that the Bank of England also maintains the working balances of other important transactors, notably the British government. The main theme running through our discussion in the next few sections will be the difference in their effects on London clearing bank balance sheets between transactions confined to customers of the London clearing banks (including, as we indicated above, customers of other banks which maintain working balances with London clearing banks) and transactions between customers of the London clearing banks and the government or the Bank of England itself.

2. TRANSACTIONS AND BANK DEPOSITS

A. *Transactions confined to customers of the London clearing banks*

In order to portray the effects on clearing bank balance sheets of various types of transaction we need a method of presentation which will concentrate on the essential elements in the balance sheets and not obscure the picture through too much detail. For this reason we shall show only those parts of bank balance sheets which are relevant to the point under discussion, but the method of setting out these balance sheets will differ somewhat from the conventional one. Normally the schematic balance sheets of banks used in illustrations of this kind are in the form of 'T-accounts', so called because two lines are set out in the shape of a letter T, with liabilities listed on one side of the vertical line and assets on the other. Our own form is to list liabilities and assets one under the other, with a horizontal line dividing assets from liabilities. The main reason for adopting this unconventional method is to economise on space. For clarity figures which have changed from one balance sheet to the next in the same sequence will be identified in bold type; italic type will be used for ratios.

In the schematic balance sheets which follow the banks are named, but there is no pattern about the choice of names and no significance attaches to the behaviour ascribed to any particular bank. They are named solely to avoid the rather clumsy use of 'Bank A' and 'Bank B'. The figures in the balance sheets are all rounded to make the arithmetic easy, but the orders of magnitude are intended to be realistic. For obvious reasons the changes shown from one position to the next have been magnified. These schematic balance sheets should be regarded as highly simplified accounting models designed to show clearly the processes at work. We shall begin by giving an example with the banks adhering to the balance sheet ratios which obtained under the old arrangements up to September 1971. Thereafter all our examples will refer to the new arrangements.

The first type of transaction which we shall examine is that between customers of different clearing banks, and to do this we shall look at the effect on clearing bank balance sheets of settlements between a pair of clearing banks. To focus the discussion we shall ignore all other clearing banks and all the other types of transaction which will be going on simultaneously: we are concerned only with what happens when Midland gains £10 million at the clearing from Barclays, implying that on the day before settlement took place those cheques presented at the clearing which were drawn by customers of Barclays in favour of customers of Midland were £10 million greater in total value than cheques drawn by customers of Midland in favour of customers of Barclays.

The position under the old arrangements is illustrated in Table 7.3. At the top of the table the balance sheets of the two banks before the settlement took place are shown, the next set of balance sheets shows the impact effect on the balance sheets of the settlement and at the bottom of the table we show the new position after the banks have restored their customary ratios. As we are concerned with the old arrangements, we show the banks adhering to an 8% cash ratio; 1½% of gross deposits is represented by balances with the Bank of England (shown in the right-hand column) and 6½% by till money. Under the old arrangements they also adhered to a *minimum* liquidity ratio of 28%, but in order to avoid falling below 28% at any time of the year they kept to a higher level during most of the year. We show them working to 30%.

In position (b) balance sheets are shown immediately after the settlement for the previous day's clearing has taken place. Since the cheques in favour of the customers of Midland exceeded those in favour of customers of Barclays by £10 million, Midland's deposit liabilities have increased by £10 million, while the deposit liabilities of Barclays have gone down by £10 million. The actual settlement took place by means of a transfer of £10 million from the bankers' deposits of Barclays with the Bank of England to the bankers' deposits of Midland, and this is reflected in identical gains and losses under the heading of 'cash' in the two balance sheets. The most important point to note is that the movements of deposits and cash are exactly equal. Since the denominator of the cash and liquidity ratios is gross deposits, equal changes in cash and deposits have the effect of changing numerators and denominators of both ratios by the same amount and thus throwing the ratios out of line. The cash ratio of Midland has gone up

Table 7.3   Transactions between customers of the London clearing banks (old arrangements)

£ million

	Midland	Barclays	Bank of England	
(a) Position before settlement				
Deposits	2,000	3,000	Bankers' deposits	
			Midland	30
			Barclays	45
Cash	160 (8.0%)	240 (8.0%)		
Money at call	200	300		
Bills	240 (30.0%)	360 (30.0%)		
(b) Position immediately after settlement				
Deposits	2,010	2,990	Bankers' deposits	
			Midland	40
			Barclays	35
Cash	170 (8.5%)	230 (7.7%)		
Money at call	200	300		
Bills	240 (30.3%)	360 (29.8%)		
(c) Equilibrium restored				
Deposits	2,010	2,990	Bankers' deposits	
			Midland	31
			Barclays	44
Cash	161 (8.0%)	239 (8.0%)		
Money at call	209	291		
Bills	240 (30.3%)	360 (29.8%)		

to 8·5% and its liquidity ratio has gone up to 30·3%; the two ratios of Barclays have gone down to 7·7% and 29·8% respectively.

Both banks have a strong incentive to restore their cash ratios to 8%, Midland because it is losing interest by holding excess cash and Barclays because it is below the required 8%. Midland gets rid of its excess cash by advancing it at call to the discount market, while Barclays restores its 8% by calling from the discount market. Rounding to the nearest £1 million, we can see that Barclays calls £9 million and that Midland advances the same amount. The overall position of the discount houses remains unchanged because Midland has exactly replaced the call money withdrawn by Barclays. The changes in the figures for cash resulting from the transactions in money at call are reflected in bankers' deposits at the Bank of England. The total of deposits in the banking system (as represented by these two banks) is unchanged, but the distribution of this total between Barclays and Midland has been changed by the settlement. After the cash ratios of both banks have been restored to 8%, the liquidity ratios remain as they were in position (b) because the transactions in money at call have done no more than change the sizes of items which both count as liquid assets. We do not need to pursue the matter further, however, because the banks are still close enough to the 30% which is assumed to be their rough target.

In Table 7.4 we portray the same transaction, a settlement of £10 million by Barclays in favour of Midland, under the new arrangements. The first change is that till money no longer counts as cash, but it will be noted that the balances with the Bank of England are of exactly the same size as before since the clearing banks have an understanding with the Bank of England that they will maintain balances equal to $1\frac{1}{2}\%$ of eligible liabilities. (We have not altered the deposits figure to indicate the difference between gross deposits under the old arrangements and eligible liabilities under the new.) Instead of liquid assets we are now concerned with a rather wider range of reserve assets, but, as we shall see, money at call still plays the key role in adjustment of cash positions. Once again we assume that the clearing banks are working to a reserve assets ratio somewhat above the obligatory minimum of $12\frac{1}{2}\%$—in this table 15%.

A quick comparison of Tables 7·3 and 7·4 will show that the sequence of events is identical. In position (b) Midland's cash and deposits go up by £10 million and cash and deposits of Barclays go down by £10 million exactly as before. There is a slight difference in position (c) in that the amount of money at call withdrawn by Barclays and advanced by Midland is now £10 million instead of £9 million, but this difference arises only because we are rounding all figures to the nearest £1 million. Once again the secondary ratio, the reserve assets ratio, remains out of line at the end of the transaction; as before we assume that the banks would not adjust further.

We can see from this comparison that the system remains unchanged in all essentials, with two ratios operative—a primary (cash) ratio of $1\frac{1}{2}\%$ adhered to day by day and a secondary (reserve assets) ratio of $12\frac{1}{2}\%$ also adhered to day by day but usually protected by excess reserve assets. This may seem somewhat surprising, but the mechanism depends essentially on the fact that the London clearing banks have some target level for their cash balances with the Bank of England. The fact that this target level is imposed by the Bank of England

Table 7.4   Transactions between customers of the London clearing
banks (new arrangements)

£ million

	Midland	Barclays	Bank of England	
(a) Position before settlement				
Deposits	2,000	3,000	Bankers' deposits	
			Midland	30
			Barclays	45
Cash	30 *(1.5%)*	45 *(1.5%)*		
Money at call	200	300		
Other reserve assets	70 *(15.0%)*	105 *(15.0%)*		
(b) Position immediately after settlement				
Deposits	2,010	2,990	Bankers' deposits	
			Midland	40
			Barclays	35
Cash	40 *(2.0%)*	35 *(1.2%)*		
Money at call	200	300		
Other reserve assets	70 *(15.4%)*	105 *(14.7%)*		
(c) Equilibrium restored				
Deposits	2,010	2,990	Bankers' deposits	
			Midland	30
			Barclays	45
Cash	30 *(1.5%)*	45 *(1.5%)*		
Money at call	210	290.		
Other reserve assets	70 *(15.4%)*	105 *(14.7%)*		

under the new arrangements is incidental; if the target level were self-imposed and undeclared, we should have had to assume some level for our tables. There is, however, one important difference between the old arrangements and the new. The 8% cash ratio under the old arrangements applied to the totals of gross deposits day by day, whereas the $1\frac{1}{2}\%$ ratio under the new arrangements is related to the total of eligible liabilities *at the last make-up day* (the day in the month, the second Wednesday in December and the third Wednesday in other months, on which the banks publish their figures and submit returns to the Bank of England). It would therefore be more correct, although it makes no difference to the figures, to regard the banks as acting to restore their unchanged cash balances between make-up days rather than reacting to changes in their deposit totals. From now on we shall confine our illustrations to the position under the new arrangements in the knowledge that these have not changed the essentials of the banking mechanism.

The sequence of events outlined in Tables 7.3 and 7.4 arises in this exact form only because we have made a tacit assumption that the whole of the £10 million received by Midland from Barclays as a settlement of the previous day's clearing went to the credit of accounts with credit balances; in practice many of the cheques would have ended up as credits to overdrawn accounts.[4] In order to emphasise the position Table 7.5 is drawn up on the assumption that the whole of the £10 million settlement is for the credit of overdrawn accounts. In this case we must add one further asset, advances, to those specified in Tables 7.3 and 7.4.

As far as Barclays and the Bank of England are concerned there is no change between Tables 7.4 and 7.5, but the position of Midland is altered. Instead of gaining £10 million of deposits in position (b) Midland reduces one of its asset headings, advances, by £10 million. Midland's cash position is as before, and it reacts in the same way as before by advancing money at call to use up its excess cash. The essential difference between Table 7.4 and Table 7.5 is that Midland's deposits are unchanged, while the deposits of Barclays have gone down by £10 million as before. Hence the deposits of the entire banking system (as represented by these two banks) have been reduced by £10 million, the amount of credits to overdrawn accounts. We shall see later how the total of deposits in a banking system can grow; the sequence of events in Table 7.5 shows that deposits are reduced by the repayment of advances.

B. *Transactions with the government*

The position which we have reached is that transactions between customers of the same group of banks have no effect on the totals of

4. When it comes to computing eligible liabilities under the new arrangements, adjustments of sterling deposits are made for transit items on the assumption that 60% of these items will affect accounts with credit balances and 40% overdrawn accounts.

cash and deposits within that group unless the transactions result in the repayment of advances. For the purpose of this statement the London clearing banks, other deposit banks (excluding the Banking Department of the Bank of England) and secondary banks form one group of banks. Transactions between customers of banks within the

Table 7.5   Credits to overdrawn accounts

£ million

	Midland		Barclays		Bank of England	
(a) Position before settlement						
Deposits	2,000		3,000		Bankers' deposits	
					Midland	30
					Barclays	45
Cash	30	*(1.5%)*	45	*(1.5%)*		
Money at call	200		300			
Other reserve assets	70	*(15.0%)*	105	*(15.0%)*		
Advances	1,000		1,500			
(b) Position immediately after settlement						
Deposits	2,000		2,990		Bankers' deposits	
					Midland	40
					Barclays	35
Cash	40	*(2.0%)*	35	*(1.2%)*		
Money at call	200		300			
Other reserve assets	70	*(15.5%)*	105	*(14.7%)*		
Advances	990		1,500			
(c) Equilibrium restored						
Deposits	2,000·		2,990		Bankers' deposits	
					Midland	30
					Barclays	45
Cash	30	*(1.5%)*	45	*(1.5%)*		
Money at call	210		290			
Other reserve assets	70	*(15.5%)*	105	*(14.7%)*		
Advances	990		1,500			

same banking group result in the movement of cash and deposits in equal amounts from one bank to another, but what one bank loses another bank gains. We are now going on to see what happens when a customer of one banking group has a transaction with the customer of another banking group. In bald terms the result is obvious: cash and deposits will be transferred from one banking group to another just as previously they were transferred from one bank to another within the same group. The consequences must be spelt out in some detail, however, because the difference between the two sorts of transaction is crucial to the working of the banking mechanism.

For practical purposes there is only one other group of banks which need concern us, the Bank of England and its customers. All the transactions between customers of the London clearing banks and their group of banks and the customers of any other group of banks take place through the Banking Department of the Bank of England, and result, as we shall see, in movements between bankers' deposits and public deposits at the Bank of England instead of from the banker's deposits of one bank to those of another. Put in another way, transactions between customers of the British deposit banking group and customers of other banking groups all take the form of transactions with the British government.[5]

As can be seen from Figure 7.2, the Bank of England is banker not only to the London clearing banks but also to the central government. We can begin our analysis by considering the effects on clearing bank balance sheets of the simplest of transactions between customers of the clearing banks and the government, the payment of taxes. This is shown in Table 7.6. We are now concerned with what happens to the London clearing banks as a whole, and we have substituted aggregate figures of the London clearing banks for the balance sheets of individual banks. The assumptions are still the same as in previous tables: the clearing banks have required cash balances equal to $1\frac{1}{2}\%$ of eligible liabilities on the last make-up day and they are assumed to be working to a 15% reserve assets ratio. In previous tables the function of the Bank of England was that of a passive recorder of changes in the cash balances of different banks, but in Table 7.6 the Bank of England has an active role to play.

The table portrays the effects of the payment of £10 million in taxes by customers of the London clearing banks. In position (b) the clearing bank deposits have dropped by £10 million, and the Bank of England has transferred £10 million from bankers' deposits to public deposits; as a result clearing bank cash has dropped by £10 million, from £150 million, to £140 million. Since all the clearing banks are now below their required cash balances they all behave as Barclays did in

5. This statement is true only of transactions in sterling and transactions which involve a switch between sterling and foreign currencies. Transactions between bank balances denominated in foreign currencies, euro-dollars for example, do not have the same effect.

our previous examples and call in £10 million from the discount houses to restore these balances to £150 million. So far all is plain sailing for the London clearing banks because they have restored their cash balances, but the discount houses are in trouble. In the previous examples the money at call withdrawn by Barclays was replaced im-

Table 7.6   Payment of taxes by customers of London clearing banks

£ million

London clearing banks		Bank of England	
(a) Position before settlement			
Deposits	10,000	Bankers' deposits	150
		Public deposits	10
Cash	150 (*1.5%*)		
Money at call	1,000		
Other reserve assets	350 (*15.0%*)		
(b) Position immediately after settlement			
Deposits	9,990	Bankers'.deposits	140
		Public deposits	20
Cash	140 (*1.4%*)		
Money at call	1,000		
·Other reserve assets	350 (*14.9%*)		
(c) Equilibrium restored			
Deposits	9,990	Bankers' deposits	150
		Public deposits	20
Cash	150 (*1.5%*)	Advances to discount	
Money at call	990	houses	10
Other reserve assets	350 (*14.9%*)		

mediately by Midland, and the discount houses remained in overall balance. This time, however, all the clearing banks have called together; if we assume that no other lender on the discount market is in a position to replace the withdrawn money at call, the discount houses have no option but to use their borrowing facilities at the Bank of England, which acts as 'lender of last resort'. This is shown in position (c) by the Bank of England's advance to discount houses of £10 million. The Bank of England, which has no rigid ratio constraints, has balanced an increase of £10 million in its deposit liabilities by an identical increase in its assets.

This sequence illustrates a most important feature of the British banking system. The Bank of England, in its role as lender of last resort, has supplied without question the cash needed by the banking system. At the end of the day, however, the total money supply, as measured here by the total of clearing bank deposits, has gone down by £10 million. The Bank of England has supplied the cash needed to restore the clearing banks' balances; it has not acted in any way to restore the level of deposits.

Exactly the same sequence of events will occur with any other type of transaction between the general public, in their role as customers of the British deposit banking system, and the government. The sequence will occur in reverse, resulting in an increase in bank deposits, when the central government makes its disbursements. Examples of these are payments to doctors under the National Health Service, grants to local authorities (which do not bank with the Bank of England but with the deposit banks) and the payment of interest on the national debt.

The fact that any of these transactions in either direction have a permanent influence on the level of bank deposits, and hence on the stock of money, opens the way for the government to initiate transactions with the direct object of controlling the stock of money. Such transactions are called *open market operations*, and they may be carried out in either treasury bills or in government stocks (bonds). Table 7.6 can be used to illustrate the sequence of events when open market operations are conducted by the sale of government bonds to the general public (customers of the British deposit banking system). The purchasers of the bonds draw cheques on their bank accounts just as they did for the payment of taxes, and these cheques result in an increase of public deposits at the Bank of England and a running down of bankers' deposits. Once again the Bank of England will act to restore the cash lost to the banking system, but it will not act to restore the deposits which have been lost. If the government in its operations in the gilt-edged market buys government bonds from the general public the effect is the opposite, an increase in bank deposits.

It is very important to note that these effects are secured because the transactions are between the general public and the government and not because it is treasury bills or government bonds which are being traded. Had one set of customers of the clearing banks sold government bonds to another set of customers when the Government Broker was inactive in the market, the effect on the total of bank deposits would have been neutral, just as it is with any other transaction between customers of the clearing banks (Table 7.4). Equally the government does not have to use treasury bills or government bonds for its open market operations; any other object which it can buy or sell—Army surplus stores, for example—will do just as well, at least in theory. It is interesting to note that the same effect could be obtained if the government maintained accounts with the clearing banks since movements of balances on the accounts between the Bank of England and the clearing banks would alter clearing bank cash and deposits by equal amounts.

The open market operations which we have considered above are transactions between bank customers and the government, but some open market operations take place between the banks themselves and the government. This situation is illustrated in Table 7.7. The initial position is that the clearing banks have excess reserve assets, and we assume that they wish to restore the 15% reserve assets ratio to which they are working at this time of the year. One way in which they can do this is to allow maturing treasury bills to run off and to replace them with assets outside the range of reserve assets. In Table 7.7 the clearing banks allow £10 million of maturing treasury bills to run off, and replace them with bonds (investments) purchased from the Government Broker. The main point to note is that there is no change

Table 7.7 Purchase of bonds from Government Broker by London clearing banks

£ million

London clearing banks		Bank of England	
(a) Position before settlement			
Deposits	10,000	Bankers' deposits	150
		Public deposits	10
Cash	150 (*1.5%*)		
Bills	260		
Other reserve assets	1,100 *(15.1%)*		
Investments	300		
(b) Position immediately after settlement – equilibrium			
Deposits	10,000	Bankers' deposits	150
		Public deposits	10
Cash	150 (*1.5%*)		
Bills	250		
Other reserve assets	1,100 *(15.0%)*		
Investments	310		

*

at all in bank deposits because the customers of the clearing banks are not involved in any way. Bank cash is also unaffected since the £10 million received for the maturing treasury bills is immediately laid out in a purchase of government bonds. Likewise public deposits remain unchanged because the debit of £10 million for maturing treasury bills is cancelled out by a credit for the sale of bonds.

The last two types of transaction between the general public and the government which we shall consider both involve the banks in replenishing stocks of assets which they can purchase only from the

Table 7.8   Withdrawal of notes and coin by customers of London
                    clearing banks

£ million

London clearing banks		Bank of England	
(a) Position before withdrawal			
Deposits	10,000	Bankers' deposits	150
Cash	150 *(1.5%)*	Notes and coin	50
Money at call	1,000		
Other reserve assets	350 *(15.0%)*		
Till money	650		
(b) Position immediately after withdrawal			
Deposits	9,990	Bankers' deposits	150
Cash	150 *(1.5%)*	Notes and coin	50
Money at call	1,000		
Other reserve assets	350 *(15.0%)*		
Till money	640		
(c) Clearing banks replace till money			
Deposits	9,990	Bankers' deposits	140
Cash	140 *(1.4%)*	Notes and coin	40
Money at call	1,000		
Other reserve assets	350 *(14.9%)*		
Till money	650		
(d) Equilibrium restored			
Deposits	9,990	Bankers' deposits	150
Cash	150 *(1.5%)*	Notes and coin	40
Money at call	990	Advance to discount	
Other reserve assets	350 *(14.9%)*	houses	10
Till money	650		

government. Table 7.8 illustrates what happens when the customers of the clearing banks withdraw notes and coin. The initial position is the same as in Table 7.6 except that we show the clearing banks' holding of till money immediately below the reserve assets and the Bank of England's holding of notes and coin in the Banking Department. The immediate effect of the withdrawal of £10 million in notes and coin is to reduce both deposits (because customers have cashed cheques drawn on their accounts) and till money by that amount. Nothing further need happen if the clearing banks are content with the reduced holding of till money, but we assume that they want to replenish their stock of notes and coin to its former level. They 'buy' £10 million of notes and coin from the Bank of England, thus reducing their cash below its required level. In position (d) they restore their cash by calling from the discount houses, which then have to borrow from the Bank of England. Apart from the fact that there is one extra step in the sequence, the situation is the same as in the payment of taxes by clearing bank customers illustrated in Table 7.6. Naturally a deposit of notes and coin by customers works in the opposite direction: if the banks feel themselves to be holding excess till money, they can 'sell' notes and coin to the Bank of England.

With a slight change of description the details of Table 7.8 apply to foreign exchange transactions. The clearing banks maintain stocks of foreign currencies in the form of balances with correspondent banks abroad, and these are replenished and run down in the same way as stocks of notes and coin. Again the source of supply, this time the Exchange Equalisation Account, is approached through the Bank of England, and replenishment of foreign currency balance involves loss of cash to the clearing banks and surrender of currencies to the authorities gains cash. In this case the level of the balances is closely controlled by the authorities, and any currencies in excess of permitted balances have to be surrendered to the authorities immediately.

3. THE GENESIS OF BANK DEPOSITS

A. *Principles involved*

One of the oldest topics of discussion in banking theory is the power of banks to 'create' deposits. Bankers themselves have usually held that such creation was impossible because they could lend only after first receiving a fresh deposit, but from early times economists have insisted that deposit liabilities could be 'manufactured' by the banking system. The first systematic exposition of the process of deposit creation in the form of a multiplier model came in a book by C. A. Phillips, published in the United States in 1920, but it was followed soon afterwards by one of the seminal articles in banking theory by W. F. Crick.[6] The concept of the banking multiplier was recognised by the Macmillan Committee, which reported in 1931.

The basis of the alleged power of banks to 'create' (the word must remain in inverted commas until we have examined what is implied by this doctrine) deposits lies in the fact that bank deposits are generally accepted as money by the public. This acceptance depends on the belief that bank deposits can always be converted into legal tender money (notes and coin) at any time. The process is very similar to that by which the medieval goldsmiths were able to issue banknotes (originally receipts for the deposit of gold with them) in excess of the gold held in their strong rooms because they found from experience that only a small proportion of their customers wanted to withdraw their gold at any one time and that a proportion of what was withdrawn by some customers would be replaced by others. Because both banknotes and bank deposits are accepted as means of payment, goldsmiths and bankers are able to buy assets by creating liabilities against themselves; the seller is not concerned whether this is done out of recently acquired gold stocks or out of a deposit freshly received by the banker. Since the seller regards a bank deposit as part of his money stock, he is quite content to receive payment in the form of a cheque drawn by (say) Lloyds Bank on itself, which he will pay into his bank account in the same way as he would any other cheque. The form of 'buying an asset' with which we shall be particularly concerned is that of lending, making an advance; as the borrower draws on his overdraft limit by writing cheques in favour of others, the cheques are paid into their bank accounts and serve to increase their bank deposits (or to reduce their overdrafts). From what has been said it can be seen that the power to 'create' bank deposits is inherent in the fact that bank deposits are money: the deposits of a particular bank cease to be money immediately we begin to query their origin.

The immediate question which concerns us is the extent to which banks can go in this process of creating deposits. There is one obvious limitation to the power of the banks. Just as the banknotes of the

6. C. A. Phillips, *Bank Credit* (New York: Macmillan, 1920) and W. F. Crick, 'The genesis of bank deposits', *Economica* (1927) (reprinted in American Economic Association, *Readings in Monetary Theory*, 1952, pp. 41–53). The title of this main section comes from the title of Crick's article.

medieval goldsmith became worthless as soon as there was the slightest suspicion that he would not be able to redeem them in gold, so the deposits of the modern banker would be unacceptable if there were the slightest suspicion that he could not redeem them in legal tender. The limitation, in other words, lies in the maintenance of confidence in the integrity of the bank. In recent times the maintenance of confidence has depended on the adherence of the bank to certain customary or legal ratios concerning the liquidity of its assets, in particular to a specified ratio of cash to deposits. In fact the power to create deposits has usually been seen as deriving from 'fractional reserve' banking.

The top half of Table 7.9 demonstrates the simplest version of the

Table 7.9   Early versions of the banking multiplier

	(a)	(b)	(c)
(1) 'Macmillan' model			
Deposits	10,000	10,010	10,100
Cash	1,000 *(10.0%)*	1,010 *(10.1%)*	1,010 *(10.0%)*
Advances	9,000	9,000	9,090
(2) 'Radcliffe' model			
Deposits	10,000	10,010	10,033
Cash	800 *(8.0%)*	810 *(8.1%)*	803 *(8.0%)*
Other liquid assets	2,200 *(30.0%)*	2,200 *(30.1%)*	2,207 *(30.0%)*
Advances	7,000	7,000	7,023

'banking multiplier' process, drawn up on the assumptions appropriate to the time of the Macmillan Report. At that time the clearing banks kept to a 10% cash ratio, although this was somewhat of a fiction because the banks made up their monthly statements on different days of the week, so that each in turn could withdraw money from the discount market to inflate its cash on the make-up day and then return the money at call the following day for another bank to use in the same way. It was not until 1946 that the Bank of England insisted on a common day for the making up of monthly statements and the adherence to an actual ratio of 8%. The table differs in form from the previous accounting models of the banking system: instead of the three positions ((a) position before disturbance, (b) position immediately after the disturbance and (c) position when equilibrium has been restored) being listed below each other down the table, they are here placed in successive columns of the table. Only the aggregate position of all the London clearing banks is shown.

As before we assume that the clearing banks have received £10 million in cash and increased their deposits by the same amount. For the purpose of exposition it does not matter how this gain of cash and deposits came about, but it can be taken as the result of the deposit of £10 million in notes and coin by customers of the banks. As before the clearing banks find themselves with excess cash, and in this case they use this excess cash to support extra deposits by making advances of £90 million. As the customers draw on the advances, cheques are paid into the accounts of other customers within the banking system, and the aggregate deposits of the clearing banks rise by a further £90 million, making them £10,100 million in position (c). The banking multiplier, defined as the ratio of additional deposits to the initial gain of cash, is $100/10 = 10$. This is the reciprocal of the cash ratio of 10%. The same result could be arrived at quite simply by stating that, with a cash ratio of 10%, an extra £10 million of cash is able to support an additional £100 million of deposits.

Before we go further we must explain two points. The first is the actual process by which the banks moved from position (b) to position (c), and the second is the difference if advances are made by loans rather than by overdrafts.

If a banking system consisted of only one bank, it would be fairly easy to accept that it would soon learn the simple arithmetic relating an increment of cash to the additional deposits which that cash could support and that it would proceed straight from position (b) to position (c). Most banking systems consist of many banks, each operating on its own and for its own profit. Even though the four large and two small London clearing banks differ greatly in number from the more than 14,000 independent banks in the United States, there is a problem to consider as soon as we move from a single bank to more than one.

The process can be understood most easily if we assume that the original gain of £10 million in cash and deposits came to a single bank. This bank, knowing that it must work to a cash ratio of 10%, will retain 10% of the extra cash (£1 million) in order to support the £10 million of deposits which it has gained, and will lend out the remaining 90% of the extra cash. As its customers draw cheques on their advances, we can assume that they are all paid into accounts with a second bank, which in turn will receive £9 million of cash and deposits through the settlement for the clearing. This second bank will behave in exactly the same way as the first one: it will retain £900,000 in cash and lend out £8,100,000 (90% of £9 million). The £8,100,000 now becomes a gain of cash and deposits for a third bank, and so on down the line. For the first four banks in the sequence the position will be as follows, each bank starting off with £1000 million in deposits:

	Bank A	Bank B	Bank C	Bank D
Deposits	1010	1009	1008·1	1007·29
Cash	101	100·9	100·81	100·729
Advances	909	908·1	907·29	906·561

For these first four steps in the sequence the original £10 million of cash has generated an additional £34,390,000 of deposits, and the same process will continue for many more stages. At the end of the first ten and twenty steps respectively over £62 million and more than £83 million of additional deposits will have been generated. At each step the growth in deposits is exactly 9/10 of what it was at the previous stage, and readers will recognise that we are dealing with an infinite geometric series. The value of the multiplier as 10 follows from the formula for the sum of such a series,[7] and the process ends when an additional £100 million of deposits has been generated.

The assumptions behind this simple sequence model are not very realistic. Just as the original increments of cash and deposits are likely to accrue to several banks within the system, so the subsequent gains of cash and deposits arising from lending are likely to be diffused throughout the system, some indeed coming straight back to the lending bank as the borrower makes a payment to another customer of the same bank. These considerations do not upset the logic of the process, however, which depends only on the supposition that each banker will behave in the same way in the process of adhering to his cash ratio. We can see immediately that the whole process of deposit creation would come to a halt if any one of the banks in the sequence took no action when it found itself with excess cash. The multiplier process depends on all banks acting together.

It is apparent from this simple model that both the practical banker and the economist are right about the 'creating' of deposits. The prac-

7. The formula for the sum of an infinite geometric series is

$$S_n = \frac{a}{1 - r}$$

where a is the first term (1) and r is the common ratio (0.9). Thus

$$S_n = \frac{1}{1 - 0·9} = \frac{1}{0·1} = 10.$$

tical banker is right because each banker in turn has received additional cash and deposits before he has increased his lending, and he has lent only 90% of the amount received. And yet the economist is also correct in stating that additional deposits have been 'created', because the original increment of £10 million has grown to an ultimate sum of £100 million.

There is a close analogy between the multiplier process of deposit creation which we have just described and the Keynesian investment multiplier. The banking mutiplier has a value equal to the reciprocal of the cash ratio, whereas the investment multiplier is equal to the reciprocal of the marginal propensity to save. At the present time in Britain the Keynesian multiplier should theoretically have a value of at least 10, but all empirical measurements of the multiplier process have ended with values in the range between 1 and 2. This is because the process is subject to severe 'leakages' in the form of transactions between the private sector and the government and the rest of the world. In exactly the same way the banking multiplier is subject to leakages which arise from the same causes, and its actual value is nowhere near the theoretical one of the reciprocal of the cash ratio. Our subsequent argument will depend almost entirely on the identification of these leakages, but for the moment we shall note only one of them which was mentioned in the early discussions of the banking multiplier. This was the fact that there would be a leakage of notes and coin as the public needed more legal tender because of rising incomes associated with the increased lending and because some of the payments would end up in the pockets of people without bank accounts.[8]

So far the discussion has been about advances made in the form of overdrafts. These do not lead to an increase in deposits until the overdraft limits are used by drawing cheques against them. If the advances had been in the form of loans, personal loans perhaps, the process would have been slightly different because a loan is made by immediately crediting the customer with a deposit to an equal amount; total deposits are therefore affected immediately. In due course the customer draws cheques, and some of the deposits (all of them on the assumptions of the discussion in the last few pages) are transferred to other banks.

The second half of Table 7.9 shows a multiplier model based on the assumptions of the Radcliffe Report. The Radcliffe Committee did not

8. See J. E. Meade, 'The amount of money and the banking system', *Economic Journal* (1934) (reprinted in American Economic Association, *Readings in Monetary Theory* (1952) pp. 54–62).

themselves argue that it was necessary to base a multiplier on the liquid assets ratio of 30%; they limited themselves to the obviously true proposition that, when such a secondary ratio was operative, deposits could not be more than 3⅓ times liquid assets. Other economists argued, however, that the base of the multiplier should be liquid assets and that the multiplier had a value of 3⅓.

The figures in the second half of Table 7.9 are based on assumptions appropriate to the period of the Radcliffe Report. Clearing banks are working to an 8% cash ratio, and in the table they are shown without excess liquid assets, that is with a liquid assets ratio of just 30%. (The minimum ratio for liquid assets was not lowered to 28% until 1963.) Once again the clearing banks receive an injection of £10 million in cash, and again the same amount in deposits. Their total liquid assets are now £3010 million, and this total will support deposits of £10,033 million. The multiplier is now 3⅓ or 100/30, the reciprocal of the liquid assets ratio.

Two different lines of argument are used to justify this departure from the earlier version of the multiplier. The first is that clearing banks did not observe a secondary ratio until after the last war, and this adoption of the liquid assets ratio reduced the value of the multiplier. A moment's reflection will show that this argument is a nonstarter. We have only to discover that clearing banks observe other rigidities in their asset structure to alter the value of the multiplier almost at will. For example, we might observe that they habitually held investments to an amount equivalent to 10% of gross deposits. We should now have a tertiary ratio based on the aggregate percentages of liquid assets *plus* investments (30 + 10 = 40), and the multiplier would become 100/40, or 2½. It is most unlikely that observed rigidities in asset structure could by themselves alter the value of the multiplier or that the labelling of certain assets as 'liquid assets' or 'reserve assets' could alter the case.

The second line of argument used to justify the change in approach is that treasury bills are always interchangeable for cash because of the way in which the Bank of England is prepared to act without question as lender of last resort to the discount market. This by itself is not very convincing as an explanation, but it contains a valuable clue to the truth.

If we look at the second half of Table 7.9 in more detail, we shall note what has happened to the £10 million of cash which the clearing banks received in position (b): only £3 million has been retained as cash, while £7 million has been used to purchase other liquid assets

—probably treasury bills. In the terminology which we were using a short while ago, this £7 million is a 'leakage' of cash, and only the £3 million which is retained as cash is available to support additional deposits. The additional deposits of £33 million generated are the sum of the original gain of £10 million and the £23 million of additional deposits created by advances. The significance of the asset heading 'advances' is now clear: advances are assets the purchase of which does not lead to a leakage of cash. The 'Macmillan' multiplier had its value of 10 because there were no leakages.

B. *Leakages and the banking multiplier.*

Our first task is to specify what constitutes a leakage, and for this purpose we must revert to the distinction between transactions within the banking group and those with 'outsiders' which we made in our discussion of the effects of settlements for clearing on bank balance sheets. We saw that transactions within the same banking group redistributed cash and deposits between banks but left the totals unchanged, whereas transactions with outsiders were all channelled through the Bank of England and resulted in losses of cash and deposits to the banking group. Table 7.7 showed what happened when the clearing banks bought bonds from the Government Broker by not replacing maturing treasury bills: the maturing bills brought a gain of cash, and the subsequent purchase of bonds transferred the cash back again to public deposits. Similarly in Table 7.8 the clearing banks lost cash when they replenished their stocks of till money. The same processes are at work in the multiplier sequence. When the banks acquire assets from their customers, they can do so on the basis of 'created' deposits, but this posibility is not open for those assets which they acquire through the Bank of England; they must pay cash for them. Thus whenever the clearing banks acquire assets through the Bank of England in the course of the multiplier process, there is a leakage, and the value of the multiplier is reduced accordingly.

From our previous discussion we can easily identify those assets the purchase of which is likely to constitute a leakage. Because the authorities are constantly intervening on the gilt-edged market, the purchase of government bonds (investments) is often from the Government Broker; treasury bills are acquired by the clearing banks after having been purchased from the government by the discount houses and held for a time by them against money at call. We may refer to the leakages represented by these transactions as 'internal' because the transactions are initiated by the banks themselves. 'External' leakages are those initiated by customers, and involve the clearing banks in the replenishment of their stocks of till money (because customers have withdrawn notes and coin) and foreign currency balances (because customers have an excess of payments to make in foreign currencies over their receipts in foreign currencies). If customers purchased bonds from the Government Broker, these transactions would also be external leakages.

It is important to note that it is the nature of the transaction and not the particular kind of asset involved which causes a leakage. Leakages arise only when clearing banks are involved in a transaction which causes a transfer out of bankers' deposits at the Bank of England. Thus banks can purchase government bonds from their customers without suffering a loss of cash, although, if the Government Broker were to sell the customers other government bonds in replacement, the net effect would be the same as if the banks had bought their bonds direct from the Government Broker. In the other direction the banks can gain cash (a 'leakage' in reverse) when the Bank of England purchases commercial bills from them or from the discount houses. It must be remembered that we are concerned here with what happens to the clearing banks as a group. It is always open to an individual bank to expand on the basis of cash and deposits received from another bank.

The examples of multiplier processes which we have given so far refer to periods when the clearing banks were following ratios different from those which apply under the new arrangements of September 1971. A word of caution is necessary before we go on to apply the new ratios in a multiplier model because these have a different significance from previous ratios. (1) There is no intention on the part of the authorities to use these ratios as the basis for any multiple contraction or expansion of deposits. (2) They apply to all banks and not just to the London clearing banks. (3) The denominator of both the primary (cash) and secondary (reserve assets) ratios is no longer the gross total of deposits but a smaller and carefully defined magnitude, eligible liabilities, although we continue to refer to 'deposits' in the tables. The ratios thus apply only to a part of the balance sheet. (4) By 1971 the liquid assets ratio was somewhat higher than the clearing banks would have followed if they had been left to their own devices, whereas the $12\frac{1}{2}\%$ ratio of reserve assets is probably smaller than the ratio of assets which the clearing banks would choose to hold for purposes of liquidity. Our whole argument, however, will be that the multiplier process depends only on the banks' adhering to some target figure for their balances at the Bank of England and that the value of the multiplier depends solely on the way in which the banks lay out any increment of cash or react to any loss of cash as between assets which involve leakages and those which do not. Liquid assets ratios and reserve assets ratios may affect the kinds of assets which the banks acquire, but the ratios themselves do not determine the value of the multiplier. For this reason we can continue the argument in terms of the ratios appropriate to the new arrangements. The only caveat to be made concerns the primary (cash) ratio. Required cash balances remain unchanged between make-up days no matter how the total of eligible liabilities may change, but in the illustrations which follow we show the banks reacting to changes in their eligible liabilities ('deposits') by adjusting their cash balances. Effectively we are assuming that the multiplier process takes longer to work itself out than the period of one month between make-up days.

In Table 7.10 we give four examples of the multiplier at work. They all show the expansion of deposits resulting from an injection of £10 million in cash on four different sets of assumptions. Although we shall see later the institutional reasons which prevent the multiplier from producing a multiple contraction of deposits in the English banking system when cash is withdrawn, there is nothing in theory to prevent the multiplier from working equally well in a downward direction. The four accounting models in Table 7.10 are concerned only with internal leakages. In order to simplify the exposition we assume that the purchase of other reserve assets and investments always constitutes a leakage and that advances and other assets do not involve leakages.

The first model makes an assumption which is certainly realistic for large injections of cash and for the medium term—that the clearing banks maintain the existing proportions of their different kinds of asset. This assumption would not, of course, be realistic if the banks were not in equilibrium to start with—if, for example, they were only waiting for an opportunity to expand their advances relatively to other assets. The balance sheets in the models are complete in the sense that total assets equal total deposits (we ignore capital and reserves). The proportion of assets in model (1) which involve leakages (cash, other reserve assets and investments) is exactly 25% or one-quarter. It is not surprising therefore that the multiplier should be 4, the reciprocal of $\frac{1}{4}$.

The next model is particularly interesting because it refers to a number of possible situations. The American expression 'loaned-up' implies that the banks do not want to make further advances, probably because their proportion of advances is already high enough for comfort. The same assumption also applies when the banks are prevented from making further loans because their lending is subject to a quantitative ceiling or because the demand for loans is weak. The third situation to which it applies is the initial stage of expansion when advances

Table 7.10   The banking multiplier (new arrangements)

	(a)	(b)	(c)
(1) Banks maintain same asset proportions			
Deposits	10,000	10,010	10,040
Cash	150 (1.5%)	160 (1.6%)	151 (1.5%)
Other reserve assets	1,350 (15.0%)	1,350 (15.1%)	1,355 (15.0%)
Investments	1,000	1,000	1,004
Advances	5,500	5,500	5,522
Other assets	2,000	2,000	2,008
(2) Banks are fully 'loaned-up'			
Deposits	10,000	10,010	10,010
Cash	150 (1.5%)	160 (1.6%)	150 (1.5%)
Other reserve assets	1,350 (15.0%)	1,350 (15.1%)	1,352 (15.0%)
Investments	900	900	908
Advances	5,800	5,800	5,800
Other assets	1,800	1,800	1,800
(3) Banks have excess reserve assets I			
Deposits	10,000	10,010	10,667
Cash	150 (1.5%)	160 (1.6%)	160 (1.5%)
Other reserve assets	1,450 (16.0%)	1,450 (16.1%)	1,450 (15.1%)
Investments	1,000	1,000	1,000
Advances	5,500	5,500	6,157
Other assets	1,900	1,900	1,900
(4) Banks have excess reserve assets II			
Deposits	10,000	10,010	10,402
Cash	150 (1.5%)	160 (1.6%)	156 (1.5%)
Other reserve assets	1,400 (15.5%)	1,400 (15.6%)	1,404 (15.0%)
Investments	950	950	950
Advances	5,500	5,500	5,892
Other assets	2,000	2,000	2,000

take the form of overdrafts rather than loans: the banks increase overdraft limits or grant limits to fresh customers, but it may be some time before the limits are used; in the meantime the banks purchase investments and any additional reserve assets which are needed to support the new level of deposits. Because all the purchases of assets in this case are leakages, the expansion is limited to the original £10 million, and the multiplier is unity.

The next two models both illustrate cases in which the banks have excess reserve assets; with our assumptions this implies that they are well above the 15% which we take to be their target level for this time of the year. In model (3) the excess reserve assets are so large that a full expansion can take place without involving any leakages through the purchase of reserve assets. The multiplier is the reciprocal of the cash ratio—66⅔. In model (4) the excess of reserve assets is not so large, and some additional reserve assets are necessary before expansion is completed. In this case the multiplier is 40.2. There are two points to note. In the first place neither of these high-value multipliers would be operative for long. They represent the impact effect of an injection when the banks have excess reserve assets, and the multiplier would probably drop down to the level of model (1) or thereabouts once the excess reserve assets had been exhausted. In the second place we should note that the banks could have started an expansion on their own initiative, for example by allowing treasury bill holdings to run off.

Before we look at external leakages, we shall see what has happened to the original increment of cash in each of the models. Our whole argument has been that certain transactions represent leakages of the original cash, and we should check that the leakages *plus* the cash retained as a basis for deposit expansion together exhaust the £10 million of cash.

	(1)	(2)	(3)	(4)
Retained as cash	1	—	10	6
Purchase of other reserve assets	5	2	—	4
Purchase of investments	4	8	—	—
Total	10	10	10	10
Value of multiplier	4	1	66⅔	40.2

It is easy to see that the value of the multiplier is highest when all the increment of cash can be retained in cash as a basis for deposit expansion and lowest when it is all used in a form that involves leakages.

It would be possible to construct rather more complicated models, on the lines of Table 7.8, to show the effects of external leakages, but the easiest way is to assume that the external leakages (withdrawals of notes and coin and of foreign currency) have a value of £2 million and that the original increment of cash was £12 million. The external leakages do not show up in the four accounting models, but we can demonstrate their effect on the multiplier by relating the expansion of deposits to a denominator of 12 instead of 10. On this basis the multipliers become: (1) 3⅓, (2) ⅚, (3) 55·6 and (4) 33·5.

The rationale of the banking multiplier is that the banks receive a given amount of cash, which they proceed to lay out to the best advantage. The constraints under which they operate are the observance of a secondary ratio (the reserve assets ratio in our models) and the need to purchase certain other assets which will involve a leakage. On the basis of the cash which they can retain in that form they build a 'pyramid' of deposits by acquiring assets with created deposits. The additional deposits created are always equal to the *retained* cash multiplied by the reciprocal of the cash ratio (·015 in our models). External leakages reduce the amount of the original cash gain which is available either to purchase assets involving a leakage or to retain in the form of cash.[9]

C. *Uses of multiplier analysis*

We have spent some time analysing various accounting models, and it may seem perverse to end by arguing that the multiplier analysis which we have derived is of little operational importance. However, these accounting models are a most useful device for emphasising the mechanism of the banking process. Like the more elaborate mathematical models in other fields of economics they force us to state our assumptions clearly and to follow through a process to the end. They have enabled us to underline the basic distinction, which lies at the root of the banking mechanism, between transactions in which deposits remain trapped within the banking system, because they are between customers of the same group of banks, and transactions with outsiders, in which cash and deposits leak out of the banking system.

9. The banking multiplier can be reduced to a formula in the same way as any other multiplier process. Using the symbols Δ for 'additional', D for deposits and C for cash, we can write

$$\frac{\Delta D}{\Delta C} = \frac{1}{r + l_i + l_e},$$

where r, l_i and l_e stand for retained cash, internal leakages and external leakages respectively, all expressed as proportions of total assets acquired.

To be of practical value a multiplier, however well grounded it may be in theory, must fulfil one basic condition: it must be stable and hence predictable. The banking multiplier is neither stable nor predictable. We have demonstrated this by taking four different sets of assumptions, none of them far-fetched, and arriving at widely different values of the multiplier. Even so, these models were simplified by assuming that all reserve assets and all investments were purchased from the authorities, thus involving a leakage. In practice reserve assets (and liquid assets before them) include items like commercial bills and local authority securities which are unlikely to involve leakages, and not all investments are purchased from the authorities. The multiplier process involves the banks' decisions on the *marginal* disposition of their assets. In the long run, it is true, the average proportions of different kinds of asset give some guide to the value of the multiplier, but in the short run the possibilities are numerous, and the value of the multiplier is correspondingly unpredictable.

These considerations apply if we consider only the internal leakages; the external leakages pose even greater problems. The additional demand for notes and coin and the demand for foreign currencies arise out of the increased income generated by the expenditure of the credit extended by banks, and here the banking multiplier becomes interwoven with the Keynesian income multiplier, and credit extended by banks becomes interwoven with credit granted by other financial intermediaries. If the 'close-in' multiplier, which looks only at the process internal to the banking system, is unpredictable, how much more so is a multiplier process in which several expansionary processes are at work, each subject to its own set of leakages.[10]

There are good institutional reasons for denying the operational importance of the multiplier in British conditions. These are that the arrangements between the London clearing banks, the discount houses and the Bank of England are such that the multiplier is not allowed to work as a contractionary weapon since the Bank of England acts without question as lender of last resort. The authorities have confirmed that they will continue to act in this way under the new arrangements for the control of banks.

One last point needs to be made clear. We have limited our analysis to the London clearing banks because it is they who are involved closely with the Bank of England through the discount market; the

10. For a multiplier model which brings in both the Keynesian multiplier and the effect of non-bank financial intermediaries see A. N. McLeod, 'Credit expansion in an open economy', *Economic Journal* (September 1962).

same analysis would apply with minor modifications to other deposit banks, but it would apply hardly at all to secondary banks. This is because multiple expansion and contraction are possible with any degree of certainty only to banks whose main concern is the transmission of payments; it is only for them that a high proportion of payments is trapped within the system. Secondary banks are in much the same position as non-bank financial intermediaries, at which we shall look shortly: some of their loans may come back to them, but the proportion will be very small. Any multiplier process originating with secondary banks or non-bank financial intermediaries is different in kind from the banking multiplier and depends on quite a different process. The banking multiplier depends on the fact that bank deposits are used for payments, so that, leakages apart, they remain trapped within the deposit banking system. The multiplier for other kinds of bank and financial intermediary depends on a propensity to hold the deposits of the particular type of institution out of an increment of income caused by loans made by the same institutions.

4. CONTROL OF BANKS

A. *Types of measure*

Although our concern is mainly with the weapons which have actually been used in this country and with the form in which they have been used, it is useful to start with a short list of the main types of weapon. Such a list would consist of four main items:

(1) open market operations
(2) ratio controls
(3) qualitative and quantitative control of bank advances
(4) interest-rate controls.

It is customary in any country for a combination of these weapons to be in use at any one time. Although the authorities are always indulging in open-market operations in the course of managing the national debt, they do not have the primary objective of controlling the level of bank deposits. Interest-rate controls, in the sense of prescribing a maximum interest rate which banks are permitted to offer on their deposits, have never been used as a weapon for controlling banks in this country. We are thus concerned with the second and third items in our list of possible weapons.

Ratio controls have been imposed on the London clearing banks since 1946, and with the new arrangements they have been extended to all other banks, discount houses and finance houses. With the exception of the new arrangements, the general course of events has been a 'request' from the Governor of the Bank of England that the clearing banks should continue to observe certain ratios to which they were voluntarily adhering at that time. Thus the 8% cash ratio was being followed by the clearing banks immediately after the war (once the practice of 'window-dressing' had been dropped), and the 30% (later 28%) liquid assets ratio had been followed by the clearing banks since about the mid-thirties.

There are certain conditions which must be fulfilled for the successful operation of ratio controls. (1) The nature of the assets which can count towards the fulfilment of a particular assets/deposits ratio must be carefully specified. (2) It is desirable that the supply of the specified assets should be under the influence if not the control of the authorities. For this reason the assets are mostly public sector assets; if certain private sector assets are included, it may be necessary to limit the extent to which they may be counted. (3) It is desirable that the banks should not be able to obtain large quantities of additional deposits by bidding up their price; if the banks can do this, ratio controls are virtually useless for controlling bank lending. (4) There should be some mechanism whereby the authorities can mop up any excess reserve assets which the banks may hold. For this purpose the power either to vary the ratio or to call for special deposits is necesary. Even this power may not be sufficient if the banks hold large quantities of a further type of highly marketable asset (investments, for example) which can be sold without risk of loss to replenish reserve assets or to furnish special deposits. For this reason the Bank of England has had to modify its tactics in the gilt-edged market so that the banks cannot count on receiving a price not far removed from the ruling one whenever they sell gilts.

This is a formidable list of conditions, and it is not surprising that the ratio controls operative until recently, the 8% primary (cash) ratio and the 28% minimum secondary (liquid assets) ratio, have always had to be buttressed by quantitative controls whenever monetary policy was tight. Of the two ratios the cash ratio fulfils all the conditions; the secondary ratio is necessary only because the authorities choose to make the primary ratio ineffective by always supplying the cash needs of the banking system.

Since 1957 there have been only short periods when bank lending has been completely free of restraint. In the early part of the period the main emphasis of the authorities' 'requests' to the banks was qualitative (to favour lending for exports and to cut back on consumer finance, for example), but from 1965 there were strict quantitative ceilings, which were not removed until the spring of 1971. Thus, the immediate past history of the control of bank lending in this country has been one of the virtual prohibition of any increase in lending, and it is small wonder that quantitative controls as such have been blamed for the lack of competition among banks and for the diversion of lending to institutions outside the scope of the quantitative controls. It is important, however, to distinguish between the idea of quantitative control and the particular form in which it was applied.[11] There is one obvious advantage of ceiling controls on bank lending, that of operating directly on the magnitude which the authorities wish to influence. It is true that the form in which they have been applied has led to a stifling of competition and innovation, but the same effects would result from any form of control which did what it was supposed to do —limit bank spending.

B. *The new arrangements*

We have already described the new arrangements for the control of bank lending in their effect on deposit banks (Chapter 6), and we shall examine their effects on discount houses and secondary banks in Chapters 8 and 9. Here we are concerned only with their relationship to the various weapons of control described in the previous section.

At first sight the new arrangements for the control of credit appear to be no more than the old ratio controls of the cash ratio (for London clearing banks alone) and the liquid assets ratio, refurbished with new definitions, both of the total of deposits to which the ratios relate and of the assets admissible within the secondary ratio, and made to apply to all banks, discount houses and finance houses. First appearances are misleading in this case. In the previous section we looked at ratio controls as a method of restricting (or encouraging) the growth of bank lending, but it is always possible for the authorities to use ratio controls as an indirect weapon designed to influence the *demand* for bank credit by enforcing changes in the prices charged by the banks.

11. Elsewhere the author has suggested a form of applying lending ceilings which would be compatible with competition among banks and between banks and other financial institutions: J. Revell, 'A "crawling peg" for bank lending', *The Bankers' Magazine* (July 1971).

It is in this latter way that the authorities apparently intend to use their new methods of control.

The reasoning behind the new arrangements was spelt out by the Governor of the Bank of England in an address on 28 May 1971 to the International Banking Conference in Munich;[12] the quotations which follow are from that address. The Governor began by stating that the authorities, while still regarding bank lending as of especial importance, were increasingly shifting their emphasis towards the broader monetary aggregates—the money supply or domestic credit expansion. One of the main reasons for abandoning quantitative control of bank lending was that, with this change of emphasis, it was no longer appropriate to attempt a precise control of the volume of bank lending.

The Governor described the basic aim of the new arrangements as 'a system under which *the allocation of credit is primarily determined by its cost*' (italics in original). The reserve assets ratio was 'designed to provide a known firm base on which the Bank of England can operate, both in market operations and by calls for Special Deposits, to neutralise excess liquidity which the banking system might acquire'. Bank rate would be used more flexibly than in the past to affect short-term interest rates, and the authorities would no longer provide, as in the past, 'outright support for the gilt-edged market in stocks having a maturity of over one year'. With this change in debt management, calls for special deposits 'can be used not only to mop up any abnormal excess liquidity, but also to oblige the banking system to seek to dispose of assets not eligible for the liquidity [reserve assets] ratio, for example gilt-edged stocks of over one year's maturity'. This would enable the authorities to exert upward pressure on interest rates, including those in the inter-bank market, the local authority market and the short-term gilt-edged market.

It will be some time before we have any direct evidence of the effectiveness of the new methods of control. While there is much to be welcomed in the new arrangements, we may perhaps doubt whether they will prove effective enough under difficult conditions. If they do not, the authorities will have no option but to restore direct controls on lending in some form or other.

12. 'Key issues in monetary and credit policy', *Bank of England Quarterly Bulletin* (June 1971). The same issue of the *Bulletin* contains the text of the Bank's discussion document outlining the proposed arrangements.

5. COMPETITION BETWEEN BANKS AND NON-BANK FINANCIAL INTERMEDIARIES

The relationship between banks and non-bank financial intermediaries has been widely discussed in economic literature of recent years. Although the discussion takes us to the heart of many theoretical issues in monetary theory, the conclusions are of considerable practical importance. One side of the discussion has been concerned with the possibility of frustration of monetary policy by non-bank intermediaries and another with whether banks are in a position to increase the total of their deposits by competing actively with non-bank intermediaries.

We shall begin by analysing what happens when a non-bank financial intermediary succeeds in persuading a holder of an idle bank balance to transfer this balance to itself. For this purpose we can really restrict the discussion to a particular set of non-bank financial intermediaries, the non-bank deposit institutions or near-banks. In order to entice the deposit away from the banks the near-banks must offer a claim which is a close substitute for a bank balance, one which is almost as liquid as a bank balance. The bait is nearly always a higher interest rate, but the closer substitute the competing claim is, with convenient withdrawal facilities on demand, for example, the smaller the differential in interest rates needs to be. The near-bank then uses the deposit which it has secured to lend to a deficit unit. The whole process has been referred to as 'activating idle balances' or 'increasing the velocity of circulation of money'. An alternative way of looking at it would be to consider that the near-bank had borrowed a bank deposit which was not required for immediate spending.

One point needs to be made clear. The process is often described in terms of a near-bank operating with a smaller margin than the bank and 'coming between' the borrowing and lending rates of the bank, paying more interest on the deposit and lending more cheaply. This, however, is necessary only when the near-banks are competing with banks in both markets, the market for deposits and the market for lending. Typically the near-bank is lending in a separate market or one which has only marginal contact with the market for bank loans.

So far we have assumed that a near-bank has secured (or 'borrowed') a deposit from the holder of an idle bank balance; we must now see whether this deposit is lost to the banking system. Let us suppose that the near-bank in question is a building society. Like all near-banks it keeps its working balances with a deposit bank; it receives its deposit in the form of a cheque drawn on a bank account, and immediately pays the cheque into its own bank account. The building society then uses the deposit to lend to a house purchaser; it sends him a cheque, which he pays into his bank account, and shortly afterwards he sends a further cheque to the seller of the house. At no stage does the money leave the banking system, and it would seem that the building society lending is a clear addition to lending by the bank on the basis of the same money balance. The process is shown diagrammatically in Figure 2.2 (p. 39), in which we make a distinction between the industrial circulation of money and the financial circulation.

The process is, however, subject to leakages just as bank lending is. These leakages are of the same kind as we found when we were examining the banking multiplier process. In the first place near-bank lending will increase incomes, and there may be leakages in the form of withdrawals of notes and coin and foreign currencies. We have already seen that the banks suffer losses of cash and deposits when their customers initiate leakages, and so these withdrawals are leakages for banks, reducing the total of bank deposits. In the second place the near-banks maintain liquid assets in a similar fashion to the banks, and many of these (government bonds and treasury bills, for example) will involve a leakage of bank deposits when they are acquired. Out of every fresh deposit which it receives the near-bank lends only a proportion, using the remainder to purchase liquid assets. Near-banks differ in the proportions of leakage to which they give rise. The transfer of a bank balance to the ordinary department of a savings bank causes a 100% leakage, because deposits are automatically used to purchase government stocks. In round figures the leakage proportions for other near-banks vary as follows: investment accounts of the National Savings Bank 50%, special investment departments of trustee savings banks 25%, building societies 6% and finance houses (which before the new credit control arrangements held virtually no government claims) 10%.[13] Savings banks, particularly in their ordinary departments, thus seem to be close competitors of banks, but building societies and finance houses appear to reduce the total of bank deposits only marginally when they receive a deposit out of an idle bank balance.

The process which we have described will obviously work in reverse when near-bank loans are repaid. It also follows that a building society deposit received over the counter in the form of notes and coin represents a gain of cash to the deposit banks because the building society will pay the notes and coin into its bank account.

13. We ignore any holdings of local authority claims because the purchase of these is not immediately a leakage.

Thus far the argument was often used to justify the lack of competition in the banking system. If banks lost only marginal amounts of deposits when near-bank deposits were increased, they could by the same token gain only marginal amounts of additional deposits by competing in terms of price with near-banks. The banks could easily find themselves paying considerably more in interest, it was argued, for virtually the same volume of deposits. Economists who accepted the basic truth of the above analysis but who nevertheless wished to see banks competing vigorously (for the good of their souls if for no other reason) were often driven to advance special arguments. Thus the P.I.B. suggested that the response of the authorities to an increase in near-bank lending, with its expansionary effects on spending and income, would be offsetting action, which was bound to reduce clearing bank lending.[14] At its best this argument indicated that a competitive spirit paid off in the long run, but the invocation of the authorities as a *deus ex machina* does not provide a very satisfying theoretical argument.

If we delve a little further into the theory of competition between banks and near-banks, we are immediately faced with the hotly debated issue of whether the money supply is exogenous or endogenous, whether it is determined solely by the amount of cash reserves supplied by the central bank and the working of the banking multiplier or whether the supply is determined by the demand for money balances. It would be too far outside the scope of this book to pursue the issue in detail here. We must limit ourselves to making a few simple points, and referring the reader to more detailed expositions elsewhere.[15]

On the basis of our previous analysis we can think immediately of one point in support of the thesis that competition between banks and near-banks can be effective. At any time that the demand for bank loans from creditworthy customers is below the level that the banks would like to see, the 'fully loaned-up' version of the banking multiplier (model (2) in Table 7.10) applies. If, by diversifying their

14. National Board for Prices and Incomes, *Bank Charges*, Report No. 34, Cmnd. 3292 (1967) p. 29.

15. An excellent summary of the theoretical issues against a background of macro-economic theory will be found in A. B. Cramp, *Monetary Management: Principles and Practice* (London: George Allen & Unwin, 1971) especially Chapter 6. A useful analysis of the controversy will be found in J. A. Cacy, 'Alternative approaches to the analysis of the financial structure', Federal Reserve Bank of Kansas City, *Monthly Review* (March 1968) (reprinted in *Money and Banking: Theory, Analysis and Policy*, ed. S. Mittra, pp. 99–105).

lending to compete directly with near-banks, the banks could increase their lending to the private sector, they could increase bank deposits through raising the value of the banking multiplier.

The basic point, however, is whether the monetary authorities in any country have ever set the money supply without taking the demand for money into account. If the money supply is set too far below the quantity of money demanded at the time, some measure of financial crisis, evidenced by large movements of interest rates and by general economic contraction, will occur. There is very little if any evidence that monetary authorities have been prepared to continue on their course in the face of financial crisis; inevitably their support function comes to the fore, and they reverse their contractionary policy. The action of the U.S. authorities over the past five or six years is a good example. If this point is conceded, it follows that the demand for money plays a considerable part in the money supply decisions of the monetary authorities, that the money supply is largely endogeneous. It is then an inevitable corollary that changes in asset preferences of the private sector as between liabilities of banks and of near-banks can become effective, and that competition between them for deposits can be effective.

Since an era of aggressive competition by banks is just beginning in this country, we shall doubtless have some empirical evidence before long. Only a few years ago the Canadian banking system was reformed on somewhat familiar lines as a result of the recommendations of the Porter Commission. There it was quickly found that the chartered banks could not only compete effectively but that the effect of their competition on certain non-bank intermediaries was great enough to necessitate the restraining of the banks. If our arguments are correct, the danger of the British banking reforms lies in this direction rather than that the banks will be found impotent.

FURTHER READING

R. S. Sayers, *Modern Banking*, 7th ed. (Oxford: Oxford University Press, 1967).

W. M. Dacey, *The British Banking Mechanism* (London: Hutchinson, 1952).

W. M. Dacey, *Money under Review* (London: Hutchinson, 1960).

8 The Discount Market

All banking systems need a highly developed money market so that banks may adjust their liquidity positions day by day and occasionally during the same day. Until September 1971 it was true to say that there were two money markets corresponding to the two banking systems—the discount market serving deposit banks and the parallel sterling money market serving secondary banks. For some time there had not been a rigid separation between them; secondary banks operated in a small way in the discount market, and discount houses had begun to assume an important role in the parallel market. The new arrangements for the control of banks will bring these two money markets much closer together. The basic difference between them will remain, however, that the discount market is predominantly a market on which lending is secured, while on the parallel market all lending is unsecured. On the discount market the Bank of England acts as lender of last resort to the discount houses, whereas the parallel market lacks a lender of last resort.

In this chapter we shall deal with the discount market, using that term to refer to the market on which the discount houses and certain other bodies operate instead of restricting its use, as the Bank of England does, to the discount houses themselves. The parallel sterling money market is described in Chapter 10, after we have analysed the working of secondary banks.

1. DISCOUNT HOUSES

A. *Functions*

The discount houses can trace their history back about 150 years, but during this time their main line of business has changed several times.

To begin with their staple trade was in inland bills of exchange, which formed the normal method of bank lending in the early nineteenth century: the function of the bill brokers, as they were then called, was to enable the small local 'country banks' to adjust their liquidity by the purchase and sale of these bills. Later the bill of exchange became more important in foreign trade, and the 'bill on London' developed as an international currency; the discount houses were an indispensable part of the mechanism, acquiring a specialised knowledge of the 'names' on these bills. The bill on London declined with the First World War, but at the same time the treasury bill assumed importance as a means of government financing, and the discount houses organised the secondary market for treasury bills. During the late 1930s they also began to act as jobbers in the short end of the gilt-edged market (stocks with less than five years to maturity). Finally, in the past few years bill finance has once again become important in both internal and international trade, and discount houses have resumed some of their old functions. They have also begun to operate on the parallel money market in several ways. They act as dealers in both dollar and sterling negotiable certificates of deposit (CDs) and in local authority negotiable ('yearling') bonds; they have begun to act through subsidiaries as brokers in the parallel money markets and in the foreign exchange market.

Through this somewhat chequered career several threads can be traced. (1) Since the early days of the nineteenth century the discount houses have operated, not as brokers, but as principals, buying and selling for their own account. (2) One important aspect of their functions has always been the service provided to banks of all kinds of enabling them to adjust their liquidity as conveniently as possible; the discount houses accepted deposits on call or at short notice, and employed the funds in the financing of a 'book' of bills and short bonds, which they were prepared to sell to the banks when required. (3) All but a tiny part of their borrowing has always been secured. Discount houses thus borrow money to finance the purchase of assets, which they then use as security for their borrowings. (4) The services which the discount houses provide have always been regarded as so useful that both the banks and the Bank of England have found new types of business for the discount houses to do when their old lines of business were in decline.

B. *Balance sheet*

Table 8.1 shows the aggregate balance sheet of discount houses, defined as the houses which are members of the London Discount Market Association, as at 31 December 1970. The discount houses have as their main liabilities very short-term deposits (here called 'borrowed funds'), and hold as assets a wide array of both public and private sector debt.

Table 8.1   Balance sheet of discount houses, 31 December 1970

	£ million	Percentages of borrowed funds
Liabilities		
Borrowed funds		
Secured	1,995	88.3
Unsecured	264	11.7
Total	2,259	100.0
Capital and reserves	59	2.6
Assets		
British government stocks (NV)	160	7.1
British government treasury bills	876	38.8
·Other sterling bills	697	30.9
Non-sterling bills .	10	.4
Local authority securities	224	9.9
Negotiable certificates of deposit		
Sterling	268	11.9
U.S. dollars	39	1.7
Money at call and short notice	1	—
Loans to U.K. local authorities	5	.2
Loans to U.K. financial institutions	15	.7
Loans to other U.K. non-bank residents	7	.3
Other assets	50	2.2
Contingent liability on re-discounted bills	*103*	*4.6*

Source: *Bank of England Quarterly Bulletin,* December 1971,
Tables 7, 8(1), 8(3) & 10(1).

Note: Unsecured borrowing is.assumed to be (1) borrowing from non-bank sources and (2) excess of total borrowing from secondary banks over money at call to discount houses reported by the same banks.

The 'other sterling bills' are mainly commercial bills, but local authority bills and treasury bills of the Northern Ireland government are
included here. The local authority securities are yearling bonds, in
which the discount houses 'make a market' and local authority stocks.
Other assets include small working balances which the discount houses
maintain with London clearing banks. The holdings of various parallel
money market assets will be commented on in later chapters.

Discount houses do not maintain rigid proportions between their
holdings of different classes of asset. Table 8.2 demonstrates that over

Table 8.2   Assets of discount houses, 1958–69

£ million

	December			
	1958	1963	1966	1969
British government stocks *(NV)*	321	442	542	364
British government treasury bills	594	529	424	399
Other sterling bills	70	249	404	629
Negotiable certificates of deposit				
Sterling	–	–	–	97
U.S. dollars	–	–	–	31
Local authority securities }	68	17	101	192
Other }		67	95	104

Source: *Bank of England Statistical Abstract*, No.1, Table 7.

the years the proportions have fluctuated quite widely. The Radcliffe
Committee, reporting in 1959, referred to the commercial bill business
of the discount houses as 'vestigial', and the figures for 1958 bear this
out. Since then the holdings of other sterling bills have grown year by
year, and in 1969 they were the largest single item. Holdings of British
government treasury bills declined between 1963 and 1969 in line with
the holdings of deposit banks, but the total was up again in 1970.
British government stocks are the most volatile item. Discount houses
act as jobbers for these stocks, and trade quite vigorously; it is nothing
for the total held to change by £100 million or even £200 million from
one quarter to another.

Discount houses have considerable constraints on their choice of
assets. These constraints are imposed both by the Bank of England and
by the banks for which the discount houses are performing specialised
services. Discount houses are the main providers of both treasury and

commercial bills for the portfolios of deposit banks, and their holdings of these items are largely determined by the demand of deposit banks for bills. Their holdings of commercial bills are also determined by the fact that they are specialist discounters of such bills; as deposit banks and accepting houses make more use of bill finance, the discount houses are expected to play their part by discounting the bills. The Bank of England influences the choice of assets in three ways. (1) Whenever they want to enter a new field, the discount houses have to approach the Bank of England for permission, and only a small proportion of their proposals proves acceptable. (2) The Bank of England takes regular samples of both bank and trade bills held by discount houses. If it disapproves of certain bills, the Bank of England informs both the discount house and the accepting house concerned. (3) Perhaps the most important constraint is imposed by the fact that the Bank of England determines which assets are eligible for re-discount with it, and on occasion prescribes the proportions in which the various eligible assets must appear in parcels of securities used as collateral for borrowing from the Bank. Although this constraint operates only at the margin as far as borrowing from the Bank of England is concerned, the deposit banks themselves follow the lead of the Bank of England in declaring their wishes on the composition of parcels of securities offered as collateral; they go beyond the list of the Bank of England, but only for relatively small amounts of ineligible assets.

Since nearly all the borrowing of discount houses is secured, collateral has to be given against borrowed funds, and the discount house has to provide an additional margin of 5% of the market value of the security. This margin must come from its own resources, capital and reserves.

As part of the new arrangements for controlling banks the discount houses and the other participants in the discount market are required to hold public sector assets to a minimum ratio of 50% of borrowed funds. Public sector assets are: (1) U.K. and Northern Ireland government treasury bills; (2) local authority bills eligible for re-discount at the Bank of England; (3) local authority negotiable bonds; (4) government-guaranteed public sector bills; (5) company tax reserve certificates; (6) British government stocks, stocks of nationalised industries guaranteed by the government and local authority stocks having less than five years to final maturity. The interesting addition to this list is the local authority negotiable bond.

These requirements are not a great sacrifice for discount houses under present conditions, since for some time they have been holding more than 50% of the required assets. In Table 8.1 we cannot work out public sector debt figures accurately, but the ratio could not have been lower than 54%. On the first two reporting dates under the new arrangements the discount houses had public sector debt ratios of 59·8% and 58·8%.

C. *Borrowed funds*

As we can see from Table 8.3, all but a small part of the funds of discount houses are borrowed from banks. In addition any borrowing from Continental banks without London branches would appear under 'overseas residents'. An increasing part of the business of discount houses is now conducted by telephone, but each discount house still sends a representative to pay a daily visit to nearly all the banks in

Table 8.3　　Sources of borrowed funds of discount houses, 1963–71

Percentages

| | 31 December | | | |
	1963	1966	1969	1971
Banks				
Bank of England	.3	5.5	–	2.6
London clearing banks	55.8	65.9	75.6	41.9
Scottish clearing banks	8.1	6.3	5.7	3.0
Other deposit banks	1.1	.7	.7	1.5
Secondary banks	21.5	13.5	11.7	37.7
Other sources				
Financial institutions	1.3	.7	2.3	5.6
Companies	5.6	4.1	1.9	3.8
Other U.K. residents	2.2	1.7	1.3	2.3
Overseas residents	4.1	1.5	.9	1.7
Total	100.0	100.0	100.0	100.0
Total borrowed funds (£ million)	*1,232*	*1,484*	*1,725*	*2,961*

Sources:　(1) *Bank of England Statistical Abstract*, No.1, Tables 7 & 8(2);
　　　　　(2) *Bank of England Quarterly Bulletin*, June 1972, Tables 7 & 11(2).

London. Many discount houses visit several hundred banks on the Continent at least once a year. One or two of the larger houses conduct what amounts to deposit banking business for certain industrial customers.

The figures of Table 8.3 show interesting trends in the sources from which discount houses derived their borrowed funds over recent years. From 1963 up to the introduction of the new arrangements for control of banks the proportion of funds coming from the London clearing banks increased, and the proportions from all other sources except financial institutions declined. The change was not so smooth as these selected dates would indicate, and in particular the proportion of 75·6% coming from London clearing banks in 1969 is something of a freak. When we come to look at secondary banks in the next chapter, we shall see that their declining use of the discount market has been complemented by an increased use of the parallel money market. The final column shows the position after the introduction of the new arrangements, and the change is startling, although clearly in line with what we should expect. The new arrangements, by requiring secondary banks, other deposit banks and finance houses to hold a prescribed minimum ratio of reserve assets, most of which are traded on the discount market, are clearly going to restore to that market something of its old character in the days when it could be referred to without qualification as *the* money market. Of all the reserve assets available, money at call is likely to prove one of the most popular. On the figures from which Table 8.3 was derived the money at call of secondary banks rose from £202 million at the end of 1969 to £1116 million by the end of 1971; other deposit banks increased their money at call over the same period from £12 million to £43 million. On the other hand the money at call of both London and Scottish clearing banks fell, probably the result of trimming of liquid assets in line with the new requirements for reserve assets. In total the money at call of the secondary banks had increased to a figure which was around three-quarters of that of the London clearing banks. It should be noted, however, that some of the secondary bank lending to discount houses consisted of unsecured inter-bank balances; this unsecured lending amounted to £113 million at the end of December 1971.

Up to September 1971 the London clearing banks agreed two rates among themselves. The first was the basic (minimum) rate at which they would lend to the discount houses; this was fixed at $1\frac{5}{8}$% below Bank rate (or $\frac{3}{8}$% over the rate paid on deposit accounts). The second was the rate which the discount houses would be charged when they called on 'privilege money' available to them at the end of the day for balancing their books; this was fixed at $1\frac{1}{2}\%$ below Bank rate. These two agreements have now lapsed. The London clearing banks differed considerably among themselves in the ways in which they determined the proportions of money to be lent at basic rate and at various higher rates. Each bank probably had in mind an average rate to be charged for lending which it regarded as reasonable, but different banks arrived at the average in different ways.

The London clearing banks still operate according to a convention that they will not call money from the discount houses after noon, and some of them restrict their calling to the morning 'parade', when the top-hatted representatives of the discount houses call on them between 10.30 a.m. and 12 noon. Some of the money lent to the discount houses by the London clearing banks was lent for long periods at fixed rates (not necessarily basic rate), which changed only when Bank rate changed. The banks differed considerably in their practices over fixing a proportion of the money at call, and they invariably retained the right to call all of this money in emergencies. The remainder of the money at call was lent at rates reflecting the conditions on each day.

Up to September 1971 there was one further agreement which restricted the power of the discount houses to seek funds outside the banking system. As part of their general compact with the London clearing banks the discount houses agreed not to offer the market rate for call money to bodies which were not listed as banks in the *Bankers' Almanac and Year Book*. To these outside bodies the discount houses could offer only the London clearing bank deposit rate (2% under Bank rate), but they could offer it for periods less than seven days and could add an extra $\frac{1}{4}\%$ for periods over seven days. The attraction of placing money for these outside bodies was thus the securing of bank deposit rate for periods of less than seven days, particularly for overnight balances.

D. *Margins*

The profits of discount houses come from two sources: (1) dealing profits on bonds, bills and certificates of deposit and (2) the margin between the average cost of borrowed funds and the average running yield on assets. Discount houses hold very short-term assets, but their borrowing is even shorter term. A sudden and unexpected rise in short-term interest rates leads to the realisation of capital losses when marketable securities are sold and erodes the margin between the running yield on assets and the average cost of borrowed funds. Likewise a sudden and unexpected fall in interest rates provides capital gains and widens the margin. Even though discount houses are good at forecasting future movements in interest rates, they are not completely free to alter the balance of their portfolios because of the demand from the banks for bills, and both the London clearing banks and the Bank of England can alter the average cost of borrowing to the discount houses. It is a risky and unpredictable business.

We can obviously provide no statistics on dealing profits, but even the average cost of borrowing and the average running yield on assets are impossible to plot. Table 8.4 gives the best impression available. Two borrowing rates are shown, the average call money rates of the London clearing banks and the inter-bank rate for overnight lending.

Table 8.4   Discount market rates, 1964–71

Percentages

Last Friday of year	Bank rate	London clearing banks call money	Inter-bank overnight	Yield on treasury bills
1964	7	5.375 – 6.0	2.0 – 6.25	6.74
1965	6	4.375 – 5.75	4.0 – 5.75	5.60
1966	7	5.375 – 6.75	5.625 – 7.875	6.64
1967	8	6.25 – 7.438	8.0 – 8.375	7.62
1968	7	5.375 – 6.75	6.5 – 7.0	6.90
1969	8	6.375 – 7.625	2.0 – 7.5	7.80
1970	7	5.375 – 6.625	5.875 – 6.0	6.93
1971	5	1.5 – 5.0	1.0 – 5.25	4.46

Source: *Financial Statistics*, January 1972, Table 106.

The figures are the ranges quoted in *Financial Statistics*, and this is the closest that we can get without knowledge of the volume of trading at each rate within the range. We have no knowledge either of the proportions of money obtained from the two sources shown and from other lenders on the discount market, including the Bank of England. The yield figures for bills suffer from similar defects; in addition they show the yields of newly-acquired treasury bills only.

Traditionally the margin to which attention is directed is that between the average cost of call money and the running yield on treasury bills, and it is in relation to this margin that borrowing at Bank rate can be called 'penal'. As we have seen, however, discount houses have had large amounts of bonds and commercial bills in their portfolios over recent years, and they may have been slightly less concerned about the penal nature of Bank rate borrowing. The real significance of Bank rate borrowing is that it raises the average cost of borrowing, and it does so quite substantially, even if it is only for a limited period and for marginal amounts.

2. OTHER PARTICIPANTS

On the borrowing side of the market the main participants are obviously the discount houses, with whose operations we have dealt at length. What distinguishes them from most other borrowers in the market is that they have unrestricted access to the Discount Office of the Bank of England as lender of last resort. This access is unrestricted both as to amount borrowed and as to frequency of borrowing. Unlike the Federal Reserve Board in the U.S.A. the Bank of England cannot deter houses from borrowing from it, except, of course, by making the cost of borrowing prohibitive. For their short bond operations the discount houses have the quick registration facilities at the Bank of England known as Z Accounts.

The other borrowers in the discount market can be divided into two groups: (1) those who use call money mainly to finance a book of treasury and other bills, and who perform similar functions to those of the discount houses, and (2) those who use call money to finance transactions in the gilt-edged market. None of these other borrowers has access to the Discount Office of the Bank of England: they could obtain loans from the Chief Cashier, but not as of right.

The other borrowers who use call money mainly to finance a book of bills consist of the discount brokers (sometimes called 'running brokers') and the money traders (or money trading banks). There are three discount brokers (Norman & Bennet Ltd.; Gerald Quin, Cope & Co.; Page & Gwyther). The six money trading banks consist of an accepting house which also does bullion business (Samuel Montague & Co. Ltd.), two foreign banks (Algemene Bank Nederland N.V. and Banque Belge Ltd.) and three other U.K. secondary banks (Ionian Bank Ltd.; Keyser Ullman Ltd.; Leopold Joseph & Sons Ltd.).

Although they are called 'brokers', the *discount brokers* act as principals and behave in much the same way as discount houses. They do not have the full privileges of the members of the London Discount Market Association, but equally they are not bound by the conventions of the market. This meant that up to September 1971 they were not bound by the agreement with the London clearing banks not to pay the market rate for call money to anybody but banks, and that they took no part in the syndicated bid of the discount houses for treasury bills. On the borrowing side they have the great advantage that their call money needs are very small in relation to the resources of the large banks (£62 million at both 15 September and 20 October 1971), and they can often rely on sympathetic treatment because the banks know that they have no access to a lender of last resort.

For the *money trading banks* bills and call money are only relatively small parts of wider arrays of assets and liabilities. They behave in every way as normal secondary banks; what distinguishes them is that, because they have traditionally supplied treasury bills to the London clearing banks, they have been given access to the cheap money obtainable in the form of secured loans on the discount market. During the recent past the discount houses have on occasion been unwilling sellers of treasury bills, and during these periods the money traders and the discount brokers supplied a disproportionate share of the London clearing banks' treasury bill needs. The total call money advanced to the money trading banks was £68 million on 15 September 1971 and £80 million on 20 October 1971.

Both the discount brokers and the money trading banks are required to observe the same public sector debt ratio as the discount houses. In the case of the money traders this requirement applies only to the money trading departments of the banks, and they are treated as ordinary banks for the remainder of their business. On the first two reporting days, 15 September 1971 and 20 October 1971, the discount brokers had public sector debt ratios of 57·7% and 61·1% and the money trading banks 93·2% and 86·9%.

The second group of other participants in the discount market is connected with the gilt-edged market, and consists of three firms of stockbrokers (increased to 6 in July 1972) who are known as *money brokers* and the main firms of *gilt-edged jobbers*. These firms all have the quick registration facilities at the Bank of England known as Z Accounts, covering stocks of all maturities; the discount houses also have Z Account facilities, but these are only for stocks with five years or less to run to maturity.

The background to the participation of these two groups of bodies in the discount market is really the shortage of capital of jobbing firms in the gilt-edged market, which prevents them from holding sufficient stock on their own books to meet demand at all times. The money brokers help them over this difficulty by borrowing stock from institutional holders until the jobbers are able to buy the lines of stock which they have already sold in the market. The jobbers also borrow money direct from the banks and from the money brokers on call money terms.

In the case of money brokers the term 'broker' is a correct description, since they act mainly as intermediaries between the institutions lending stock and the jobbers. Their stock in trade is a list of institutions which are willing to lend stocks of different maturities. Such a list might consist of some forty or fifty names, ranging from discount houses for the short-dated stocks, clearing banks, merchant banks and industrial companies for the short- and medium-dated to insurance companies and pension funds for the longer-dated stocks. To the lender of the stocks the attraction is the $\frac{1}{2}\%$ commission, which helps to boost the yield of gilt-edged stocks.

If we suppose that stock to the value of £1 million has been borrowed, we can now show the different possibilities, using illustrative rates of interest appropriate to a Bank rate of $6\frac{1}{2}\%$. As soon as he has received the stock from the money broker, the jobber pays over £1 million in cash as security for the loan of the stock; on this £1 million balance he will be paid around $3\frac{3}{4}\%$. If he wants to do so, the jobber is then allowed to borrow back the £1 million at a privileged rate of around $4\frac{1}{2}\%$. The Z Account certificate registering the borrowed stock in the name of the jobber is passed to the money broker as security for the loan of the £1 million, and he passes it to the lender of the stock as security for the loan of the stock. If the jobber wants to borrow more than the £1 million, the money broker will obtain call money in the market and pass it on to the jobber at the market rate. If the jobber is 'bearish', he will probably not want to borrow back even the original £1 million, and the money broker is left with a balance on which he is paying $3\frac{3}{4}\%$. The money broker will then try to lend the £1 million as call money to a discount house, which will provide security in the form of bills or bonds.

The money brokers thus operate both ways in the discount market, as borrowers and as lenders, quite apart from their functions as agents in facilitating the borrowing of stock by jobbers from the institutions. When they borrow call money, they have useful lines of money at market rates, but on occasion they may have to pay up to $\frac{1}{4}\%$ more than the discount houses. The gilt-edged jobbers themselves appear in the discount market as borrowers of call money, although their overnight facilities are often with City branches of the London clearing banks rather than with the discount market operator. The jobbers normally borrow direct from the banks only when they cannot obtain accommodation from the money brokers, because the banks charge jobbers a fixed rate only slightly below Bank rate. The London clearing banks are, in a sense, the lenders of last resort to the gilt-edged jobbers.

The extent of the discount market has now been officially recognised as covering the discount houses, the discount brokers, the money trading banks, the money brokers and gilt-edged jobbers by the fact that, under the new arrangements, secured money at call qualifies as a reserve asset only if it is with one of these bodies. In the case of gilt-edged jobbers there is a further requirement that the call money must be secured on British government stocks or stocks of nationalised industries guaranteed by the government. Neither the money brokers nor the gilt-edged jobbers have any public sector debt requirements.

In a market which fluctuates so much according to stock exchange conditions it is difficult to give even orders of magnitude for the sums involved. Perhaps £10 million could be regarded as a 'normal' figure for the amount of borrowed stock outstanding at any one time and £30 million as the total of call money borrowed by the gilt-edged jobbers, both directly from the banks and indirectly from money brokers. This means that the total of call money advanced to all the other participants in the market probably lies in the range from £150 million to £200 million.

3. THE TREASURY BILL TENDER

Legally the treasury bill is not a bill of exchange because it is not an unconditional promise to pay, but the possibility that the Consolidated Fund would not be in a position to repay it on maturity is obviously so remote that we can look on it as a bill of exchange issued by the government. All treasury bills now mature 91 days after the date of issue (with adjustments if the 91st day happens to be a public holiday), but between 1955 and 1962 some 63-day bills were issued to mature during the tax-gathering season from January to March. Treasury bills are issued in denominations of £5000, £10,000, £25,000, £50,000, £100,000 and £250,000. It is one of the attractions of treasury bills for those who trade in them that the round sums simplify accounting. There are two methods of issuing treasury bills—by weekly tender and by direct issue to government departments. Bills issued by the second method are known as 'tap' bills; they are indistinguishable as pieces of paper from tender bills, and they often find their way into the market as a result of the operations of the Bank of England. Only banks (including discount houses and money brokers) are permitted to tender for treasury bills, and the minimum tender is £50,000.

The mechanics of the weekly tender are quite simple. Each Friday the Bank of England announces the amount of treasury bills to be offered for tender on the next Friday. The authorities cannot subsequently increase the amount on offer, but they often reduce it slightly. Tenders are submitted in £p (to the nearest $\frac{1}{2}$p) for £100 of bills. A tender at £98.50 represents a rate of discount of $1\frac{1}{2}\%$ for 91 days or 6.02% per annum, which is equivalent to a yield of 6·11% per annum. Tenderers can choose the day in the following week on which they will take up the bills, and large tenderers such as the discount houses normally take up some bills on each day of the week. Tenders must be received at the Bank of England by 1 p.m. on Friday. The Bank of England makes a rough calculation of the allotment by around 1.45 p.m., and announces the exact results by 3 p.m. The announcement at 3 p.m. states the total amount of tenders, the amount allotted, the average rate of discount and the amount to be offered on the following Friday.

The allotment of bills is made by first arranging the tenders in descending order of price. All tenders above the minimum price needed to exhaust the allotment are allotted in full, and the tenderers at the minimum price receive that proportion of their joint tenders which exhausts the amount to be allotted. Each tenderer pays the price at which he has tendered, and payment is made when the bills are taken up during the following week.

Up to September 1971 the treasury bill tender was dominated by certain rigid conventions, most of which have now ceased to operate. The most important of these was that the members of the London Discount Market Association submitted tenders at an identical price agreed among themselves—the 'syndicated bid'. The other conventions were: (1) the discount houses accepted an informal obligation to submit tenders for at least the total amount of bills on offer—'to cover the tender'; (2) the London clearing banks agreed not to tender on their own behalf and not to buy bills less than seven days old; (3) the London clearing banks do not normally sell on their own initiative bills which they have taken into their portfolios, but hold them to maturity unless the Bank of England wishes to buy them as part of its operations. The last convention was more a matter of custom than of agreement, and probably still obtains. Of the other conventions only the informal obligation to cover the tender remains.

The syndicated bid, like many other conventions of the discount market, dates back to 1935, and came into being as a means of enabling the discount houses to survive in the face of declining yields on treasury bills. Each Friday the London Discount Market Association met to agree a common rate at which members would tender for treasury bills, and at the same meeting they agreed prices at which they would sell treasury bills and the minimum price at which they would discount prime bank bills (bills payable in the United Kingdom and accepted by an accepting house, a London or Scottish clearing bank, one of the larger British overseas banks or one of the Commonwealth banks which have had branches in London for many years). The other side of the coin to the syndicated bid was the informal obligation to cover the tender. Each house was given a quota calculated according to a formula based on its capital and resources, and its total bid was for this quota, or occasionally for slightly more. All members were bound by the agreed price, except that each house could bid at a price equivalent to $\frac{1}{16}\%$ per annum higher for up to 15% of its quota if it had special commitments to customers.

Although the authorities stated to the Radcliffe Committee that they set great store by this arrangement, all that remains after the drastic changes of September 1971 is the informal obligation to cover the tender. Each discount house now bids on its own for as many bills as it wants. In order to make the obligation to cover the tender effective, however, a remnant of the syndicated bid still exists. In addition to bidding for the bills which it really wants at its own price each house has to submit a bid for the remainder of its quota, and this part of the bid is at a rate agreed by the L.D.M.A. each week; if the rate for this part of the bid were not agreed, individual houses could effectively leave the others to take up the bills by bidding extra low.

If the discount houses were completely free agents, they would decide their bids solely on their assessment of the profitability of holding treasury bills over the next three months, and the most important factor would be their guess as to the future level of interest rates. If rates were expected to go up, the houses would not want bills because the cost of borrowing would rise and they would suffer capital losses when they sold the bills. Conversely they would want as many bills as possible if they thought that rates were likely to go down. However, the discount houses are not completely free agents. They are relatively small bodies, poised uneasily between the Bank of England on one side and the large banks on the other, and both the Bank of England and the large banks are in a position to raise the average cost of borrowing to the discount houses if they are displeased.

The bidders at the tender can be divided into three groups: (1) the discount houses, (2) the Bank of England on behalf of its customers (mainly overseas central banks) and (3) all the others (known collectively as the 'outsiders'). When the syndicated bid was in force, things were so arranged that the bid of the Bank of England on behalf of its customers was always satisfied in full, but since September 1971 even the Bank of England has been unsuccessful at the tender on occasion. The proportion of the amount of treasury bills allotted which the discount houses secure at the tender fluctuates widely from week to week. When the syndicated bid was in force, an approximation to the allotment received by the discount houses could be made by assuming that it was equal to the proportion allotted at the minimum price: because the syndicate covered the tender, nobody bidding below the discount houses received any bills. During the first six months of 1971 the discount houses received no allotment on four occasions; taking this into account an estimate of their average allotment over the period is 45%.

Table 8.5   Holdings of treasury bills outside the government and
             Bank of England, 1963–70

Percentages

	31 December			
	1963	1966	1968	1970
Deposit banks	33.7	26.3	14.9	19.8
Secondary banks	2.0	2.3	1.3	2.2
Discount houses	17.3	16.0	12.7	39.0
Overseas central monetary institutions	34.1	46.9	66.6	34.4
Other overseas	3.8	3.2	2.2	1.2
Other	9.1	5.3	2.3	3.4
Total	100.0	100.0	100.0	100.0
Total outstanding (£ million)	*3,066*	*2,642*	*3,704*	*2,244*

Source: *Financial Statistics* (e.g. October 1971, Table 21).

Because only banks can tender for treasury bills, the only information which we have about the other tenderers is the amount of treasury bills held by them at different dates. Table 8.5 gives the figures for four dates between 1963 and 1970. The most interesting feature is the build-up and subsequent decline in the holdings of the overseas central monetary institutions—the customers of the Bank of England to which we referred previously. In the 1950s both other overseas residents and other holders were important. At that time 'hot money' from overseas normally went into treasury bills, and the treasury bill rate, adjusted for forward exchange cover, was the interest rate that determined the movement of funds from overseas. Under these circumstances it could reasonably be said that hot money was neutral in its impact on the domestic credit situation: more treasury bills were issued to finance the purchase of foreign currency by the Exchange Equalisation Account, but the hot money was invested in these bills. The bulk of overseas money now goes through the parallel money market, and this happy neutralisation no longer occurs. Similarly a lot of industrial money went into treasury bills in the late 1950s as corporate treasurers reacted to higher interest rates by economising on working cash balances and investing in the short-term markets. This money, too, was diverted into the parallel market as it grew up.

4. OPERATION OF THE MARKET

A. *Daily operation*

So far we have looked at the operation of the new issue side of the market for treasury bills and at the behaviour of the various participants. We must now turn to the daily operation of the discount market as a secondary market for treasury bills, commercial bills and short bonds and in the daily renewal of borrowing to finance the holding of these claims. The market has two important characteristics. (1) Deals are conducted entirely by word of mouth, and no written confirmation is passed. (2) All but a tiny fraction of the deals involve the deposit of security with the lender, and twenty to thirty minutes after the deal has been concluded verbally a messenger will arrive at the lender's office to deposit a new parcel of securities or to withdraw an existing parcel.

To understand the daily working of the discount market we must know the objectives of the various participants. The objective of the discount houses and the other borrowers of call money is simplicity itself: by 3 p.m. they must have obtained sufficient borrowed funds to balance their books, that is to bring their total liabilities into equality with their assets. The London clearing banks have an equally simple objective—to maintain as exactly as possible the $1\frac{1}{2}\%$ ratio of their overnight balance at the Bank of England to eligible liabilities at the last make-up day. The other major operator in the market, the Bank of England (often referred to as 'the authorities'), appears in two guises and has two objectives. In its role as banker to the government the Bank of England aims to keep the accounts of the Exchequer (including the Paymaster General and the National Debt Commissioners) down to an overnight level of about £2 million. In its role as agent of government monetary policy the Bank of England aims to control the market so as to further policy on short-term interest rates; in practice it does not aim through the market to control the supply of money. Leaving aside this policy aim of the Bank of England, we can see that the main function of the discount market in the eyes of the major participants is that of converting all cash balances beyond the indispensable minimum into earning assets; the English banking system does not voluntarily hold excess cash reserves. For the other participants in the discount market, including all commercial banks other than the London clearing banks, the discount market is not central to their control of the level of cash reserves, and in our exposition we can regard them as autonomous (with a caveat that the Scottish banks are probably in an intermediate position).

The daily working of the discount market is dominated by a strict timetable. Between 10.15 a.m. and noon representatives of the discount houses, in their distinctive 'uniform' of a black top hat, visit 100 or more banks to ask whether the bank wants to lend or to call back money already lent, to adjust the rates on money already lent and to buy or sell treasury bills or commercial bills. By midday the clearing banks will have ceased to call back money already lent, and at this time each discount house reports its position to the Bank of England bill broker[1] so that the Bank of England can calculate the overall deficiency or surplus in the market. From then on most transactions are conducted by telephone. The Bank of England will often intervene by dealing in certain securities held by the discount houses, but if the discount houses need to borrow from the Bank of England this must be done by 2.30 p.m., and there is usually a hectic scramble for call money just before that time when some houses are short. Since money often comes on offer between 2.30 and 3 p.m. it is often a matter of fine judgement on the part of a discount house to decide whether and how much to borrow at the Bank of England. By 3 p.m. discount houses must have balanced their books, and business in the discount market proper ceases.

Each of the participants in the discount market maintains a work-

1. He is the chairman of the smallest discount house, Seccombe, Marshall & Campion Ltd., but other directors act in his absence.

sheet in some form or other, on which are recorded all changes in its cash position. For clearing banks the cash position is the total of deposits at the Bank of England as affected by movements during the day. Although discount houses maintain nominal balances with the Bank of England, their real bankers are the London clearing banks. Discount houses are thus concerned with changes on their accounts with London clearing banks, and balancing their books implies that incomings must equal outgoings, so that the net change is zero. The Bank of England is concerned particularly with the cash positions of two of the main groups of its customers—the London clearing banks and the Exchequer.

Table 8.6 gives an illustration of the daily operation of the discount market; in order to show the intervention by the Bank of England a day on which the market is short of cash has been chosen. By tabulating changes in the balance sheets of the London clearing banks and the Banking Department of the Bank of England, changes in the cash positions of the four main groups of participants are shown in the following columns: (1) discount houses; (2) all 'outside bodies' lumped together, whether they are banks or not; (3) and (5) London clearing banks; (6) the Exchequer. The table is completed with columns for other assets of the London clearing banks and advances and other assets of the Bank of England. Because both balance sheets must balance throughout, changes on the assets and liabilities side of each balance sheet must be equal; this is achieved by entries of opposite sign on the same side of the balance sheet or by entries of the same sign on opposite sides. The changes in the cash positions are consolidated for each group of participants, because fluctuations between individual discount houses and London clearing banks are ironed out automatically and do not affect the overall position of the market. Figures are imaginary but realistic.

The various transactions that take place can be summarised into four classes, each class having a different effect on the cash positions of the participants. (1) All transactions between the 'authorities' on the one hand and London clearing banks, discount houses and outside bodies on the other affect the cash position of the London clearing banks in columns (3) and (5). Examples of transactions between the authorities and the three groups of bodies are the maturing of treasury bills held by the London clearing banks, the taking up of treasury bills by the discount houses and the payment of taxes by customers of the London clearing banks. (This last transaction telescopes two transactions into one, since the taxpayers' cheques are banked by local

Table 8.6 A day's operation in the discount market   £ million

	Clearing banks				Bank of England			
	Deposits		Assets		Deposits		Assets	
	Discount houses (1)	Other (2)	Cash (3)	Other (4)	Bankers' (5)	Public (6)	Advances (7)	Other (8)
Position as seen at 10 a.m.								
Tax payments		− 30	− 30		− 30	+ 30		
Exchequer disbursements		+ 5	+ 5		+ 5	− 5		
Gilt-edged bought from Government Broker by clearing banks (6)								
Gilt-edged bought from general public by discount houses and their customers (4)	**− 2**	− 4	− 10	+ 6	− 10	+ 10		
Foreign exchange received from customers and surrendered to Exchange Equalisation Account		**+ 2**						
Treasury bills held by clearing banks mature		+ 3	+ 3	− 10	+ 3	− 3		
Treasury bills taken up by discount houses	− 8		+ 10		+ 10	− 10		
Commercial bills held by discount houses	+ 5	− 5	− 8		− 8	+ 8		
Repayment of Bank of England advances by discount houses	− 7		− 7		− 7		− 7	
10 a.m. − 12 noon	− 12	− 29	− 37	− 4	− 37	+ 30	− 7	
Treasury bills sold to clearing banks by discount houses	+ 2			+ 2				
Call money withdrawn by clearing banks	− 55	− 5		− 55				
Call money advanced by other banks	+ 5							
Commercial bills discounted by discount houses	− 5	+ 5						
12 noon − 3 p.m.	− 65	− 29	− 37	− 57	− 37	+ 30	− 7	
Direct help: Bank of England buys treasury bills from discount houses	+ 5		+ 5		+ 5			+ 5
Indirect help: Bank of England buys treasury bills from clearing banks			+ 10	− 10	+ 10			+ 10
Call money advanced by clearing banks	+ 33			+ 33				
Bank of England advance to discount houses	+ 24		+ 24		+ 24		+ 24	
Privilege money	+ 3			+ 3				
Exchequer buys treasury bills						− 30		− 30
	−	− 29	+ 2	− 31	+ 2	−	+ 17	− 15

Collectors of Taxes with the London clearing banks, which pay the total amounts over to the Exchequer twice a week on Wednesdays and Fridays.) (2) Transactions between London clearing banks and discount houses affect the cash position of discount houses but not that of the London clearing banks. Thus the act of calling from the market by a London clearing bank does not restore the latter's cash position; this will not happen until the discount house replaces the called money by borrowing from another London clearing bank or from the Bank of England. An example is the calling from the market by London clearing banks between 10 a.m. and noon and the subsequent help extended to the market by the Bank of England. (3) Transactions between discount houses and outside bodies affect only their respective deposits with London clearing banks. An example is the maturing of commercial bills held by discount houses. (4) Transactions between the Exchequer and the Bank of England, such as the final transaction of the day, affect only the balance sheet of the Bank of England.

Although most of the important types of transaction are included in Table 8.6, there are one or two deliberate omissions. Some of these arise, as we have noted, because we have consolidated the positions of both the clearing banks and the discount houses, and we have shown no demand by the clearing banks for additional notes. The most important omission, however, arises because we have not wanted to complicate the table further by showing a separate coloumn for the other customers of the Bank of England, particularly the overseas central banks. On many occasions these assume an important role in the market. The most noteworthy occasion occurs on the fifteenth of each month, when oil royalties, which have been accumulated by the oil companies with their London banks, and lent to the discount market, are paid over to the Middle East central banks; because the central banks bank with the Bank of England, the withdrawal of the call money and its paying over represent a drain of cash to the system.

We can now go briefly through the events of the day. The day starts with the London clearing banks determining the likely effects on their Bank of England balance of items settled in the Clearing House during the day. These items will comprise, for example, any large movements of funds by their bigger corporate customers and transfers of money to and from the authorities in respect of tax, government disbursements, notes and similar items. The net amount of these items is then applied to the Bank of England balance at the close of business on the previous day, and a decision is reached on whether to call money from the discount houses or to lend additional money. Each bank thus has a target figure for its balance at the Bank of England. In Table 8.6 the London clearing banks are assumed to be aiming at increasing their aggregate balances with the Bank of England by £2 million.

Some of the transactions referred to above will be known with complete accuracy because they are payments to be made in settlement of transactions of the previous day, but many others can only be estimated at this stage. Because the clearing banks refrain from calling from the market after midday, they will not take credit in their estimates for any sums that could be delayed and thus not reach them until the following day. For this reason the clearing banks always call more or lend less at the beginning of the day than would be warranted by an estimate of the likely position, and the Bank of England takes this factor into account in deciding how much help the market will eventually need. In the nature of things Table 8.6 has to show exact figures for those items which can only be estimated, and it shows the clearing banks as starting off the day at 10 a.m. with an estimated cash deficiency of £37 million. During the course of the morning 'parade' the clearing banks call the much larger sum of £55 million, and at midday, after various transactions in treasury bills and commercial bills have taken place, the discount houses report a total deficiency of £65 million to the Bank of England's bill broker.

Because of the relatively large deficiency in the market on this day, the stage is dominated in the period from 12 noon to 3 p.m. by transactions initiated by the Bank of England, and the first four lines of figures for this period refer to transactions which are of this nature. We shall examine further the factors determining the Bank of England's choice of methods for helping the market when we have seen what the authorities are aiming at in their control of the market.

The last two transactions of the day show the discount houses making a final adjustment to their books by borrowing £3 million of privilege money from the clearing banks and the Exchequer overnight balance being reduced to its customary level of £2 million by the purchase of £30 million of treasury bills from the Banking Department of the Bank of England. Privilege money had an origin dating back many years, and it arose because the discount houses received late parcels of commercial bills from overseas after the 2.30 p.m. deadline for borrowing from the Bank of England; without special accommodation from the London clearing banks they would not have been in a position to discount the bills. It survived as a means of balancing the books if the discount houses had made slight errors in their sums. The privilege facilities with the clearing banks have ceased to exist since the new arrangements came into force in September 1971; they have been replaced by limited borrowing facilities from the Bank of England at market rates.

B. *Balance of the Market*

As the marginal provider of funds to the discount market when there is a deficiency the Bank of England is in a monopoly position, and it is this which gives it the possibility of controlling the market. No monopolist can ever control both price and quantity, and the authorities have to choose which variable they will control—the supply of cash to the banking system or the general level of short-term interest rates. If the authorities chose to control the supply of cash, they would be operating a variant of the classical open-market operations, in which the central bank determines the level of bank cash by initiating sales or purchases of government securities; it would be a variant because they are not initiating sales or purchases of securities but taking advantage of the flows of money between the private sector and the government and deciding to what extent they should be offset. In fact it is quite clear from the evidence of the Bank of England to the Radcliffe Committee and from their behaviour in the market that the authorities take advantage of the flows between the private sector and the government to control short-term interest rates, and that they always provide the cash that the banking system needs to maintain its level of deposits.

The balance of the market can be seen quite easily from the table. At 10 a.m. the London clearing banks have a cash deficiency of £37 million, and this is composed of two elements: (1) the Exchequer surplus (balance on public deposits) of £30 million and (2) the £7 million repayment by the discount houses of an advance from the Bank of England. In addition the banks are aiming to increase their cash balances by £2 million, making a total need for cash of £39 million. In its intervention after 12 noon the Bank of England provides just this sum (5 + 10 + 24).

The balance for the discount houses is somewhat more complicated. They were made to suffer the full impact of the clearing banks' need for cash from the beginning, and so the Bank of England intervention filters back to them to the full extent of £39 million. In terms of borrowed funds they start the day with a repayment of £7 million to the Bank of England and a withdrawal of £55 million by the London clearing banks, a total withdrawal of £62 million. Against this they borrow fresh funds as follows: £5 million from other banks, £33 million from the London clearing banks, £24 million from the Bank of England and £3 million of privilege money; this is a total of £65 million, and a net gain of £3 million. On the assets side of their balance sheet they sell £7 million of treasury bills (5 + 2) and £5 million of commercial bills, and they purchase £8 million of treasury bills, £2 million of gilt-edged and £5 million of commercial bills. Their balance sheet remains in balance because the excess of purchases over sales of £3 million is exactly matched by the gain in borrowed funds.

There are interesting implications in the method of operation of the discount market. Since the authorities are concerned only with the cash of the clearing banks, the real business of the discount market is conducted between the authorities and the clearing banks, with the discount houses as go-betweens.

If the position were as rigid as we have indicated, there would obviously be many occasions on which the clearing banks would have attained their target figure while the discount houses were still a long way from balancing their books. Even if we ignore the 'outside' transactions of the discount houses, we can see that there must be some element of flexibility in the system if the clearing banks are to attain their target figure simultaneously with the balancing of their books by the discount houses; this is provided by the fact that the Banking Department of the Bank of England operates without rigid ratios. In practice, however, the flexibility in the system extends far beyond this. Table 8.6 depicts a happy world in which everybody has exactly attained his objective by the end of the day, but such a situation must be exceptional. All the participants in the market are working with partial information and making allowance for events that are expected to happen later in the day, and they often get their sums wrong in consequence. The Bank of England may not have provided enough assistance before 2.30 p.m., and the discount houses may have underestimated their need for borrowing from the Bank of England; at the end of the day the clearing banks may well have a surplus or deficiency on their cash position. As long as it is plain to the clearing banks that the Bank of England is willing to see the situation righted, the clearing banks will lend all that is necessary to the discount houses, particularly as such action does not make their cash position any worse. If the Bank of England clearly wants the discount houses punished, the clearing banks will not help, but the discount houses can always obtain funds from outside bodies by bidding high enough; at times they probably have to bid over Bank rate to attract funds from the inter-bank market. Any surplus or deficiency in the cash of the clearing banks at the end of the day just has to be tolerated.

On the whole the market works extremely well, and it is certainly the most efficient money market in the world if efficiency is measured by the small extent to which cash balances remain unlent. As long as the dialogue between the Bank of England and the clearing banks is conducted through the discount houses, some miscalculations are inevitable, but the experience of the operators reduces them to a minimum. It is easy to poke fun at the discount houses because of their top-hatted representatives or because their presence hides the realities of the system, but their justification is that they are part of a remarkably efficient system.

C. *Bank of England intervention*

We have seen that the Bank of England makes no attempt to control the level of cash held by the London clearing banks, but that its main concern is with the level and stability of short-term interest rates. Although its attitude towards stability of short-term interest rates has undergone some change in recent months, there is nothing in the new arrangements which indicates a wish to operate directly on bank cash; indeed this intention has been specifically disavowed. Once it has decided how much help is needed in the market, the Bank of England has to fix the terms on which it will provide assistance. These terms affect the average cost of borrowing of the discount houses, and are factors to be taken into account by the houses in fixing their bids at the next treasury bill tender. The Bank of England uses the terms on which it supplies funds as signals of its wishes on the level of the treasury bill rate. When it acts to raise the treasury bill rate nearer to Bank rate, the Bank of England is said to be 'making Bank rate effective'.

The Bank of England has several channels through which it can assist the market, but there are only two choices open for the terms on which help is given—'penal' borrowing at Bank rate or over and help at the market rate of interest. When the syndicate of discount houses fixed not only the bid for the tender but also the rates at which long bills would be dealt in, the Bank of England used to accept these rates for its own assistance. Apparently the Bank has not yet decided how it will react to the absence of dealing rates fixed by the syndicate. In practice, on a day such as that depicted in Table 8.6, the authorities might well supply some help both at market rates and at Bank rate or over; the signal would then consist of the proportions supplied on the different terms. The Bank of England also has some signals which fall short of enforcing penal borrowing. For example, its operator in the discount market can quite often induce a rise in rates just by taking an extra long lunch hour and thus delaying the provision of help to the market.

Bank rate is spoken of in so many contexts that it comes as something of a shock to realise that the only occasion on which it is actually used is when the discount houses are obliged to borrow from the Bank of England as lender of the last resort. It occurs in so many other contexts only because it is used as a base point for the calculation of other interest rates, but its use for this purpose is declining. For some time secondary banks and finance houses have based their rates on those for inter-bank lending in the parallel money market, and the deposit banks now set their own base rate independently of Bank rate. Originally Bank rate was the rate at which the Bank of England would re-discount bills, but in recent years the discount houses have nearly always preferred a loan; the loan is for not more than seven days, whereas re-discounting meant incurring the effects of penal borrowing for a period equal to the maturity of the bills, which on average must be not less than twenty-one days.[2]

There are three channels through which the Bank of England can provide assistance at market rate, and the first two of these involve purchases of treasury bills by the Bank of England bill broker, who in this context is referred to variously as the 'special buyer', the 'hidden hand' or the 'back door'. If there is a surplus of cash in the market, the bill broker can 'mop it up' by selling treasury bills. The Bank of England normally buys or sells bills of maturities which will assist its operations on later days. The two channels through which the Bank of England can assist the market by buying treasury bills are purchases

2. The final blow to the importance of Bank rate came on 9 October 1972, when the Chancellor of the Exchequer announced that in future the penal rate for assistance to the discount market would be calculated each week according to a simple formula, which would link it automatically to the prevailing discount rate on treasury bills at the end of the previous week. The 'Bank's minimum lending rate', as it would be known, would be announced by the Bank of England at about 3 p.m. each Friday. It would be calculated at $\frac{1}{2}\%$ above the average discount rate on treasury bills at the Friday morning tender, rounded up to the nearest $\frac{1}{4}\%$, and this rate would then rule for the following week. The authorities reserved the right to bring back traditional Bank rate if they wanted to secure the peculiar psychological effects associated with changes in that rate. This change came too late for references to Bank rate in other parts of this book to be amended. (See *Bank of England Quarterly Bulletin* (December 1972) p. 442.)

from the discount houses, when it is called 'direct help', or from the clearing banks, when it is called 'indirect help'. We have seen enough of the working of the market to know that the reality of the situation would require the reversal of the two labels. When the help is through the clearing banks, these are in honour bound to pass it on to the discount houses as 'made money', which commands a rate based on the treasury bill tender, with a 'turn' of $\frac{1}{8}\%$.

The third channel for assistance at market rate is a loan by the Bank of England. This method has been in use only since June 1966, and its adoption has been a direct consequence of the general shortage of treasury bills. The normal loan is overnight, but longer periods have been used on several occasions. In many ways this method gives the Bank of England a better control of the market. A system of overnight loans means that almost every day starts with a repayment to the Bank of England, thus often converting a cash surplus into a cash deficit. The ability of the Bank of England to impose its will on the market is non-existent when the market is in surplus, so that this measure must have increased its power quite a bit. Since the new arrangements came into force, assistance by overnight loans has been at Bank rate.

The use made by the Bank of England of penal borrowing has varied quite a bit in recent years. For the whole of 1968 and 1969 all assistance was at market rates, but the use of assistance at Bank rate or above was restored early in 1970. Under the new arrangements the Bank of England has made two changes in technique, to which we have already referred. The first is that of deciding the rate at which it will deal in treasury bills each day. The second is that of extending to the discount houses limited borrowing facilities, which each house may use at its discretion. The object of this change is to give the discount houses time to adjust their portfolios in the face of larger and more frequent fluctuations in short-term interest rates.

In summary two points can be made about the effects of the new arrangements on the discount market: (1) they will restore some of its lost importance to the market and (2) they will bring the discount market and the sterling parallel markets much closer together. We shall defer consideration of these points and the impact of the new arrangements on the Bank of England's powers to control short-term interest rates until we look at the parallel money markets in Chapter 10.

FURTHER READING

W. M. Scammell, *The London Discount Market* (London: Elek Books, 1968).

Gillett Brothers, *The Bill on London*, 3rd ed. (London: Chapman & Hall, 1952).

The following articles from the *Bank of England Quarterly Bulletin*:

'Commercial bills' (December 1961).

'The management of money day by day' (March 1963).

'The treasury bill' (September 1964).

'The U.K. and U.S. treasury bill markets' (December 1965).

'The London discount market: some historical notes' (June 1967).

'Competition and credit control: the discount market' (September 1971).

'Reserve ratios: further definitions' (December 1971).

'Competition and credit control: extract from a lecture by the Chief Cashier' (December 1971).

9 Secondary Banks

1. SECONDARY BANKING

A. *The nature of secondary banking*

While the deposit banks form the main banking network in this country, in terms of numbers they are only a small part of the bank population. At first sight the remaining banks are so heterogeneous a group that it would be wrong to give them all one label, but in recent years most of them have been drawn into a secondary banking system in which, despite their different origins and geographical interests, they compete for similar types of business. All these banks have one factor in common: they do not attempt to compete with the deposit banks for the business of transmitting payments, although all of them have a proportion of current accounts among their deposits. Because the current accounts are such a small part of their business, these banks can concentrate on the financial intermediary side of banking, and they can do so relatively untrammelled by the rigid ratios of deposit banks or by the self-imposed conventions about the types of business which it is proper for them to undertake. They have the same obligation to behave with extreme prudence, but the criteria by which prudence is judged are different.

The main features of secondary banking are five in number. (1) It is wholesale banking, in which both deposits and loans are for large sums. (2) The bulk of both deposits and loans is fixed for a definite period—term deposits and term loans. (3) The business is international in scope, around 80% of deposits and loans being in foreign currencies and attributable to overseas residents. (4) The secondary banking system is highly competitive, and agreements about rates are, with very few exceptions, unknown. (5) The system operates with a structure of interest rates which is higher than that of the deposit banks, at least for deposits if not for advances.

In this main section we are concerned only with the commercial banking business conducted by these banks. For many of them other services are often of equal importance, but we shall look at these in subsequent sections as we consider each group of secondary banks separately.

B. *Balance sheet*

Table 9.1 shows the aggregate balance sheet for all secondary banks— or 'accepting houses, overseas banks and other banks in the United Kingdom', as the Bank of England calls them. It must be remembered that for nearly all the banks whose statistics are aggregated in this table the figures represent only a partial balance sheet, relating to that part of their total business which is conducted in the United Kingdom. For British-owned banks it is the balance sheet of the head office and of any other U.K. branches; varying proportions of the total business of the bank will be conducted overseas, and all this will be missing. For foreign banks it is the balance sheet of their U.K. offices.

The table separates the assets and liabilities into sterling and other currencies, and so brings out the dominance of foreign currencies in secondary banking. It is in the nature of things that the classification of sterling assets is much finer than that of assets in other currencies.

Perhaps the first instinct of anybody confronted with a bank balance sheet is to work out a liquidity ratio, but there are certain difficulties with the balance sheets of secondary banks. If we are prepared to count everything down to negotiable certificates of deposit as liquid assets, the ratio to total deposits works out at 38·5%, a reassuringly high figure. There are three difficulties with this approach. (1) As we shall see later, liquidity is largely irrelevant for secondary banks. (2) The aggregate balance sheet conceals very large differences in the liquidity ratios of individual banks. (3) Three of the asset headings which we have counted as liquid include items with maturities ranging up to at least a year and sometimes beyond.

One thing is clear from this table: secondary banks make very little use of the discount market when they need short-term assets, but go instead to the parallel money markets, where yields are higher. Of the 'liquid' assets, balances with other U.K. banks, loans to local authorities and negotiable certificates of deposit are parallel market assets; together they represent 35·8% of total deposits, while the discount

Table 9.1   Balance sheet of secondary banks, December 1970

£ million

	Sterling	Other currencies	Total
Liabilities			
Current accounts	593 ⎱	19,423	24,788
Term deposits	4,772 ⎰		
Negotiable certificates of deposit	1,089	1,649	2,738
Total	6,454	21,072	27,526
Assets			
Coin, notes and balances with Bank of England	5	–	5
Balances with other U.K. banks	1,747	5,431	7,178
Money at call and short notice			
Discount houses	450	–	450
Other borrowers	112	–	112
Sterling bills discounted			
British government treasury bills	50	–	50
Other U.K. bills	71	–	71
Other	48	–	48
Loans to U.K. local authorities	1,727	–	1,727
Negotiable certificates of deposit	575	355	930
British government stocks	354	–	354
Advances	1,639	15,012	16,652
Other assets	393	406	799
Total	7,171	21,204	28,376
Acceptances	...	...	*890*

Sources: (1) *Bank of England Quarterly Bulletin*, June 1971, Tables 10(1) & 12;   (2) Table 10.5.

market assets of money at call and sterling bills discounted account for only 2·7%. This point will be important when we look at the impact of the new control measures on secondary banks. The 1970 position represents a considerable reversal of the proportions before the parallel money markets were fully developed: in 1958 those secondary banks which were then established in London covered 40–45% of their total deposits with discount market assets.

We have already looked at the deposits of secondary banks analysed in two different ways in Tables 5.3 and 5.5. Table 5.3 in particular showed us that £1694 million of the sterling deposits and £5357 million of the deposits in other currencies came from other U.K. banks. Table

9.2 carries this analysis a little further, for a slightly different date, by showing the proportion of deposits from overseas residents which came from banks abroad. (For the purposes of this analysis, which came from a special inquiry, the Bank of England has introduced another classification of banks into British, Commonwealth, American and

Table 9.2   Source and destination analysis of liabilities and claims in non-sterling currencies of banks in the United Kingdom, February 1971

£ million

Source and destination	Type of bank				Total
	British	Common-wealth	American	Other	
Liabilities to					
Other U.K. banks	1,714	338	2,482	1,206	5,740
Other U.K. residents	272	30	266	44	612
Banks abroad	2,956	390	5,901	2,194	11,441
Other overseas residents	899	459	1,734	480	3,572
Total	5,841	1,217	10,383	3,924	21,365
Claims on					
Other U.K. banks	1,615	603	2,451	1,237	5,906
Other U.K. residents	622	144	279	145	1,190
Banks abroad	1,937	277	4,890	1,697	8,801
Other overseas residents	1,695	196	2,724	854	5,469
Total	5,869	1,220	10,344	3,933	21,366

Source: *Bank of England Quarterly Bulletin*, June 1971, pp. 222-3.

other.) The proportion of deposits from banks abroad is particularly high for the American banks, which use their vantage point in London to collect deposits from banks in Western Europe. Most of these deposits are then lent to their head offices in New York and other branches (counted as 'banks abroad'), although this traffic had passed its peak by this date.

As we have seen, the characteristic deposits in secondary banking are interest-bearing and fixed for a definite period. Table 9.1 shows that only about 9% of total sterling deposits in December 1970 were current accounts; some of the large multinational companies are known to have euro-dollar current accounts in London, but they are likely to be somewhat smaller in total than sterling current accounts. We shall be looking at the different maturities of non-sterling deposits later, but we must now go on to describe the nature of advances.

We know even less about advances than we do about deposits, but we can safely assume that they take a variety of forms, since a feature of secondary banking is the tailoring of loan terms and conditions to the particular circumstances of each case. Some of the banks which have been long established in London continue to do overdraft lending to some extent, but the proportion of overdrafts to total loans is probably small. The remaining loans are for a fixed period, ranging from a few months up to five or seven years. Some will be repayable in instalments, and some repayable in full on maturity. Similarly some will have a fixed rate of interest throughout their terms, while others, probably the majority of recent years, will provide for changes in the interest rate every six months, usually according to the prevailing rate on six-month euro-dollar deposits or deposits in the inter-bank sterling market.

It is worth pausing to inquire why term loans should have become so popular in this country, which pioneered the overdraft and still relies so heavily on it. Some measure of this popularity can be obtained from Table 5.5. Since nearly all deposit bank advances are overdrafts and the majority of secondary banks advances are term loans, we can compare the total lending of deposit banks and secondary banks to industrial and commercial companies. Table 5.5 shows that at December 1970 secondary banks lent just over 50% as much as deposit banks to non-financial companies.

There are several reasons for the popularity of term loans. (1) During a period of credit squeezes, when overdraft limits might be drastically reduced, the security of a term loan was particularly attractive. (2) While overdrafts are suitable for working capital and represent a generalised form of finance for all the activities of a company, term loans tie in with the newer forms of investment appraisal (such as discounted cash flow) and facilitate budgeting. (3) Because the basis for the granting of a loan is generally the cash flow of a particular project rather than the assets of a company, the creditworthiness of companies is extended by the use of term loans; even first-class companies can borrow more from the banking system than they could on overdraft alone. (4) The liquidity which companies built up during the war was not finally exhausted until about 1960, and since then companies have leaned heavily on the banking system to finance capital investment because new issues could not grow fast enough to compensate for the decreased availability of finance derived from internal sources—the cash flow.[1]

C. *Operation*

The contrast between secondary banking as we have described it and deposit banking as it had been practised in Britain up to September 1971 is complete. Deposit banking was almost entirely in sterling, and virtually no deposits were fixed for a period longer than seven days. The deposit banker has a very large number of accounts and, relying on the law of large numbers, he can safely treat these as largely a revolving fund. He protected himself by covering as much as one-half of his deposits with assets which were held, wholly or partly, for reasons of liquidity, and by restricting the bulk of his advances to the safest and most liquid forms. The secondary banker deals with a relatively small number of large accounts on both sides of his balance sheet, which are fixed for varying periods ahead and which have a large proportion expressed in currencies other than sterling. Normal banking prudence requires that he should think in terms of two further dimensions beyond straightforward liquidity—the maturity of his assets and liabilities and the currency in which they are expressed. He has no guarantee that a matured deposit or loan can be replaced by one on similar conditions or for a similar period, and so his most prudent course is to match his assets and liabilities, both in terms of maturity and in terms of currency. If he is completely 'matched', the maturity of a loan in a particular currency will occur at precisely the same time as the maturity of a deposit (or deposits) for the same amount in the same currency. A completely matched balance sheet has been likened to a Christmas tree, on which branches opposite each other are of equal size. Providing nobody defaults, it is a self-liquidating balance sheet. There is no need for liquidity as such, only for short-term assets to match short-term deposits. A perfectly matched balance sheet in which long-term deposits support long-term assets is every bit as safe as one in which short-term deposits support short-term assets, although, when it is set out in conventional form, the latter will appear more liquid.

An imaginary example of a perfectly matched balance sheet is given in Table 9.3. It covers one currency only; in practice similar balance sheets would be needed for each currency separately. The difference from a balance sheet set out in conventional form is immediately

1. See 'Company finance: 1952–65', *Bank of England Quarterly Bulletin* (March 1967).

apparent. With a conventional balance sheet the only information given is usually the total value of different kinds of asset and liability; in this balance sheet we are given in addition the maturity of both assets and liabilities, and our attention is directed, not to the row totals, but to the column totals. As long as the total at the foot of each maturity column is equal for assets and liabilities, we can say that the balance

Table 9.3   A completely matched balance sheet

	Sight	1 day to under 8 days	8 days to under 3 months	3 months to under 1 year	1 year and over	Total
Liabilities						
Customers' deposits	18	7	5	20	5	55
Inter-bank deposits	2	1	3	5	6.	17
Certificates of deposit	–	–	3	15	10	28
Total	20	8	11	40	21	100
Assets						
Balances with other banks	8	1·	3	5	4	21
Local authority loans	12	1	5	10	–	28
Certificates of deposit	–	6	–	–	–	6
Advances	–	–	3	25	17	45
Total	20	8	11	40	21	100

sheet is perfectly matched. In practice things are not quite so simple as this imaginary example makes out because there are certain kinds of asset whose maturity is uncertain. These are marketable securities like bills, bonds and certificates of deposit; they can be sold at any time, and bankers do not agree on whether they should be matched against overnight money or deposits fixed for longer periods. Loans repayable by instalments can be worked into the general scheme by treating each instalment as a separate loan for matching.

'Matching' is the basic principle of secondary banking as liquidity is of deposit banking. (The term is not always used; some bankers talk of 'managing their money book'.) But this statement should not be taken to imply that secondary bankers always keep their assets and liabilities exactly matched by maturity and currency. Very few of them do this rigorously, although some are naturally more conservative than others. The statement means only that the basic principle of secondary banking is the comparison of assets and liabilities by maturity and currency, and that departures from a completely matched position are the results of a deliberate decision. Matching is a well-established principle of banking, but its application in British banking is new. The need for it has arisen from the growth of large deposits and loans for fixed terms and in foreign currencies.

At one end of the maturity scale secondary banks are almost bound to be unmatched: there is a large demand for medium-term loans (two to seven years), whereas deposits fixed for periods of more than one year are still uncommon and expensive. As to the rest of their 'money book', there are two considerations that urge them towards a moderately unmatched position. (1) The secondary banking system is so competitive that margins between deposits and loans of the same maturity are very narrow, and there is very little profit in just 'putting business through'. On the other hand interest rates rise with maturity, and making their lending somewhat longer than their borrowing widens the margin. (2) 'Taking a view' on the future level of interest rates and exchange rates is a normal part of banking business, and many decisions cannot be made without taking these expected levels into account. Secondary banking in this country is so new that there are no agreed principles on the degree of matching; bankers range from the ultra-conservative to the mildly venturesome according to temperament and background.

The direction in which bankers will go unmatched when they take a view of future interest rates can be seen quite easily. If interest rates are expected to rise, bankers will have their assets as short as possible and their liabilities as long as possible; they can switch into higher-yielding assets when the interest-rate change comes, but continue to pay the lower rates on a high proportion of deposits. Conversely, if interest rates are expected to fall, liabilities will be shortened to take early advantage of the lower rates, while assets will be lengthened to secure the benefit of the present higher rates for as long as possible. The banker will also keep in mind the possibility of capital gain and loss on holdings of marketable securities, such as bills, bonds and certificates of deposit. When interest rates are expected to rise, capital losses will be feared, and holdings of marketable securities will be avoided; when interest rates are expected to fall, holdings of marketable securities will be increased.

It is only for non-sterling liabilities and claims that we have any knowledge of the maturities. The figures for February 1971 are shown in Table 9.4. When it comes to interpreting actual figures of maturity, certain technical factors have to be borne in mind. We have already mentioned the problem of deciding the appropriate maturity for market-able securities; in this case the banks were instructed to regard bills and negotiable certificates of deposit (CDs) as sight assets. It is clear that there is an excess of claims at the long end; the excess of sight claims may consist largely of bills and CDs.

Table 9.4   Maturity analysis of liabilities and claims in non-sterling currencies of banks in the United Kingdom, February 1971

£ million

Maturity	Liabilities	Claims	Net liabilities(-)/ claims(+)
Sight	3,067	3,554	+ 487
Less than 8 days.	1,469	1,275	− 194
8 days to less than 3 months	10,490	8,816	− 1,674
3 months to less than 1 year	5,446	4,963	− 483
1 year and over	893	2,758	+ 1,865
Total	21,365	21,366	+ 1

Source: *Bank of England Quarterly Bulletin*, June 1971, pp. 222–3.

D. *Inter-bank deposits*

Balances with other U.K. banks figure prominently among the assets of secondary banks, and in aggregate they are offset by roughly equivalent amounts of deposits from other U.K. banks. Secondary banks keep their working balances with London clearing banks, but these balances are usually quite small, often as little as 1% of daily turnover, and they are normally kept to a conventional level, which is changed only at infrequent intervals. All the other balances with banks are interest-bearing and fixed for a definite period, from overnight up to one year.

The background to the importance of inter-bank deposits, both in sterling and in other currencies, lies in two features of secondary banking. (1) Both deposits and loans are for relatively large sums. The normal minimum unit in which a secondary bank will accept a deposit is £50,000 and it will not look at business for less than £10,000. On

the lending side the units are usually larger still, and many banks regard £500,000 as the norm. (2) No bank likes to refuse either deposit
or loan business when it is offered on acceptable conditions. The
secondary banker is thus perpetually in the position of obtaining
business which upsets the matching of his assets and liabilities. If he
has just made a loan for £500,000, he will be looking for a deposit of
the same sum and for roughly the same maturity. Since he has relatively few customers, it is most unlikely that a customer will offer
spontaneously just the deposit he is looking for, but it is far more
likely that another secondary bank somewhere in the system will have
received a deposit of the required amount and maturity which it cannot match immediately with a loan to a customer or a local authority
(or, of course, that two or three banks between them are anxious to
place a total of £500,000). Inter-bank deposits thus fulfil an essential
role in the process of matching the maturity of assets and liabilities:
they are used to fill in the gaps in a bank's maturity structure on
either side of its balance sheet.

More recently negotiable certificates of deposits (CDs) have come to
play an important part in the process of matching, and they do so
both as liabilities and as assets. Because holders are more willing to
hold a long-dated CD than a deposit of similar maturity, the issuing of
CDs enables secondary banks to match their medium-term loans (two
to seven years) more closely. In issuing CDs banks are effectively tapping the customers of all secondary banks, and they are therefore more
likely to be able to match loans with a CD of the same maturity than
if they relied on term deposits. It is on the assets side that CDs have
played an even more important part; Table 9.1 shows that in December
1970 54% of the sterling CDs and 22% of the dollar CDs were held
by secondary banks other than the bank of issue. They have partly
supplanted inter-bank deposits as the instrument for filling gaps in the
maturity structure of assets. For this purpose they have one advantage
over inter-bank deposits: being marketable they can be sold at any
time, thus allowing the bank to change its maturity structure quickly
without waiting for fixed-term inter-bank deposits to run off.

E. *Interest rates and margins*

In the markets for wholesale deposits secondary banks compete fiercely,
and there are no agreements on rates to prevent a true market rate
for deposits from emerging. For deposits in non-sterling currencies the
market is international, and the secondary banks in London are compet-

ing with banks throughout the world. We shall be looking at the international money (euro-dollar) market in Chapter 11, and we do not need to go into the rate structure here. For sterling deposits secondary banks form part of the parallel money markets, on which rates for inter-bank, local authority and finance house deposits are determined. The minimum level for rates is determined by the 2% below Bank rate for seven-day money, which was the only kind of interest-bearing deposit offered by the deposit banks before September 1971. The secondary banks competed by offering whatever rate above this level was necessary to attract deposits and by offering a wide choice of maturities. The rates for deposits in this market fluctuated freely and frequently, although probably not so much as inter-bank sterling deposits. The rates depend on maturity, and rarely go above Bank rate.

We have little firm information on the rates which secondary banks charge for advances, but there are many reasons for thinking that they operate with much narrower margins than apply in deposit banking as a whole. (1) They do not incur the costs of operating the payments mechanism through an extensive branch network. (2) They concentrate on the larger deposits and loans and thus avoid the costs of operating a large number of small accounts. (3) Their customers are large companies with first-class names. (This statement does not sound so impressive as it would have done before the recent troubles experienced by Rolls Royce and several other large organisations with first-class names.) (4) Their business is highly competitive. (5) They can satisfy their need for short-term assets without much sacrifice of income because they concentrate on the higher-yielding assets offered by the parallel money markets.

Secondary banks are thus in the position of having to add a much smaller margin on to a higher cost of deposits than for deposit banks. The resultant interest rate on advances is probably not much out of line with the rates charged by deposit banks; secondary banks are unlikely often to undercut deposit banks, but the general level of their rates is not much higher.

In their replies to a questionnaire from the Monopolies Commission the American banks in London reported rates covering the same range as those of the London clearing banks.[2] Because few of the large corporate customers would have to pay the most expensive rate of the clearing banks, it seems likely that secondary bank loans are slightly dearer than clearing bank overdrafts on average.

2. Monopolies Commission, *Barclays Bank Ltd., Lloyds Bank Ltd. and Martins Bank Ltd.: a Report on the Proposed Merger* (1968) Appendix 9.

F. *The new controls and the future*

The essence of the new arrangements for the control of banks which we described in detail in Chapter 6 is that they should apply to all banks and (with slight modifications) finance houses. Secondary banks will thus have to hold reserve assets amounting to a minimum of $12\frac{1}{2}\%$ of their eligible liabilities, comprising total sterling deposits with an original maturity of two years or under and sterling CDs issued, offset by inter-bank deposits placed and CDs held. On the first two reporting days, 15 September and 20 October 1971, accepting houses and overseas banks had reserve ratios well in excess of $12\frac{1}{2}\%$, but the other secondary banks were $10\cdot8\%$ on the first date and $9\cdot9\%$ on the second. Individual banks were given some grace, not extending beyond the end of 1971, to build up their reserve asset holdings.[3]

Although one may hold that the whole concept of reserve assets, consisting exclusively of short-term, relatively 'liquid' assets, has no application to secondary banking based on the matching of maturities, it is clear that the new arrangements are not a great sacrifice to secondary banks. When we looked at their use of the discount market and the parallel money market in relation to conventional liquidity, we showed the proportions which these short-term assets bore to total deposits. The reserve asset ratios are bound to be much higher than our earlier figure for discount market assets as a proportion of total deposits because eligible liabilities consist only of *sterling* deposits and CDs and because these are offset by inter-bank deposits and CDs on the assets side of the balance sheet. It seems that in aggregate the secondary banks have voluntarily held more than $12\frac{1}{2}\%$ of reserve assets: the figure at December 1970 was at least $13\cdot9\%$ and probably somewhat higher. The difficulty is, however, that the use of the discount market was not spread evenly among all banks. It was those banks doing accepting business which discounted bills and which were under some pressure from the discount houses to provide them with money at call. For the other banks there is some sacrifice in the new arrangements—that represented by the lower yield on the excess of reserve assets over what they would have had voluntarily; this will slightly widen their margins.

Secondary banking in sterling grew over the past decade because the deposit banks were unwilling to alter the structure of their business to meet the demand that had arisen for term loans and term

3. 'Reserve ratios: further definitions', *Bank of England Quarterly Bulletin* (December 1971) p. 486.

deposits, and the secondary banks (including deposit bank subsidiaries) were able to 'cream off' the profitable large unit, low cost business. Since September 1971 the deposit banks have begun to compete for wholesale term deposits and to make term loans under their own names, but it is difficult to see that this will make a great deal of difference to the field of secondary banking because the deposit banks have used their subsidiaries for wholesale banking since 1965. The business of term loans based on term deposits and CDs will go on much as it has before. The main change is that it will be less true in the future to talk of two banking systems operating side by side. Deposit banks are not likely to face strong rivalry in the operation of the payments mechanism, but wholesale banking will now be operated by both deposit banks and secondary banks. An important aspect of the new arrangements was the breaking down of the barriers between the two banking systems.

2. U.K. SECONDARY BANKS

A. *Accepting houses*

The definition of an accepting house is simplicity itself: an accepting house is a member of the Accepting Houses Committee. Membership of this Committee is open to banks which have the following three qualifications: (1) that a substantial part of their business consists of accepting bills to finance the trade of others; (2) that bills accepted by them can be sold at the finest rates in the discount market; (3) that their acceptances are freely taken by the Bank of England from the discount market.

Accepting houses operate in three main fields: (1) commercial banking, (2) international banking and (3) investment banking. These fields are not mutually exclusive, because a part of both commercial and investment banking is international. We have already dealt sufficiently with the commercial banking business in the last main section, and we can go on to deal with the functions of accepting houses in the other two fields.

The difference between an accepting house and a deposit bank can be summarised readily: whereas a deposit bank lives on its deposits and branches, an accepting house lives on its name and wits. The characteristic function of an accepting house is to use its name to mobilise funds of other institutions for the benefit of its customers. Its traditional business of accepting bills of exchange linked with particular

consignments of commodities is an 'off-the-peg' solution to a recurring problem, but in its newer functions the accepting house has become more and more concerned with producing 'tailor-made' solutions
for a much wider range of problems, using expertise in a number of
different techniques and a long list of contacts in the City. Thus a
high proportion of an accepting house's income is received in the
form of fees for specialist services. As the secondary banking system
has developed over recent years, accepting houses are more able to use
their own resources and to rely correspondingly less on the mobilisation
of other people's funds. The accepting houses remain small organisations, and they concentrate on business involving large sums and the
use of expertise, leaving the small transactions and the routine clerical
work that they bring with them to the deposit banks.

The traditional business of the accepting houses is the acceptance of
bills of exchange. Many of the prominent houses began as commodity
merchants, using bills of exchange in their own transactions. They soon
found that 'lending their names' to less well-known merchants was a
lucrative sideline; after a time it developed into their main business.
The traditional accepting business is tied to a particular consignment of
goods, and the bills of exchange are backed by shipping or insurance
documents; for this reason the credits provided are known as 'docu-
mentary credits'. A credit arises when an accepting house 'accepts' a
bill of exchange drawn on it by endorsing its name on the bill; since it
bears a first-class name, this bill can then be discounted in the discount
market at the finest rate, and the accepting house normally arranges
to do this for its customer. If the customer is a buyer of commodities,
he is able to pay his supplier immediately; if he is a seller, he receives
payment immediately instead of having to wait for anything from 90
to 180 days until the purchaser settles the transaction according to the
normal custom of the trade. Such acceptance credits are used to finance
both foreign and domestic trade, and they are also used to provide funds
for finance houses. As the acceptor of the bill, the accepting house is
liable to pay the full value of the bill on maturity, but under the terms
of the credit the customer undertakes to put the accepting house in
funds before the due date. Unless the drawer defaults, or unless it also
discounts the bill, the accepting house uses none of its own resources;
it merely facilitates the raising of funds from other sources by providing what amounts to a guarantee of payment.

Business such as this, tied to individual consignments of goods, remains the bread and butter of acceptance business, but accepting
houses are tending to concentrate on the business for relatively large

sums, revolving credits to cover a whole series of shipments or a seasonal movement of goods. Often these credit lines run into several millions of pounds, and when they do one accepting house will organise a syndicate of other accepting houses and banks to parcel out the credit line between them.

The value of acceptances made by accepting houses rose just under three times from 1960 to 1970, and a lot of this increase is accounted for by a new type of business. This is the granting of 'clean' (unsupported by documents), unsecured facilities for first-class British industrial and commercial companies. These facilities are very large, often as much as £20–30 million, and they are syndicated among a group of accepting houses and overseas banks, with one accepting house as leader of the syndicate. The credit revolves, so that at the end of the quarter the company has to settle only the amount of discount to pay off the previous quarter's bills.

The traditional acceptance credit facilities remain an important part of international banking and contribute to the export drive, but in post-war years a large part of our exports has taken the form of capital goods, and for such exports the less-developed countries have demanded longer and longer credit terms. The accepting houses have been active in arranging these credits for periods far beyond the term of normal acceptance facilities. With this kind of credit the accepting houses have again been mobilising the funds of others, in this case mainly deposit banks, and the guarantee of the government Export Credits Guarantee Department (E.C.G.D.) has been essential.

At first sight there would not seem to be much scope for an accepting house to organise the provision of finance by deposit banks, but these banks probably prefer to have a bank outside their own number conducting negotiations between them. In most of these large-scale capital projects several British firms are involved, as main and subcontractors, and each deposit bank contributes towards the finance needed according to the participation in the contract of its own customers.

There are indications that the scale and extent of this long-term credit business will continue to grow. It is already extending beyond the provision of finance for specific capital projects to 'shopping-list' finance, whereby a development bank or similar institution is given credit to finance the import of any capital goods. Accepting houses, along with overseas banks, are also active in business that arises out of long-term export credit. The E.C.G.D. guarantee covers only 80% of the total cost of the contract, whereas the foreign buyer often wants to obtain credit, not only for the remaining 20%, but also for various local costs incurred with the project.

Long-term export credits of this sort are used by countries which are not able to raise funds on the international bond market by the issue of the so-called euro-bonds—mainly the less-developed countries. The London accepting houses were the first to organise euro-bond issues, although their early dominance is being strongly challenged by American banks; as so often happens with financial innovations, the big boys 'muscle in' when the market is established.[4] This activity of the accepting houses lies in the area of overlap between international banking and investment banking, but it is in the historical tradition of their investment banking activity: until the1930s nearly all the new issue activity of merchant banks was in the field of foreign bonds, and it was not until the depression that they moved over to domestic issues.

Their first ventures in the raising of capital on the market for industrial companies were for debenture issues, but since the last war they have been concerned also with the raising of ordinary share capital. All the members of the Accepting Houses Committee are members of the Issuing Houses Association, along with many other merchant banks and specialist issuing houses without banking business. Merchant banks are obviously well placed to conduct new issue business because their contacts in the City enable them to organise underwriting syndicates.

Since the organisation of the raising of new capital for companies or arranging the quotation of shares in previously private companies involved a thorough appraisal by the merchant banks of a company's finances, it was a short step for them to be involved in the giving of general financial advice to companies. The best publicised part of this activity is their conduct of negotiations between companies when mergers or take-overs are involved, although only a small proportion of mergers between industrial companies hits the headlines. But the service of giving financial advice to companies is not limited to such situations. More and more companies retain merchant banks for advice on all aspects of their financial affairs.

Under the heading of investment banking we can also consider several other important functions of merchant banks. Their new issue activity often involves them in taking a stake in a small but promising company with a view to grooming it for eventual quotation on the stock exchange. To a growing extent recently they have become in-

4. For a description of the euro-bond market see Chapter 3.

volved in the management of portfolios of securities for clients, and pension funds and the larger charities have been the growing field of activity. They have long managed investment trusts, but more recently they have added the management of unit trusts to their activities. Like deposit banks they have begun to take stakes in companies specialising in factoring, leasing and similar relatively new fields of financial activity. Some of them retain their original interests in a particular sphere of commodity trade, and two of them are concerned in the bullion trade.

B. *Subsidiaries of deposit banks*

In 1964 and 1965, when the secondary banking system had assumed its present shape, the deposit banks began to form subsidiaries to operate in secondary banking. In origins these subsidiaries were of three distinct types. (1) Several of the London clearing banks already had subsidiaries with branches in France and Belgium originally intended to cater for the needs of British residents and tourists, and the new business was grafted on to these banks. (2) Some deposit banks had small deposit banks as subsidiaries, and in at least two cases these were turned towards secondary banking. (3) The remainder were specially formed for the purpose, often in association with overseas banks or with accepting houses.

There are several possible ways of operating subsidiaries to compete in secondary banking, and the banks still display some diversity in their methods of conducting business. In the early days some of them were seen just as ways of attracting extra deposits for the benefit of the parent bank. This particular phase was short-lived, and one of the main attractions of these subsidiaries soon became the possibility of holding against the more expensive deposits assets which have an average earning power considerably above that of deposit bank assets; this possibility is open only if the subsidiaries operate as independent banks.

These subsidiary banks differed from all other banks operating in the secondary banking system in one respect: they had no other kinds of business which they had traditionally carried on, and they were able to become pure secondary banks. They were extremely successful in this. As Table 5.1 shows, by 1970 they had become the second largest group of secondary banks; their total deposits surpassed those of the accepting houses, and were exceeded only by those of the American banks.

Table 9·5 sets out the aggregate balance sheet structure of eight of these subsidiary banks, accounting in total for about 47% of the deposits of all subsidiaries. Even though this is not the complete picture, one important fact sticks out. The subsidiary banks were mostly founded just at the time when credit controls in the form of quantitative limits on bank lending in sterling were imposed on all banks, and these limits, adjusted from time to time, remained in force until 1971.

Table 9.5   Balance sheet structure of subsidiaries of deposit banks, 1970

Percentages

Liabilities	
Capital and reserves	2.9
Deposits	92.9
Intra-group accounts	2.8
Other liabilities	1.3
Total	100.0

Assets	
Cash and money at call and short notice	23.4
Deposits with local authorities and banks	35.3
Bills discounted and certificates of deposit	2.5
Investments	1.2
Loans	29.6
Intra-group accounts	6.6
Other assets	1.4
Total	100.0

Source: Published accounts for dates between September 1970 and January 1971 of 8 banks with total deposits of £1,650 million.

The subsidiaries could attract deposits readily enough, but they were not permitted to employ them in profitable sterling lending. Instead a large part was placed in the parallel money markets. In this balance sheet loans represented only 32% of deposits and money market assets 66% of deposits.

At the moment a big question mark hangs over the future of these subsidiaries of the deposit banks. Two of the deposit banks have rationalised the business of their subsidiaries by combining the overseas business of the subsidiary with that of a British overseas bank under their control and by forming a separate subsidiary for domestic business. The Prices and Incomes Board was vehement in its denunciation of the practice of deposit banks operating through subsidiaries, although it failed to make clear what this had to do with its general advocacy of more competition between deposit banks. From the point of view of public information there is a good deal to be said for keeping different kinds of business in different balance sheets. Now that the deposit banks have begun to conduct wholesale banking in their own right, the future of these subsidiary banks is not clear. They may well be allowed to wither away.

3. BRITISH OVERSEAS BANKS

British overseas banks are those British-owned banks which carry on deposit banking business overseas. As we have seen, several of them are wholly or partly owned by British deposit banks, and in recent years American banks have acquired substantial stakes in some of them. In their overseas operations they are joined by a group of banks owned by Commonwealth countries. The areas in which they operate their deposit banking business are (1) the former British colonial empire, (2) other countries of the Middle and Far East, (3) Latin America and (4) Australasia. At one time it was sensible to consider as separate groups those banks whose main interests were in the sterling area and those whose main interests were elsewhere; this distinction is nowhere near so important under present conditions.

To begin with we must consider the traditional business of British overseas banks as it was operated in countries of the sterling area. The banks normally had a surplus of local deposits beyond what could profitably be employed in the colonies. This surplus was employed in London. Similarly expatriate British and the wealthier sections of the native population sent their savings to London, and the overseas banks were their agents. Most of the colonial territories were primary producers, so that a large part of the advances went to finance crops, either to British plantation companies or to native producers. Because of the different seasonal needs for crop finance in different territories, the bank was able to switch funds from one territory to another to meet the seasonal demands. In this it was acting in the same way as a head office in a domestic branch banking network, which switches funds from one region to another according to need. It was able to act in this way without risk because the colonies formed part of one unified monetary system, so that there were no hindrances on transfer and no exchange risk. In addition the overseas bank has always been concerned to finance trade between Britain and the countries in which it operates. This is necessarily an over-simplified picture, but it approximates to the traditional pattern of overseas banking.[5]

This traditional pattern never applied to the full extent outside the colonies and dominions because the exchange risk precluded large scale switches of funds from one country to another, but it has been disrupted even within the sterling area by recent events. The former colonies have mostly obtained political independence, and they are in the first stages of industrialisation. In certain of the countries the business of the British overseas banks has been nationalised; in others the state has taken a controlling interest or enforced local incorporation so that local inhabitants could participate in ownership.

Other changes affecting the operation of British overseas banks have taken place. (1) Central banks have been formed in most of the newly independent countries. Overseas banks have been forced to make deposits with the central banks, and they have lost the government balances which they formerly held. (2) The new central banks have demanded the local employment of funds in loans to the government and in instruments of newly established local money markets. (3) Exchange controls have kept the transfers to London down to agreed amounts. (4) As the failure of many sterling area countries to follow the British devaluation of 1967 showed, an exchange risk must be assumed even for currencies of other sterling area countries. In these circumstances each country must be treated almost as a watertight compartment.

Despite these handicaps the British overseas banks have shown remarkable powers of adaptation, and the deposits of their overseas offices have continued to grow from about £1730 million in 1957 to around £3200 million in 1966, an 85% increase over the decade. On imperfect figures, it seems, however, that the deposits of their London offices grew from about 16% of total deposits in 1957 to 24% in 1966, and the advances of London offices grew from about 9% of total advances to 19% over the same period.

As these figures show, British overseas banks have adapted them-

---

5. By the time of the Radcliffe Committee overseas banking was in a state of transition, but the memorandum of the British Overseas Banks Association (Committee on the Working of the Monetary System, *Memoranda of Evidence*, II, 64–9) and the oral examination of its representatives (*Minutes of Evidence*, QQ. 4327–4759) are useful sources of information as long as the recent changes described below are borne in mind. See also F. Seebohm 'The role of the British overseas banks', *Journal of the Institute of Bankers* (June 1967) pp. 162–73.

selves by increasing the importance of their international banking business conducted in London. They were among the pioneers in the euro-dollar market. They have been spurred on to this by the fact that the surplus of funds in the territories in which they operate has given way to a deficit—an increased demand for loans for development, partly from local enterprises and partly from British companies making direct investments. International banking represents the scouring of the entire world for funds in dollars and other currencies for employment in development, a complete reversal of their former role.

They have also moved in other directions. Because the trade of the developing countries is no longer tied largely to the metropolitan country, the banks have opened offices in Hamburg, Frankfurt, Zürich and New York. One has moved into branch banking in California, and others have taken over controlling interests in accepting houses. Many of them compete with accepting houses in the organisation of syndicates for export credits.

Table 9.6 shows the aggregate balance sheet of the British overseas banks, with separate figures for U.K. offices and overseas offices. Because

Table 9.6   Balance sheet of British overseas banks, December 1966

£ million

	U.K. offices	Overseas offices	Total
Liabilities			
Deposits: U.K. residents	509 ⎫	3,210	4,200
Overseas residents	481 ⎭		
Notes issued	–	12	12
Capital and reserves	–	–	108
Loan capital	–	–	15
Assets			
Cash & balances with banks	316	268	584
Money at call & short notice	36	–	36
Treasury bills	21	291	312
Other bills	26	202	228
Loans to U.K. local authorities	90	–	90
Investments *(BV)*	352	354	706
Advances	371	1,611	1,982

Source: (1) Bank of England with the authority of the British Overseas and Commonwealth Banks Association;   (2) published accounts.

the estimation of these separate balance sheets is a complicated exercise, the latest date for which we give the estimates is December 1966. They should be taken as an indication of orders of magnitude and not as completely accurate figures. The overall balance sheet is recognisably that of a deposit bank: the liquidity ratio is just under 30%, and advances represent 47% of total deposits. Despite the changes in operation which we have noted, the function of the head office as holder of a large part of total liquidity still persists and is apparent in the above average percentages of liquid assets and investments for the U.K. offices. One interesting feature is the presence of loan capital.

4. CONSORTIUM BANKS

As their name implies, consortium banks are groupings of other banks. Most of these groupings are international (hence the name of 'multinational banks' or 'multi-banks' sometimes given to them), but recently several consortia have been formed with participation from banks of a single country. They are the newest type of bank with which we have to deal. The first was formed in 1964, but the rapid expansion of their numbers did not come until 1969 and 1970. The first consortium bank was Midland & International Banks Ltd. (referred to generally as 'MAIBL'); Midland Bank owns 45% of the shares, and other partners are a British overseas bank, a Canadian bank and an Australian bank. Because London is the centre of the euro-dollar market, it is a favoured location for consortia, but others are established in Brussels, Zürich, Milan, Paris and Luxembourg. Australia is the location for many recent consortia, but several of these represent a means for foreign participation in Australian banking in face of the prohibition on the establishment of new foreign bank branches.

The participants in these consortia are the well-known deposit and investment banks of the world. Among British participants, accepting houses are almost as common as deposit banks. One consortium, Atlantic International Bank, contains an accepting house, banks from Italy, France and the Netherlands and four smallish American banks. There are some non-banking participants, notably the Crown Agents for Oversea Governments and Administrations, which is a member of several consortia.[6]

6. See M. von Clemm, 'The rise of consortium banking', *Harvard Business Review* (May–June 1971) for a list of consortia and an excellent description of their operations.

Many of the consortia owe their origins to the growth of a market for medium-term lending to multinational companies. We have already looked at some of the attractions of term loans, but a special feature of the last few years increasing the demand for medium-term loans has been the high level of both long-term and short-term interest rates. Over time many consortia have developed activities outside medium-term lending; they have been responsible for several innovations, which have subsequently become commonplace in international banking.

Consortium banks have two features of especial interest. The first is that many of them have loan capital as well as share capital. The second is the extent to which they syndicate their loans, showing that the borrowing needs of large international corporations and public bodies are often beyond the means of even consortia of large banks. The syndicates for these loans are drawn together in several different ways, but there are two basic approaches: (1) to restrict the syndicate to banks which already act for the borrower and (2) to seek participa-

Table 9.7   Balance sheet structure of consortium banks, 1970

Percentages

Liabilities		
Capital and reserves		2.5
Subordinated loans		1.6
Deposits		93.8
Other liabilities		2.0
	Total	100.0
Assets		
Loans to customers and deposits with local authorities and banks		
Up to 7 days		23.8
8 days to 1 year		36.7
Over 1 year		35.8
Other accounts		1.7
Investments		.4
Other assets		1.6
	Total	100.0
Acceptances		.4

Source: Published accounts for dates between March 1970 and March 1971.

tion from outside banks. In at least one case a consortium bank broadcasts over the telex requests for participation in loans which it makes in the first place out of its own resources. The participation certificates which are issued for the loan are usually bearer documents, and are negotiable. They are not quoted on any stock exchange, but the issuing bank often stands ready to buy certificates back or to use its good offices to secure replacements for lenders who wish to withdraw. The participation certificates thus have many of the features of euro-bond isues, including floating interest rates for many issues and the occasional addition of rights to convert into equity or to subscribe for equity on a future date at a stated price (convertibles and warrants).

By December 1970 there were ten consortium banks in London, and during their short period of existence they had secured £1296 million of deposits, most of it in non-sterling currencies. A few months later the number of consortium banks had risen to fifteen. The aggregate balance sheet structure of the consortium banks is shown in Table 9.7. Because it is drawn from published accounts, which use different classifications for assets, it is not possible to differentiate between loans to customers, deposits with other banks and deposits with local authorities, or to separate sterling from other currencies, but it is possible to set out the maturity of the assets.

5. FOREIGN BANKS

A. *American banks*

We saw in Table 5.1 that at December 1970 there were thirty-two American banks with branches in the U.K., and that their total deposits were some 10% higher than the total deposits of the London clearing banks. By far the greater part of these deposits was in currencies other than sterling; the total of deposits in other currencies was, by a coincidence, just £1 million short of the London clearing bank deposit total at £10,605. The sterling deposits amounted to only just over 9% of London clearing bank deposits.

The influx of American banks has been one of the major events of the past decade. Up to 1959 banks in the United States had very few international operations, but from then on they began an aggressive expansion of overseas branches, sparked off, it is said, by Japanese industrialists who travelled throughout the United States seeking funds for capital investment. In 1959 there were only seven U.S. banks with branches abroad, and their overseas branch network amounted to 132;

the same seven banks were the only U.S. banks with offices in London. By the middle of 1966 the number of banks with branches abroad had doubled to fourteen, and they had 227 branches between them; by the end of 1970 the numbers had risen to 536 branches. Some of the effort went into building up deposit banking in Latin America, and there were branches in the Far East and Continental Europe. The branches which were established in London occupied a special position, however, because London was the undisputed centre of the euro-dollar market. In 1970 the U.K. branches accounted for 61% of the deposits of all overseas branches of U.S. banks. They became by far the biggest operators in the London euro-dollar market, having by 1970 just over 50% of all liabilities in non-sterling currencies of banks in the United Kingdom. The driving force in their aggressive exploitation of the euro-dollar market was the need to seek euro-dollar balances for lending to head office because of the tight monetary conditions in the U.S.A. in 1966 and 1969; we shall be charting this phenomenon when we look at the international money market in Chapter 11.

The aggregate balance sheet of American banks at December 1970 is shown in Table 9.8, derived from the normal Bank of England statistics. There are several other sources of figures for American banks, and in principle one could derive a most elaborate balance sheet in terms of currency, maturity, sources of deposits and types of borrower; unfortunately the various sources are not always for the same date, and they disagree slightly in their totals. We shall use them as rough indicators of percentages.[7]

Table 9.2 has already shown us that in February 1971 American banks in Britain derived 57% of their total non-sterling deposits from banks abroad. At an earlier date, December 1966, we know that current accounts were 19% of all sterling deposits, and we can deduce that 13–15% of the non-sterling deposits were current accounts. Of the sterling deposits 51% in 1964 and 39% in 1967 came from the subsidiaries of U.S. companies operating in Britain; at the latter date 48% of sterling deposits came from British-owned companies and 5% from private individuals.

On the assets side Table 9.2 showed the importance of banks abroad,

7. The sources are (1) 'The euro-currency business of banks in London: maturity analysis as at end-February 1971', *Bank of England Quarterly Bulletin* (June 1971) pp. 218–23 (and earlier references); (2) U.S. Government, *Treasury Bulletin* (e.g. November 1970, pp. 132–7); (3) *Federal Reserve Bulletin* (e.g. September 1971, p. 757); (4) Monopolies Commission, *Barclays Bank Ltd., Lloyds Bank Ltd., and Martins Bank Ltd.: a Report on the Proposed Merger*, Appendix 9.

Table 9.8   Balance sheet of American banks, December 1970

£ million

	Sterling	Other currencies	Total
Liabilities			
Current & deposit accounts			
·U.K. banks	281	2,474	2,755
Other U.K. residents	468	226	694
Overseas residents	214	7,905	8,119
Total	963	10,605	11,567
Assets			
Coin, notes & balances with Bank of England	1	–	1
Balances with other U.K. banks	244	2,411	2,655
Money at call and short notice	61	–	61
Sterling bills discounted			
British government treasury bills	2	–	2
Other	18	–	18
Loans to U.K. local authorities	169	–	169
British government stocks	3	–	3
Advances			
U.K. residents	369	285	654
Overseas residents	11	7,888	7,899
Other assets	79	38	117
Total	957	10,622	11,579
Acceptances			
U.K. residents	...	...	74
Overseas residents	...	...	51

Source: *Bank of England Quarterly Bulletin*, December 1971, Table 10(4).

Notes: (1) Balances with head office and other banks overseas are
included under advances.   (2) Negotiable certificates of
deposit issued: sterling under deposits of other U.K. residents
and dollar under overseas residents. Sterling CDs held are
under 'other assets'

and a large part of these claims is on the head office in the U.S.A. The
total amount of deposits on-lent to the head office has varied considerably according to the tightness or ease of monetary conditions in
the U.S.A. The peak was reached in July 1969 when dollar balances
with U.S. offices of the parent bank reached 47% of total assets; at the
same date balances with other branches of the parent bank outside the

U.S.A. accounted for 7% of total assets. From July 1970 there was a considerable decrease in the borrowing by U.S. banks from their over-seas branches, the total falling from $10,500 million to $6700 million in February 1971. The deposits of American banks in Britain continued to grow during this period, and there was a switch towards lending to overseas residents other than banks, banks abroad and other U.K. banks. Of their sterling advances the subsidiaries of U.S. companies took 84% in 1966 and 78% in 1967, the drop probably being accounted for by the easing of monetary conditions in the U.S.A.

We have seen the dominance of the American banks in the euro-dollar market, but we are also concerned with the competition which American banks are offering and can offer in domestic banking in Britain. The main reason for the questionnaire which the Monopolies Commission sent to the American banks was the fact that Barclays, Lloyds and Martins had given competition from American banks as one of the forces leading to the proposed merger. At that time (1967) it certainly seemed that American banks were more concerned to offer service to the subsidiaries in the U.K. of the U.S. corporate customers than to compete generally with British banks. Over recent years some of the banks have begun to open branches outside London, but there is certainly no intention of creating nationwide networks to compete in the bread and butter of deposit banking. American banks can still compete quite effectively outside this particular part of banking.

Very many large British companies are already customers of U.S. banks for their operations in the U.S.A., and whenever companies are customers of two or more banks there is a probability of competition between these banks at the margin. In this case the margin will be largely in the international sphere, and British companies could come to make more use of American banks outside both Britain and the U.S.A. Even within Britain there are many forms of profitable banking business which American banks can cream off. In one particular field some American banks (but not all) already undercut British banks. Al-though there is no specific agreement, all deposit banks and accepting houses charge a standard 1% commission for their customers on acceptances ($1\frac{1}{4}$% for finance house acceptances), and some American banks now offer the same service at $\frac{5}{8}$% or even $\frac{1}{2}$%. In the realm of 'fringe' services some American banks are offering portfolio and pension fund management. One bank made tentative steps towards attracting savings account business from individuals. Such competitive forays into profitable services offered by deposit banks and accepting houses will undoubtedly continue, but there is no indication as yet that

American banks will use the massive resources of their parent banks to enter the mainstream of deposit banking in this country.

B. *Other foreign banks*

The number of foreign banks has increased rapidly over the past decade. Including the American banks the total number of foreign banks included in the Bank of England statistics was 87 in 1966 and 120 in 1970, an increase of 38%. The great attraction has been, as for the American banks, the fact that London is the centre of the euro-dollar market, but an important factor is the attitude of the British authorities towards foreign banks. Britain, unlike many countries throughout the world, has made no attempt to protect its domestic banks from foreign competition. It is only in recent years, for example, that the United States has eased the limitation on foreign banks because of its desire for reciprocity of treatment for American banks abroad. In Britain foreign banks are free to operate, subject only to the sketchy requirements of English banking law and to 'requests' from the Governor of the Bank of England. In several cases the foreign banks have incorporated subsidiary companies under British law, but this makes no operational difference.

We have already mentioned the important group of banks from Commonwealth countries, and of these the Canadian banks deserve special attention. Canada is a Commonwealth country, but she is not in the sterling area; this places Canadian banks in rather a special position. They look to New York as their main money market centre, and American banks complain that their operations there have been all too successful in attracting U.S. dollars into Canada. Three of the Canadian banks, however, have branch networks within the sterling area in the Caribbean, and these branches look to London as their money market centre in order to avoid exchange risk. For these three banks as much as 60% of their London deposits is held to the account of these Caribbean branches. The volume of these deposits has gone up over recent years as both British and American citizens have sought to avoid the stringencies of their own tax systems by setting up trust funds in Bermuda and the Bahamas.

FURTHER READING

J. Revell, *Changes in British Banking: The Growth of a Secondary Banking System*, Hill, Samuel Occasional Paper No. 3 (1968) (summarised in J. Revell, 'The growth of a secondary banking system', *The Banker* [September 1968]).

The following articles from the *Bank of England Quarterly Bulletin:*
'Overseas and foreign banks in London' (June 1968).
'Control of bank lending: the Cash Deposits scheme' (June 1968).
'The U.K. banking sector 1952–67' (June 1969).

10 Parallel Money Markets

We have already charted the relationship between the deposit banks and the discount market, which until about 1955 was the only money market in London. In this chapter we are going to look at the various parallel money markets which grew up alongside the secondary banking system, and contributed so much to the growth of that separate banking system. We shall look at the markets in euro-dollars and other euro-currencies alongside the markets in sterling because the methods of operation are very similar in both sterling and currencies and because the development of the euro-dollar market was to some extent the engine which caused the growth of the secondary banking system. Our concern here will be only with the London markets for deposits and other claims denominated in non-sterling currencies; we shall go on to deal with the international aspects of the euro-dollar market in Chapter 11.

1. GROWTH AND WORKING OF THE MAIN MARKETS

A. *History*

Over the short space of seventeen years the parallel money markets have outstripped the discount market in size. During this period there were certain significant stages in development, to each of which we can assign a rough date.

1955   Local authorities no longer allowed to borrow at will from Public Works Loans Board
1957   Use of sterling acceptance credits for financing trade between non-sterling countries banned
       Beginning of euro-dollar market

1962   Beginning of inter-bank deposits in euro-dollars
1964   Beginning of inter-bank deposits in sterling
1966   Introduction of dollar certificates of deposit
1968   Introduction of sterling certificates of deposit
1969   Beginning of market in inter-company loans

The first two events and the introduction of both dollar and sterling certificates of deposit can be dated precisely, but the other dates are largely a matter of opinion because it is in the nature of things that new developments are not noted by observers outside the market until they have become significant.

Because local authority treasurers regarded interest rates as historically high in 1955, when they were forced to obtain most of their capital requirements from the market instead of from the Public Works Loans Board, they began to raise a large and growing part of their requirements in short-term deposits, sometimes called temporary money. Before long some secondary banks began to pay market rates for deposits in order to lend them to local authorities, so that the same event can be said to have initiated the development of both parallel money markets and the secondary banking system. The accepting of deposits denominated, not in sterling, but in other currencies was not a new departure for secondary banks. It took place during the thirties, and the most persistent story of its revival after the war attributes it to the desire of the Soviet Union and East European countries to safeguard their dollar holdings against expropriation by the U.S. authorities by transferring the deposits to banks in Europe. It was the banning in 1957 of the use of sterling acceptance credits for financing trade between pairs of non-sterling countries which led secondary banks actively to seek non-sterling deposits as an alternative method of financing this trade. These were the events which started the growth of these new money markets; we shall see the significance of the other events listed as we proceed.

B. *Working*

In our analysis of the working of the discount market we saw that its main features were that all loans were secured, that the authorities intervened actively to smooth flows and to control short-term interest rates, that the Bank of England acted unquestioningly as lender of last resort to the discount houses and that a proportion of the dealings was conducted verbally on the 'morning parade'. The characteristics of the parallel money markets are the exact opposite in all respects: (1) all loans are unsecured; (2) there is no direct intervention by the authorities; (3) there is no lender of last resort; (4) all deals are conducted by telephone.

The main claims dealt in on the parallel money markets are those listed in Table 10.1. In addition there are several less important markets

Table 10.1   Totals outstanding of parallel money market claims, December 1970 and 1971

£ million

	1970	1971
Local authority deposits	1,820	1,743
Finance house deposits	688	823
Inter-bank deposits		
Sterling	1,694	2,200
Other currencies	5,357	5,996
Certificates of deposit		
Sterling	1,089	2,242
Dollar	1,649	1,924
Total	12,297	14,928

Sources: (1) *Bank of England Quarterly Bulletin*, June 1971, Table 10(1) and March 1972, Table 8(1);
(2) *Financial Statistics*, May 1972, Tables 31 & 67.

for other claims. (1) The local authority deposits shown in Table 10.1 are all for periods of up to 364 days, but several types of local authority security are traded on the market (negotiable bonds, bills and mortgages for large amounts). (2) The inter-bank deposits shown are strictly those in which banks figure both as taker and giver, but the market deals also in secondary bank deposits placed by outsiders through the agency of deposit brokers.[1] (3) A market in inter-company loans has developed during the last few years, and this has grown into a market on which companies seek bank loans through a deposit

1. In an excellent book on the parallel money markets (*Parallel Money Markets, Volume One: The New Markets in London*) from which some of the facts in this chapter were taken, Dr P. Einzig includes deposits placed by non-bank customers through brokers as part of the inter-bank markets in both sterling and other currencies. This difference of terminology accounts for several apparent contradictions in estimates of the size of the inter-bank markets and on other points between Dr Einzig and the present chapter.

broker as well as seeking to place deposits. (4) In the euro-dollar markets bills denominated in euro-currencies and euro-dollar commercial paper are traded in a small way. We shall look at all these specialised markets in due course, but here we shall concentrate on the six main markets listed in Table 10.1.

The totals outstanding give some impression of the vast size of the parallel money markets. By way of comparison we can point to the totals of borrowed funds of discount houses—£2259 million at the end of December 1970 and £3066 million in 1971. Totals outstanding are, of course, an imperfect measure of the size of a market, and we shall look at the other measure, that of daily turnover, shortly.

Table 10.2 shows what is known of the maturity structure of the various types of claim. Among the deposits those of local authorities have the shortest average maturity, followed by inter-bank non-sterling and finance house deposits.

Table 10.2   Maturity analysis of certain parallel money market claims

Cumulative percentages

	Date	Up to				
		7 days	1 month	3 months	1 year	1 year & over
Local authority deposits	*Dec. 1970*	69.3	...	81.5	100.0	–
Finance house deposits	*1968*	...	28.2	56.7	98.3	100.0
Inter-bank deposits non-sterling	*Oct. 1971*	17.6	37.9	68.8	96.5	100.0
Certificates of deposit – sterling	*Dec. 1971*	...	10.2	36.0	89.7	100.0

Sources: (1) *Financial Statistics*, October 1971, Table 31;
(2) Chapter 12;
(3) *Bank of England Quarterly Bulletin*, March 1972, p.60;
(4) Bank of England press release.

From a maturity structure it is in principle possible to build up a rough estimate of turnover in the various markets for deposits—but not, of course, for certificates of deposit, which can be traded many times between issue and maturity. On the assumption that inter-bank sterling has much the same maturity distribution as non-sterling inter-bank deposits the average daily turnover works out at around £1000

million for inter-bank deposits (£750 million for non-sterling and
£250 million for sterling), £550 million for local authority deposits and
£25 million for finance house deposits—a grand total of around £1600
million. An estimate produced in this way is bound, however, to be
much too high as an indication of trading volume in the market.
Direct transactions between local authorities have been excluded from
the figures for local authority deposits, but in the inter-bank markets
direct dealings between banks, avoiding the payment of brokerage,
could be as much as 25% of the total. Another reason for considerable
over-estimation of trading volume in the market lies in the fact that
very many of the short-term deposits are continually renewed, usually
because they are subject to notice which is not given for some time.
The probable effect of these two factors is at least to halve the estimates of turnover given above. Some indication of the turnover in sterling
deposits can be gleaned from the fact that the daily average value of
transactions passing through the town clearing has gone up from
about £475 million in 1958, before the parallel markets had developed,
to not far short of £3000 million in 1971.

The practices of the various markets are summarised in Table 10.3.
The units quoted must be taken as no more than indications of normal
amounts, because both the standard and minimum units are smaller
for smaller bodies; it is possible with some difficulty to place amounts
of £5000 or even less in the local authority and finance house markets.
At the other end of the scale transactions running into several millions
of pounds or dollars are by no means uncommon. For each of the
markets there are several standard maturities for which quotations are
always available, but transactions for other maturities, including those
beyond the ranges indicated, can usually be negotiated.

There are around forty-five firms of deposit brokers[2] participating in
the various markets, and the bulk of the business goes through ten
large firms, each of which has private telephone lines to its larger
clients. These large firms of brokers are active in all the parallel deposit
markets, and many of them are also foreign exchange brokers. Most
of the discount houses have subsidiary companies engaged in foreign
exchange and deposit broking, and the discount houses themselves act
as principals in the inter-bank, local authority and finance house deposit
markets and in the secondary market for certificates of deposit. Other
deposit brokers combine this business with stockbroking, and one or

2. The term 'money broker' is often used in the press, but it is best avoided
because of confusion with the specialist money brokers, whose function is to
borrow gilt-edged stock from holders and to lend it to jobbers (see p. 221).

two others specialise in all sorts of local authority securities and deposits. In most respects the routine of the market follows that of the foreign exchange market, with the important difference that the names of the parties are disclosed to each other before the deal is concluded.

Table 10.3   Practices of the parallel money markets

	Units	Maturities	Brokerage
Local authority deposits	Standard £500,000 Minimum £10,000	Overnight to 364 days	$\frac{1}{8}\%$ by borrower
Finance house deposits	Standard £500,000 Minimum £25,000	Overnight to 2 years	$\frac{1}{16}\% - \frac{1}{8}\%$ by borrower
Inter-bank deposits: Sterling	Standard £500,000 Minimum £100,000	Overnight to 5 years	$\frac{1}{32}\%$ by both parties (total $\frac{1}{16}\%$)
Euro-dollar	Standard $1 million Minimum $100,000		
Certificates of deposit: Sterling	£50,000 x £10,000 to £250,000	3 months to 5 years	Nil
Dollar	$25,000 x $1,000; no upper limit	30,60,90 & 180 days and 1&2 years	

Sources: (1)   P. Einzig, *Parallel Money Markets. Volume One*;
            (2)   author's estimates.

This last provision is necessary because all loans in the parallel money markets are unsecured, and lenders achieve some measure of protection by limiting the amounts which they deposit with each 'name'. The methods by which banks arrive at limits for other banks vary, but the limits are applied more stringently in respect of smaller banks than of the largest. They cover certificates of deposit as well as inter-bank deposits. In the local authority and finance house markets limits are also applied, and they are not always based on logic. Some depositors will not place money with small local authorities even though no local authority in the U.K. has ever defaulted, and many will lend only to finance houses in which clearing banks have an interest.

Payment for sterling deposits and CDs is made by means of a cheque drawn on a clearing bank; deals concluded up to 2 p.m. are implemented the same day, and those concluded after 2 p.m. the following day. For euro-dollar items payment is made in New York in what are known as 'clearing house funds' between the correspondent banks of the two parties. Payment is made on the third working day after the deal has been concluded. For some years there has been support for the proposal to establish a clearing house in London, which could sort out the transactions on the same day, leaving only net differences between American banks to be settled in New York. The reason for the non-adoption of this apparently obvious solution to payment delays may well lie in the benefits which American banks draw from clearing house funds.[3]

C. *Interest rates*

Although there are several sources which quote interest rates on the parallel markets, there is little point in presenting these in the form of a table or graph. Invariably the rates are shown as a range between high and low figures, the outer limits of which may represent very few deals reflecting the special circumstances of one or two borrowers. It is only if we could obtain a true average rate, representing the rates at which deals were actually concluded, weighted by their size, that the statistics would enable us to talk with confidence of differentials between different markets and maturities. Instead we shall give a brief description of the factors determining interest rates, with some indication of the differentials commonly found.

In the markets for deposits in sterling it is the inter-bank rate which is the key. Up to a few years ago it was usual to talk of Bank rate or the treasury bill rate as determining other rates, but for the past three or four years it has been the inter-bank sterling rate for an appropriate maturity which has come to represent the 'cost of money' in London. Both secondary banks and finance houses now relate their rates for loans to the inter-bank sterling rate instead of to Bank rate.

The inter-bank market is by far the most volatile of all the parallel money markets in sterling, and the overnight rate is the most volatile of all. Over the past few years overnight money on this market has ranged from a low of 1% to a high of 100% and even more, and the fluctuations during the course of the day can be quite large. The market is so volatile because the banks operating on it have nowhere else to go if rates became exorbitant. On the discount market discount houses can rely on loans at Bank rate, and on the other parallel sterling markets

3. See p. 306.

local authorities and finance houses have unused overdraft facilities with deposit banks. There is very little overspill from the inter-bank market for overnight money, and supply and demand are fully reflected in the rate.

Until recently there was a differential between the rate for unsecured overnight money on the inter-bank market and the rate for secured loans on the discount market. Because of the volatility of the inter-bank rate it was never easy to determine exactly what this was, but there was no doubt of its existence, and it was larger in the early stages of the parallel markets before the unsecured loan gained widespread acceptance. Particularly since September 1971, with the abandonment of the London clearing banks' basic rate for call money, this differential has nearly disappeared: there is almost if not quite one rate for overnight money.

There are also differentials in rates between the various parallel money markets. Secondary banks have always paid less for deposits from outside the market (from non-bank customers), and both the local authority rate and the finance house rate have usually been above the inter-bank rate. The differentials vary as each market has its own technical factors. Local authorities are subject to seasonal influences during their financial years, and finance houses, particularly when they are subject to stringent controls on their lending business, are not always keen takers of funds. The normal progression of rates for any given maturity proceeds from CDs to deposits from non-bank customers through inter-bank deposits and local authority deposits up to finance house deposits, the entire spread normally being 1 or $1\frac{1}{2}$ percentage points.

Within each market there is also a differential according to maturity. In the absence of strong expectations about the future course of interest rates the yield curve rises gently towards the longer maturities, with a normal differential between overnight and one-year money of perhaps $\frac{1}{2}\%$. Non-standard maturities and deposits for longer than one year, deals in which have to be negotiated, usually have a rather greater differential. There are times when the general expectation is of falling interest rates, and on those occasions the yield curve will dip from the short end to the long end. Although the differentials on the markets are not normally very large, they are sufficient to attract arbitrage business if they get out of line temporarily, especially as banks often undertake deals with a prospect of no more than $\frac{1}{16}\%$ profit. On the more hightly developed markets there is also some trading for future dates (known as 'forward-forward').

So far we have been speaking only of the sterling markets. On the euro-currencies side there are fewer separate markets—deposits from outside the market, inter-bank deposits and (for dollars only) CDs, with small markets for euro-acceptances and euro-commercial paper. Although a large part of total business takes place in London, the euro-currencies market is international, and it is used as a vehicle for arbitrage and speculation in foreign currencies. Many of the influences affecting the euro-currencies markets naturally spill over into domestic markets and from the market for one currency into that for another. The markets are too complex for brief analysis.

If we narrow our gaze down to the largest of the euro-markets, that for euro-dollars, we can talk of a few of the influences. As we shall see in Chapter 11, the euro-dollar market is basically a market in demand deposits with U.S. banks, and the euro-dollar rates have to be above those on money market assets in New York; in the early days of the market this meant either time deposits or treasury bills, but for the greater part of the 1960s it has come to mean New York CDs. At times when U.S. banks are inhibited from raising their interest rates on time deposits and CDs, they scour the world for euro-dollar deposits to replace the CDs which have run off, and interest rates on the euro-dollar markets rise to high levels.

2. PARTICULAR MARKETS

A. *Certificates of deposit*

Certificates of deposit (or CDs for short) were first introduced in New York in 1961, but London did not follow suit for some time. Dollar CDs were introduced in London by the First National City Bank in 1966, and sterling CDs followed in 1968. One of the factors delaying matters was a general ruling of the Inland Revenue that income tax must be deducted at source, even by banks, on securities with maturities of over one year, but this was eventually relaxed in favour of CDs, thus making it possible to attract overseas residents as holders.

The details of the denominations and maturities of sterling and dollar CDs are shown in Table 10.3. CDs generally differ from treasury and commercial bills in that they bear a rate of interest, instead of being issued at a discount; a tiny fraction of the total is, however, issued at a discount or, what amounts to the same thing, subject to a repurchase agreement. Sterling CDs follow the English practice of having interest calculated on the basis of a 365-day year, but dollar

CDs (but not other euro-dollar claims) have their interest calculated on a 360-day year as is done generally in the U.S.A.

The effect of issuing a certificate for a bank deposit and of providing a secondary market on which it can be traded is to convert it into a claim similar to a bond. As a result of the marketability of the certificates banks can issue them at rates which average $\frac{1}{8}\%$ below the rates for deposits of the same maturity. The major attraction of CDs to the issuing banks, however, is that depositors can be persuaded to enter into a longer term deposit if it is covered by a negotiable certificate. Term deposits often had penalty clauses written into them allowing the depositor to withdraw his money before the full term if he had need of it, but the penalty was relatively severe. Knowing that he can sell the CD on a secondary market, the depositor is much more likely to be willing to contract for a longer period. We have already seen the increasing popularity of term loans for periods of two to seven years; CDs offered a way of matching these loans.

While the advantages conferred by the bond-like characteristics of CDs are substantial, there are also disadvantages. The most important of these is the possibility of capital loss to the holder if interest rates are expected to rise. At such times CDs become difficult to issue, and secondary market dealers often hold large unsaleable stocks.

The crucial factor in the issuing of CDs by banks is the existence of an efficient secondary market on which depositors can recover their money before maturity if they need it. The discount houses are the main dealers in the secondary markets for both types of CD. Over the year 1971 their holdings varied between 80% and 88% of all dollar CDs held by dealers and between 89% and 93% of all sterling CDs. The other dealers differ in two markets: for sterlings CDs they are three accepting houses, while for dollar CDs they are five London branches of U.S. and Canadian securities houses.

Table 10.4 analyses secondary market transactions during December 1971. The end-month balances held by market dealers represented 22% of sterling CDs in issue and 6·5% of dollar CDs, although the disparity in market transactions was not nearly so great. The extent of purchases by dealers from issuing banks in the sterling CD market (figures for dollar CDs are not available) shows that secondary market dealers are in a sense also part of the primary market since they take the initiative in persuading banks to issue particular CDs, either to hold in their own portfolios or, more often, to meet the requirements of customers, who approach them rather than issuing banks direct. Because CDs have a minimum maturity of three months on issue, the secondary market is the only source of CDs with less than three months to run; in December 1971 sterling CDs with less than three months to run represented about 14% of all sales by secondary market dealers.

For holders who need only part of the value of a CD there is an alternative to the secondary market. Issuing banks are normally willing to 'chip off' part of the value so that the remaining value represents a denomination for which CDs are issued; for sterling CDs the amounts withdrawn in this way must be multiples of £10,000 and for dollar

Table 10.4   Secondary market transactions in certificates of deposit, December 1971

£ million

		Sterling	Dollar
	Opening balance	440	86
plus Purchases:	from issuing banks	162 }	216
	from others	343 }	
less Sales		− 408	− 168
less Maturities		− 44	− 8
	Closing balance	493	126
Discount houses		*457*	*108*
Other dealers		*36*	*18*

Sources: (1) Bank of England press releases;   (2) *Bank of England Quarterly Bulletin*, March 1972, Table 7(1).

CDs multiples of $1000. Banks themselves buy and sell CDs in the secondary market, although no bank has as yet overcome inhibitions against buying back its own CDs.

The fact that CDs are not eligible collateral for loans from the Bank of England poses certain problems for the discount houses. Clearing banks will accept limited quantities of sterling CDs in parcels of security for call money, but have in the past demanded higher interest rates for call money secured in this way; now that the markets for call money and inter-bank sterling have tended to merge since September 1971, this practice has probably become irrelevant. The rest must be borrowed on the inter-bank sterling market. For the funds to hold dollar CDs discount houses have always had to look to the euro-dollar market. We can get some idea of the extent to which discount houses have had to resort to unsecured inter-bank loans in both dollars and sterling by comparing the total which they report of funds borrowed from banks with the total of call money to the discount houses reported by the banks themselves. In December 1969 and 1970 the amount of unsecured loans was around £200 million, rising to £277 million in December 1971 (including £113 million from secondary banks).

We have already seen that discount houses are liable to have large stocks of unsaleable CDs at times when interest rates are expected to rise, and in these circumstances they look to the issuing banks to help. The New York banks had agreed to help secondary market dealers because of the importance to them of the development of a broad secondary market, and similar arrangements were made in London for dollar CDs. Discount houses have dollar lines of credit with American and other banks in London. The arrangements for support of the market in sterling CDs are far less formal, and issuing banks generally are unwilling to assume any formal commitment to help out. Help is in the form of either loans or purchases of CDs issued by other banks. Whenever issuing banks are known to be willing to help out in this way, the discount houses reciprocate by extending their limits for the holdings of CDs issued by those particular banks.

The development of the markets for both sterling and dollar CDs has been somewhat slow, and this is true particularly of sterling CDs. Their early development was hampered by a period of rising interest rates, and it was not until 1971 that the amount in issue exceeded that of dollar CDs. Table 10.5 shows what a high proportion of the sterling CDs is held within the banking system itself. It would be a useful exercise for the reader to attempt to follow the steps by which the various amounts are calculated; all the necessary information is given in the tables listed and in the additional notes to them. Discount houses hold CDs in their role as dealers in the secondary market. Since they are acting as principals, they are remunerated by dealing profits; they will aim to hold a larger 'book' when interest rates are expected to fall, and they will try to reduce their holdings when interest rates are expected to rise. Secondary banks are also holders for speculative reasons, but the most important reason for their large holdings is undoubtedly the role of CDs in matching. On the liabilities side CDs have enabled the banks to match longer term loans, and as assets they have the advantage over inter-bank deposits that they can be sold when conditions change.

There are signs that the breakthrough of the sterling CD is about to occur. This can be seen in the trebling of holdings by non-bank U.K. residents between December 1970 and December 1971; over the same period the proportion held outside the banking system has gone up from a shade over 20% of the total to a little under 30%. For overseas holders sterling CDs have a special significance because they are a vehicle for holding sterling assets without the need for forward exchange cover; as long as they move quickly enough, a sale as soon as confidence in sterling changes will enable holders to withdraw their funds at a cost which will probably be lower than that of forward cover. There has also been an increase in forward dealing.

Table 10.5   Holders of negotiable certificates of deposit, December 1969–71

£ million

		Sterling			Dollar
		1969	1970	1971	1970
U.K. banks		169	593	1,160	355
Discount houses		97	268	418	39
Other U.K. residents		143	194	602	} 1,255
Overseas residents		33	34	·62	
	Total	442	1,089	2,242	1,649

Source: *Bank of England Quarterly Bulletin*, (1969 & 1970) June 1971, Tables 7, 8(2), 10(1) & 23; (1971) March 1972, Tables 7(1), 8(1) & 25.

Notes: (1) 1969 and 1970 figures are at 31 December and 1971 figures at 8 December.
       (2) The March 1972 issue of the *Bank of England Quarterly Bulletin* gave for the first time figures for the holdings of sterling CDs by different types of secondary banks. The total of these figures for 31 December 1969 agrees with the estimate given above, but the total for 31 December 1970 is only £575 million. The difference of £18 million must have been held either by deposit banks or outside the banking system.

The growth in the total issue of sterling CDs was particularly rapid between October 1971 and January 1972, when £668 million was issued. Out of this total £257 million (38·5%) was issued by London and Scottish clearing banks. On 19 January 1972 deposit banks of all kinds held £333 million of the £1355 million held as assets by U.K. banks—just under 25%. The entry of the deposit banks into the market for sterling CDs, both as issuers and as holders, has been one of the factors causing the recent growth. The other factor was probably expectations of the continuance for some time of lower interest rates.

Table 10.4 shows that dollar CDs were of greater significance for non-bank holders. Because of the changes in timing of the various banking tables beginning with the March 1972 issue of the *Bank of England Quarterly Bulletin* it is not possible to repeat for 1971 the calculation for dollar CDs given in Table 10.4. By December 1971 the total in issue had risen to £1924 million.

B. *Local authorities and finance houses*

The holder patterns of local authority and finance house deposits are shown in Table 10.6. As we should expect from our study of the second-

Table 10.6   Holders of local authority and finance house deposits, December 1970

£ million

Holders	Local authority	Finance house
Banks	420	97
Other financial institutions	629	115
Non-financial companies	220	316
Other	551	160
Total	1,820	688

Source: *Financial Statistics*, June 1971, Tables 31 and 63.

ary banking system, banks are large lenders to both local authorities and finance houses (ordinary bank advances are excluded from both sets of figures). Both other financial institutions, such as insurance companies, pension funds and trustee savings banks, and non-financial companies use these two types of deposit as part of their cash management balances. The other holders in both cases comprise mainly personal sector and overseas sector holders. In the case of finance house deposits we know that £50 million was held by overseas residents, but we do not know the comparable figure for local authorities. For local authority deposits the personal sector holdings were £310 million, but with such large unit deposits the bulk of this must have come from large charities, colleges and churches. The non-overseas element in finance house deposits was £110 million. A large part of this consists of relatively small unit personal deposits, but there was also some large unit money from charitable funds.

For technical reasons local authority deposits have a maximum maturity of 364 days, and they are not negotiable, but several types of negotiable local authority security, both long-term and short-term, are traded in the parallel money markets. Of recent years local authorities have increasingly begun to issue three-month and six-month bills, and discount houses deal in these. Because most of them are eligible for re-discount at the Bank of England, the discount houses have no problems in using them as collateral either for call money from the clearing banks or for loans from the Bank of England. Negotiable bonds, either yearlings or two-year bonds, have many of the characteristics of CDs. As with CDs it is possible to obtain a small part of the amount of the bond before maturity. The most important similarity, however, is that negotiable bonds are not eligible as collateral for loans from the Bank of England, and hence discount houses, which are the most important dealers in the secondary market for these bonds, can obtain only a limited amount of call money from clearing banks on the security of these bonds.

Local authority mortgages are issued in a wide range of denominations, from a few hundred pounds for individuals to many thousands of pounds for trustee savings banks, insurance companies and other financial institutions. There is a secondary market for the mortgages of the larger denominations, although the dealers tend to be specialists in this field.

C. *Company loans*

We now move into a part of the parallel money markets which is relatively uncharted and which grew up in the sustained credit squeeze from 1965 onwards. The market is generally referred to as the 'inter-company' (or 'inter-corporation') market, but this is something of a misnomer because banks have always been concerned with between 60% and 70% of the loans in the market. In reality there are several markets, and we must distinguish between the wholesale market, on which the borrowers are first-class companies, and the retail market, concerned with small or medium companies.

The markets can be said to have developed at the retail end from the requirement in the spring of 1968 that importers should deposit for a period of six months 50% of the value of the goods imported. The relevant Act did not specify that the deposit must be made by the importing firm itself, and provided for repayment at the end of six months to the firm which had made the deposit. It was soon realised that the import deposit receipts were equivalent to government bonds, and a market grew up for financing import deposits. There was a good demand for such finance. Much finance was provided by the suppliers in other countries (probably as much as 40% of all import deposits), but firms which were not helped in this way were precluded from seeking loans from their clearing banks because of official directives. The market consisted of a few firms of specialist import deposit brokers, whose function was to obtain money in bulk from certain banks and to break it down into smaller units, often of as little as £250. The importer paid only the interest on the amount of the deposit for six months, but he paid it in advance. The broker then completed all documents and deposited the money with H.M. Customs and Excise. The banks involved in providing the finance for this market were mostly the smaller 'merchant' banks, many of them outside the range of bodies from which the Bank of England collects statistics. One broker quoted an annual yield to them of 10–11% at a time when Bank rate was 8%. The rates charged to the importers by brokers are not known, but this cannot have been a cheap form of finance.

As in all other credit squeezes there was also a 'grey' market in loans for companies which could not obtain finance from their normal banks. The operators on this market were 'fringe' banks, charging rates of up to 20%.

In 1969 the wholesale end of the market began to develop. In the early stages a number of specialist broking firms grew up, but the deposit brokers concerned with other parallel money markets soon became involved. Although the market may have started by inter-company loans, particularly between companies with different seasonal needs for finance, banks soon took part. Some secondary banks are reported to have made short-term loans between the monthly 'make-up' days on which they had to give the figure of their advances to the Bank of England. Many banks, including clearing banks, which could not meet the demand of their customers for loans directed them to the market, and a large proportion of the loans was guaranteed (for a fee) by banks. Most of the loans were short term—two to seven days' notice, with a month's notice at most. For a first-class company borrowing on this market was cheaper than a bank overdraft, the normal rate being $\frac{1}{4}$% over the rate for inter-bank sterling. The market suffered a short setback at the time of the Rolls Royce affair early in 1971, but it soon recovered. Estimates of the size of the market vary, particularly because many genuinely inter-company loans are arranged direct between companies without the help of brokers. The largest estimates quoted for the end of 1971 have been a total size of £250–300 million, of which only about £50 million was pure inter-company.

With the introduction of the new arrangements for the control of banks in September 1971 and the aggressive search for lending outlets by all banks, the market has taken on a new shape. Treasurers of companies and other large organisations have long been accustomed to use deposit brokers to obtain the best rates for secondary bank deposits, CDs and other parallel market claims; now the market has developed into one for bank loans. Companies wanting to borrow money from banks get deposit brokers to hawk the proposal around a number of banks, including the clearing banks, and will borrow from whichever bank will meet the terms suggested within the shortest time. Banks themselves are reported to be contacting deposit brokers asking for the names of companies which want to borrow. Companies are outgrowing the concept that the goodwill to be obtained by loyal adherence to the services of one bank is valuable and are replacing it with a purely commercial concept of obtaining funds from whichever bank is offering the best terms at a particular time. If the market for bank loans develops in this form, it will considerably alter the business of wholesale banking.

As we have seen, loans between one company and another have remained a small part of the market, and could possibly decline now that bank finance is readily obtainable. It will not have been lost on company treasurers, however, that they have been able to borrow on this market on the basis of their own names at rates finer than the banks could offer. The names of first-class industrial companies have as good a standing in the market as those of even large banks. The next stage in development would appear to be a market for commercial paper (basically promissory notes), on the lines of the U.S. market which grew to such size during periods of tight monetary policy. Such a market would probably have developed before this but for legal difficulties; commercial paper is not covered by the Bills of Exchange Act, 1882, and a company issuing its own paper would probably run foul of the Prevention of Fraud (Investments) Act. A market for commercial paper remains a distinct possibility for the future, however.

D. *Euro-currency markets*

We shall be looking at the international euro-currency markets in the next chapter, and there are only a few points which need to be made here. Table 10.7 is included to show the breakdown of the markets in terms of currencies. Over the three years currencies other than the dollar have grown in importance—from 10·6% of the total in 1969 to 19·5% in 1971.

This table gives a glimpse of the extent to which U.K. banks have been prepared to run unbalanced positions in various currencies. The figures are not very good indicators because they show only the liabilities

Table 10.7   External liabilities and claims of U.K. banks in non-sterling currencies

£ million

End-year	U.S.dollars	Deutschemark	Swiss francs	Other	Total
U.K. liabilities					
1969	10,728	615	454	197	11,994
1970	13,086	1,154	676	237	15,153
1971	14,172	2,094	1,046	298	17,610
U.K. claims					
1969	10,514	795	496	201	12,006
1970	12,189	1,363˙	868	271	14,691
1971	13,104	1,953	1,341	322	16,720
Net position *(net liabilities −)*					
1969	− 214	180	42	4	12
1970	− 897	209	192	34	− 462
1971	− 1,068	− 141	295	24	− 890

Source: *Bank of England Quarterly Bulletin*, March 1972, Table 22.

to and claims on non-residents, and miss completely the fairly sizeable euro-currency deposits of and euro-currency loans to U.K. residents. The overall net positions of U.K. banks in all non-sterling currencies differ considerably from those shown in Table 10.7, but unfortunately there is no currency breakdown:[4]

	£ *million*
July 1969	+31
July 1970	−30
February 1971	+1
October 1971	+107

Two relatively small markets have grown up around the euro-dollar market. Of recent years acceptance credits have been denominated in

4. The figures will be found in the *Bank of England Quarterly Bulletin*, December 1970, p. 453; June 1971, p. 220; March 1972, p. 58.

U.S. dollars, and the bills drawn on these credits circulate in the market. The total amount at the end of 1971 was probably around $250 million. An offshoot of the tremendous growth of the New York market in commercial paper has been the development of a London market in euro-dollar commercial paper. The amounts involved are not large—probably around $50 million at end-1971.

3. SIGNIFICANCE

The development of the parallel money markets in both sterling and euro-currencies raises a number of interesting problems. Of these perhaps the most important is the significance of such a vast increase in unsecured lending in markets which have no lender of last resort. This can be regarded as yet another advance in sophistication of the financial system, but in the early days many voices were raised to point out the inherent dangers; before they themselves became the biggest users of the euro-dollar market, U.S. banks were loud in pointing to the dangers.

The dangers arise not only from the unsecured nature of the lending but from the fact that the network of inter-bank deposits means that lending banks have no control over the ultimate destination of the funds which they advance. Precautions are taken: lending is only to first-class names and each bank imposes a limit on the amount which it has at risk in each name. One could retort that the concept of 'first-class names' has been somewhat dented since the Rolls-Royce affair, but the fact remains that the markets have shrugged off with no apparent difficulty a number of failures, both of banks and of industrial companies. Certainly the markets are now much stronger than they were in the beginning, principally because all the large banks in the world now dominate them. In these circumstances the absence of a formal lender of last resort may not matter so much because no central bank could stand by and watch the failure of one of the major banks in the country.

The second problem concerns the attitude of the authorities in Britain towards the development of these markets, both in sterling and euro-currencies. From the beginning the attitude towards the euro-dollar market has been one of allowing its development without interference. The Bank of England has undoubtedly regarded the first priority as the maintenance of the position of London as an international financial centre while the role of sterling as a reserve currency was in decline. So far this policy has paid handsome dividends in invisible earnings and in attracting ever more foreign banks to set up in London.

As far as the sterling parallel markets were concerned, the issues facing the authorities were necessarily more complex, but here too they have interfered as little as possible. One of the major factors leading to this attitude has probably been the help which the parallel money markets gave in maintaining the general level of interest rates in Britain lower than it would otherwise have been. Before the parallel market grew, overseas residents wanting to hold sterling assets nearly always put their money into treasury bills. This feature had the convenient facility of neutralising any increase in the money supply: the need of the government for borrowed funds rose as the Exchange Equalisation Fund took in foreign currencies, but the extra treasury bills which were issued were immediately taken up by the overseas residents themselves. At this time the authorities had to regard the treasury bill rate (determined largely by Bank rate) as the key interest rate for attracting foreign funds to London. In the early days of the parallel markets and for some years afterwards the differential between Bank rate and rates for local authority and finance house deposits was wider than it is now. Once foreign funds were attracted into the parallel markets, the authorities could keep Bank rate at a lower level than when the funds went into treasury bills. While so many domestic interest rates were still tied to Bank rate, particularly the rates of the deposit banks, this was an important consideration.

As we have seen, the main consideration of the authorities in the markets for short-term funds has been the control of interest rates. The development of the volatile parallel markets undoubtedly weakened the control of the authorities over short-term interest rates, and yet they took no apparent steps to assert their control over the parallel markets. They limited their positive measures to encouragement for the discount houses to enter the parallel markets, both as brokers and as dealers. The Bank of England could not operate directly in the parallel money markets, because these are markets in clearing bank deposits and the Bank of England has no deposits at clearing banks with which to operate; any action which it took in the parallel sterling markets would affect clearing bank cash and hence affect the discount market.

However, there are several links between the discount market and the parallel markets by which the effect of Bank of England operations in the discount market is partially transmitted to the parallel markets. (1) Whenever conditions in the discount market are tight, discount houses know that they may have to borrow from the Bank of England, and they will limit their operations in the parallel markets, whose claims are not eligible to back loans from the Bank of England. (2) Secondary banks have always operated in both the discount market and the parallel markets, and many of them can choose between selling bills to the discount houses or borrowing on the inter-bank market. (3) Since most foreign funds switching into sterling are covered for the exchange risk, the authorities can influence the inflow of funds to the parallel markets by operating in the forward exchange market.

The new arrangements for the control of banks in operation since September 1971 have had the effect of integrating the discount market and the parallel money markets just as they have integrated the wholesale business of deposit and secondary banks. All secondary banks must now hold substantial amounts of discount market claims to fulfil their reserve assets ratio, and by January 1972 the amount of money at call to the discount houses from secondary banks exceeded for the first time that from the London clearing banks. As we have seen the market for overnight money is virtually one market, with little or no differential between secured and unsecured loans. The deposit banks have now entered the parallel money markets directly, instead of operating exclusively through subsidiaries. In this process of integration the relative importance of the discount market has been enhanced, and the influence of the authorities on short-term interest rates in both markets has been increased.

FURTHER READING

P. Einzig, *Parallel Money Markets, Volume One: The New Markets in London* (London: Macmillan, 1971).

'London's "new" markets for money', *Midland Bank Review* (August 1966).

'Recent developments in London's money markets—the clearing banks and discount houses', *Midland Bank Review* (August 1969).

E. Davis, 'Financial innovation and the credit squeeze', *The Bankers' Magazine* (November & December 1970).

11 The International Money Market

During the past twenty years a vast new international money market has grown from nothing. It is a market in which the claims are bank deposits and bank loans denominated in currencies other than that of the country in which the bank is operating. The most common name for this market is the euro-dollar market, because the largest part of the claims is expressed in U.S. dollars and because most of the banks concerned are in Europe, with a heavy concentration in London. But the market deals in claims expressed in many currencies other than dollars, and it extends throughout the world. We have already seen what a great influence this new market has had on the development of the British financial system, having been largely responsible for the growth of the secondary banking system and of the sterling parallel money markets. In this chapter we are concerned with the markets for various euro-currencies in their international context.

1. THE CREATION OF EURO-CURRENCY DEPOSITS

There is nothing mysterious about the creation of euro-currency deposits. They are merely the application on an international scale of the principle that we examined in Chapter 7, the 'borrowing' of bank deposits by another financial institution, which in this case is a bank in a different country.

This point can be made clear by considering a simple sequence in the creation of euro-dollar deposits. We shall use the device of schematic balance sheets which we introduced in Chapter 7, with liabilities above the horizontal line and assets below it. The right-hand column refers to the position in New York, and all the other columns show the balance sheets of transactors outside the U.S.A.—in 'Europe' for short. Such a system is portrayed in Figure 11.1. The deposit concerned is

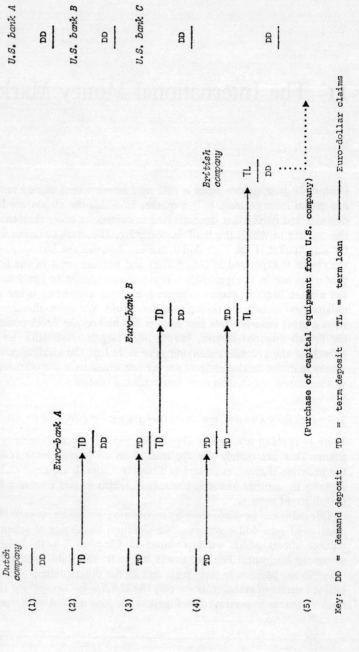

Figure 11.1 The creation of euro-dollar sequences

Dutch company

U.S. bank A

(1) DD

Euro-bank A

U.S. bank B

(2) TD | DD

Euro-bank B

U.S. bank C

(3) TD | TD | DD

(4) TD | TD | TL

British company

(5) TL | DD ········ ▶ Euro-dollar claims

(Purchase of capital equipment from U.S. company)

Key: DD = demand deposit   TD = term deposit   TL = term loan   ▬▬ Euro-dollar claims for $1 million throughout, and the figures may thus be omitted from the diagram.

In our imaginary example of the creation of euro-dollar deposits we start in position (1) with a Dutch company, which has a demand deposit for $1 million with Bank A in New York. This demand deposit may have been newly acquired as the result of trading with the U.S.A., or it may have resulted from the liquidation of a time deposit or of money market instruments such as certificates of deposit or treasury bills; when it decides to switch to the euro-dollar market, the Dutch company must first convert into a demand deposit whatever assets it holds in New York of the requisite value. This demand deposit is not a euro-dollar deposit; it is a normal demand deposit (or current account balance, as it would be called in English banking terminology) held by an overseas resident with an American bank. A euro-dollar deposit is created in position (2) when the Dutch company converts its demand deposit with U.S. bank A into a term deposit (for which the period may be anything from overnight up to over one year) with a merchant bank in London. All commercial banks outside the U.S.A. which participate in the euro-dollar market are usually called 'euro-banks', and the London merchant bank is shown in Figure 11.1 as Euro-bank A. This London bank now has a liability to the Dutch company, which it must pay back in dollars, so that the Dutch company has no greater exchange risk than it had with its demand deposit in New York. The New York correspondent of Euro-bank A is U.S. bank B, and this stage of the process is completed when the demand deposit in New York is transferred from U.S. bank A to U.S. bank B. Euro-bank A now 'owns' this demand deposit.

The next link in the chain is shown in position (3). Euro-bank A finds no immediate employment for the deposit in a loan to a customer, and so it passes the deposit on to another euro-bank, Euro-bank B, as an inter-bank deposit. This, too, is a euro-dollar deposit. In position (4) we find that Euro-bank B has a customer, a British company, in need of a dollar loan. This is a euro-dollar loan. The demand deposit in New York has passed to U.S. bank C in position (3) because this bank is the New York correspondent of Euro-bank B. When Euro-bank B makes a term loan to the British company in position (4), the demand deposit passes to the British company's New York bank, U.S. bank D. This is the end of the matter as far as the euro-dollar market is concerned. The British company uses its term loan to purchase capital equipment from a U.S. company, and the demand deposit passes into the industrial circulation of the United States and is lost from view. After its passage through the euro-dollar market this New York demand deposit leaves behind it two euro-dollar deposits for $1 million each and one euro-dollar loan for the same amount. Conceptually the euro-dollar market is an alternative financial circulation through which U.S. demand deposits may pass; it is alternative to the domestic financial circulation of the United States. The euro-dollar claims behave in exactly the same way as domestic financial claims created during the passage of a bank balance through the financial circulation: they remain in existence for their full maturity, usually some time after the demand deposit has gone back into the industrial circulation.

There are many other possible sequences for the creation of euro-dollars, and to illustrate some of them we shall use a more economical format than that of Figure 11.1. In Figure 11.2 we revert to the form and notation of Figure 2.2, which we used in Chapter 7 to illustrate the sequence of events when a current account balance was transferred to a building society. In Figure 2.2 the top line referred to deposit banks and the bottom line to their customers. The labels of the two lines have changed in Figure 11.2, but the concept is the same: the New York demand deposit moves along the top line, and on the bottom line the successive owners of the demand deposit enter into their transactions.

Sequence (a) of Figure 11.2 is the one which we have just charted in Figure 11.1. The company 'sells' its New York demand deposit to a euro-bank in return for a term deposit, and the euro-bank passes it to another euro-bank as an inter-bank deposit. It then passes to another company as the second euro-bank makes a term loan, and finally it disappears into the U.S. industrial circulation when the company spends the money in U.S. dollars.

Sequence (b) is really two sequences in one; they have no necessary connexion with each other. The sequence starts as in (a) with a term deposit by a company with a euro-bank. This bank decides, however, that the most profitable employment for this deposit is in the currency of its own country—a London secondary bank switching a euro-dollar deposit into sterling in order to make a deposit with a British local authority, for example. The euro-bank sells the dollars to its central bank and acquires a domestic financial claim with the domestic currency which it receives in return. The New York demand deposit has thus passed into the ownership of the central bank of the euro-bank's country of operation, and we assume that it is then held at a commercial bank in New York although there are several other possibilities for its employment. The matter could well stop at this

Figure 11.2 Euro-dollar sequences

(a) Existing demand deposit placed in euro-dollar market

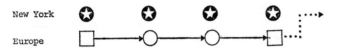

(b) Euro-dollar deposit switched into European currency, with central bank re-depositing

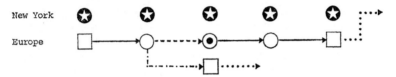

(c) Euro-dollar deposit created by switch into dollars

(d) European branch of U.S. bank lends euro-dollar deposit to parent bank

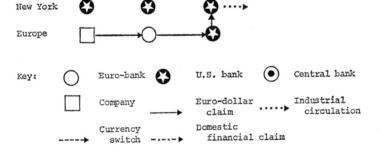

point, the central bank being content to keep its dollar reserves in this form. The second part of the sequence, however, shows the results of a decision by the central bank to earn extra interest on its reserves by transferring the deposit from the commercial bank in New York to the euro-dollar market. From then on the sequence is identical with the second half of sequence (a). Until fairly recently the central banks were one of the biggest groups of transactors in the euro-dollar market, but the central banks of most developed countries have now agreed to avoid re-depositing in the euro-dollar market.

In sequence (c) a euro-dollar deposit is created by a company which is attracted by the high interest rates of the euro-dollar market to switch from a domestic employment of its funds. We assume that there are no exchange control impediments to its switch, and show it obtaining the necessary dollars from its central bank, which, as before, kept them as a working balance at a large commercial bank in New York. The company places the funds on term deposit with a euro-bank, which immediately employs them in a term loan to another company; as before, the proceeds are spent in the United States.

Sequence (d) is one which we shall examine in more detail later on. The first two steps are the same as in sequences (a) and (b), but this time the euro-bank employs the term deposit in an inter-bank deposit to a London branch of an American bank. This branch passes the deposit on to its parent bank in New York, which employs it for lending to its U.S. customers.

The parallel between these sequences and the one in which a bank balance is transferred to a building society or other near-bank is complete. There are two particular points to note. (1) The bank balance (demand deposit) leaves behind it at least two financial claims, and more if inter-bank deposits are involved; it then disappears into the industrial circulation. As with the domestic example, it appears that the total of deposits with the U.S. banking system is unchanged throughout the process; the demand deposit passes from one owner to another and then disappears into the industrial circulation. This is a conclusion which we shall have to modify later on, just as we did with the domestic example. (2) If the euro-dollar deposit forms the basis of expenditure in U.S. dollars, as it must almost inevitably in the long run, the demand deposit disappears into the industrial circulation of the United States. If the euro-dollar deposit is switched into domestic currency, the demand deposit comes into the possession of a central bank. The proceeds in domestic currency disappear into the domestic industrial circulation, but the central bank has several choices open for the use of its New York demand deposit—retention in that form, employment in the U.S. money market or re-deposit in the euro-dollar market.

The sequences which we have considered relate to the creation of euro-dollar deposits, but the same principles apply to the creation of deposits in any other euro-currency. In every case the process starts with a bank deposit owned by a non-resident of the country concerned, and this bank deposit passes from one transactor to another as euro-currency deposits and loans are made. In the case of euro-sterling the bank deposit is a current account with a London clearing bank, and in the case of euro-lire it is an account with an Italian commercial bank.

2. DEVELOPMENT AND SCOPE OF THE MARKET

A. *History*

The taking of deposits denominated in foreign currencies has been known on several occasions in the past, but the present development of the market is traceable back to the early 1950s. Two stories have been advanced to explain the origins of the market, and both probably contain part of the truth. The first traces the origin of euro-dollar deposits to the fact that the U.S.S.R. and East European countries transferred their dollar balances from New York banks to banks in Western Europe out of a fear that the balances might be blocked by the U.S. government. The second story traces the origin of the market to the fact that the London accepting house Brown Shipley & Co. Ltd. enticed the dollar balances of British insurance companies away from the London clearing banks. In both cases the date is around 1953.

Three further events that happened in the late 1950s gave an impetus to the development of the market. (1) The sterling crisis of 1957 led the British authorities to prohibit the use of sterling acceptance credits for trade in which no U.K. resident was taking part. This caused the British banks to search for alternative ways of continuing their finance of trade between third countries. (2) In 1958 many currencies were made convertible into dollars. (3) In 1959 the beginning of tight credit conditions within the U.S.A. led American companies to seek dollar loans abroad.

Events of this kind would not have been sufficient if the basic supply and demand conditions had not been favourable. Our analysis of the creation of euro-currency deposits has shown that the process is identical in principle with the 'borrowing' of bank deposits by non-bank financial intermediaries in a domestic context, and the conditions giving rise to the two phenomena are therefore likely to be the same, namely that the euro-bank or domestic near-bank should be able to offer a financial claim which is more attractive to the holder of a bank deposit. The attractiveness of the alternative claim in both cases is often a higher interest rate, but it may well be the payment of interest on deposits of shorter maturity than the shortest term interest-bearing deposits of deposit banks, convenience or safety. In this context the factor most frequently cited is Regulation Q of the U.S. Federal Reserve Board, under which American banks are prevented from offering interest at all on demand deposits or on time deposits for periods of less than thirty days and are limited in the interest that they can offer on time deposits of thirty days or more. However, Regulation Q applies only to bank deposits, and is the effective limitation only for those holders of dollar balances which must keep them with a bank and cannot diversify into treasury bills or government bonds. A more general condition must be postulated—namely that short-term interest rates were higher abroad than in New York. However, there are many holders who cannot go beyond bank deposits, and the fact that deposit banks in most countries are limited in their rates of interest and (just as important) in the maturity of deposits on which they can pay interest was responsible for the growth of markets in the other euro-currencies. The supply and demand conditions were certainly favourable for the development of the euro-dollar market in the 1960s. Not only were short-term interest rates generally higher outside the U.S.A. but American banks were limited in their lending power, so that there were borrowers of dollars who would pay more than the lending rate of American banks.

Other conditions were also favourable. Although the dollar came under suspicion on occasion, it was generally regarded as the most stable of the important currencies. The suspicion that arose came from the successive balance of payments deficits suffered by the U.S.A., but these also increased the supply of dollar balances in the hands of foreigners and they led to pressure being applied on American companies to borrow overseas. Finally several countries which had balance of payments surpluses encouraged their nationals to place funds abroad (which meant effectively on the euro-dollar market), and some countries with balance of payments deficits encouraged their banks to borrow on the euro-dollar market. The market had become a part of the international financial system and was officially recognised as such.

B. *Extent*

In its early days the international money market lacked statistics, but in recent years the Bank for International Settlements in Basle has begun to collect figures from a number of countries. One of the earliest estimates of the extent of the euro-dollar market was $1 milliard[1] in 1960 and $3 milliard in 1961. The most recent estimates for the net size of the euro-dollar market for the years 1965–70 are shown in Table 11.1.

Table 11.1 Estimated net size of the euro-dollar market, 1965–70

U.S.$ milliard

	December					
	1965	1966	1967	1968	1969	1970
Uses						
8 W. European countries	5.0	6.3	6.9	7.9	11.6	17.4
U.S.A.	1.8	4.4	5.2	9.5	16.5	12.7
Rest of the world	3.2	3.8	5.4	7.6	9.4	15.9
Total	10.0	14.5	17.5	25.0	37.5	46.0
Sources						
8 W. European countries	5.0	8.4	9.6	13.2	18.3	21.0
U.S.A.	.8	1.1	1.7	3.2	3.8	4.2
Rest of the world	4.2	5.0	6.2	8.6	15.4	20.8
Total	10.0	14.5	17.5	25.0	37.5	46.0

Source: Bank for International Settlements, *Annual Report*.

In presenting its estimates the B.I.S. tries to eliminate the double-counting caused by inter-bank deposits, and this is the significance of the word 'net'. The aim is to show only funds supplied in the first instance to the market as sources and the ultimate borrowings as uses, but the estimates do not quite succeed in this aim. The B.I.S. relies for its statistics on reports from banks in eight West European countries (Belgium–Luxembourg, France, Italy, Netherland, Sweden, Switzerland, United Kingdom and West Germany), and it can eliminate the deposits between banks within this reporting area. It cannot, however, cope with the problem of euro-dollar deposits placed with banks outside the

1. I milliard = 1000 million. It is the same as a U.S. billion.

reporting area and then immediately re-deposited with other banks within the area. Nevertheless, the estimates are a very good indication of the net size of the market. On these estimates the net size of the euro-dollar market in 1970 was forty-six times its size in 1960.

Perhaps the most noteworthy trend in Table 11.1 concerns the U.S.A. itself. U.S. residents have always supplied a certain amount of funds to the market, and in the early days they often did so through the Canadian banks which are such big operators in the New York money market. U.S. corporations re-deposit in the euro-dollar market the proceeds of euro-bond issues. Although these two markets are quite distinct entities, there are close connexions between them, a further relationship being that banks underwriting euro-bond issues (among which U.S. banks are prominent) need to have working balances in the euro-dollar market. It is in the uses of funds that the position of U.S. residents has changed so dramatically. In both 1966 and 1969 the use of the market by the U.S.A. increased considerably over the previous year. We shall see later that this was due to the tight money conditions domestically, which led U.S. banks to scour the world for euro-dollar deposits, which their European branches secured and passed on to head office.

The fact that the euro-dollar market and the euro-currency markets generally have developed to the point of being a truly international money market implies that the pattern of sources and uses of funds will change from year to year, although this fact is largely obscured by the sparse geographical detail of Table 11.1. The B.I.S. tables do not have a standard format from year to year, and there are thus difficulties in providing further detail in tabular form. Instead we shall refer to certain specific uses which have been made of the euro-dollar market.

One of the first large scale users of the euro-dollar market was Japan, which used the market to obtain funds for industrial investment domestically. Belgium and other countries have used euro-dollar funds for government finance. Perhaps the most significant feature, however, has been the use of the market by governments to offset balance of payments deficits and surpluses. Countries like West Germany with chronic balance of payments surpluses have offered 'swap' facilities to their commercial banks, by which the banks could obtain dollars for deposit in the euro-dollar market or in the U.S.A. (normally the former) with re-conversion to Deutschemarks at a guaranteed rate. Countries in deficit have increased their reserves by persuading their commercial banks to borrow on the euro-dollar market and then to switch the proceeds of the loan into domestic currency. (A euro-dollar deposit is neutral in its impact on a country's reserves until it is switched into domestic currency.) Of recent years the Bank for International Settlements has intervened on the market to conduct smoothing operations, particularly at the end of the calendar year, when European banks and companies indulge in *ratissage* (calling back) of funds deposited abroad over their balance sheet dates. As we have seen, central banks themselves were large providers of funds to the euro-dollar market for several years up to 1969, when the depositing of reserves in the euro-dollar market was abandoned by the central banks of the major industrial countries.

A particular use of the euro-dollar market was made by British industrial and commercial companies in 1969 and 1970 as a way round the exceptionally severe restriction on bank credit. In 1969 British companies borrowed around £84 million in euro-currencies from U.K. banks for use domestically; in 1970 the figure rose to around £324 million, but it fell back to about £55 million in 1971 as a result of the withdrawal of Bank of England permission to use this source of finance.[2]

So far we have been concerned with the ultimate sources and uses of funds on the euro-dollar market, but it is now time to widen our horizon in several ways. Table 11.2 brings in the other euro-currencies, but it is dealing with the markets on a gross basis—gross of interbank deposits. One of its main purposes is to demonstrate the geographical location of the euro-banks whose assets and liabilities form the basis of the euro-currency markets. The inequality between assets dominated in euro-dollars and other euro-currencies and the equivalent liabilities arises because in most countries banks have often acquired euro-dollar assets by switching their domestic currency into dollars; this is offset by the fact that banks in some countries, notably the U.K., switch euro-currency deposits into their domestic currency on occasion. The pre-eminence of London as the main centre of the euro-dollar market stands out; banks in London had no less than 46% of all euro-dollar deposits in December 1970. London is also the largest market for all other euro-currencies except sterling, in which Paris is the main centre.

The relationships between euro-dollars and other euro-currencies and between the net and gross sizes of the markets are seen more clearly in Table 11.3. In both net and gross terms the euro-dollar

2. See E. W. Davis, 'Financial Innovation and the Credit Squeeze', *Bankers' Magazine* (November and December 1970).

component of the total euro-currency market went down from 83–84% in 1968 to 76% in 1971 (except for the liabilities of banks, for which it was still 83% in 1971). The net size of the market as a proportion of the gross size is for most years roughly the same whether we take the euro-dollar market alone or consider all euro-currency markets: in terms of bank liabilities it declined from 75% to 65% over the period, but in terms of bank assets it remained between 62% and 65%.

Table 11.2   External liabilities and assets of banks in foreign currencies, December 1970

U.S.$ milliard

Country of bank	U.S. dollars		Other foreign currencies	
	Liabilities	Assets	Liabilities	Assets
United Kingdom	31.4	29.3	5.0	6.0
France	6.7	6.0	2.5	2.3
Italy	6.9	6.7	2.5	2.7
Switzerland	4.9	9.6	1.3	2.1
Other Western Europe	8.3	8.9	5.4	4.8
Canada	5.4	7.4	.1	.2
Japan	4.7	6.9	.3	.5
Total	68.8	74.7	17.0	18.5

Source: Bank for International Settlements, *42nd Annual Report*,1971/72.

Notes: (1) Other foreign currencies are sterling, Swiss francs, Deutschemark, Dutch florins, French francs and Italian lire.
          (2) The other West European countries are Belgium-Luxembourg, W. Germany, Netherlands and Sweden.

3. SOME THEORETICAL ISSUES

A. *The euro-dollar multiplier*

During its short existence the euro-dollar market has given rise to a large volume of theoretical writing by economists. The books and articles have been concerned with such issues as the relationship be-tween the balance of payments of the U.S.A. and other countries on one hand and the working of the euro-dollar market on the other and the links between the euro-dollar market and national money stocks. We have no space to follow these particular issues, but there is one con-troversy which is of particular interest because it links up with the question of competition between banks and near-banks which we discussed in Chapter 7. Indeed one of the fascinations of the euro-dollar market as a theoretical question is the light that it throws on domestic financial relationships. The controversy in question concerns the existence of a banking multiplier in the euro-dollar market.

Table 11.3   Estimated size of euro-currency markets, 1968–71

U.S.$ milliard

	December			
	1968	1969	1970	1971
Estimated net size				
Euro-dollars	25.0	37.5	46.0	54.0
All euro-currencies	30.0	44.0	57.0	71.0
Estimated gross size				
Liabilities of banks				
Euro-dollars	33.5	54.2	68.8	83.2
All euro-currencies	40.5	64.8	85.8	110.8
Assets of banks				
Euro-dollars	38.6	59.3	74.7	84.6
All euro-currencies	46.1	70.0	93.2	114.2

Source: Bank for International Settlements, *Annual Report*.

Note: The figures for the estimated gross size are those reported by the banks in the 10 countries of Table 11.2.   Only the currencies listed in note (1) to that table are included.

The first article suggesting the possibility of credit creation through the euro-dollar market was written as early as 1964, but the controversy which we are considering started with an article in 1969 by Professor Milton Friedman.[3] Professor Friedman was concerned to rebut the theory that euro-dollars arose primarily out of the U.S. balance of payments deficit. Pointing out that the total size of the euro-dollar

3. G. L. Bell, 'Credit creation through euro-dollars?' *The Banker* (August 1964); M. Friedman, 'The euro-dollar market: some first principles', *Morgan Guaranty Survey* (October 1969). Other articles dealing with the same points are: F. H. Klopstock, 'Money creation in the euro-dollar market—a note on Professor Friedman's views', *Federal Reserve Bank of New York Monthly Review* (January 1970); F. Machlup, 'The magicians and their rabbits', *Morgan Guaranty Survey* (May 1971); G. Carli, 'Euro-dollars: a paper pyramid?' *Banca Nazionale del Lavoro Quarterly Review* (June 1971).

market was considerably greater than the cumulative deficit on the U.S. balance of payments, Friedman used the analogy of Chicago banks to explain the operation of euro-banks and declared: 'Euro-dollars, like "Chicago dollars", are mostly the product of the bookkeeper's pen— that is, the result of fractional reserve banking.' In reply Dr Klopstock asserted that the analogy with commercial banking was misleading, and that euro-banks bore a much closer resemblance to such financial inter- mediaries as savings and loan associations. Since savings and loan associations are the U.S. equivalent of our building societies, the de- scription which we have given above of the creation of euro-dollar deposits is very similar to Dr Klopstock's and quite at variance with that of Professor Friedman.

Throughout this book we have explained the creation of all sorts of financial claims (except debtors/creditors) in terms of the passage of a bank deposit through the financial circulation, where it leaves behind it one or more financial claims before disappearing into the industrial circulation once more. With this approach there is no more problem in explaining the size of the euro-dollar market than there is in explain- ing the ratio of the total value of financial claims to the money stock domestically. Because the financial claims are generally of several days, months or years maturity, they remain in existence for some time after the bank deposit has passed back into the industrial circulation. In exactly the same way euro-dollar claims remain in existence after the U.S. demand deposit has passed back into the U.S. industrial cir- culation.

As we pointed out in Chapter 7, the two kinds of multiplier, the banking multiplier and the near-bank multiplier, have different bases. The banking multiplier depends on the fact that bank deposits are used for the making of payments, so that most of them are trapped in the system, circulating from one account to another in the deposit banking system. The near-bank multiplier depends solely on the fact that there is a certain propensity to hold deposits with each type of near-bank; as incomes rise because of loans made by both banks and near-banks, the deposits of near-banks are likely to rise as well. The leakages from the near-bank multiplier process are many times greater than the leak- ages from the banking multiplier process, and so the value of the near- bank multiplier is much lower than that of the banking multiplier.

Professor Friedman's analogy between euro-banks and Chicago banks would apply if the euro-dollar system were used on a large scale for the transfer of payments. It is true that some multinational com- panies keep current accounts at euro-banks, but these are relatively small. (In Chapter 9 we estimated that roughly 13–15% of the non-sterling deposits of the American banks in London were current accounts, and it is probable that most of the euro-dollar current accounts are held by American banks.) Apart from these small current accounts, euro-banks play almost no part in the international payments mechanism. The proceeds of euro-dollar loans are used by drawing cheques on New York demand deposits, and the deposits are trapped within the U.S. banking system and not within the euro-dollar system.

B. *Lending to head office by U.S. bank branches abroad*

Twice during recent years the euro-dollar market has been dominated by the aggressive search for euro-dollar deposits by foreign branches of U.S. banks, which then lent them to head office in the U.S.A. We shall first describe the situations that arose and then go on to consider the theoretical implications.

Table 11.4 shows the extent of this lending to head office by foreign branches of U.S. banks quarter by quarter from 1966 to 1971 and its effect on the rate for three-month euro-dollar deposits in London. The two occasions on which the lending to head office reached a peak were in September 1966 and in September 1969, and on both occasions the rate for euro-dollar deposits was dragged up to levels which it had not achieved before. The background to the feverish activity of U.S. bank foreign branches in both cases was tight money conditions in the U.S.A. As domestic interest rates rose, U.S. banks came up against the Regulation Q ceiling of interest rates which could be paid on time deposits and on certificates of deposit; as the deposits and CDs came to maturity, their holders did not renew them, and the banks became short of funds at a time of heavy demand for loans. They instructed their foreign branches to seek euro-dollar deposits for on-lending to head office. In 1969 the foreign branches were so successful that the total size of the euro-dollar market was increased by 50% within a few months. In the process interest rates rose to unprecedented heights, not only in the euro-dollar market itself but in domestic markets throughout the world. The whole world was made to pay for the consequence of U.S. monetary policy.

The interesting theoretical point is how the U.S. banks could benefit from the obtaining of euro-dollar deposits which had as their basis existing demand deposits in U.S. banks. Our analysis in Figures 11.1 and 11.2 led us to the conclusion that the total demand deposits in the U.S. banking system was unaffected by the creation of euro-dollar deposits. How then could U.S. banks obtain additional funds for lending by attracting euro-dollar deposits to their foreign branches?

Table 11.4   Gross liabilities of U.S. banks to their foreign branches and euro-dollar interest rates

Year and month		Gross liabilities of U.S. banks to foreign branches U.S.$ million	3-month euro-dollar deposits in London % per annum
1966	March	1,879	5.81
	June	1,951	6.09
	September	3,472	7.06
	December	4,036	6.56
1967	March	3,412	5.38
	June	3,166	5.38
	September	4,059	5.78
	December	4,241	6.31
1968	March	4,920	6.38
	June	6,202	6.88
	September	7,104	6.25
	December	6,039	7.13
1969	March	9,621	8.53
	June	13,269	10.56
	September	14,349	11.25
	December	12,805	10.06
1970	March	11,885	8.63
	June	12,172	9.06
	September	9,663	8.50
	December	7,676	6.56
1971	March	2,858	5.38
	June	1,492	6.50
	September	2,475	7.63
	December	909	5.75

Sources: (1) *Federal Reserve Bulletin*, April 1972, A90 (last Wednesday of month); (2) *Bank of England Statistical Abstract*, No.1, 1970, Table 28 and *Bank of England Quarterly Bulletin*, March 1972, Table 29 (last working day of month).

When the size of the euro-dollar market increases as a result of the demand for euro-dollar deposits by foreign branches of U.S. banks, it is clear that some funds which have previously been held in other currencies are switched into dollars. This is the case to concentrate on because it is unlikely that the capture of an existing euro-dollar deposit by the foreign branch of a U.S. bank will increase deposits in the U.S. banking system. The general case of a euro-dollar deposit created by a switch of funds into dollars is that shown in sequence (c) of Figure 11.2. The demand deposit is already held in New York by the central bank of the country concerned, and no new deposit is created for the U.S. banking system. This conclusion applies when the central bank's demand deposit is held with a commercial bank in New York, but in the case in which the central bank liquidates U.S. treasury bills to provide the dollars demanded is more complex. The impact effect of the transaction is to increase the deposits and cash reserves of U.S. commercial banks by the value of the treasury bills sold, and it would seem that the banks could undertake multiple deposit expansion on the basis of their newly-acquired cash reserves. The argument must be taken one stage further. It is most unlikely that the requirement of the U.S. government for treasury bill finance would be reduced just because foreign holders had sold treasury bills; the U.S. treasury bill rate would rise in order to secure domestic holders for the unchanged treasury bill issue. The purchase of treasury bills by domestic holders would exactly cancel out the gain of cash reserves and deposits arising from the sale of the treasury bills. This case is thus also neutral in its effect on the total of deposits in the U.S. banking system.

There are, however, three ways in which the supply of dollars to a domestic transactor by the central bank can increase the total of cash reserves of the U.S. banking system and hence lead to a multiple expansion of deposits. (1) The dollars may have been supplied by activating the central bank's 'swap' arrangement with the Federal Reserve Bank of New York, under which it borrowed dollars from the U.S. central bank. When the dollars were deposited in the euro-dollar market, the effect would be the same as if the 'Fed.' had created new cash reserves by open-market operations. The effect would be the same if the dollars originated from the Bank for International Settlements. (2) The central bank may have supplied the dollars by selling gold to the U.S. government. The U.S. gold stock is part of the reserve base for the banking system, and so the cash reserves of U.S. commercial banks are increased by the amount of the sale. (3) If the central bank supplied the dollars by running down its working balance with the Federal Reserve Bank of New York, this also would increase the total of cash reserves and deposits of the U.S. banking system. Between them these three cases cannot have accounted for more than a small proportion of the increase in size of the euro-dollar market in 1969, and we must look elsewhere for the motives behind the aggressive search of U.S. banks for euro-dollar deposits.

Because Regulation Q does not apply to the operations of foreign branches, these branches can pay the market rate for deposits. We have seen that the competition between U.S. banks for euro-dollar deposits sent interest rates to very high levels, and the advantages must have been substantial to offset the extra cost of the deposits. These advantages arise out of certain institutional features of the U.S. banking system.

The first advantage came from the fact that up to October 1969 balances due to foreign branches were completely free of cash reserve requirements. During 1969 the cash reserve requirements against demand deposits for the larger banks were 17% for deposits under $5 million and $17\frac{1}{2}\%$ for deposits of $5 million and over; against time deposits the requirements were 3% and 6% respectively. Euro-dollar deposits repatriated by foreign branches could thus be fully employed in the most profitable way without suffering any deduction for non-interest bearing cash reserves.

The second advantage came from the clearing arrangements in New York. The operations of the euro-dollar market are settled through what are known as clearing house funds, and items in the course of clearing, which takes two days, may be deducted from gross deposits when computing cash reserve requirements. By making nearly all the loans to head office from foreign branches on an overnight basis U.S. banks ensured that they were always going through the clearing and thus deductible. The overnight loans were constantly 'rolled over' (renewed), but by this stratagem the U.S. banks secured a further economy in cash reserve requirements. It is probably because of this advantage that U.S. banks have successfully resisted attempts to set up a euro-dollar clearing in London, with only net balances settled in New York. A further advantage accrued to U.S. banks when euro-dollar funds were borrowed on a Friday: the banks had the use of the funds until they were cleared on the Monday, but they had to pay only one day's interest. This particular feature accounts for the fact that the London euro-dollar rate is always higher on a Thursday than on other days of the week.

The gains to U.S. banks from their aggressive bidding for euro-dollar deposits were thus only to a minor extent the gaining of additional cash reserves and deposits; the real advantage lay in the increased utilisation of the cash reserves which they already had. There was really no alternative for the U.S. banks. They had lost CDs and time deposits with their cash reserve requirements of 3% or 6%. To the extent that the holders were free to enter the euro-dollar market these lost deposits would come back as demand deposits with the full cash reserve requirements of 17% or 17½%. By entering the euro-dollar market on their own account the U.S. banks acquired loans from their foreign branches which were free of cash reserve requirements.

As a result of pressure from foreign governments the U.S. authorities imposed cash reserve requirements of 10% on any euro-dollar borrowings from foreign branches above a reserve-free base; this base was the level of borrowings in May 1969 or any subsequent lower level. In January 1971 the cash reserve requirement was raised to 20%. Table 11.4 shows that the borrowings from foreign branches fell drastically as a result of these requirements.

4. CONCLUSION

We have devoted more space to the euro-dollar market than would normally be justified in a survey of a domestic financial system. We have done this for two reasons. The first is the great influence which the euro-dollar market has had on the development of financial systems in most countries throughout the world. Not only has the euro-dollar market been a most efficient transmission mechanism for demands for short-term and medium term funds throughout the world and for interest-rate changes but it has also transmitted financial innovations. The present shape of the British financial system owes a lot to techniques brought here by the euro-dollar market. The second is the light which the euro-dollar market throws on domestic theoretical questions, particularly on the question of competition between banks and other financial intermediaries. Our detailed analysis of the motives which drove U.S. banks to enter the euro-dollar market in such a big way has also shown how important a close knowledge of institutional arrangements is for the understanding of theoretical questions in this field.

FURTHER READING

P. Einzig, *The Euro-dollar System*, 4th ed. (London: Macmillan, 1970).
F. H. Klopstock, 'Euro-dollars in the liquidity management of U.S. banks', *Federal Reserve Bank of New York Monthly Review* (July 1968).

PART C

Other Deposit Institutions

12 Finance Houses

1. TYPES OF INSTITUTION

A. *Range of bodies covered*

To most people finance houses are those bodies which undertake consumer finance in the form of instalment credit, and they are often qualified as 'hire purchase finance houses'. This is indeed the way in which they are regarded for the purposes of official statistics, which cover only those bodies dealing in instalment credit; other activities of the same bodies are included, but activities outside the range of instalment credit are not covered if they are the business of separate subsidiary companies. Since finance houses are the main bodies providing consumer finance for purposes other than house purchase, we shall need to look briefly at consumer finance in general and at certain other types of body providing it, but our main concern will be with finance houses as institutions and with the wide range of activities which they conduct.

From our point of view finance houses are closely akin to secondary banks. Their business covers a similar range to that of secondary banks, the main difference being that they deal in much smaller units and with much smaller customers: they are retail secondary banks. Their method of operation is also similar to that of secondary banks in many respects, but they have much wider margins and do not match the maturities of assets and liabilities at all closely.

We are fortunate that the field of consumer credit, with many side-long glances at the business loans of finance houses, was recently investigated by the Committee on Consumer Credit under the chairmanship of Lord Crowther (the Crowther Committee).[1] We cannot do

1. *Consumer Credit: Report of the Committee*, 2 vols., Cmnd. 4596, 1971. We shall not be giving page references for all the points quoted from the Report.

better than survey the types of body engaged in consumer credit from estimates prepared by the Crowther Committee as shown in Table 12.1. We have excluded all loans for house purchase as being outside the scope of this chapter; the esimates relate only to consumer finance, but there are no bodies other than those listed which we need to consider, except in the fields of leasing and factoring.

Table 12.1   Consumer credit outstanding, December 1966 and 1969

£ million

	1966	1969
Sellers of goods and services		
Retail shops & itinerant credit traders	612	605
General mail order houses	113	170
Other	180	239
Total	905	1,014
Account credit	*363*	*442*
Instalment & other credit	*542*	*572*
Lenders of money		
Finance houses	508	499
Check traders	52	93
Credit card issuers	3	5
Pawnbrokers	3	3
Moneylenders	25	28
Small loan societies & companies	1	1
Second mortgage lenders	10	25
Other	7	8
Sub-total	609	662
Banks	497	501
Insurance companies	128	184
Building societies	(140)	(150)
Local authorities	(70)	(75)
Total	1,444	1,572

Source: *Consumer Credit: Report of the Committee*, Vol.1, Tables 2.1
and 2.9

Notes: (1)   All identifiable loans for house purchase have been
excluded, but loans for home improvements are included.

(2)   Block discounted credit is shown under finance house
credit.

The top half of Table 12.1 covers credit extended to consumers by retail shops and other sellers of goods and services, excluding that which was subsequently financed by finance houses under the system of block discounting. The 'other' category covers all those selling organisations which are not included in the Census of Distribution—motor traders; hotels and restaurants; builders' merchants and builders; suppliers of solid and oil fuels; gas, electricity and telephone services; travel agents; passenger transport undertakings. Of the credit advanced by sellers of goods and services a high proportion consists of normal trade credit, here referred to as 'account credit'—the credit arising because it is the custom not to pay immediately on receipt for the goods and services. The true consumer credit in the form of instalment and other loans advanced by sellers of goods and services is of the same order of magnitude as that provided by finance houses.

The remainder of the institutions listed are financial in nature: the advancing of credit is their business. Since we cover banks, insurance companies and building societies elsewhere, we are concerned only with those bodies listed down to the sub-total. Of these finance houses are by far the largest, and we shall leave them on one side for detailed examination. The information shown for the other bodies was obtained by special surveys conducted by the Crowther Committee.

Check traders fall into two groups—those conducting traditional business and the newer bodies offering relatively high-value vouchers. The traditional check trading business is done by doorstep sellers, who are often part-time agents. Originally the business was concerned largely with clothing, but more recently consumer durables have been included in the trade. The typical form is for the customer to buy a check, which can be exchanged for goods to its face value in any shop accepting those particular checks. The purchaser pays 5p down for each £1 check and a further 20 weekly payments of 5p, making a total payment of £1.05. The service charge of 5% represents a nominal annual rate of interest of about 25% without compounding, but the Crowther Committee regarded this as reasonable for the type of business. In addition the check trader charges a discount of between $12\frac{1}{2}$% and 15% to the retailer. Most of the 626 check traders reported in the Census of Distribution for 1965 were small, but one large company accounted for about 50% of the total business. As check trading has been extended into consumer durables, the period of payment has also been extended. The Crowther Committee thought that the average period of payment was as much as fifty weeks in 1969.

Voucher trading is of recent growth. The vouchers are for much larger sums than checks, and the period of payment is much longer. Often the payment is made monthly by banker's order. It has become of importance in television, radio, furniture and home handyman materials. The Crowther Committee had no definite information, but guessed that the voucher trade amounted to £15 million in 1969, with £10 million outstanding at the year-end.

There are three kinds of *credit cards*. The first kind does not concern us because it is a card issued to identify persons who are entitled to charge their purchases to accounts in certain shops and department stores. The second kind of card is exemplified by Diners' Club and American Express. A charge is made to the card holder, and the card issuer also levies a discount of between 2½% and 5% on the retailer selling the goods; there is normally no credit beyond that involved in charging monthly purchases on one account. Barclaycard (operated by Barclays Bank) and Access (operated jointly by Lloyds, Midland and National Westminster Banks) are the only examples at present of the third kind of credit card. No charge is made to the cardholder, and the operator receives his remuneration from the 2½–5% discount levied on the retailer and from interest charged to those cardholders who take advantage of a revolving credit facility offered. If North American experience is anything to go by, we can expect a great extension of the use of credit cards over the next few years. English visitors to the United States often report great difficulty in paying in cash for purchases for which American citizens would use their credit cards.

The number of *pawnbrokers* in business declined from 1417 in 1950 to 363 in 1966 according to official statistics, although the Crowther Committee's own survey found 402 in business in 1968. It is a trade which has declined with increasing affluence, and the total credit outstanding is estimated to be only £3 million.

The business of *moneylending* also exhibited a declining trend from before the war down to the early nineteen-fifties, but the number of licensed moneylenders rose from 1500 to nearly 2350 in 1967. The explanation may well be certain new types of business involving loans for the purchase of consumer durables like motor cars in a form which took them outside the Hire Purchase Control Orders.

Small loan societies are the sole examples of mutual help in lending to be found in Britain; in the United States and elsewhere credit unions of this kind are important financial institutions. In 1969 there were at least 125 societies and companies of this type in existence, but the restrictions of individual loans to £15 in some cases and £50 in others means that the total debt outstanding is tiny.

Second mortgage lenders greatly increased their loans between 1966 and 1969, largely as the result of the controls on hire purchase and bank lending. The fast rate of inflation of property values during the nineteen-sixties has meant that many owner-occupiers have a growing equity in their houses, particularly after the mortgage has been running for some years. Many of the loans have undoubtedly been used for home improvements, but there is nothing to prevent loans from being used for any other purpose.

The *other lenders* consist largely of reversionary companies, lending on the security of a person's right to a financial interest which will accrue on the death of another person under a will or settlement or under a life policy left in trust. Other companies in this group advance loans for the purchase of ordinary shares or units in unit trusts.

B. *Finance houses*

Table 12.2 shows the size distribution of finance houses as reported in the official statistics. The nine largest houses accounted for nearly 60% of total debt outstanding, and the twenty-six largest for 78%. Since these figures exclude the outstanding debt of some specialised subsidiaries of the larger companies conducting business other than instalment credit and since there have been mergers since 1965, it is likely that the present degree of concentration is even greater.

Table 12.2   Size distribution of finance houses in Great Britain, 1965

Net amounts outstanding	No. of companies	Total outstanding	
		£ million	*Percentages*
Over £25m.	9	557	*59.7*
£5m. – £25m.	17	171	*18.3*
£1m. – £5m.	40	100	*10.7*
£500,000 – £1m.	33	22	*2.4*
£100,000 – £500,000	211	51	*5.5*
£25,000 – £100,000	400	22	*2.4*
Under £25,000	1,193	10	*1.1*
Total	1,903	933	*100.0*

Source: *Board of Trade Journal,* 10 December 1969.

All the largest finance houses and several of the medium-size houses are members of the Finance Houses Association, and Table 12.4 shows that in 1970 these forty or so houses accounted for 88% of all instalment credit, 94% of other loans and advances and 77% of leasing business. In fact the field is dominated by eleven large groups of finance houses. Their total outstandings in all fields except leasing and factoring as listed by the Crowther Committee accounted for 95% of all finance house outstandings as shown in Table 12.4 (including overseas business); the two sets of figures are probably not truly comparable, but there is no doubt of the domination of the field by these eleven giants.

Of the total outstandings of these eleven largest finance houses at the end of 1969 no less than 29% was accounted for by four wholly-owned subsidiaries of deposit banks and a further 9% by one finance house jointly owned by two deposit banks. The minority interests of deposit banks in the remaining six finance houses amounted to another 25% of total outstandings, and there were several holdings by secondary banks and insurance companies.

Among the large finance houses outside these eleven there are several which are wholly-owned subsidiaries of manufacturing companies, particularly in the fields of motor manufacturing and consumer durables. These 'captive' houses advance instalment credit only for the sale of the parent's products. The largest is Ford Motor Credit Co. Ltd.

Table 12.2 gives the total population of finance houses in 1965 as 1903. Of these, no fewer than 500 were dormant, and the population of active finance houses can be taken as around 1000. There are so many small finance houses largely because of control of capital issues from 1951 to 1958, a period during which the demand for hire purchase facilities was growing rapidly. The limit of £50,000 above which consent for the raising of new capital was necessary and the fact that consent was invariably refused to finance houses provided the opportunity for the formation of hundreds of small houses.

Table 12.3 gives a somewhat surprising picture of the business of finance houses since no less than 59% of outstanding balances in Great Britain was for business purposes, and only 41% for consumers. The Radcliffe Committee estimated that the business proportion of instalment credit for 1958 was only around 15%[2] The explanation lies in the stringent controls under which instalment credit business has suffered for many years past; business credit was free of many of the con-

2. Committee on the Working of the Monetary System, *Report*, para. 203.

trols applied to consumer finance, and the finance houses were able to flourish only by providing more business credit, by extending into new fields such as leasing and factoring and by mergers.

Instalment credit remains the most important field of activity shown in Table 12.3, accounting for 67% of outstanding balances in Great Britain. The new activities of leasing and factoring accounted for 10%

Table 12.3   Outstanding balances on finance house credit to consumers and business, end-1969

£ million

	Consumers	Business	Total
Great Britain			
Instalment credit	**498**	322	820
Non-instalment credit & loans			
Instalment credit subsidiaries	–	107	107
Other subsidiaries	*10*	*154*	*164*
Leased assets	–	127	127
Factored receivables	–	*15*	*15*
Total	508	725	1,233
Overseas	...	...	*213*

Source: *Consumer Credit: Report of the Committee*, Vol.1, Table 2.19.

Note: Figures in italics are for items not included in the official statistics on finance houses.

and 1% respectively, and non-instalment credit and loans for 22%. This last activity falls into two parts. The credit advanced by finance houses and their instalment credit subsidiaries consists largely of the stocking loans for motor dealers to which we shall refer later; that advanced by other subsidiaries consists of personal loans, second mortgage loans and loans for property development. Several of the larger finance houses have flourishing business in Commonwealth countries and some in Europe; this is largely of the same types as in Great Britain. Some major finance houses are also active in providing export credit through four different international credit clubs. These clubs are mutual arrangements between finance houses of several countries, each of which undertakes the provision of instalment credit for the importers of goods from the other countries.

Like deposit banks, finance houses have recently extended their activities into fields outside their main line of business with loans for school fees, travel, professional fees and the purchase of partnerships. They have also begun to compete directly with deposit banks for savings accounts and personal loans by opening 'money shops' in shopping districts. By the end of 1973 there will probably be over one hundred of these, operated by finance houses and an American bank. Some finance houses have moved into investment banking, property development and the management of investment trust companies and unit trusts, and several have manufacturing subsidiaries.

2. OPERATION

A. *Balance sheet*

The first point to be made about the aggregate balance sheet of finance houses as compiled from the official statistics shown in Table 12.4 is its inadequacy for obtaining accurate figures about the operation of finance houses. It is based on a sample grossed up on the basis of census inquiries every few years. The balance sheet leaves out of account a number of items, and the deficiencies are greater for liabilities than for assets. Long-term borrowing is completely absent, and provisions for tax and dividends are not shown. Since the official statistics are concerned with instalment credit and not with finance houses as institutions, subsidiaries undertaking non-instalment credit business are omitted, the book value of the shares in these subsidiaries held by the parent companies being included under trade investments. In Table 12.3 we were able to show the Crowther Committee's estimate of these missing items, as well as the value of overseas business. The practice of netting cash and bank balances against bank overdrafts makes it impossible to obtain clean figures for sources of borrowing and for liquid assets. The official analysis of bank advances gives a figure for advances to finance houses, but it is at the middle of each quarter whereas the other figures for finance houses are at the end of the quarter.

Rough estimates of cash and bank balances can be obtained by interpolating between the figures of advances for the middle of each quarter on either side of the end-quarter date, and on this basis it seems that cash and bank balances have risen from around £20 million in 1963

Table 12.4   Balance sheet of finance houses, December 1969 and 1970

£ million

	1969	1970 Total	1970 F.H.A. members	1970 Others
Liabilities				
Deposits	636	688	663	25
Bills discounted	97	97	90	7
Bank overdrafts, net	37	23	9	14
Other borrowing	31	7	2	5
Unearned finance charges	99	110	94	16
Capital & reserves	201	230	205	25
Total	1,101	1,155	1,063	92
Assets				
Instalment credit outstanding				
Direct	787 }	877	737	140
Block discounted	32 }			
Non-instalment advances & loans	107	109	103	6
Leased assets	127	164	127	37
Assets with other U.K. financial institutions	10	4	4	–
Trade investments	55	61	57	4
Other securities	23	7	5	2
Total	1,141	1,222	1,033	189

Source: *Credit*, June 1971.

Note: Bank overdrafts are shown net of cash and balances with banks.
In 1970 gross bank overdrafts were about £110 million, and
cash and balances with banks about £80-90 million.

to around £85 million in 1970. The other liquid assets shown in the
statistics are assets with U.K. financial institutions other than banks
and other securities. Counting these together with estimated cash and
bank balances we arrive at a ratio of liquid assets to total assets shown
of just under 6% in 1963, rising to 7% in 1970. We shall need these
figures again when we look at the impact of the new regulations introduced by the Bank of England for the control of credit.

Instalment credit is the main asset heading, but its proportion of the total has declined from 79% in 1963 to 67% in 1970. This is mainly because of the tight control which was imposed on consumer instalment credit from 1965 to 1971. We have already seen how the finance houses were able to expand their total business by increasing loans for business purposes, which were not so tightly controlled. They also started new lines of activity in the less rigidly controlled sectors; the most notable examples are leasing and factoring, although there were also specialised types of non-instalment credit. The mix of assets is thus not entirely under the control of the finance houses themselves, since their main line has been singled out for especially stringent controls. The item entitled 'non-instalment advances and loans' is another example of an asset which is not entirely under control. It consists largely of loans to motor dealers at a low rate of interest, to enable them to hold stocks of cars. As we shall see, most of the finance house business in motor cars is conducted through car dealers, and these loans are a means of tying dealers to a particular finance house. At a time when instalment credit controls are relaxed and consumer demand for cars is rising, finance houses have no option but to advance the dealers large sums to enable them to stock up.

On the liabilities side of the balance sheet the incomplete coverage of items makes it difficult to work out borrowing ratios, the ratios of borrowed funds to capital and reserves, although these are of great importance in the operation of finance houses. On the figures in Table 12.4 the members of the Finance Houses Association had capital and reserves in 1970 equal to about 27% of the borrowing shown, and for the smaller houses the figure was 49%; this implies borrowing ratios of 3·7:1 for the larger houses and 2·0:1 for the smaller companies. There is considerable diversity of borrowing ratios among finance houses, the actual level depending on size, conservatism of management and whether or not the house has a close link with a large bank. The published accounts of larger finance houses in 1969 showed a range of borrowing ratios from 1·82:1 to 7·88:1. The market obviously regards the business of finance houses as more risky than many other types of financial intermediation.

The three main types of borrowed funds shown in the balance sheet are deposits, bills discounted and bank overdrafts, and these are further analysed in Table 12.5. We shall be looking at the considerations which affect the choice between these sources in the next section; here we shall limit ourselves to a short description of each source. Table 12.5 shows how the proportion of deposits in the total of borrowed funds has risen from 1964 to 1970, and it can be seen that the proportion of borrowed funds obtained from the largest single source, deposits by non-financial companies, has risen in line. Deposits from U.K. banks (secondary banks), bills discounted and bank overdrafts are all funds obtained from the banking system, and the proportion of these taken together has tended to decline over the period from 1964 to 1970. Even so, a proportion of one-third of borrowed funds obtained by one

Table 12.5   Sources of finance house borrowed funds, end-years
               1964–70

Percentages

	1964	1966	1968	1970
Deposits				
U.K. banks	10.9	9.3	13.3	10.7
Other U.K. financial institutions	7.1	7.8	10.8	12.7
U.K. non-financial companies	26.4	29.4	32.9	35.0
Other U.K. residents	8.6	13.1	12.6	12.2
Overseas residents	11.2	15.0	5.3	5.5
Total	64.2	74.7	74.9	76.2
Bills discounted	14.4	12.2	13.3	10.7
Bank overdrafts, gross	19.4	11.6	9.9	12.3
Other borrowing	2.1	1.4	1.8	.8
Total	100.0	100.0	100.0	100.0
Total from banks (%)	*44.7*	*33.2*	*36.6*	*33.8*

Source: *Financial Statistics* (e.g. October 1971, Tables 39 & 63).

Note: Bank overdrafts are computed as the arithmetic mean of
         November and February figures.

type of financial institution from another is very high; only discount houses have a higher proportion of funds raised from the banks.

Deposits are of two kinds: (1) those obtained on the parallel money market and (2) those obtained by advertisement or through branch offices from the general public. We have already looked at the parallel money markets in Chapter 10, so that there is little need to develop the points further. The deposits are commonly raised in hundreds of thousands of pounds, with a minimum often as low as £1000. Finance houses are competing for corporate and other money with local authorities and to some extent secondary banks, although they are more interested in longer-term deposits than local authorities. The differential between overnight or seven-day money and 12-month deposits is usually of the order of 1%. Only the large and well-known finance houses are able to raise funds in this way, but there is little difference in the rates for similar maturities which each company has to pay. Finance houses do not normally refuse the offer of a deposit, but they shade their rates to attract or repel funds.

At present only a few houses are active in the market for deposits obtained from the general public, although some other houses have declared their intention of entering or re-entering the market. This is basically savings account business, usually with a period of notice for withdrawal of several months. Since building societies offer the advantage of quick and easy withdrawal, finance houses will have to offer higher rates than building societies for their money, and they compete more directly with the investment departments of savings banks and with items of National Savings. This is not a market which can be entered and left quickly according to the need for funds at a particular time, but it provides a basic source of money for several houses. The figures for deposits from other U.K. residents in Table 12.5 give a fair indication of the relative importance of this source of funds, although some 'money market' deposits from large non-profit bodies are also included.

There is no official information on the maturity structure of deposits, but many of the larger houses provide an analysis in their published accounts. The following distribution was shown in the 1968 accounts of eight large houses with total deposits of £575·5 million:

Percentages

	Under 1 month	1–3 months	3–12 months	Over 12 months
Mean	28·2	28·5	41·6	1·7
Highest	41·1	41·1	71·0	9·8
Lowest	10·7	3·2	18·2	—

Since all houses will have broadly similar maturities of instalment credit contracts, the wide dispersion of liability maturities indicates that there is no agreement among finance houses as to the degree of matching which is desirable or as to future changes in interest rates. It is the smallest of the eight houses which have the greatest percentages of deposits with a maturity of over three months, and those houses which have conservative borrowing ratios also tend to go longer in their borrowing.

Table 12.6 puts the role of borrowed funds into their context by showing the total sources and uses of funds for the twelve largest finance houses over the period from 1964 to 1968.[8] This table shows

Table 12.6   Sources and uses of funds of finance houses, 1964–68

Percentages

Sources

Internal
Retained profits	4.3
Depreciation	8.8
Increase in tax and divided liabilities	1.4

External
New issues (a) fixed interest	2.5
(b) equity capital	3.1
Increase in borrowed funds and creditors	76.1

Other sources	7.6
	103.8
less Increase in cash and securities	– 3.8
Total	100.0

Uses

Increase in fixed assets	17.8
Increase in outstandings and debtors	80.5
Increase in other current operating assets	1.4
Increase in other assets	.3
Total	100.0

Source: Hoare & Co., Govett.

3. The table is taken from a privately circulated survey of the hire purchase industry prepared by Mr P. Redmond of the firm of stockbrokers Hoare & Co., Govett. Permission to quote and use this and other material from the survey is gratefully acknowledged.

that the increase in borrowed funds represented just over three-quarters of the total sources of funds, and that the increase in instalment credit and other outstandings accounted for over 80% of the uses of funds. The rapid rise in importance of leasing is reflected in the increase in fixed assets as a use of funds and in depreciation as an internal source of funds. Altogether internal sources accounted for 14·5% of total sources of funds, and external sources for 81·7%.

B. *Management of liabilities*[4]

Like most other financial institutions finance houses face a conflict between cheapness of funds and prudence. By far the cheapest way of financing their business at any particular moment would be by overnight or seven-day money continually turned over; their assets, however, consist largely of loans for two or three years on which the rate has been fixed at the drawing up of the contract. If the general rate of interest rises sharply during the currency of the contracts, they therefore run the risk of having their margins whittled away if their borrowing is largely short-term. Prudence would lead them to behave like secondary banks and to match their borrowing by maturity with their assets. When we looked at the concept of matching as applied by secondary banks, we spoke in terms of discrete deposits, repayable in total on maturity. We mentioned the possibility of repayment by instalments, but this is the norm for finance houses. Under these circumstances finance houses could be perfectly matched and hence immune from the effects of changes in interest rates if they had deposits maturing each month to the value of the repayments on outstanding contracts. The principle is identical; all that has happened is that each instalment is regarded as a separate loan.

As we saw above when we looked at the maturity of deposits with the larger finance houses, there is no evidence that finance houses go any distance towards a matched position. Some houses have a longer average maturity of deposits than others, but none of those whose accounts we examined had anything like a matched position. In practice finance houses take a view on the course of interest rate changes over the life of each contract and incorporate a risk premium in their charges. Since credit charges are fairly uniform, those houses with a relatively large proportion of longer-term deposits face a higher average cost of

4. This section and the next lean heavily on an article by Professor A. D. Bain, 'The cost of motor vehicle hire purchase', *Journal of Industrial Economics* (May 1966) and on the survey by Hoare & Co., Govett mentioned in the previous section.

borrowing (and hence a narrower margin) but are correspondingly less at risk than those houses which borrow shorter.

It is important, however, not to overstate the risks involved in the neglect of matching. Finance houses have an extremely stable cash flow generated by their instalment lending. Although the initial terms of contracts are usually two or three years, early repayment is very common, and the effective maturity is well under two years; it will be higher when business is expanding because of the large proportion of new contracts. For any contract the risk of erosion of the margin through a rise in interest rates which has not been foreseen is reduced by the fact that outstanding balances are largest in the early stages, when it is easiest to predict interest rates.

To show how the cost of borrowing from different sources has varied over the past few years Table 12.7 quotes annual average rates

Table 12.7   Average cost of borrowed funds, 1964–70

Annual averages

Year	Bank rate %	Differential (%) on Bank rate				
		Money market deposits		Deposits from the public	Bank overdrafts	Acceptance credits
		3 months	6 months			
1964	5.0	+0.3	+0.5	+0.1	+1.3	+1.2
1965	6.4	+0.6	+0.5	−0.4	+1.2	+1.2
1966	6.5	+0.8	+0.7	−0.5	+1.2	+1.3
1967	6.2	+0.3	+0.4	−0.2	+1.3	+1.3
1968	7.5	+0.6	+0.6	−0.8	+1.3	+1.1
1969	7.8	+1.7	+1.7	−0.6	+1.4	+2.0
1970	7.3	÷1.2	+1.4	...	+1.5	+2.2

Sources: (1) *Financial Statistics*; (2) Hoare & Co., Govett.

for three kinds of deposits, bank overdrafts and acceptance credits, expressed as a differential on Bank rate. It is clear that the cost of borrowing has no constant relationship with Bank rate, and that the costs of different sources are not in constant relationship with each other. It was because of the loosening of the link between Bank rate and the cost of deposits over recent years that the Finance Houses Association began to compile its own base rate in September 1970.

This is calculated as a monthly average of daily rates at 11 a.m. for three-month money in the inter-bank market; the resulting figure is rounded up to the nearest $\frac{1}{2}$%.[5] The base rate applies only to longer term loans, the rate on which formerly varied with Bank rate.

Only two rates of finance house money market deposits are reported in *Financial Statistics*, those for three-month, and six-month deposits. In the early part of the period it was generally reckoned that the average cost of money market deposits lay in the range between Bank rate and Bank rate $+\frac{1}{2}$%. With the generally higher structure of rates towards the end of the period the differential on Bank rate has tended to widen, partly, of course, to maintain the differential expressed as a percentage of Bank rate. It will be noted that the rate for six-month deposits is often below that for three-month deposits, and that this has usually happened when Bank rate was high.

The fourth column of figures in Table 12.7 quotes rates for deposits obtained by press advertisement from the general public. The smaller units increase administrative costs, but the advertising which attracts the deposits serves a double function since it also advertises the finance house as a lending institution. As we saw above, finance houses in this market are in competition with building societies and savings banks, whose rates are sticky. As a result of this deposits from the general public are relatively cheaper than money market deposits (and may well be absolutely cheaper after allowing for the additional costs) when Bank rate is high. These rates are those quoted by the larger finance houses: smaller houses have to pay considerably more for money of this type. The main advantage of size to finance houses (at least up to balance sheet totals expressed in millions of pounds) lies in the ability to achieve a lower average cost of borrowing by tapping the parallel money market and to secure deposits from the general public at fine rates.

In obtaining deposits from the parallel money market finance houses have a free choice among the various maturities; their choice will depend on interest rate differentials and the extent to which they want longer-term deposits to give some immunity to interest-rate changes. They are not so free to choose between different maturities in obtaining deposits from the general public. Table 12.7 shows that the search for the cheapest sources of funds would normally lead them to prefer deposits over either bank overdrafts or acceptance credits, but there are constraints on the choice. Smaller finance houses will often find that

5. The basis of calculation and the implications of base rate are considered in *Credit* (September 1970).

bank overdrafts are the cheapest source of funds because of the high rates which they must pay on deposits secured from the general public.

Both overdrafts and acceptance credits are lines of credit to the larger finance houses. Acceptance credits are bills of exchange drawn on and accepted by accepting houses and discounted in the market. The total cost consists of a commission of $1\frac{1}{4}\%$ and the discount rate on bank bills, and this is often competitive with the cost of overdrafts. This is especially true when Bank rate is low because during the period considered the banks imposed a minimum rate of interest on overdrafts of 6%, which was raised to $6\frac{1}{2}\%$ in October 1969. This upward shift in the structure of overdraft rates widened the minimum charge for overdrafts to finance houses from 1% over Bank rate to $1\frac{1}{2}\%$ over Bank rate. Banks have also begun to levy commitment fees for unused overdraft facilities, although these are quite small.

In choosing between acceptance credits and overdrafts as lines of credit finance houses have to consider certain differences between them. (1) Acceptance credits are for a fixed term of three months, whereas overdrafts are on a day-to-day basis. If a need is judged to be temporary, overdrafts will be preferred even if they are considerably more expensive than acceptance credits. (2) Bank lending to finance houses has been strongly discouraged during recent credit squeezes, and thus overdrafts are vulnerable; acceptance credits are secure for a period, usually twelve months. (3) There is no particular pressure on a finance house to make full use of its overdraft facility even when credit is easy, but finance houses feel compelled to make some use of their various acceptance credit facilities at all times in order to keep the lines of credit open. For this reason they are likely to make more use of acceptance credits than would be justified by considerations of cost or of availability of deposit funds.

C. *Expenses and margins*

We have looked at the cost of borrowed funds in some detail. We must now go on to consider the charges levied by finance houses and their other costs so that we can determine their margins.

Finance houses have many 'products' in the sense that they advance credit on a number of different types of commodity. Each area of lending has its own costs and risks, and the charges therefore vary considerably. This is illustrated by the flat-rate charges shown in Table 12.8, which in 1965 varied between a minimum of $6\cdot5\%$ and a maximum of $13\cdot5\%$.

The charges quoted in Table 12.8 are in a form which is appropriate for considering the operation of finance houses, since the total amount of the advance is calculated by adding the total finance charge over the period of the contract to the purchase price of the commodity; the equal repayment instalments are then calculated by dividing the resultant sum by the number of instalments. For example, the total finance

Table 12.8   Average flat rates of charge on new U.K. business, 1960–69

Percentages

	1960	1965	1969
Hire purchase and credit sale agreements			
Private cars			
New	7.0- 7.5	9.0- 9.5	11.2
Used: under 3 years old	8.0- 9.5	10.0-11.5	
over 3 years old	9.5-11.0	11.5-13.5	14.4
Commercial vehicles			
New	6.5- 7.5	8.5- 9.5	
Used	8.5-10.0	11.0-12.5	12.75
Motor cycles	9.5-10.0	11.5-12.5	...
Industrial equipment	5.5- 7.0	6.5- 9.5	8.7
Agricultural equipment	7.5- 9.5	8.5-10.5	...
Personal loans			
Private cars, new & used	...	8.5-11.5	10.6
Home improvements	...	7.0- 7.5	9.0
Non-instalment credit			
Factoring	...	8.4	...
Loans to motor dealers	...	7.9- 8.9	...
Loans to property developers	...	9.9-11.9	...
Loans to private individuals	...	9.9-12.4	...

Source: Hoare & co., Govett.

charge on a car costing £500 over a period of three years at a flat rate of interest of 7% is £21 (7 × 3), and the equal monthly instalments are £14.47 (521/36). This form of stating the finance charge takes no account of the fact that the outstanding balance is reduced progressively throughout the contract, and is thus not directly comparable with the cost of a bank overdraft, which is calculated as x% of the average daily balance outstanding. In order to compare one cost of borrowing with another it is necessary to reduce them all to a true rate of interest, which takes account of the reducing balance of the amount outstanding. The Report of the Crowther Committee contains a memorandum contributed by the Government Actuary's Department on the mathematics of true (or 'effective') rates of interest.[6] The formulas become quite complicated, but the memorandum suggests that a simple rule of thumb gives adequate results. This is to multiply the flat rate by 1·85 for quarterly instalments, 1·95 for monthly instalments and 2·05 for weekly instalments. Thus in Table 12.8 the flat rate of 6·5% represents a true rate of 12·675% for monthly instalments, and the flat rate of 13·5% similarly represents a true rate of 26·325%. We can see that the true rate of interest is not far short of double the flat rate for quarterly and monthly instalments and slightly over double for weekly instalments.

Our immediate concern is with total finance charges rather than with rates of interest, whether they are flat rates or true rates, and we want to examine the parts played by different types of cost in determining the margin. Here two approaches are possible. One is to take each type of business separately, and to identify the margin over the whole period of the contract; the other is to compute the average experience of finance houses over all types of business during a given period, usually one year. We shall use both approaches, although limitations of space prevent our giving more than one example of the first approach.

Table 12.9 shows the calculation of the gross return on new car business at different flat rates of charge. In each case the contract is assumed to be for three years, but to be settled at the end of the second year. The gross finance charge is obtained by multiplying the amount financed by three times the annual flat rate charge (e.g. 88·2 = 420 × 0·07 × 3), and the average outstanding balance is then calculated. The various expenses (other than the cost of borrowed funds) are deducted from the gross finance charge to give a gross return, which is then expressed as an annual rate of return on the funds employed, which are equal to the average balance outstanding. Each of the flat rates of charge is appropriate to a different cost of borrowed funds. For example, with the cost of borrowing at 5% per annum a flat charge of 7% gives a margin of 2·2% (7·2 − 5·0).

The behaviour of the various elements of expenses with different levels of flat-rate charge will be noticed. Dealer's commission and the rebate on early settlement are expressed as percentages of the gross finance charge, and thus increase with higher flat-rate charges. Administrative expenses are independent of the level of charge, and the

6. *Consumer Credit*, Vol. 2., Appendix IV.

provision for losses is calculated as a percentage (here 0·25%) of the total amount financed, which does not change with the level of charges. All the figures in Table 12.9 relate to the period of two years over which the contract is running, but we can see the relation of the different types of expense to each other much better on an annual basis.

Table 12.9   Calculation of gross return on new car business

£

| | Flat rate of charge | | | |
	7%	8%	9%	10%
Amount financed	420	420	420	420
Average outstanding balance	312	316	320	323
Gross finance charge	88.2	100.8	113.4	126.0
Dealer's commission (20%)	17.6	20.2	22.7	25.2
Administrative expenses	16.0	16.0	16.0	16.0
Rebate on early settlement (10%)	8.8	10.1	11.3	12.6
Provision for losses	1.1	1.1	1.1	1.1
Total expenses	43.5	47.4	51.1	54.9
Gross return	44.7	53.4	62.3	71.1
Return on funds employed *(% per year)*	7.2	8.4	9.7	11.0

Source: A. D. Bain, The cost of motor vehicle hire purchase, *Journal of Industrial Economics*, May 1966.

Note: The calculation is for a 3-year contract settled at the end of 2 years.

Table 12.10 presents estimated figures of the structure of costs during each of three years for all instalment credit business of the larger finance houses.

The second line of Table 12.10 shows the proportion of total repayments in each year which consists of gross finance charges realised. The level of flat rate charges has risen fairly steadily since 1964, and so the ratio of total repayments to gross finance charges realised has fallen; the remainder of the repayments consists of capital repaid. The finance charges realised are expressed as 100·0%, and from these are deducted the various items of expenses, taking credit for the excess of provision for loss over actual losses. The bottom three lines of the table then show how the gross finance charges realised are split between expenses, interest paid and surplus.

The identification of gross finance charges realised presents some problems. The practice is to add the total finance charge to the amount of the contract at the signing of the contract. Since finance charges are

Table 12.10   Cost structure models for finance house U.K. instalment credit business

Percentages

	1964	1968	1969
Repayments	563.0	453.0	409.9
Gross finance charges realized	100.0	100.0	100.0
less Dealers' commission on new business	16.7	14.3	12.6
Initial costs on new business	9.2	9.7	8.9
Running costs	12.2	13.5	14.3
Provisions for future losses	4.9	3.9	3.5
Rebates on early settlement	6.5	5.7	5.0
plus Excess of provision for loss over actual losses	.1	.8	.3
Total expenses	49.4	46.5	43.9
Interest paid	24.7	30.3	32.4
Surplus	25.9	23.2	23.7

Source: Hoare & Co., Govett.

realised as a proportion of each equal instalment, it would be wrong to take credit for them all at the beginning of that period. Instead a variety of methods is used to identify the finance charges appropriate to each period. The two commonest methods are the actuarial method and the use of a formula known as the 'sum of the digits'; both have as their object the allocation of revenue in line with the declining balance of capital outstanding, and so they allocate a progressively decreasing proportion of revenue with each instalment.

The costs of administration are split into two groups—initial and running costs. Since motor business is such a large proportion of finance houses' instalment credit, the major part of initial costs for all instalment credit business consists of dealers' commissions. The other initial costs are for credit status inquiries, advertising and the costs of entering the new agreements on the records. The running costs are mainly those of recording payments as they are received, although a large proportion of general head and branch office expenses, such as rent, rates, heating and lighting, would be allocated to this head. One source suggests that salaries represent around 50% of total administration costs; since a large part of dealers' commissions is payment for administrative services performed, this estimate would bring finance houses roughly into line with the general level of staff costs as 70% of total costs which prevails in many other fields of finance.

Finance houses have on occasion suffered heavy losses from two causes. The first is the default of motor dealers on loans when times are difficult. It is just at these times that used car prices tend to slump, and the finance houses suffer losses when they try to sell the cars which they have repossessed from defaulting hire purchase debtors. Overall, however, they have managed to keep losses down to about 0·75% of credit extended. The provision is at different levels according to the risks of the particular types of business, and one source suggests the following rates as typical: new cars 0·25%, good used cars 0.75%, old used cars 1·75% and used commercial vehicles 2·5%.[7]

The remaining item shown under expenses is the rebate for early settlement of contracts. Finance houses have no obligation to make any allowance, but it can be reckoned that on average the rebate amounts to 10% of total finance charges for new cars and about 5% in other cases. The calculation of the rebate would normally be on the same formula as that used for allocating finance charges to different periods. If a customer is entering immediately into a new agreement, a larger rebate is sometimes given. Rebates for early settlement are an important item in the cost calculations of finance houses since over the period from 1963 to 1967 about 60% of all hire purchase contracts for both new and used cars were settled ahead of the contract date.[8]

Over the period covered by Table 12.10 interest rates have risen faster than the various cost items reflected in expenses, and as a result interest paid has risen as a proportion of gross finance charges realised. The surplus as a percentage of finance charges has declined, on these estimates, from 25·9% in 1964 to 23·7% in 1969. This figure of surplus is not one which enters directly into the calculations of finance houses; they are concerned with the rate of return on their funds, and as proprietary institutions primarily with the rate of return on shareholders'

7. Bain, *Journal of Industrial Economics*.

8. 'Hire purchase contracts for cars', *Bank of England Quarterly Bulletin* (September 1967).

funds, the ratio of surplus as calculated in Table 12.10 to equity capital and reserves. This rate of return on shareholders' funds depends not only on the level of costs of the finance house, but critically on its borrowing ratio. Table 12.11 shows the great effect of 'gearing' on rates of return. It assumes that a finance house is aiming at a target rate of return of 15% on equity capital and reserves, and calculates

Table 12.11   Borrowing ratios and return on capital

Annual percentage returns

Cost of borrowed funds % per annum	Borrowing ratios								
	1:1	2:1	3:1	4:1	5:1	6:1	7:1	8:1	9:1
5	10.2	8.5	7.7	7.1	6.8	6.6	6.4	6.2	6.1
6	10.7	9.2	8.4	8.0	7.7	7.4	7.3	7.1	7.0
7	11.2	9.9	9.2	8.8	8.5	8.3	8.2	8.0	8.0
8	11.7	10.5	9.9	9.6	9.4	9.2	9.1	9.0	8.9

Source: A. D. Bain, The cost of motor vehicle hire purchase, *Journal of Industrial Economics*, May 1966.

Note: The figures show the annual rate of return on outstanding balances which must be earned to provide an annual return of 15% on equity capital and reserves.   Fixed assets are assumed to be 2% of total assets.

what rates of return on outstanding balances (or total funds employed) are necessary to achieve this for several different costs of borrowed funds and several different borrowing ratios. As an example, we can see that, when the cost of borrowed funds is 6%, a finance house with a borrowing ratio of 1:1 would need to earn 10·7% on funds employed, while a house with a borrowing ratio of 9:1 could achieve the same rate of return for its shareholders if it earned only 7·0% on total funds employed.

We can now summarise the factors determining the margins of finance houses. In calculating their finance charges the companies will start with a target rate of return on shareholders' funds, assess the likely cost of borrowed funds during the contract period and add on a margin which will yield the required rate of return. They are not, however, in a position to make a cost-plus calculation without reference to competition from other finance houses. It is true that consumers appear to make little comparison of finance charges in deciding on their purchases, largely because the credit facilities are offered along with the article by the same dealer, but finance houses are under pressure from dealers to keep their charges in line with those offered else-where. We can see competition as affecting the target rate of return.

Quite apart from any economies of scale in administration costs, the larger finance houses are able to operate with much narrower margins than small companies for two reasons: (1) they are able to tap cheaper sources of borrowed funds and (2) they are able to have higher borrowing ratios. In practice the small houses have to concentrate on those lines of business in which the major finance houses are not par-ticularly interested and to service the less creditworthy customers and dealers. Because the finance charge is fixed for the duration of the contract and because finance houses generally borrow much shorter than they lend, the houses will take expected future movements in the cost of borrowing into account when deciding on the finance charge: if a general rise in interest rates is feared, the margin will be wider than when interest rates are expected to remain unchanged or to fall.

D. *New credit controls*

Since 1965 the larger finance houses have been subject to the same lending ceilings as banks of all kinds. These have applied to the whole of their business, instalment credit, loans and leasing, to business bor-rowers as well as to consumers. Likewise the new system of credit controls which we have been describing for banks has been applied to the larger finance houses.[9]

The new system applies only to finance houses whose total eligible liabilities are £5 million or more. At the outset there are only fourteen houses covered, and it is estimated that they provide between 80 and 85% of all finance house instalment credit. The definition of eligible liabilities is all deposits with an original maturity of two years or less received from U.K. residents other than banks and from overseas resi-dents. Borrowing from banks has been excluded from eligible liabilities because the banks will already have been required to hold reserve assets against the funds which financed the lending to finance houses. The definition of reserve assets is exactly the same as for banks, but the holding of these assets is a much greater burden for finance houses than for banks because the yields on the assets are generally below the cost of borrowing to even the largest finance houses. For this reason the finance houses are required to hold only 10% of reserve assets, and they have been given 12 months to build up the required propor-

9. The details have been given in 'Reserve ratios: further definitions', *Bank of England Quarterly Bulletin* (December 1971).

tion of reserve assets in four equal stages. At the first reporting date (20 October 1971) the fourteen houses had eligible liabilities of £756 million and reserve assets of £12·6 million (1·7%).

The new requirements are an even greater distortion of their normal commercial practice for finance houses than for banks. Both deposit banks and secondary banks need to hold short-term assets to cover demand or short-term deposits, but finance houses have been in the habit of relying far more on lines of credit for their liquidity and keeping few liquid assets. From the figures quoted in the last paragraph it is clear that few of the liquid assets which they did hold qualified as reserve assets, but even if all the assets with other U.K. financial institutions and the other securities which the members of the Finance Houses Association held in June 1971 had been reserve assets, the proportion would have been only 3·1%. (Cash balances are not eligible reserve assets unless they are held with the Bank of England.)

The large finance houses affected by these new measures may, however, apply for banking status, and already five of them have been successful. On achieving banking status they have to hold $12\frac{1}{2}\%$ of reserve assets to eligible liabilities instead of 10%, but this is outweighed by substantial advantages. (1) They can issue negotiable sterling certificates of deposit. (2) Their bills of exchange are treated as bank bills, and they do not need the backing of a bank in the form of an acceptance credit. (3) Various administrative costs imposed by the Protection of Depositors Act are avoided. (4) They obtain the protection in the handling of negotiable instruments which is accorded to banks.

3. INSTALMENT CREDIT

A. *Forms and history*

There are two main classes of transaction coming within the definition of instalment credit: (1) hire purchase and (2) credit sale. A hire purchase agreement is a document peculiar to the law of Britain and of those countries whose legal systems are based on the British model. It provides that the title to the goods remains vested in the finance house or trader throughout the contract, and that the customer is legally a hirer. The hirer is given the option to purchase the goods, usually for a nominal sum of £1, once all the instalments have been paid and also to terminate the hiring and to return the goods at any time. In nearly every case the hirer does, in fact, purchase the goods. Because the legal title to the goods remains vested in the finance house or trader, repossession of the goods is a recourse if the customer defaults. A credit sale, on the other hand, is an outright sale of goods. The customer agrees to buy the goods and to pay for them by instalments. Ownership passes to him immediately, and he is an ordinary unsecured debtor.

The Crowther Committee took a very robust view of the legal complexities of instalment credit under the English legal system. It held that the purpose of all forms was to advance credit, and recommended that all consumer credit should be dealt with under unified legal provisions. For our purposes the legal forms are not very important, although occasionally the choice of one legal form rather than another for tax reasons or in order to avoid controls on certain types of credit becomes of economic importance.

On the face of it the fact that hire purchase contracts enable the 'lender' to repossess the goods is of economic importance. Since the security is in the goods, hire purchase contracts will be limited to those types of goods which are of standard design and readily movable, so that they have a good second-hand market. The finance house or trader will also need to protect his interests by ensuring that the second-hand value is always greater than the outstanding debt throughout the period of the contract. This he does by demanding a substantial deposit and by limiting the length of the contract. Repossession is very much a last resort, however, and finance houses and traders are far more concerned with the borrower's ability to pay and his honesty. Unlike banks, lenders on instalment credit usually have little or no knowledge of a customer's financial affairs. For this reason they obtain reports on potential borrowers from credit bureaux, which keep records of customers' previous instalment credit transactions.

Although there were traces of hire purchase transactions as early as the beginning of the nineteenth century, hire purchase first became important in the middle of the nineteenth century. On the consumer side the first transactions were in pianos and sewing machines, while in business the hire purchase of railway wagons flourished. The real development came, particularly after the Second World War, with the spread of ownership of motor cars, radio sets, television and other consumer durables. More recently instalment credit has been extended to the provision of central heating and other home improvements (for which the hire purchase contract is obviously unsuitable) and into the financing of vehicles, plant and equipment for industry and agriculture.

In terms of instalment credit outstanding per head of population

Britain is a long way behind the U.S.A., Canada and Australia, but well ahead of West European countries. In 1967 the estimated outstanding credit per head was as follows: [10]

U.S.A.	£95·4
Canada	£79·9
Australia	£48·8
U.K.	£25·4

The West European countries all fell into the range from £10 to £15 per head.

The most recent figures for the proportion of consumers' expenditure financed by instalment credit are for 1969, when the overall proportion was about 8·4%. The instalment credit was naturally concentrated on certain types of goods, and for these it represented much higher proportions of consumers' expenditure: motor vehicles, caravans, etc. 45%; radio and electrical goods and other household appliances 42%, furniture and floor coverings 41%; clothing and footwear 20%. [11]

B. *Market arrangements*

It is a characteristic of instalment credit that it is generally arranged as part of the sale of goods. This means that the dealer plays a key role in nearly all instalment credit, and that much of the competition between finance houses consists of persuading dealers to use the facilities of one house rather than of another. As we have already seen, the seller of goods can provide his customers with instalment credit finance in three different ways: (1) he can provide the credit himself, (2) he can provide the credit initially and then block discount his agreements with a finance house or (3) he can act as agent for a finance house in arranging for it to advance the instalment credit. If the legal form of instalment credit in the third method is hire purchase, the dealer sells the goods to the finance house and passes a completed hire purchase proposal form from his customer along with his invoice for the goods.

Table 12.12 gives a commodity analysis of instalment credit outstanding to finance houses, and provides separate figures for the larger houses which are members of the Finance Houses Association. These larger houses find nearly 80% of their business in providing finance for

10. Quoted by Hoare & Co., Govett.
11. Estimates of the Crowther Committee (Vol. 1, p. 111 of the Report).

motor vehicles and caravans and for industrial and building plant and equipment. The growth of finance for home improvements and central heating is reflected in the growth of the 'other' category. It is obvious that only the smaller finance houses play any large part in the provision of finance for the so-called 'small unit' business—instalment credit for furniture, furnishing, radio and other household durables. It is here that the great part of retailers' own credit is advanced, and goods of this type probably account for most of the block discounting. We are

Table 12.12   Commodity analysis of instalment credit outstanding to finance houses, December 1967 and 1970

Percentages

	1967	1970		
		Total	F.H.A. members	Others
Motor vehicles and caravans	72.2	64.7	63.6	71.3
Farm equipment (including tractors)	1.7	1.4	1.5	.5
Industrial & building plant and equipment	14.4	13.6	15.5	3.1
Furniture, furnishings, radio, etc.	2.7	2.2	1.3	7.1
Other	9.0	18.1	18.1	17.9
Total	100.0	100.0	100.0	100.0

Source: *Credit*, March 1970 and 1971.
Note: Block discounted credit is excluded.

more interested in finance houses than in instalment credit as such, and we shall be covering a very large part of their activities if we concentrate on the relationship between dealers and finance houses in motor business.

The Crowther Committee referred to the 'triangular relationship' between finance house, dealer and customer as typical of the motor trade. The main fact to be borne in mind is the great growth in competition between finance houses since the last war. Before the war it was customary for finance houses to charge dealers for providing their customers with hire purchase facilities; since the war finance houses have competed by offering larger commissions to dealers and by providing other inducements. The Finance Houses Association had an agreement limiting dealer commission to a maximum of 20% of gross finance charges, but in 1965 the Restrictive Practices Court ruled that this agreement was against the public interest. Since then dealer commission seems to have remained fairly stable at about 22½% of gross finance charges. A reasonably high rate of dealer commission is obviously justified by the selling and administrative costs which are saved to the finance houses by their close link with dealers.

The second major form of inducement to dealers has been the provision of finance for their stocks of cars. The demand for motor cars is largely seasonal, whereas assembly line manufacture requires continuous production. The manufacturers therefore want the dealers to take steady delivery of cars as they are produced so that the storage problem is overcome. Although motor dealers obtain some bank finance for this purpose, banks are not keen on this type of business because of the lack of security—a floating charge over highly mobile assets is not very good security. In an effort to tie dealers more closely to them finance houses have competed fiercely to provide stocking finance for car dealers, and the competition has resulted in uneconomic rates. Under a part of the Finance Houses Association's Code which survived the judgement of the Restrictive Practices Court the minimum rate of interest on stocking finance was 1½% over Bank rate. This rate gave a very narrow margin over the cost of borrowed funds, barely enough to cover the administration costs and leaving nothing to cover the risk, which was often substantial with largely unsecured lending to relatively small companies. The business is obviously uneconomic to the finance houses unless they can subsidise it from increased instalment credit brought to them by the dealer; one house aims to secure a ratio of 3:1 of additional instalment credit business to stocking finance. The facilities provided to the dealers often consist of a current account, on which the dealers draw by cheque up to the agreed limit.

Although we cannot explore the relationship between finance houses and dealers in other types of business, we can establish one conclusion. This is that dealers are the source of competitive pressure on finance houses. Even though credit customers may not compare finance charges at all closely, finance houses have to compete fiercely on charges and other facilities in order to secure dealer outlets.

Of recent years certain types of business have come to finance houses through other channels. In motor business two large finance houses have made special agreements to provide instalment credit at competitive rates to members of the motoring organisations. Other examples of the same tendency for links between large organisations and the bigger finance houses are the personal loan scheme provided for users of the National Giro by Mercantile Credit and loans for central heating installations arranged in conjunction with nationalised industries and oil companies.

In the near future finance houses are going to face fierce competition for consumer and industrial credit from the deposit banks, liberated by the new arrangements for competition and credit control. Since so many of the larger finance houses are directly owned by deposit banks, it is not easy to see how this competition will go. Certainly the deposit banks are in a strong position to divert a great deal of finance house business in their direction if they want to do so. Not the least of their competitive advantages is the fact that they are given warning of a customer's intention to use a finance house when the house applies for a banker's reference. Because of their intimate knowledge of their customers' financial affairs, the banks will be able to choose the less risky business, and they are able to offer it with a much narrower margin than finance houses have to secure.

C. Legal controls

It was largely because consumer credit and the activities of finance houses were subject to so many different legal provisions under different sets of legislation that the Crowther Committee was set up to survey the whole field. The recommendation of the Committee has been to unify the legislation and to subject all bodies advancing consumer credit to licensing and supervision by a Consumer Credit Commissioner. At present finance houses are subject to legislation for the protection of depositors as takers of deposits; on the lending side of their business they must steer clear of the Moneylenders Acts, and their instalment credit activities are subject to legislation on hire purchase designed to prevent gullible consumers from being persuaded to accept credit which they cannot repay and to limit the rights of finance houses to repossess goods. All these types of legislation have had their influence on the development of instalment credit and the activities of finance houses, but we are more concerned with regulations imposed on all grantors of instalment credit and on finance houses in particular in furtherance of credit control and monetary policy.

These regulations have taken two forms. (1) Terms control, covering the proportion of downpayment and the maximum repayment period for instalment credit, was in force from 1943, with only short periods free from control. (2) From 1965 finance houses were subject to the same overall lending limits as banks—the so-called control by

Governor's letter. Both these forms of control were removed in September 1971 as part of the new arrangements for credit control.

Terms control on instalment credit has been very popular with the authorities because of its large and immediate effect, and no credit squeeze has been complete without a turn of the screw in the form of raising the deposit (or downpayment) required as a percentage of the total cost of the goods and of reducing the maximum period over which repayment may be made. Of the two halves of terms control it is probably the initial deposit which has the greater effect: many consumers find themselves having to save up for an additional period before entering into an agreement, whereas their reaction to the shortening of the repayment period may be to 'trade down', that is to buy a cheaper good on which the instalments are within their reach.

The Crowther Committee estimated that credit on goods subject to terms control amounted to no more than $2\frac{1}{2}\%$ of total consumer expenditure, but this expenditure represented a very high proportion of the total business of finance houses. Table 12.13 shows the effects on new credit extended in the motor vehicle sector of changes in terms control. During the period covered by the table commercial vehicles were exempt from terms control, and the last column of the table gives some indication (although very imperfect) of what the course of events might have been without terms control. It can be seen that the effects of changes in terms control are quite large in their impact on credit extended, and that the effect of a relaxation of controls has been proportionately greater than that of a tightening; the effect on total finance house credit would be even greater as a result of relaxation than is shown in the table because of the additional demand from car dealers for stocking finance. New cars have been affected more than used cars, largely because of the 'trading down' effect mentioned above.

The Crowther Committee examined the advantages and disadvantages of terms controls and recommended that they should not be used any more.[12] Much has been written in economic literature on this subject, and one particular controversy is of interest. This started from the hypothesis that motorists tended to trade in their old cars when the hire purchase contract was completed, and held that the effect of changes in terms control would be to impose booms and slumps on the car market; this contention did not stand up to empirical investigation.[13] Our main concern with terms control, however, lies in another

12. Part 8 of Vol. 1 of the Report.

13. The controversy can be followed in articles by J. R. Cuthbertson (*Economica*, May 1961 and *Economic Journal*, September 1963), J. R. Cuthbertson and Brian

direction—the effect of terms control in diverting the course of credit.

As with all forms of administrative control, loopholes in terms control were always being stopped by the authorities. At the end terms control applied to all hire purchase contracts, to credit sales where

Table 12.13   Effects of changes in terms controls on vehicle business, 1965–68

Percentages

Period	Controls *Deposit %/repayment period (months)*		New credit extended as % of new credit extended in same period of previous year			
	Current	Previous year	New cars	Used cars	Motor cycles	Commercial vehicles
August 1965–January 1966	25/30	20/36	86.2	98.9	74.7	93.1
February 1966–May 1966	25/27	20/36	84.2	92.7	79.9	102.6
August 1966–January 1967	40/24	25/30	54.3	64.1	44.3	77.7
February 1967–May 1967	40/24	25/27	64.3	73.0	70.5	83.6
September 1967–November 1967	25/36	40/24	315.0	243.8	228.6	148.8
December 1967–May 1968	$33\frac{1}{3}$/27	40/24	147.1	143.5	135.4	131.0
June 1968–August 1968	$33\frac{1}{3}$/27	30/30	81.5	84.9	94.5	101.5

Source: Hoare & Co., Govett.

repayments were spread over nine months or longer and to all except short-term rental contracts. Check and voucher trading, credit advanced by mail order houses and personal loans remained uncovered, however, and the inevitable result was the loss of credit business by finance houses to check traders and mail order houses and a switch by finance

Motley (*Credit,* March 1962) and A. Silbertson (*Economic Journal,* March 1963 and September 1963). Hire purchase contracts for cars, *Bank of England Quarterly Bulletin* (September 1967) also refers.

houses towards personal loans. This is one of the clearest examples over recent years of the diversion of credit channels resulting from controls.

Although terms control is now ended, the finance houses themselves would welcome some means of imposing restraint on competition in this form. The memories are still fresh of bad debts arising in the period between 1958 and 1960, when terms were uncontrolled and a 10% deposit and a 48-month repayment period were common. Because of the judgement of the Restrictive Practices Court finance houses cannot regulate this matter by agreement among themselves, and their evidence to the Crowther Committee favoured legislative restriction of terms.

4. LEASING

A. *Growth*

Leasing represents a divorce between the ownership and use of physical assets, and such a divorce has long been known. For many years companies have operated in rented premises and have chartered ships from their owners; households have rented houses or flats, and more recently about 50% of all television sets in Britain have been hired from radio dealers or specialist hiring firms. There has been growth recently in the practice of sale-and-leaseback, under which companies with chains of shops or other premises have sold them to an insurance company or pension fund and then leased them back at a rental which was significantly lower than the interest cost of raising a mortgage.

We have already noted the rapid growth in the leasing business of finance houses, and now we must look briefly at the growth of leasing in general over the past ten years. It is an area in which statistical information only scratches the surface. The only identifiable leasing operations are those by finance houses and accepting houses shown in Table 12.14. Starting from practically nothing in 1960 the leasing of finance houses expanded more than threefold between 1965 and 1970; the leasing operations of accepting houses showed an even faster rate of growth, although the total value of assets on lease was only just over one-third of that of finance houses. In addition to the direct operations noted in the table, both finance houses and accepting houses have joined other financial institutions in a number of leasing consortia. The consortium known as Computer Leasings consists of four finance houses, an accepting house and a consortium bank, and in 1967 it announced that as a result of new financial arrangements it would be able to expand its leasing by £100 million over the next four years. A consortium for the leasing of aircraft, Airlease International, had as its participants all major deposit banks, a British overseas bank, an insurance company and four accepting houses. There are also several specialist leasing firms operating, many of them subsidiaries of U.S. leasing companies, of which Leasco is perhaps the best known.

Table 12.14   Assets leased by finance houses and accepting houses

£ million

	1965	1966	1967	1968	1969	1970
Finance houses	50	52	64	95	127	164
Accepting houses	6	9	18	26	38	...
Total	56	61	82	121	165	...

Sources: (1)   E. W. Davis, Leasing and factoring: a study in
                 financial innovation, *Credit*, September 1970;
          ·(2)   *Credit*, March 1971.

The types of asset covered by leasing are often those of new technology, such as computers, aircraft, hovercraft, containerships and the associated containers and port facilities; a great deal of plant and equipment, ranging from complete production lines to individual items, and the more expensive items of office equipment are also leased. Statistics of the importance of leasing in various types of asset are as hard to come by as are those of the total values of assets on lease by different kinds of leasing company. Among items gleaned from the press recently are that about 50% of all computers sold in Britain are leased, and that British Rail has encouraged private industry to lease its own bulk freight wagons for use on the railways; nearly 4000 of the 19,000 privately-owned wagons on British Rail are now leased. British Rail itself has been responsible for an ingenious scheme, whereby it leased ships and other assets from a specially formed company; the essence of the scheme was to exploit, largely to its own advantage but partly to that of the leasing company, the large tax losses piled up by British Rail. Many privately-owned companies, notably the major oil companies, are potentially able to operate similar schemes if they can get government permission to do so, and there may well be a major extension of leasing as a result.

The rapid growth in leasing over recent years owes something to special factors. One of these was the Treasury restriction on the sterling borrowing of the U.K. subsidiaries of foreign companies; leasing provided a way round this difficulty, and was much used by subsidiaries of U.S. companies. The general shortage of credit and the various credit squeezes were also important factors. Leasing has the same attraction on the demand side as a term loan or instalment credit of being available for the period required no matter what restriction of credit takes place subsequently. Leasing was included within the over-all ceiling of finance house and bank lending covered by the Governor's letters, but for finance houses leasing was a way of using resources released by the reduced demand for instalment credit. Towards the end of the period the Bank of England removed restrictions from leasing operations financed by equity capital rather than by borrowed funds.

B. *Operation*

The terminology of leasing can be confusing. Leasing proper is defined as a hiring without the option to purchase, and it is normally for the economic life of the asset. The terms 'hiring' or 'renting' are used for shorter periods. However, there is an intermediate form of hiring without the option to purchase which covers several years but a period less than the economic life of the asset. This is known to the finance houses as 'contract hiring', but we shall consider it as part of leasing. The most common form of contract hiring is when motor dealers arrange for finance houses to finance the hiring of fleets of vehicles to their customers; there is usually a clear intention to return the vehicles to the dealer after one or two years and to replace the fleet with new vehicles. This leaves outside the scope of leasing such items as plant hire, in which a specialist company, sometimes owned by a finance house, hires items of plant to contractors or others for relatively short periods; the main difference from leasing is that the plant is used by a number of different operators in succession.

Corresponding to the distinction between leasing for the whole economic life of the asset and contract hiring there are two types of lease. A finance lease is one in which the period is split into two parts: a primary period during which rentals are paid monthly or quarterly and in total cover the cost of the asset and the finance charge; the secondary period is of indefinite extent, and during this the hirer can continue to use the equipment for a nominal rental of $\frac{1}{2}\%$ or 1% of the cost of the equipment. In general the primary period on fixed equipment is five years and on mobile equipment three years; it thus covers most of the expected useful working life of the equipment. Corresponding to contract hire there are risk leases, in which the rental payments allow for a certain residual value in the asset at the end of the agreement.

From the points of view of both the lessor (the leasing company) and the lessee (the company renting the asset) leasing is a clear alternative to purchase of the asset financed by a term loan or instalment credit, and which method will be more advantageous depends on circumstances. Both leasing and a term loan ensure that finance is available for the whole period irrespective of credit squeezes, although leasing is more likely to be at a fixed rate throughout than is a term loan. The cost is likely to be in line with that of a term loan or instalment credit. Because ownership of the asset remains with the leasing company throughout, it is the leasing company which secures all tax allowances and investment grants, although competition between leasing companies has ensured that these are passed on in the calculation of rentals. It is perhaps the main advantage of leasing that the benefit of the investment grant or tax allowances is felt immediately in the cash flow through reduced rentals instead of after one or two years as with owned assets. The example of the British Rail scheme quoted above shows that under the present system of investment allowances leasing may have substantial advantages over loan-financed purchase: tax allowances are of no use to companies which are not making profits, whereas a leasing company can obtain the allowances and pass them on to companies which are not making sufficient profits to receive the benefit of allowances.

Leasing companies point out certain advantages of leasing. They stress particularly that leasing involves no capital outlay, even for a deposit, and that neither the leased asset nor the leasing agreement is mentioned in the company's accounts. This is certainly of advantage to companies which are already at the limit of their borrowing powers permitted by the memorandum of association, but it is probably a trifle naive to suggest that leasing leaves borrowing power unimpaired, since any sophisticated lender is going to inquire about leasing and to regard leasing as effective borrowing. It is also suggested that leasing has accounting advantages with discounted cash flow calculations, because the cost of the equipment is clearly related to the cash flow, but we have already made this point as applying to term loans.

5. FACTORING

Factoring involves the provision of one or more of the following services for clients: (1) collection and management of clients' trade debts; (2) short-term finance by purchasing trade debts from clients and advancing up to 80% of their value immediately; (3) credit insurance against bad debts. Most factoring involves the provision of all three services, but an important form of factoring consists of providing only the last two services. If credit insurance alone is wanted, this is available from specialist insurance companies and not from factors.

Factoring has been practised for something like 120 years in the U.S.A., where it grew up from the practice of finance houses on the eastern seaboard paying for the imports of traders in the west while the country was being opened up. At present the turnover of factoring in the U.S.A. is in excess of £3000 million a year. Factoring was introduced to Britain in 1959, and its progress since then has been slow. One source gives the following figures of total turnover of factored trade debt:

	£ million
1966	105
1967	121
1968	150
1969	155

Press reports agree broadly with these estimates, but there are no reliable statistics. Most industries follow the custom of monthly payment, and thus credit is outstanding for about forty-five days. On this basis the amount of credit outstanding at the end of 1967 was around £15 million, rising to about £20 million at the end of 1969. Of the total turnover of factored debt in 1967 it was reported that about £10 million was for export sales. The Bolton Committee estimated the total annual turnover of factoring at between £150 million and £200 million, but added a further £140 million for confidential invoice discounting.[14]

Several of the larger finance houses have factoring subsidiaries, but there are other companies in the field. The largest factor is the subsidiary of a finance house owned jointly by two deposit banks, and the second largest is a direct subsidiary of National Westminster Bank. Several of the other large factors are consortia, in which accepting

14. *Small Firms: Report of the Committee of Inquiry on Small Firms*, Cmnd. 4811, 1971, paras. 12.28 & 12.29.
　*

houses, American banks, U.S. factors, insurance companies and export houses[15] play a prominent part. The two largest factors have their own overseas links, but the other factors are members of an international organisation called Factors Chain International.

Factoring is suitable for companies selling on fairly standard terms to a large number of outlets, but these outlets must themselves be other companies and not the general public since part of the factor's service consists of a better knowledge than any manufacturing company can have of the creditworthiness of individual companies. Some factors will accept clients with turnovers of as little as £25,000, but the preferred levels of turnover lie between about £250,000 and £1 million. A recent press report stated that fewer than 5% of all companies with turnovers between £100,000 and £1 million were using the services of a factor.

There are four standard forms of factoring. (1) *Confidential invoice discounting* provides short-term finance and credit insurance but no debt management. (2) *Non-recourse factoring* provides debt management, short-term finance and credit insurance. (3) *Recourse factoring* provides debt management and short-term finance but no credit insurance. (4) *Maturity factoring* provides debt management and credit insurance but no short-term finance.

In confidential invoice discounting the client company offers trade debts to the factor as and when it wants to, and it may use the facility as much or as little as it requires. The factor immediately advances up to 80% of the value of the debts, and he normally has no recourse to his client if one of the trader's customers fails to pay. The main feature of this form of factoring, from which its name derives, is that the trader's customer does not know that the debts have been assigned to another company; this is regarded as important for preserving goodwill. The client company continues to collect its debts, and pays the proceeds into a bank account in its own name but held in trust for the factor. Out of this account the factor pays the outstanding 20% immediately on receipt. The usual cost quoted for this service is 1% per month, or 12% per annum.

The common feature of the other three forms of factoring is that the factor takes over the management of the entire trade debts of the client company. By specialising in this function the factor is able to perform it more economically than all but the largest of client companies, using computers to the full. He is able to use sophisticated credit control methods, and to employ specialised staff, with a know-

15. See below, p. 350.

ledge of the trade credit customs of each industry. He will have records on the payment regularity of the customers of all his clients, and many customers will appear among the trade debtors of several clients. He can thus reduce the risk of bad debts by this knowledge, and it is because of this that a large part of factoring involves credit insurance by not giving the factor recourse to his client in the event of bad debts. It is customary in non-recourse factoring for the client to require the factor's approval for each transaction; this is usually given in the form of limits set for each of the customers of the client. The client may still sell to his customers beyond the limit, but in that case the factor has recourse.

The factor's charges consist of two elements. The first is for finance provided by paying immediately for up to 80% of the value of each invoice as the goods are sold. This charge is usually 2–3% over Bank rate. The second element consists of a charge for debt management and credit insurance. For a company with a turnover of £100,000–£250,000 this would be around 2% of turnover or possibly somewhat higher; for a company with a turnover of £1 million the charge would probably be less than 1% of turnover.

Although most companies of the size suitable for factoring would have to pay 2–3% over Bank rate (or base rate) for bank overdrafts, factoring as a whole would be an expensive service if there were not substantial economies to set against it for the client company. (1) The advancing of 80% of the value of invoices represents an immediate increase in liquid resources and working capital, which can be put to profitable use. The use of a factor often allows a company to take advantage of the $2\frac{1}{2}$% discount for prompt payment normally allowed by suppliers. Like leasing, the use of a factor does not appear in the company's accounts. (2) The debt management service enables the client company to employ a smaller office staff and to avoid the costs of office space. The superior management of the debts will also be of advantage. (3) Credit insurance will prevent the failure of an important customer having a disastrous effect on the cash flow of the company. (4) Because the debts are bought outright, factoring does not count as credit, and it is thus immune to credit controls of the direct variety.

Factoring is a classic example of the exploiting by a financial intermediary of the economics of scale. The factor uses his superior creditworthiness to borrow on bank overdraft or acceptance credit at fine rates. He pools the risks of a large volume of trade debts, and is able to employ specialised management. The factor is able to avoid the staffing problem arising from the seasonal nature of the sales of individual companies, and he is able to secure economies of clerical labour in dealing with a large volume of accounts.

6. EXPORT HOUSES

We have already mentioned in passing the role of factors in export trade. Potentially the use of a factor can be especially advantageous to a medium-size or small manufacturer in connexion with export sales because he can then benefit from the factor's superior knowledge of overseas buyers. While factors mostly operate in overseas trade as well as for domestic markets, there are many specialist export houses, which between them are reported to assist in about 20% of Britain's exports. They have a number of functions, and some of them combine several functions. Among these are: (1) merchants, who act as principals in buying goods in one market and selling in another; (2) export managers, who act as the complete export department for a number of manufacturers; (3) manufacturers' agents, holding sole rights for the promotion of the sale of some of the manufacturer's goods in one or more markets, usually on an agency basis; (4) buying agents, serving overseas buyers; (5) confirming houses, serving overseas buyers by confirming orders already placed.

The confirming houses are the biggest category of all, and they and factors are the only ones which can be said to perform a financial service. Some of the factoring companies had their origins as confirming houses or as overseas merchants. Confirming agents have a function very similar to that of factors, except that they act for the overseas buyer rather than the British exporter. In effect they substitute their credit for that of the overseas buyer, and receive payment from him in the form of interest and commission. After paying the exporter, the confirming house will normally draw a bill on the overseas buyer. Like factors, confirming houses obtain their own funds by way of bank overdrafts and acceptance credits.

FURTHER READING

Consumer Credit: Report of the Committee (Crowther Report), 2 vols., Cmnd. 4596, H.M.S.O., 1971
> Parts 1, 2, 3, 8 and 9 and Appendix are especially important. Vol. 2 contains an extensive bibliography.

N. Runcie, *The Economics of Instalment Credit* (London: University of London Press, 1969).

Statistics

Statistics on instalment credit and finance houses will be found in *Trade and Industry* (formerly *Board of Trade Journal*), *Financial Statistics* and *Credit* (the quarterly journal of the Finance Houses Association; this also contains articles of general interest).

13 Savings Banks

In this chapter we move away for the first time from banks and near-banks which are operated for profit into a field in which institutions were established for the good of the 'deserving poor'. Both savings banks and building societies, at which we look in the next chapter, were founded during the industrialisation of Britain around the turn of the eighteenth century, and they both still operate on a non-profit basis. The savings banks in Britain differ considerably from their counterparts in many other countries. In most countries savings banks play a large part in the financing of house purchase, but in Britain this is a function of the specialised savings banks called building societies; only one savings bank (the Birmingham Municipal Bank) does any mortgage business. In Britain savings banks form a special financial circuit, channelling deposits from the personal sector exclusively into the public sector.

1. TYPES OF SAVINGS BANKS

Table 13.1 shows the deposits and numbers of active accounts in the different types of savings bank. The two largest are the National Savings Bank (formerly known as the Post Office Savings Bank), accounting for around 40% of total savings bank deposits, and the trustee savings banks, with 57% of total deposits. The Birmingham Municipal Bank and the railway savings banks account for the remaining 3% of total deposits. The main savings banks are split into ordinary departments, with 57% of total deposits, and investment departments, with 41% of total deposits (in both cases including the equivalent departments of the Birmingham Municipal Bank). In the ordinary departments deposits received from the public are automatically passed on to the National Debt Commissioners for investment in government securities.

Table 13.1   Savings bank deposits and numbers of accounts, 1970

Type of Bank	Total deposits £ million	Number of active accounts Thousands
National Savings Bank		
Ordinary department	1,445	21,705
Investment accounts	308	646
Trustee savings banks		
Ordinary departments		
Savings accounts	1,050	10,297
Current accounts	14	194
Special investment departments	1,474	1,918
Birmingham Municipal Bank	100	762
Railway savings banks	28	113
Total	4,419	35,635

Sources: (1) Department for National Savings; (2) Trustee Savings Banks Association; (3) Birmingham Municipal Bank (at 31.3.71); (4) Registry of Friendly Societies.

Any interest received over and above that required for paying a fixed rate of interest to depositors and for the management expenses of the savings banks is divided equally between the Exchequer and writing down the underlying investments. In the investment departments savings banks have greater freedom of investment, and receive the whole of the interest on the securities held, thus enabling them to pay a market rate of interest to depositors.

We shall be looking at the National Savings Bank and the trustee savings banks in more detail in the remainder of this chapter, but we can deal with the remaining types of savings banks in this section. The Birmingham Municipal Bank was founded in 1919, and is organised into three departments. Of these No. 2 Department is equivalent in every respect to an ordinary department and No. 3 Department is equivalent to investment departments in other savings banks. No. 1 Department is, however, unique in several respects. At 31 March 1971 it had £55 million of savings accounts and £606,000 of current account balances, and these funds were invested in house mortgages (£6 million), loans to the City Corporation and government securities. It pays a fixed rate of interest to depositors, which is $\frac{1}{2}\%$ higher than that payable on deposits in ordinary departments.

The two railways savings banks are the only ones remaining from a large number associated with the many railway companies operating before the First World War. There are several other small savings banks not included in the table. In Scotland there are several small municipal banks and some 'uncertified' savings banks still remaining. As one can see from the notes to income tax assessment forms, there is also a Seamen's Savings Bank; the funds of this are now under £1 million, and are in process of transfer to the National Savings Bank. The railway companies were not the only employers to form savings banks for their workers, and there are still a few savings banks associated with long-established industrial companies.

2. TRUSTEE SAVINGS BANKS

A. *History and organisation*

The history of trustee savings banks, like that of building societies and friendly societies, is tied up with the industrial revolution. At the end of the eighteenth century many small local banks were set up by the gentry to help the poor. Most of these operated in the same way as the 'goose clubs' still to be found in working class areas—weekly contributions, withdrawn at Christmas with the addition of a bonus or interest. The first savings bank which operated on a continuous principle, allowing free facilities for deposit and withdrawal at any time, appears to have been the Tottenham Benefit Bank, opened by Mrs Priscilla Wakefield in 1804. The next stage in development followed soon afterwards in Scotland. This consisted of the elaboration of a suitable constitution, with the funds of the savings bank under the control of voluntary managers and trustees; Ruthwell in 1810 and Edinburgh in 1813 provided different constitutional frameworks, but between them they are the immediate forerunners of the present trustee savings banks.

An essential feature of a savings bank is that the depositors should have a guarantee of the nominal value of their savings, that every pound of deposits should be withdrawn at its full face value *plus* interest no matter how long it has been with the savings bank. This guarantee cannot be achieved unless the savings bank can invest its funds in assets which have a similar guarantee. In Scotland the savings banks had the co-operation of the joint-stock banks, with which the balances were invested at interest, but this was not possible in England and Wales, to which the idea of savings banks quickly spread. The solution was contained in an Act of Parliament of 1817, which provided for the

payment of all money received, other than that needed for the transaction of day-to-day business, into the Bank of England for the credit
of the National Debt Commissioners. The Act also specified the duties
of the treasurers, trustees and managers of the savings banks, none of
whom was to derive any benefit whatever from his office. This is still
the basis of the trustee savings banks.

The savings bank movement grew during the first half of the nineteenth century, the number of banks reaching a peak in the year 1861
at 645. It was in that year that the Post Office Savings Bank was established by Mr Gladstone, and the competition from the new institution
drove many trustee savings banks out of existence, particularly in the
south of England and Wales. The surplus funds of these closed banks
were retained by the National Debt Commissioners, and it was these
funds, enhanced by accumulated interest, that were used as capital for
expansion when the trustee savings banks were recognised in 1928 as
an integral part of the National Savings Movement and encouraged
to open new branches, particularly in the south of England.

The trustee savings banks have remained on a geographical basis,
and there has been no parallel to the development of nationwide organisations by the building societies. The size distribution of trustee savings
banks is shown in Table 13.2, which demonstrates the wide disparity

Table 13.2   Size distribution of trustee savings banks, 1970

Size of total funds	No. of banks	Total funds £ million	Total funds Percentages
Over £100m.	5	697	24.8
£50m. – £100m.	14	987	35.2
£25m. – £50m.	21	717	25.6
£10m. – £25m.	18	325	11.6
Under £10m.	17	80	2.9
Total	75	2,806	100.0

Source: *Trustee Savings Banks Year Book*, 1971.

in the sizes of the savings banks as measured by their total funds. The
largest banks are all in areas of large population (the three largest are
the London and South Eastern (formed by a merger at the end of 1971),
Glasgow and Belfast), but among the twenty largest banks are many
which represent amalgamations of smaller banks over a wide area.

The smaller local banks are all in the areas where the trustee savings bank movement has always been strong—Scotland and the North of England. Amalgamations are still taking place among these small banks; the total number of trustee savings banks declined from seventy-nine in 1966 to seventy-three in 1971. Because each bank serves a separate area, there is no direct competition between trustee savings banks, although they face competition from other outlets for savings such as the National Savings Bank, other national savings and building societies.

The strength of trustee savings banks still remains in their traditional areas of Scotland and the north of England. The north of England accounts for just under 50% of all funds, the south of England and Wales for about 27%, Scotland for 19% and Northern Ireland for less than 5%. If we relate the numbers of active accounts to the population of the different regions, a somewhat different picture emerges. In its evidence to the Radcliffe Committee[1] the Trustee Savings Banks Association said that about two persons out of five in Scotland had trustee savings bank accounts, one person out of five in the north of England and a few southern counties like Devon and one person out of twenty in London and the home counties.

Trustee savings banks are organised into two departments, the ordinary department with a fixed rate of interest and the special investment department with a market rate of interest. The ultimate control of the affairs of each savings bank is in the hands of a body of trustees, whose services are by law entirely voluntary. These trustees are usually chosen from among local men prominent in business and the professions. The running of the savings bank is carried out by salaried officials.

The depositors in the ordinary departments of trustee savings banks receive the benefit of a guarantee that the National Debt Commissioners will always repay to the trustees the sums invested with interest. As the price paid for this guarantee trustee savings banks are subject to a great deal of government supervision. The National Debt Commissioners are directly responsible for the investment of ordinary department funds, and their permission is necessary for each investment of the funds in the special investment department. In addition there is a statutory body, the Trustee Savings Banks Inspection Committee, which inspects the affairs of each bank and makes an annual report to Parliament. Whenever they wish to extend the services they offer, trustee savings banks have to enter into lengthy negotiations with the Treasury.

1. Committee on the Working of the Monetary System, *Memoranda of Evidence*, Vol. 2, p. 78.

In this and other negotiations with the authorities they are represented by the Trustees Savings Banks Association, a body formed in 1887.

B. *Operation*

The balance sheet of trustee savings banks is shown in Table 13.3, and the income and expenditure account in Table 13.4. Although the

Table 13.3 Balance sheet of trustee savings banks, 20 November 1970

£ million

		Ordinary departments	Special investment departments
Liabilities			
Deposits		·1,064	1,474
Loans		8	–
Other liabilities		1	–
Superannuation reserves		23	–
Other reserves		18	29
	Total	1,114	1,503
Assets			
Cash		67	32
Loans to local authorities		–	786
Investments	*BV*	1,028	653
Loans to other savings banks		1	–
Premises		17	1
Other assets		1	32
	Total	1,114	1,503

Source: *Report of the Inspection Committee of Trustee Savings Banks.*

operations of the banks are split into two departments, ordinary and special investment, each bank is a single organisation, with staff and premises common to both departments. This situation and the fact that banks cover a geographical area create some operational problems, which we shall examine by considering the working of each department in turn. Of the two departments it is the special investment department which has shown the faster growth rate over recent years, with deposits rising from £116 million in 1951 to £1474 million in 1970 as against the comparable rise from £817 million to £1050 million *plus* £14 million of current account balances in the ordinary department. This faster growth of the special investment departments is a function of high and rising interest rates; in the past there have been periods when the rate of interest offered in special investment departments was below that in the ordinary departments, and the former have declined in importance.

Table 13.4   Income and expenditure of trustee savings banks,
                       20 November 1970

£ million

		Ordinary departments	Special investment departments
Income			
Interest on invested funds		38.9	98.0
Other income		4.4	2.7
	Total	43.3	100.7
Expenditure			
Interest paid to depositors		23.8	89.2
Management expenses		16.7	6.0
Other expenditure		1.7	2.5
	Total	42.2	97.7
Surplus (added to reserves)		1.2	3.0

Source: Trustee Savings Banks Association.

Each depositor in the ordinary department is subject to a maximum of £10,000. Amounts of up to £100 are usually withdrawable on demand, and larger sums require only a few days' notice. The rate of interest is at present 4%, but this is one of the stickier interest rates in our financial system because it remained unchanged at $2\frac{1}{2}$% from 1861 to 1970, when it was raised to $3\frac{1}{2}$% until 20 November 1972. The first £21 of interest (£42 for joint accounts of married couples) is completely exempt from income tax; from 1974 the first £40 (£80 for joint accounts) will be exempt.

Apart from sums needed as till money, all the money deposited is immediately passed to the National Debt Commissioners, who invest it at their entire discretion in British government securities. Mr Gladstone is reported to have said that it would have made no difference if the National Debt Commissioners had chucked the money into the sea, because the yield obtained by the Commissioners does not affect the fixed rate paid to depositors. The banks receive the fixed rate of interest payable to depositors with an addition to cover their expenses of management and surplus. From 1920–49 and again from 1953–8 this addition remained fixed at 37½p for each £100 of deposits, with a drop to 30p between 1949 and 1953. In 1958 the addition was raised to 55p, and since then it has climbed steadily up to its present figure of £1.95. The present rate of payment means that trustee savings banks receive 5·95% interest on deposits, out of which 4% is passed on to the depositor. Any surplus earned by a bank remains on deposit with the National Debt Commissioners at the same rate of interest (5·95%).

Seventy out of the seventy-three trustee savings banks had a special investment department in 1972. The maximum deposit for each individual is £10,000, and interest is subject to income tax and surtax in full. In order to qualify for the right to deposit in the special invest-

Table 13.5   Investments of savings bank investment departments, December 1970, market values

£ million

	National Savings Bank	Trustee savings banks
Cash and balances with banks	–	22
Local authority deposits	5	91
British government securities	153	320
Local authority securities and long-term debt	132	971
Overseas government securities	–	4
Total	290	1,408

Source: *Financial Statistics*, August 1971, Tables 61 and 62.

ment department a person must have at the time a minimum balance of £50 in the ordinary department. The deposits are invested in a range of public sector (British government and local authority) securities and the securities of Commonwealth governments and public authorities prescribed by regulation. The investments held in December 1970 are shown in Table 13.5. The permission of the National Debt Commissioners is necessary for each investment, but the banks are responsible for arranging their own portfolios. In deciding whether or not to give permission for an investment one of the considerations which the

Commissioners will have in mind is the maturity balance of the port-folio. Not only must a liquidity margin be maintained to meet with-drawals, but it would be unwise of savings banks to concentrate ex-clusively on the higher yields obtainable on longer-term securities because of their vulnerability to changes in the general level of interest rates.

It is largely the different maturity distributions of savings bank portfolios which cause the wide spread of rates offered by special investment departments throughout the country: those banks which have a high proportion of short-term securities can adjust the rates offered on special investment department deposits quickly when the general level of interest rates changes, while those with a preponderance of longer-term securities have to wait for maturities on their securities. One month's notice is obligatory in the special investment department, and at 21 November 1970 this was the only type of deposit offered by twenty-two banks; a further thirty-six banks offered a choice of one and three months, and fourteen banks offered a choice of one, three and six months. The one-month rate varied between 5% and 7½%, the three-month rate between 6½% and 7½% and the six-month rate between 7% and 7½%.[2] The margin secured in the special investment department is thus one determined by competitive conditions and by the allocation of management expenses between the ordinary depart-ment and the special investment department; this allocation must be agreed by the National Debt Commissioners.

Table 13.4 shows that the greater part of income in both depart-ments consists of interest received on invested funds. In the ordinary department interest received on bank deposits represented 55% of other income, charges for specific services 17%, grants from the Mutual Assistance Scheme (described below) 16% and commissions for sale of national savings items and unit trust units 5%. In the special investment department bank interest accounted for 36% of other income and profits on realisation of securities 40%.

While income is standard for all trustee savings banks in the ordin-ary department and varies between banks according to investment skill in the special investment department, the expenditure side varies widely between banks and between departments. The overall average of man-agement expenses for 1970 was 92p gross (87p net of sundry income) per £100 of mean balance of depositors. Of this roughly 70% repre-sented staff costs (including transfers to pension reserves) and 19%

2. The rates were quoted in the *Report of the Inspection Committee of Trustee Savings Banks.*

expenditure on accommodation and computers. (The savings banks have combined in a number of consortia for computer services.) In the ordinary departments average expenses were £1.58 gross (£1.47 net) and in the special investment departments 42p, both gross and net. The overall average conceals a very wide variation in total management expenses for different savings banks from 34p to £1.82 (both net). This reflects the different circumstances under which individual banks operate. Size is obviously one of the important factors, since a trustee savings bank operating in a populous area is likely to be relatively large, and it can achieve economies of scale through a large volume of business in each branch. The most important factor, however, appears to be the extent to which each bank has expanded its branch network during recent years. The total number of trustee savings bank offices has risen from 811 in 1946 to 1505 in 1970, and the expansion has been greatest in the southern half of England and Wales. It is here that most of the highest expense ratios are to be found.

Every financial institution with a branch network faces similar problems. New branches must operate for many years before they show a profit, and some branches will always be more profitable than others. Such disparities can be ironed out within a single organisation, and some means of doing so must be found as between savings banks covering geographical areas of the country. This is done in two ways—by loans and by a Mutual Assistance Scheme. These two devices enable the resources of trustee savings banks to be pooled on a national scale, while retaining the advantages of local initiative and control.

Loans are of several sorts. At 20 November 1970 the outstanding total of loans was £7·5 million, of which just under £1 million consisted of inter-bank loans, £3·1 million of loans from a Mutual Assistance Capital Fund (which has ceased to operate) and £3·4 million from the Fund for the Banks for Savings. These last loans were made under a provision of the Trustee Savings Banks Act, 1968, which gave banks the right to obtain loans up to a total of £10 million for all capital expenditure; of this sum £5 million was unofficially earmarked for computers and £4 million for premises. The Mutual Assistance Scheme applies only to ordinary departments, and under the scheme which came into operation on 21 November 1971 all banks which make an annual surplus contribute an equal proportion of the surplus to a General Fund. Grants from this Fund are made to cover the operating deficiencies of banks which are not covering expenses.

C. *Services*

Of recent years the trustee savings banks have offered two new services—a current account service and a unit trust of their own. The former was started in 1965 and the latter in 1968.

The current account service is open to any person who holds £50 in the ordinary department or who has had an ordinary department account for at least six months. A fixed charge is made for each cheque used for payment to a third party, while cheques drawn for cash at the drawer's own branch attract no charge. The charges are offset by an allowance of 50p for every £50 retained in the account over a six-month period. Like all trustee savings bank facilities the current account service is not available for business purposes, although it may be used by non-profit organisations and clubs. Progress in building up the current account service has been somewhat slow; after five years of operation there were only 194,000 accounts with total balances of £14·4 million. Associated with the service are the usual range of facilities, such as cheque cards and standing order payments, so that with previously existing facilities for safe deposit, standing orders on savings accounts in the ordinary department, travellers' cheques and foreign exchange the trustee savings banks have become competitors of the deposit banks in a modest way.

The TSB Unit Trust offers all the normal facilities of income units, accumulation units and a monthly savings plan associated with life assurance. On 20 September 1970 the total value of units in the trust was £18 million.

Since they were recognised as part of the National Savings Movement in the nineteen twenties, the trustee savings banks have acted as agents for the sale of all national savings items. They have their own SAYE (save-as-you-earn) scheme, in which there were 109,000 contracts by 20 November 1970 with total accumulated contributions of £6·6 million. They also operate a stock department, in which there is a simple procedure for the purchase of British government securities, the holdings of which are recorded in the National Savings Stock Register. One of the attractions of holding government stocks on this register is that interest is paid without deduction of income tax, so that persons who are not liable to the standard rate of income tax do not have the trouble of making repayment claims. At 20 November 1970 the stock department had 287,000 accounts with total holdings to a nominal value of £197 million.

One facility which causes the savings bank much trouble is that of direct transfer, in which employers make arrangements to pay some of their wages and salaries direct into trustee savings bank account. In their oral evidence to the Radcliffe Committee the representatives of the Trustee Savings Bank Association complained that this service, particularly the receipt of weekly wages, was uneconomic, despite a charge levied on the employer, because nearly all the money was usually drawn out in cash shortly after it had been credited to the accounts. The representative of the Post Office Savings Department (as it then was) also complained about the use made of the Post Office Savings Bank for 'current account' purposes. It is unlikely that either the trustee savings banks' current account service or the National Giro will have greatly improved the position since then, because most of the persons in receipt of direct transfer credits and weekly wages will probably have continued to use cash for all their payments.

All that the trustee savings banks are now lacking before they can offer a complete range of services in competition with the deposit banks is a personal loan service. They have been pressing for one for some time, but their negotiations with the Treasury for permission to operate new services have always lasted several years. An interesting development is the link formed between the Bank of Scotland and several of the larger Scottish trustee savings banks whereby the Bank of Scotland operates and underwrites a personal loan scheme for customers of the trustee savings banks. This scheme was started in the autumn of 1972.

3. NATIONAL SAVINGS BANK

With the exception of unit trusts, foreign exchange and travellers' cheques the services available through post offices are almost identical to those offered by the trustee savings banks. We are concerned here only with the ordinary department and investment accounts of the National Savings Bank: the current account service is provided by the National Giro (already described in Chapter 6), and the other facilities are functions of the Post Office itself.

The basic difference between the National Savings Bank and the trustee savings banks is that the former is a nationwide service with a completely centralised system of accounts, using Crown post offices and many sub-post offices as its branch network. The operation of the ordinary department and investment accounts is so similar to the equivalent facilities of the trustee savings bank that we need mention only the differences.

The only difference in the operation of the ordinary department concerns management expenses. Whereas the trustee savings banks are given a fixed margin to cover expenses and surplus, the National Savings Bank works on the basis of actual expenses. Sub-postmasters are mostly paid a unit charge for each transaction, irrespective of its value, and a payment is made for the time spent on savings bank business by Post Office staff in Crown post offices. To these items is added the cost of the National Savings Bank staff and such items as printing and stationery.

The National Savings Bank has one significant feature—the presence of a vast number of tiny accounts. As can be computed from Table 13.1, the average holding in the ordinary department of the National Savings Bank is only about £67, compared with about £102 in the savings accounts of the trustee savings banks. In its evidence to the Radcliffe Committee the Post Office Savings Department stated that in 1956 more than one-quarter of depositors had balances under £1, and about one-half had balances under £10; at the other end of the scale 0·8% of depositors had balances over £1000, and their balances amounted to 17% of the total.[3] Since 1956 the total balances in the ordinary department have declined from around £1700 million to £1445 million, and the average balance has gone down from £76 to £67. It would seem likely that the proportion of large balances has declined over this period, leaving behind an even greater proportion of tiny accounts.

In the year 1970/71 the expenses in the ordinary department of the National Savings Bank were £1.63 per £100 of mean balances, only marginally higher than the comparable figure of £1.58 for the ordinary departments of trustee savings banks. It would seem that the preponderance of small accounts in the National Savings Bank is largely balanced by the fact that many of them are relatively inactive. Like the trustee savings banks the National Savings Bank has invested heavily in computers, and it has had to bear the costs of moving its accounting centre from London to Glasgow.

The investment accounts of the National Savings Bank are a recent innovation, having been started in 1966, and they are so similar to the special investment departments of the trustee savings banks that the only point to note is the somewhat different spread of investments shown in Table 13.5. By maturity the National Savings Bank had a smaller proportion of short-term local authority deposits, a smaller pro-

3. Committee on the Working of the Monetary System, *Memoranda of Evidence*, Vol. 1, p. 212.

portion of British government and local authority securities maturing within five years (23·6% at nominal value compared with 37·5% for trustee savings banks) and a much larger proportion of stocks over fifteen years and undated (35·9% against 13·6%).

14 Building Societies

1. THE BUILDING SOCIETY MOVEMENT

A. *Characteristics of building societies*

Building societies are specialised savings banks. The claims which they issue, called shares and deposits, are all short-term, even large amounts being withdrawable virtually on demand. On the assets side of their balance sheet they have the overwhelming proportion in the form of mortgages on owner-occupied houses; 15–20% of cash and investments and the premises from which they operate are the only other important items.

Building societies are unique among British financial institutions in the extent to which they operate within the personal sector. More than 97% of their shares and deposits come from individual persons, and a similar proportion of their mortgage lending is to individual persons. They account for around 90% of institutional lending for house purchase, and the purchase of around 70% of new houses built for owner occupation in recent years has been financed by them. Next to life assurance they have been the largest single outlet for personal savings in the past few years. Although building societies operate almost entirely within the personal sector, the lenders and borrowers are basically two separate groups of people; there is no necessary connexion between them as there used to be in the early days of the movement.

The first recorded building society was founded by a Birmingham publican named Ketley in 1775, and the early building societies were part of the self-help movement of the skilled workers during the Industrial Revolution, which also found its expression in friendly societies. The original societies were 'terminating' societies, in which the savers obtained houses in turn, often by drawing lots, the society terminating when the last member had obtained his house. In this form of society savers and borrowers were the same people. The present form of building society, with its separation of savers and borrowers, has long been dominant, but at the end of 1967 there were still eight terminating societies in existence, although their total assets were only £143,000.

The origin of building societies as part of the friendly society movement is still of importance to their method of operation today. It accounts for the fact that government supervision over the societies is exercised by the Chief Registrar of Friendly Societies, but more important it accounts for the fact that they are non-profit institutions. Building societies are mutual organisations, in which there are no proprietors distinct from the persons who hold shares in the society; there is no set of persons to whom any part of the excess of receipts over outgoings has to be distributed. Building societies make surpluses, but these are accumulated and retained as reserves, and there is no attempt to make any larger surplus than is necessary to maintain their reserves at a prudent level. Building societies operate on a 'cost-plus' basis, setting the rate which they pay to savers at the level necessary to attract sufficient funds and charging a rate of interest on mortgage advances that covers tax and expenses and yields the required surplus. They do not charge what the market will bear, and they are reluctant to raise the mortgage rate of interest. Although building societies compete with each other and strive for commercial efficiency, they conceive of their function as partly a social service, and it is this aspect which justifies our use of the term 'the building society movement'.

B. *Structure of the movement*

At the end of 1970 there were 481 building societies in Great Britain, but these were of widely different sizes. The largest society, the Halifax, with £1996 million of assets, alone had 18·4% of the total assets of the movement. The remainder of the size distribution is shown in Table 14.1 Notionally, we can divide them into three separate groups according to their scope of operations, although it would be difficult to assign many individual societies with certainty to any one group. First there are the few very large societies operating throughout the country. These have nation-wide branch networks, and advertise in the national press. Then there are the medium-size societies, which have branches and operate only in restricted areas of the country. Finally there are the small societies, most of which have only one office, which is often the premises of a local professional man, who runs the society more or less

on his own. Many of the very small societies are moribund, and most
of the growth of the total assets of the movement over recent years has
come from the large and medium societies.

The number of building societies has been declining steadily over
recent years. In 1890 there were 2795 societies, and it was not until
the middle of the 1930s that the number fell below 1000. A large part
of the explanation for the decline in number to the level of 481 in 1970
is the continuing process of mergers between societies. These mergers

Table 14.1   Size distribution of building societies, 1970

Size of total assets	Societies		Total assets	
£ *million*	Numbers	*Percentages*	£ million	*Percentages*
A. Over 250	10	*2.1*	6,956	*64.3*
B. 50 – 250	19	*4.0*	1,976	*18.3*
C. 10 – 50	63	*13.1*	1,278	*11.8*
D. 1 – 10	158	*32.8*	545	*5.0*
E. 1 & under	231	*48.0*	64	*.6*
Total	481	*100.0*	10,819	*100.0*

Source: *Report of the Chief Registrar of Friendly Societies,*
          Part 2, 1970.

consist partly of the taking over of the engagements of small societies
by larger ones, but there is also a considerable number of mergers
between pairs of fairly large or medium-sized societies. This is obviously
a tendency which will continue into the future because the pressures
which make for mergers are growing.

From the passing of the first Building Societies Act in 1836 building
societies have come under government supervision, exercised by the
Chief Registrar of Friendly Societies. This supervision has been carried
out by requiring annual returns to the Chief Registrar in sufficient
detail for him to ensure that the societies are fulfilling all the requirements laid on them by the Building Societies Act in force at the time
and that they are not exceeding the powers granted to them by the
Acts. Supervision has never gone so far as visits by government inspec-
tors, as it has with trustee savings banks. In 1959 and 1960 the Chief
Registrar was given two important new powers. (1) As a means of
combating the use of moribund building societies by property specu-
lators for purposes of private profit he was given the power to prohibit

advertisements and the taking of further deposits by societies which were being misused. (2) Shares and deposits in designated building societies were made trustee investments[1] for the first time, and the Chief Registrar was given the duty of designating societies according to certain criteria. For designation societies must have total assets of not less than £½ million (£1 million for societies applying for designation after 28 March 1968), their reserve ratio must be above a prescribed minimum level varying with the size of total assets and their liquidity ratio must be at least 7½%. Even when all these conditions have been fulfilled, the Chief Registrar still has discretion, and he has explained that in particular he would need to be satisfied that the building society was not so closely tied to a firm of estate agents, solicitors or accountants that it was not in control of its own destiny. At the end of 1970 there were 241 societies which had been designated. The designated societies accounted for 98·9% of the assets of all building societies.

Although building societies come under supervision by a government agency, they receive no special concessions from the government by way of subsidy, tax concessions or guarantees. There are special tax arrangements for personal savers in building societies, which are described later, but these do not result in any loss of tax to the government.

At the end of 1970 the Building Societies Association had a membership of 287 societies in the United Kingdom, and these member societies accounted for no less than 98% of the total assets of the movement. The Association acts as the collective voice of building societies in negotiations and discussions with the government. It also recommends rates of interest to its members, both on mortgages and on borrowed funds, but members are not bound to follow these recommendations. Membership of the Association is open to societies of any size, with prescribed minimum reserve and liquidity ratios, which are the same as for trustee status.

1. Unless they have been given wider powers by the trust deed or by the courts, trustees of personal trusts, charities, pension funds and similar bodies are permitted to invest only in certain types of asset specified by statute. In recent years the trustees of most large funds have taken care to obtain very wide investment powers.

2. BUILDING SOCIETY ACCOUNTS

A. *Balance sheet*

Table 14.2 shows the bare essentials of the collective balance sheet of all building societies as at the end of 1970.[2]

The main liabilities are shares and deposits. Shares have nothing in common with company ordinary shares, except that shareholders are members of the society, whereas depositors are creditors. Because of their privileged position in the event of liquidation of the society,

Table 14.2   Balance sheet of building societies, 1970

		£ million	*Percentages*
Liabilities			
Shares		9,788	*90.5*
Deposits		382	*3.5*
Government advances		56	*.5*
Other liabilities		190	*1.8*
Special reserves		11	*.1*
General "		392	*3.8*
	Total	10,819	*100.0*
Assets			
Mortgages		8,752	*80.9*
Investments *(BV)*		1,760	*16.3*
Cash		188	*1.7*
Other assets		120	*1.1*
	Total	10,819	*100.0*

Source: *Report of the Chief Registrar of Friendly Societies,*
         Part 2, 1970.

2. The statistics for most of the tables in this chapter are drawn from the *Report of the Chief Registrar of Friendly Societies.* This is the only source providing sufficient detail for our purposes, but it has the disadvantage that the figures relate to the accounting dates of the societies. Most societies end their financial year on 31 December, but three of the largest do not (Halifax 31 January, Woolwich Equitable and Leeds Permanent 30 September). The figures in *Financial Statistics* are for all societies as at the year-end or quarter-end. Societies in Northern Ireland are not covered by the Chief Registrar's statistics, but they are covered in *Financial Statistics*; some of them are members of the Building Societies Association.

depositors are rewarded with a slightly lower rate of interest (normally $\frac{1}{4}\%$ less) than that on shares. In recent years savers have been quite prepared to accept the nominally more risky position of being shareholders, and deposits have declined as a proportion of the total of shares and deposits from over 8% in 1957 to under 4% in 1970.

Building society shares are highly liquid. Over recent years societies have considerably eased their withdrawal conditions as a means of competing with other outlets for personal saving, and most societies will now pay out £50 or £100 over the counter and larger sums within a few days. There is effectively a maximum holding of £10,000 for each individual (£20,000 for a married couple) because the composite tax arrangements, which are described below, do not apply to holdings above this size.

Many societies issue shares with special features. These fall into four main groups. (1) Term shares, which receive an extra $\frac{1}{2}\%$ of interest as long as they are not withdrawn for a specified period of years, have never become very important. (2) Savings (or subscription) shares offer an extra $\frac{1}{2}\%$ or $\frac{3}{4}\%$ in return for a contractual saving commitment. They account for around 3% of all shares outstanding.[3] (3) Building societies have participated in the government SAYE (save-as-you-earn) scheme, and by the end of 1970 45% of the total amount contributed was with building societies—about £13 million out of a total of £9788 million outstanding in shares; assuming the same proportion the figure would, however, have risen to around £30 million by the end of 1971. (4) More than 100 societies have formed links with life assurance companies to issue 'building society bonds', similar in form to the property bonds which we shall examine in Chapter 17, which secure for investors in building societies the tax reliefs associated with life assurance. By the end of 1970 only £3 million has been deposited with building societies by assurance companies, and just under half of this amount was with one society.[4] The attraction to building societies of all these forms of share as a contribution to stability in their liabilities is obvious, but in aggregate shares of all four types represent less than 5% of all shares outstanding.

The remaining liabilities can be summarised readily. Government advances were made to building societies in the years 1960–2 to facilitate the purchase of older houses, although the scheme was officially discontinued in 1961, when a peak amount of £89·6 million was out-

3. A. R. Roe, 'The stability of contractual saving', *Building Societies' Gazette* (August 1970).

4. *Report of the Chief Registrar of Friendly Societies*, Part 2, 1970, p. 12.

standing. Reserves are the accumulated surpluses, to which we shall refer in detail below. Other liabilities were £89,000 of bank loans, all of which were to societies with total assets of less than £1 million, and creditors (tax payable, accrued interest and similar items).

On the assets side of the balance sheet the major item is mortgages. Of these around 85% are normal annuity mortgages, with equal monthly instalments. The remaining 15% are mortgage loans associated with endowment assurance policies. Many societies dislike this form of lending because there is no repayment of principal until the policy matures. The overwhelming part of the mortgage advances is to individuals for the purchase of owner-occupied houses, but building societies have always seen part of their function as providing finance to developers to enable houses to be built. This activity has been curtailed over recent years. Under the Building Societies Act, 1960, societies are permitted to make up to 10% of their advances in any year in the form of 'special advances', although the proportion is reduced if a society already holds excessive amounts of this type of advance. Special advances cover two separate categories—advances to an individual person which make his total indebtedness to the society over £10,000 (increased to £13,000 in 1971) and advances to bodies corporate. In practice over the past few years special advances have been running at just over 2% of all advances. In the Housing Act, 1964 special arrangements were made for building society loans to housing societies; advances totalling £14·4 million were made to housing societies in 1970.

The next two items, cash and investments, are both held for purposes of liquidity. The cash holdings are till money and accounts with deposit banks. The investment holdings are shown in detail in Table 14.3, from which it can be seen that they consist of roughly equal amounts of British government securities and local authority debt. Table 14.4 gives the maturity distributions for 1961 and 1970, showing the considerable shortening of the average life of the portfolio which has taken place. The investments which building societies are permitted to acquire are specified in statutory orders, and both quoted and unquoted securities are divided into three 'parts' according to maturity as indicated in the table. Acquisition of securities in Part II is permitted only when the overall liquidity ratio has reached a certain level, and a liquidity ratio of a still higher level is necessary before Part III investments may be purchased.

The other assets, which complete the balance sheet in Table 14.2, consist almost entirely of premises.

Table 14.3   Investments of building societies with total assets of over
£1 million, 1970

		£ million	Percentages
British government stocks (BV)		780	45.1
Other quoted (BV)		46	2.7
Local authority mortgages		500	28.9
Local authority deposits		332	19.2
Other unquoted		72	4.2
	Total.	1,729	100.0
Quoted: book values		825	47.7
market values		846	...

Source: *Report of the Chief Registrar of Friendly Societies,*
Part 2, 1970.

Table 14.4   Maturity distributions of investments of building societies
with total assets over £1 million, 1961 and 1970

Percentages

	Period to redemption	1961	1970
Quoted			
Part I	Up to 5 years	17.9	36.4
Part II	Over 5 and up to 15 years	31.3	11.0
Part III	Over 15 years	4.6	.4
Unquoted			
Part I	Up to 6 months	33.7	49.5
Part II	Over 6 months and up to 2 years	4.6	2.6
Part III	Over 2 years	8.0	.2
	Total	100.0	100.0

Source: *Report of the Chief Registrar of Friendly Societies,*
Part 2, 1969 and 1970.

B. *Balance sheet ratios*

Building societies operate with two balance sheet ratios, the reserve ratio and the liquidity ratio, and these are crucial to the mechanics of building society working. Minimum levels of both ratios are laid down by the Chief Registrar of Friendly Societies for trustee status, applying only to societies with over £1 million of total assets, and the same ratios must be followed by all members of the Building Societies Association irrespective of size. The minimum liquidity ratio is at a flat 7½%, but the minimum reserve ratio is based on a sliding scale— 2½% on all assets up to £100 million, 2% for assets between £100 million and £500 million, 1½% for the next £500 million of assets and 1¼% for all assets over £1000 million. A very large society, like the Halifax with £1996 million of total assets, thus calculates its minimum reserve assets ratio on successive tranches of its assets, and ends up with a minimum of around 1·6%.

For each ratio there are two definitions, an 'unadjusted ratio', which is used for most purposes, and a 'statutory ratio', which is used for defining eligibility for trustee status and membership of the Building Societies Association. The unadjusted reserve ratio is defined as

$$\frac{\text{general reserves and balances carried forward}}{\text{total assets}}.$$

This definition has the effect of excluding from the calculation specific reserves (except those against depreciation of or losses on investments) and amounts set aside for future taxation, which together amounted to £11 million in 1970. The unadjusted liquidity ratio is defined as

$$\frac{\text{cash and investments}}{\text{total assets}}.$$

For this purpose investments are taken at book value, including accrued interest.

The adjustments which are made in the calculation of the respective statutory ratios consist of the following elements:

(1) any excess of book value over market value of investments
(2) bank loans and overdrafts
(3) other liabilities as shown in the balance sheet
(4) government advances under the defunct scheme for aiding the purchase of older properties

(5) amounts recommended for distribution as interest, dividend or
bonus and not provided for in the annual return.

Items (1) and (4) are deducted from total assets in the denominators of
both statutory ratios. Items (1) and (5) are deducted from general
reserves and balances carried forward in the numerator of the reserve
ratio. Items (1), (2) and (3) are deducted from cash and investments in
the numerator of the liquidity ratio. Since item (1) is deducted throughout, the ratios are calculated at market value whenever this is less than
book value, and building societies are unique among British financial
institutions in calculating their ratios in this way.[5]
The differences between the unadjusted and statutory ratios naturally
vary from year to year, particularly with fluctuations in the market
prices of fixed-interest securities. For 1969 and 1970 the figures are as
follows (in percentages):

		Unadjusted	Statutory
Reserve ratio	1969	3·67	3·59
	1970	3·63	3·64
Liquidity ratio	1969	15·94	14·15
	1970	18·00	16·33

These figures serve to illustrate the extent to which building societies
operate with ratios much higher than those prescribed as minima by
the Chief Registrar of Friendly Societies and the Building Societies
Association; in fact building societies regard the prescribed levels as
unusable minima, and aim to keep a considerable cushion above
the minimum levels of both ratios. To some extent this behaviour is
based on a misunderstanding, because the Chief Registrar has made it
clear that he would not withdraw trustee status for a temporary short-
fall, but it does raise the question of the optimum levels of both these
ratios. It was to this question that a committee (usually known as the
Hardie Committee from the name of its chairman) appointed by the
Building Societies Association addressed itself following the examination of building societies by the Prices and Incomes Board.[6]

5. See L. E. H. Williams, *Building Society Accounts* (London: Franey, 1966) pp.
161–70 for calculation of the ratios. This book is a most useful source for detailed
information on building society accounts and management accounting.
6. *The Report of the Inquiry into Building Society Reserves and Liquidity to the
Building Societies Association*, 1967, and National Board for Prices and Incomes,
Report No. 22, *Rate of Interest on Building Society Mortgages*, Cmnd. 3136, 1966.

We have dealt at some length in Chapter 4[7] with the general purposes of reserves in financial institutions, and building societies have no peculiarities in this respect. Reserves are the accumulated surpluses. Although no specific assets can be identified as the counterpart of reserves, total assets must exceed total liabilities by the amount of reserves (since there is no equity capital). The main assets which are at risk from loss or depreciation of value are mortgage balances and investments. In one year, 1964, losses on mortgages were as high as 0·01% of total balances, but in recent years the average has worked out between 0·01% and 0·02%. Specific provisions against mortgage losses in 1970 were around 0·05% of outstanding balances, but the general reserves would be at risk in the event of a severe economic depression. Before 1960, when societies held large amounts of undated stocks, losses on investments, realised or potential, were large, but the general shortening of portfolios has much reduced the risk from this element.

Liquid assets have similar functions in all kinds of financial institution—mainly to adjust the unevenness in the flows of income and expenditure and to meet the possibility of sudden withdrawals of liabilities. There is a considerable seasonal element in the payments of building societies, whereas their receipts are much more even, since the basic receipt is the monthly repayment of mortgages. Nearly all the tax payments are made in the month of January, and interest is nearly always paid half-yearly, with heavy concentrations in the periods 1 December–31 January and 1 June–31 July. As Table 14.5 shows, these two items account for a very large part of outgoings, and the need for a cushion of liquid assets to cover the seasonality of them is correspondingly large. There is also some seasonal element in the withdrawals of deposits and in the placing of new deposits, but with these the seasonal element is often overlaid by increased withdrawals or by a reduced intake of new deposits because building society deposit rates are out of line with those on competing financial claims. A very important function of liquid assets is therefore to enable the lending business of the society to be continued while a decision on the raising of deposit rates is being taken and implemented.

The levels at which societies aim to keep both ratios are of great relevance to the amount of new mortgage advances which they can make during a period. There is an intimate connexion between the reserve ratio and the possible rate of growth of building society assets, but the level of the liquidity ratio is also important because new funds

7. See pp. 103–6.

diverted to the acquisition of liquid assets cannot be employed in making mortgage advances. The Hardie Committee made recommendations about the levels of both ratios. It felt that the minimum liquidity ratio of $7\frac{1}{2}\%$ should remain unaltered, but it recommended that societies should aim to operate with lower actual ratios than they had

Table 14.5   Revenue and appropriation account of building societies, 1970

	£ million	£p per £100 mean total assets
Income		
Mortgage interest	706	7.02
Investment interest	98	.97
Other	24	.24
Total *(A)*	828	8.23
Outgoings		
Management expenses	68	.68
Share and deposit interest	465	4.62
Other interest	5	.05
Income tax on shares & deposits	226	2.25
Total *(B)*	764	7.60
Gross surplus *(A–B)*	64	.64
Corporation tax	26	.26
Net surplus	37	.37
Other credits and appropriations (net)	15	.15
Balance added to reserves	52	.52

Source: *Report of the Chief Registrar of Friendly Societies,* Part 2, 1970.

in the recent past. For reserve ratios the Committee was impressed by the extent to which actual reserve ratios varied according to the size of society, with the larger societies keeping relatively low ratios. It therefore proposed a sliding scale of minimum reserve ratios. The Chief Registrar followed this recommendation when he laid down the present scale of minimum reserve ratios, but the scale adopted was not quite so easy on the large societies nor so harsh on the small societies as the Hardie Committee had suggested. Over recent years the actual reserve ratios (unadjusted) in aggregate have declined steadily from 4·18% in 1965 to 3·63% in 1970.

C. *Revenue and appropriation account*

Table 14.5 sets out the revenue and appropriation account of building societies for 1970, with the proportions of each item expressed in the way that is customary for building societies, as ratios to £100 total assets, taking the mean of total assets at the beginning and end of the year.[8] Because mean total assets are £10,054 million, 1p per £100 mean total assets is roughly equivalent to £1 million in absolute terms.

The major items of the revenue and appropriation account consist of interest received and interest paid out, the margin between receipts and payments having to cover management expenses and taxation as well as providing a net surplus, which is the main source of additions to reserves. In this particular year the average rate of interest on mortgages (calculated on mean balances) works out at 8·58%, on investments at 6·35%, on shares at 4·94% and on deposits at 4·53%. Of the other income shown about 50% consisted of commissions received from insurance companies. These arise because building societies insist that borrowers insure their properties against fire and storm with a company nominated by the society. The society acts as an agent for the company in collecting premiums, and it receives commission for this as well as for any extensions of the compulsory cover which the householder elects to have on the same policies. 30–35% of the other income consisted of valuation fees and expenses, most of which also figure as an outgoing when they are passed on to the professional valuers by the society, and the bulk of the remainder was rent received from letting surplus office space.

Management expenses vary quite a bit with the size of society. Table 14.6 gives detailed information on the composition of management expenses for the different size groups of building societies. Staff costs work out at roughly 50% of total management expenses for all size groups, but commission and agency fees decline steadily as a proportion of total management expenses from 12·3% in size group A (total assets of over £250 million) to 1·5% in size group E (total assets of £1 million and under).

Even though they are non-profit bodies, building societies are liable to corporation tax on the surpluses which they earn, and before corpor-

8. Since these ratios are sometimes expressed in terms of £100 total assets *at the end of the year*, care is necessary to establish the exact basis.

ation tax was introduced they had to pay income tax and profits tax on them. They have often urged that they should not be taxed at all, but no government has been willing to concede the point.

The figure for income tax shown in Table 14.5 is not a tax on the societies themselves but on the interest paid out to holders of shares

Table 14.6   Management expenses of building societies by size group, 1970

Cost (p) per £100 mean total assets

	A	B	C	D	E	Overall
Directors' fees and expenses	.4	1.2	3.3	5.8	12.8	1.2
Staff	33.5	36.9	33.4	32.1	49.2	34.2
Office accommodation & expenses	15.1	16.9	14.8	12.4	16.7	15.3
Advertising	4.3	4.2	4.2	3.7	2.6	4.2
Commission and agency fees	8.2	8.3	5.9	3.6	1.4	7.7
Other (including depreciation)	5.0	6.3	6.0	5.9	9.0	5.4
Total	66.6	73.9	67.6	63.4	91.7	68.0

Source: *Report of the Chief Registrar of Friendly Societies*, Part 2, 1970.
Note: The size groups A to E are defined in Table 14.1.

and deposits. Under arrangements made with the Inland Revenue holders of building society shares and deposits are not themselves liable for income tax on the interest received. Instead the society pays income tax on their behalf at a special rate, known as the 'composite rate'.[9] The intention of this arrangement is that in total the Revenue shall receive the same amount of tax as if each individual had paid according to his own appropriate rate. The composite rate is re-negotiated every year between the Building Societies Association and the Inland Revenue; every three or four years the Inland Revenue analyses a sample of account-holders to provide a benchmark estimate.

There are three main factors which can change the composite rate from year to year: (1) changes in the standard rate, (2) rising incomes causing higher marginal rates of tax with an unchanged standard rate and (3) changes in the composition of persons holding building society shares and deposits according to the marginal rates of tax to which

9. The special arrangements apply only to personal holdings up to £10,000. They do not apply to surtax; for the purpose of assessing a person's liability to surtax any interest received from a building society is grossed up, not at the composite rate, but at the standard rate.

＊

they are liable. The combined effect of these factors over recent years has tended to bring the composite rate closer to the standard rate— from 65% of the standard rate in 1957/58 to 84·5% in 1970/71.

The main consequence of the composite tax arrangements is that the gross yield (pre-tax equivalent) represented by the interest received by holders of shares and deposits varies according to their individual marginal rates of tax. Since it is a part of the arrangements that persons whose marginal rate of tax is below the composite rate shall not be able to claim refunds, these people are subsidising standard rate tax-payers. There is also an element of subsidy to borrowers in these tax arrangements. If they did not exist, building societies would have to operate with a rate of interest equivalent to the present grossed-up yield to a standard rate taxpayer in order to offer a competitive outlet for these people, who account for about 70% of the holders of shares and deposits. With an unchanged margin building societies would have to raise their mortgage rate of interest; the composite tax arrangements thus enable societies to operate with a lower structure of interest rates on both liabilities and assets.

The other credits and appropriations (net), which are added to net surplus in Table 14.5 to give the balance added to reserves, are almost entirely dealing profits on the realisation of investments. With a port-folio of British government securities amounting to £780 million at the end of 1970 building societies have become important operators in the gilt-edged market, and the larger societies have made sizeable profits in favourable years; 75% of these profits in 1970 accrued to the ten societies whose total assets were over £250 million.

D. *Sources and uses of funds*

The last account which we shall consider, the sources and uses of funds statement given in Table 14.7, is a very important one because it shows the determinants of the volume of lending during a period. These are: (1) the repayment of mortgage principal, (2) the net inflow of shares and deposits, (3) the extent to which holders of shares and deposits are content to have the interest added to their holding instead of with-drawing it every half year and (4) the addition which is necessary to liquid assets or the extent to which these can be run down. The repay-ment of mortgage principal is of two different kinds: (1) the element of capital repayment included in the monthly payments to societies by borrowers and (2) premature redemptions of mortgages. Premature redemptions arise because people move house periodically, and very few mortgages run to their full term: the average 'life' of a building society mortgage is less than ten years. The proportion of total repayments represented by premature redemptions has tended to rise over recent years, and seems to be slightly in excess of 50%.[10] Since premature redemptions are usually associated with moving house, they

Table 14.7   Sources and uses of funds of buildings societies, 1970

	£ million	*Percentages*
Sources		
Repayment of mortgage principal	907	*37.2*
Increase in shares and deposits	1,162	*47.6*
Interest credited to accounts	284	*11.6*
Additions to reserves	52	*2.1*
Other	35	*1.4*
Total	2,440	*100.0*
Uses		
Mortgage advances	1,954	*80.1*
Increase in cash and investments	467	*19.1*
Increase in premises and other assets	16	*.7*
Other	3	*.1*
Total	2,440	*100.0*
Commitments for advances, end-1970	*514*	*...*

Sources: (1)   *Report of the Chief Registrar of Friendly Societies,* Part 2, 1970;
(2)   *Financial Statistics,* March 1972, Table 69.

Note: The figure for commitments refers to the U.K., whereas all other figures refer to Great Britain.

normally give rise to a demand for a new mortgage. The proportion of interest on shares and deposits which is actually paid out in cash has been declining over the years, and stood at only 39% in 1970.

Nearly all building society mortgages work on the annuity principle, in which equal monthly repayments are made throughout the life of the mortgage. These repayments are calculated in such a way that the

10. See S. K. Edge, 'Repayment of capital on building society mortgage loans', *Building Societies' Gazette* (December 1967) and A. R. Roe, 'The stability of contractual saving', *Building Societies' Gazette* (August 1970).

correct amount of interest is paid throughout, the capital repayment being a residual. The examples in Table 14.8 show the effects of this method. In the early years the payment of interest is a much higher proportion of each repayment than it is in later years. The examples also show that an increase in the interest rate and an extension of the initial term of the mortgage both reduce the proportion of capital repayment in the early years. An extension of the term does, however,

Table 14.8   Repayment of building society mortgages

Rate of interest & term in years	3%			6%			9%		
Year	15	20	25	15	20	25	15	20	25

Percentages of level periodic payment consisting of repayment of principal

Year	15	20	25	15	20	25	15	20	25
1	64	55	48	42	31	23	27	18	12
5	72	62	54	53	·39	29	39	25	16
10	84	72	62	70	53	39	60	39	25
15	97	84	72	94	70	53	92	60	39
20		97	84		94	70		92	60
25			97			94			92

Level annual payments (£p) on loans of £100

8.38	6.72	5.74	10.30	8.72	7.82	12.41	10.96	10.18

reduce quite considerably the amount of periodic repayment needed for a loan of a given size. When the interest rate on mortgages is raised by societies, they often allow existing borrowers to extend the term instead of increasing the monthly repayment. The flow of regular repayments available as a source of funds for further lending thus depends on four factors: (1) the level of the mortgage rate of interest, (2) changes over the recent past in the mortgage rate of interest, (3) the initial term of mortgages and (4) the rate of growth in lending over recent years. The last factor comes in because a quick expansion of mortgage lending means that a high proportion of monthly instalments is on recent mortgages, for which the interest element far outweighs the repayment of principal.

3. OPERATION

A. *Competition for funds*

Despite temporary setbacks, holdings of building society shares and deposits have increased in recent years at a rate faster than those of any other liquid asset. Building societies have many competitors, and they have had to fight to keep up the rate of progress needed to meet the high demand for mortgages. In this section we shall examine the nature of the competition and the selling methods of building societies.

Because of the composite tax arrangements building society shares and deposits are attractive particularly to standard rate taxpayers, people in the middle ranges of the income and wealth scales. Various surveys have shown that around 70% of the total is owned by persons aged 55 and over and that rather more than half is owned by women. Most holders seem to regard shares and deposits as a medium-term form of saving, to which access in case of need is easy and quick; the average 'life' of a share is around five years, and it has tended to shorten over recent years.

From this it is easy to see what are the main competitive outlets: (1) bank deposit accounts, (2) investment departments of savings banks, (3) other forms of national savings and (4) local authority mortgages. Building societies must therefore set their interest rates on shares and deposits at such a level that the grossed-up yield to a standard rate taxpayer is roughly in line with that on the competitive forms of saving. Not all of the competition takes the form of yield, especially as the interest rates on many of the alternatives are sticky: liquidity and the convenience of nearby branches are also important. On occasion the increase in permitted maximum holdings of national savings affects building societies, because of the considerable tax advantages which these forms of saving are able to offer. At the margin building societies are also in competition with unit trusts.

Building societies often benefit from sudden influxes of funds or suffer from sudden withdrawals for reasons other than the yields and other conditions offered on assets which are truly competitive. Although it is difficult to provide statistical evidence, building society managers often refer to sudden flows of funds to and from stock exchange securities. When persons wish to 'go liquid', they often regard building societies as a temporary haven for money released by the sale of securities, and these funds are withdrawn as suddenly when the general sentiment on the stock exchange improves or when there are particularly attractive new issues to be applied for. Building societies also suffer from sudden withdrawals designed to finance consumption, followed in the normal course by a slower build-up as persons aim to restore their holdings of liquid assets. The classic example of this is the 'spending spree' during the first half of 1968. During this period withdrawals were £208 million higher than during the comparable period of 1967, resulting in a drop of £173 million in the net increase in shares and deposits.

Any institution which aims to tap personal savings by offering liquid assets needs an extensive branch network. In 1962 building societies in the United Kingdom had 1138 branches, and by 1966 the number had risen to 1552, only thirty-seven of which were branches of societies with total assets of less than £½ million. By 1970 societies whose total assets were over £1 million had 2016 branches, and 83% of these branches were of societies whose total assets were over £50 million.

Although the large and very large societies have relied to a great extent on branches to expand their total assets, business obtained from agents (accountants, solicitors, stockbrokers and estate agents) still represents a high proportion. One effect of the expanded branch network is that less business is done by post, but there is little evidence that the proportion of shares and deposits obtained through agents has declined markedly; even for a very large society it could still be as much as 45% of the total. The proportion of mortgage business introduced through agents is higher than that for investment business. On this side there are some firms of mortgage brokers operating, who specialise in finding mortgages from building societies or other sources even when funds are tight, often by discovering a building society which is temporarily in an easy position.

B. *Setting interest rates*

Building societies set two basic rates of interest—that on shares and that on mortgages. When the share rate of interest changes, the rate on personal deposits and that on various special types of share (savings, subscription and term shares) normally maintain a constant differential with the rate on ordinary shares, although this has not always been so. Building societies have complete freedom in setting their own interest rates, since adherence to the recommended rates of the Building Societies Association is not a condition of membership. They may alter the rates of interest on existing contracts both for shares and deposits and for mortgages.

The basic calculation which individual societies and the B.S.A. carry out in setting their interest rates is very simple in form, although there are many complications, not all of which can be taken explicitly into account. The basic decision is to set the rate offered on borrowed funds, which we shall call the deposit rate (d'), high enough to obtain the funds funds judged to be necessary in the next few months, and then to obtain the mortgage rate (m') by adding a margin to d' sufficient to maintain the desired level of reserves. Building societies have a strong dislike of high interest rates on mortgages; as we have seen, they regard their business as partly the social service of making home ownership available as cheaply as possible, and in recent years their own feelings on this score have been supplemented by government pressure to keep down the cost of borrowing to owner occupiers. In esimating the future need for borrowed funds societies rarely operate with a concept of the total effective demand for building society mortgages. Unless changes in the market situation are readily apparent, they are more likely to project the rate of growth in lending from the recent past and then to assess d' at a level which they think will yield them the net inflow of funds necessary to maintain the estimated rate of growth.

Since about 1952 building societies have nearly always been faced with a bigger demand for housing finance than they can provide. They have never attempted to fix a market rate of interest on mortgages, but instead they have been content to ration mortgages whenever demand is excessive. When rationing is necessary, a society will allocate lending quotas to each region and branch, and then leave the local managers to keep within them; some societies will undoubtedly instruct managers on desirable methods of rationing, while others will leave the managers fairly complete discretion. Among the methods of rationing used are: (1) discrimination against older properties, (2) more conservative valuation of properties, (3) a tighter attitude towards including earnings which may not continue when deciding whether an applicant's income is sufficient to support a given loan and (4) the advance of a smaller proportion of the purchase price. Even if these methods of rationing are not used consciously, the general feeling of stringency will induce managers to be less charitable in all these respects.

Whatever may be the current level of interest rates, societies face an inertia against making a change, and changes in rate are by no means frequent. During the 16¼ years from January 1955 to April 1971 Bank rate changed thirty-seven times, but the B.S.A. made only sixteen changes in recommended rates, and seven of these affected only part of the rate structure (d' alone or m' alone). Societies have to take account of the costs of making a change in rates. Depositors and borrowers have to be notified of the change, and, unless the society has its accounts on a computer, the clerical costs of calculating the half-yearly interest payment are increased if the change occurs in the middle of a period. The considerable lag before a change in interest rate works itself fully into the society's financial results means that a society or the B.S.A. will have to be satisfied that the current situation will continue for some time before it makes a change. When interest rates are raised, the lag operates to reduce the society's surplus for several months. On the borrowing side a changed d' can be made effective within a few weeks, but within a similar period only m' for new mortgages can be changed because existing borrowers are usually entitled to several months' notice. When interest rates are lowered, the same factors operate to increase the society's surplus for several months.

The signals of a need for readjustment of interest rates are of two kinds, the first of which relates to d' and the second to m'. The first sign that a rise in d' may be necessary is a reduced net intake of shares and deposits. Societies cannot immediately couple this with reduced lending because the pipeline of committed advances is very close to three months' lending: next quarter's advances are committed by the end of the current quarter. The result is that the committed lending must be financed by running down liquid assets. Conversely a rise in liquid assets greater than can be attributed to seasonal factors is often (but not necessarily) a sign that d' could be lowered. There is no direct indication that a change is needed in m' because this is not a market rate of interest, but the result of adding a margin to d'. The indication that the margin has become too small is a drop in the reserve ratio.

The margin beteen d' and m' has to cover management expenses and taxation as well as to provide a surplus for augmenting reserves. The pressures on the margin have not been constant over recent years. Management expenses maintained a fairly constant ratio to total assets for some years, but recently they have begun to climb. Income tax on shares and deposits has tended to rise, but the margin has had the benefit of one reduction in standard rate in recent years. The rate of corporation tax has declined from 45% to 40% since its introduction in 1965, and its impact has been considerably less than that of income tax and profits tax before 1965. The main pressure on the margin has probably come from the fast rate of growth of total assets. As we saw in Chapter 4,[11] there is a simple mathematical relationship linking the rate of growth, net surplus and the reserve ratio, such that a faster

11. See p. 101.

rate of growth leads to the need for a larger surplus if the reserve ratio is not to decline.

We have already seen that the bulk of building society mortgages are on the annuity principle, in which equal monthly instalments contain varying amounts of interest and the repayment of principal from year to year, with the interest element predominating in the earlier years of the mortgage.[12] With mortgages of this type changes in m' affect the proportions of the monthly instalments going to interest and capital repayment respectively and hence the sum total of funds available for further lending. When m' is raised, societies can either (1) recalculate the monthly repayments corresponding to the new interest rate or (2) permit the borrower to continue his monthly repayments at the old rate and extend the term of the mortgage. In recent years, despite the frequent increases in m', many borrowers have kept their monthly instalments at the same level and extended the term of their mortgages. Even if monthly repayments are increased to correspond with the rise in m', the proportion of capital to interest declines, but the proportion declines much more sharply if the term is extended. For example, with a twenty-year mortgage, five years of which have elapsed, a rise in m' from 6% to 7% reduces capital repayments by 7·4% if the monthly payments are increased but by 23·3% if the term is extended. The converse is true, of course, when m' is reduced, but over recent years the tendency has been for a sustained rise in m'. It is difficult to estimate what is the total effect on the flow of capital available for further lending by the building society movement as a whole under present circumstances; Miss Edge has calculated that a 1% rise in m' possibly reduces the flow of capital from regular repayments by around 10%, but the estimate is rather uncertain.[13]

Building societies thus face a kind of 'scissors movement' when they raise or lower interest rates. If they raise d', with an unchanged or increased margin, they necessarily raise m', and this in its turn leads to a reduced availability of funds accruing from the regular monthly repayments. There is no evidence that building societies take this factor into account in their computations, since the effects are probably within the margins of error on the calculation as a whole. Strictly speaking d' should be raised further or reduced more than is justified on an assessment of market conditions for shares to compensate for the effect on other capital flows.

12. See pp. 381–2.
13. S. K. Edge, 'Repayments of capital on building society mortgage loans', *Building Societies' Gazette* (December 1967).

This conclusion is reinforced by another factor which operates independently of changes in interest rates. Of the total flow of repayment of mortgage principal available to societies for further lending probably rather more than 50% comes from premature redemptions and rather less than 50% from regular repayments. There is no connexion between a rise in m' and the volume of premature redemptions, but there are grounds for supposing that the conditions necessitating a rise in d' and m' will also have caused a concurrent drop in premature redemptions. In our society it is becoming more common for people to change houses two or three times during their lifetimes. The movement is both geographical with change of employment and towards better-class housing with progression up the income scale, and the result is that few mortgages run their full term, the average 'life' of a building society mortgage working out at rather less than ten years. The common situation in the housing market under present conditions is for a number of transactions in houses to be linked together in a 'chain'; somebody will move into a newly-built house and sell his existing house to somebody else, who cannot provide the purchase money until he has sold his house, and so on. Such a situation is inevitable when there are few houses standing empty. When mortgage finance is easy to come by, these chains move fast, and the various transactions are completed at around the same time; when mortgage finance is difficult, the chains move very slowly, and many transactions which have reached the stage of an offer being made and accepted do not materialise at all. Since the conditions which have led to a rise in m' are likely to have been accompanied by a tightness in the mortgage market, premature redemptions will probably have been reduced at the same time.

The various elements that enter into decisions on changes of interest rates and the consequences that flow from a change are summarised in diagrammatic form in Figure 14.1.

C. *Demand for mortgages*

Building societies are not the only sources of mortgage advances for owner-occupied dwellings, although they dominate the market. Since we must deal with the global demand for mortgages, it is useful to begin by comparing the position of building societies with that of other suppliers of funds to the market. Table 14.9 shows the total advances (net of repayments) made by the various institutional lenders during the period from 1967 to 1970 and the totals of their outstanding house purchase loans at the end of 1970.

Figure 14.1 Rates of interest and funds available for lending

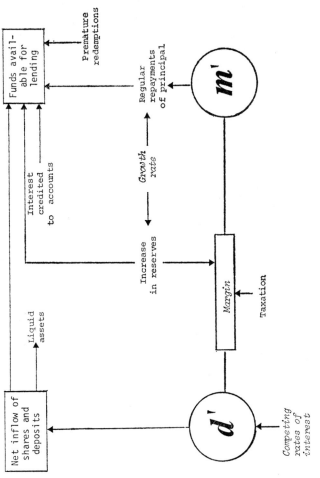

Of the institutions considered in Table 14.9 banks occupy a somewhat special position. A large part of their house purchase loans is to
their own staffs, and much of the remainder has been short-term loans
to enable borrowers to bridge the gap which arises if they buy a new
house before the existing one is sold; since September 1971 the deposit
banks have begun to make longer-term house purchase loans. Local

Table 14.9   House purchase loans, 1967–70

£ million

	Net advances				Amount outstanding Dec. 1970
	1967	1968	1969	1970	
Building societies	823	860	782	1,088	8,810
Insurance companies	˙34	71	83	36	1,154
Banks	40	25	− 5	40	411
Local authorities	68	9	− 30	37	988
Other public sector	18	15	16	9	90
Total	983	980	846	1,210	11,453
Percentage by building societies	*84*	*88*	*92*	*90*	*77*

Source: *Financial Statistics*, January 1972, Supplementary Table D.

authorities have often run up against cuts in government expenditure,
and they have to withdraw completely from the market when they have
exhausted the quota of lending which the government allows them.
Insurance companies rarely seek loans for house purchase, regarding
them merely as a means of selling endowment policies; for this reason
they tend to be the residual lender in the market. It is because the
other institutions are influenced by different factors from building
societies that the proportion of net advances made by building societies
fluctuates from year to year. In addition to the institutional lenders
shown in the table many other bodies like pension funds, charities and
trade unions make some house purchase loans to their members, and
there is still a considerable amount of inter-personal lending, either
within families or arranged through solicitors. All told these additional
sources probably amount to much less than £1000 million of outstanding debt.

We must begin our analysis of the global demand for mortgage
finance in physical terms, the number of extra dwelling units available

for owner-occupation. The main element in this quantity is obviously new construction for private owners, but there are several other elements to be added or subtracted before we arrive at the net increase in owner-occupied dwellings. There are three sources of new owner-occupied dwellings other than construction: (1) sales by private landlords of rented dwellings, (2) sales by local authorities and new town corporations and (3) conversion of single dwellings into a number of flats for owner-occupation. On the debit side about 5% of new construction for private owners is for renting, and the stock is reduced by slum clearance and sales to local authorities for re-development. The net effect of all these factors can be seen from the fact that during the period 1962–70 the number of new dwellings constructed for private owners was 1·76 million, whereas the increase in the number of owner-occupied dwellings was estimated at 1·95 million.[14]

Even the total increase in the number of owner-occupied dwellings does not equal the total demand for mortgages because of the 'chains' of transactions to which we referred earlier. Most of the people who sell existing houses will buy another house, either new or existing; they will redeem one mortgage and take out another. Since 1963 the statistics of numbers of mortgages advanced by building societies have been split into those on newly-built houses and those on existing houses. Some of the mortgages advanced on existing houses will be to persons who are becoming owner-occupiers for the first time, but the bulk will be to finance a move of house. In rough terms two-thirds of mortgages granted are on existing houses and one-third on new houses, but the proportion varies somewhat from year to year.

So far we have talked in rather nebulous terms of the 'numbers of applicants for advances', and we have not distinguished between those who are eligible for an advance and those who are not. We must now go on to consider the effective demand for advances and the factors that determine it. Although we shall be dealing in money terms, we shall still be concerned for a while with the numbers of applicants, and only later shall we translate demand in these terms into the total money demand for mortgages.

Applicants for building society mortgages are first screened by an income qualification. The requirement broadly is that the basic weekly wage shall be greater than the monthly repayment. For any given

14. A small part of the increase in the number of owner-occupied dwellings was caused by an upward revision of the estimated total stock as a result of the 1966 sample census of population. The figures come from *Annual Abstract of Statistics*, 1971, Tables 66 and 69.

mortgage advance the monthly repayment rises with m' and declines with an extended period of mortgage. To illustrate this we may consider a person who is earning £20 per week and see for what size of advance he could qualify under two different interest rates and for three different terms of mortgage:

Term	4%	8%
20 years	£3262	£2356
25 years	£3749	£2562
30 years	£4150	£2702

Not only is there a large drop in the loan possible with the higher value of m', but the proportionate relief brought by a longer mortgage term is less when interest rates are high.

These examples make the position look much more clearcut than it is in practice, since societies can vary both the income and the monthly repayment that enter into the calculation. Effective income can be varied by taking account of (1) regular overtime and bonuses, (2) probable future income for persons on a salary scale and (3) a wife's earnings. The monthly repayment figure can be varied by taking account of (1) maintenance expenditure and (2) rates. Building societies differ considerably in their attitudes to the various elements that can enter into the calculation, and the same society may change its attitude according to the ease or tightness of funds. The person who is in the best position of all is probably somebody on a salary scale; even if he has a young wife, the society will probably take account of her earnings for a period, by which time the husband's income will have risen.

We have seen that the term of the mortgage has a marked influence on the monthly repayment for a given size of advance, and building societies have been under pressure recently to grant longer-term mortgages to enable people with lower incomes to become owner-occupiers. There are several societies which will grant thirty-year and thirty-five year mortgages, but there are many more which will not go beyond twenty-five years. Of advances granted in 1970 only 6% had a term over twenty-five years. Even those societies which grant mortgages for thirty or thirty-five years pay considerable attention to the age of the borrower and to the age and condition of the property. A person who could look forward only to a state pension would not normally receive a mortgage extending beyond his retirement, and the maximum term for properties on the margin of acceptability as security for an advance would not be over fifteen years. There is no evidence of any marked trend towards an extension of the average term.

All the factors that we have considered so far affect the numbers of persons qualifying for an advance. None of them affects the size of loan demanded by an eligible applicant, although the period of repayment affects the availability of funds for re-lending from the regular repayments, since the longer the term the greater the proportion of interest in each monthly repayment. We now move on to factors that directly affect the size of the advance demanded. The first of these is the proportion of the purchase price demanded. This, of course, also affects the number of eligible applicants, since a person who qualifies on income may have few savings to provide a deposit.

The maximum proportion of its own valuation (or the actual purchase price if it is lower) which a building society will advance is normally 75–80%. It will, however, go up to 95% of valuation if it has additional security for the remaining 15–20%. This additional security can take three forms: (1) a single-premium insurance policy, indemnifying the society against default (the amount of the premium can be added to the advance), (2) a guarantee by a person or company, which is often backed by a sum left on deposit with the society and (3) a guarantee by a local authority under the Housing (Financial Provisions) Act, 1958. There is also provision for government guarantees of mortgages of up to 100% in connexion with the option mortgage scheme, which we examine at the end of the chapter. The average proportion of actual purchase price advanced by building societies in 1970 was 75% on new houses and 71% on existing houses. Once again we have no evidence of a rise in the average proportion in recent years. In their own loans for house purchase local authorities are much more inclined to grant loans for a higher proportion of valuation; in fact, about one-half of the authorities in England and Wales are prepared to grant 100% mortgages.

The major factor entering into the money demand for building society mortgages over recent years has undoubtedly been the steep rise in house prices. This has, of course, affected the number of eligible applicants, but the major effect has been the constant rise in the average size of mortgage advance. The relevant statistics are shown in Table 14.10.

Table 14.10 shows that the prices of new houses have risen much faster than the general price level, and that as a consequence the average value of building society advances has risen by 114% since 1960. Part of the rise in house prices can be attributed to increased construction costs, and a further part to improvements in quality (central heating, fitted furniture and larger garages, for instance). These two factors cannot explain the whole of the rise in prices of new houses; that the situation is basically one of demand exceeding supply is shown by the fact that prices of existing houses have risen rather more steeply than those of new houses.

Table 14.10   House prices and average values of mortgage advances, 1960–70

Index numbers (1960=100) of annual averages

Year	Average value of advance	Price of new houses	Retail prices
1960	100	100	100
1965	144	148	131
1967	171	168	140
1968	183	176	147
1969	196	189	155
1970	214	201	165

Sources: (1) *Report of the Chief Registrar of Friendly Societies*;
           (2) Department of the Environment;
           (3) *Monthly Digest of Statistics*.

We have already looked at the 'chains' of transactions in existing houses as adding to the numbers of applicants for building society mortgages, but we must now consider their effect in money terms. At first sight it would seem that persons who had redeemed one mortgage would demand a much smaller mortgage for their next house, but there are factors operating in the other direction. Part of the capital gain realised on the old house goes in removal expenses, solicitors' and estate agents' fees, curtains and floor coverings for the new house and so on, and part of the remainder may be treated as a windfall gain and spent on consumer durables that could not previously be afforded. But the main factor which operates to keep up the level of the advance demanded on the new house is the desire for improved quality of housing; many if not most people will decide on the price of house that they can afford by looking at the level of monthly repayments in relation to their income. The fact that on average in 1970 building societies advanced 71% of purchase price on existing houses as against 75% on new houses shows that realised capital gains do not keep down the money demand for mortgage advances to any great extent. When many people are moving house and the 'chains' of transactions are lengthy, the money demand for mortgages goes up by almost as much as if all the applicants were becoming owner-occupiers for the first time.

Figure 14.2 summarises in diagrammatic form all the various factors that we have been considering, but it is also useful to see the broad effect of recent trends on the operation of building societies. The main trends have been (1) a reduction in the contribution to funds available for lending from repayments of mortgage principal on outstanding loans and (2) a steep increase in the average value of mortgage advance. In 1962 building societies were able to finance loans totalling £613 million to 378,145 borrowers by attracting £296 million of new shares and deposits (a ratio of new lending to new borrowing of 2·07); in 1970 they needed £1162 million of new shares and deposits to lend £1954 million to 624,000 borrowers (a ratio of 1·68).

4. THE OPTION MORTGAGE SCHEME

On 1 April 1968 the government introduced an option mortgage scheme, which provided for a subsidy to the lending institution in the case of borrowers who agreed to forgo their right to tax relief on mortgage interest. At the same time an option indemnity scheme was introduced, under which the government would participate in a guarantee enabling borrowers to secure up to 100% mortgages. Both schemes are operated by all types of lending institution, so that competition between them is unaffected.

The background to the subsidy in the option mortgage scheme is the present arrangement for tax relief on the interest element in mortgage repayments, whereby the interest is deducted from income before the liability to tax is calculated.[15] This inevitably means that those who pay tax at high rates get the most relief, and that those who are not liable for income tax get no relief at all. The scheme copes with this problem by providing a straight government subsidy of

15. The rate of relief is equal to the marginal rate of tax only if it can all be set off against unearned (investment) income. When interest has to be set off against earned income, the earned income allowance of $\frac{2}{9}$ is lost on the equivalent slice of earned income, reducing the tax relief to just over 30% instead of 38·75%. When all income is earned, the tax relief reduces the effective rate of interest on an 8% mortgage rate to 5·59%; when all the interest can be set off against unearned income, the effective rate is 4·9%.

Figure 14.2 Demand for building society mortgages

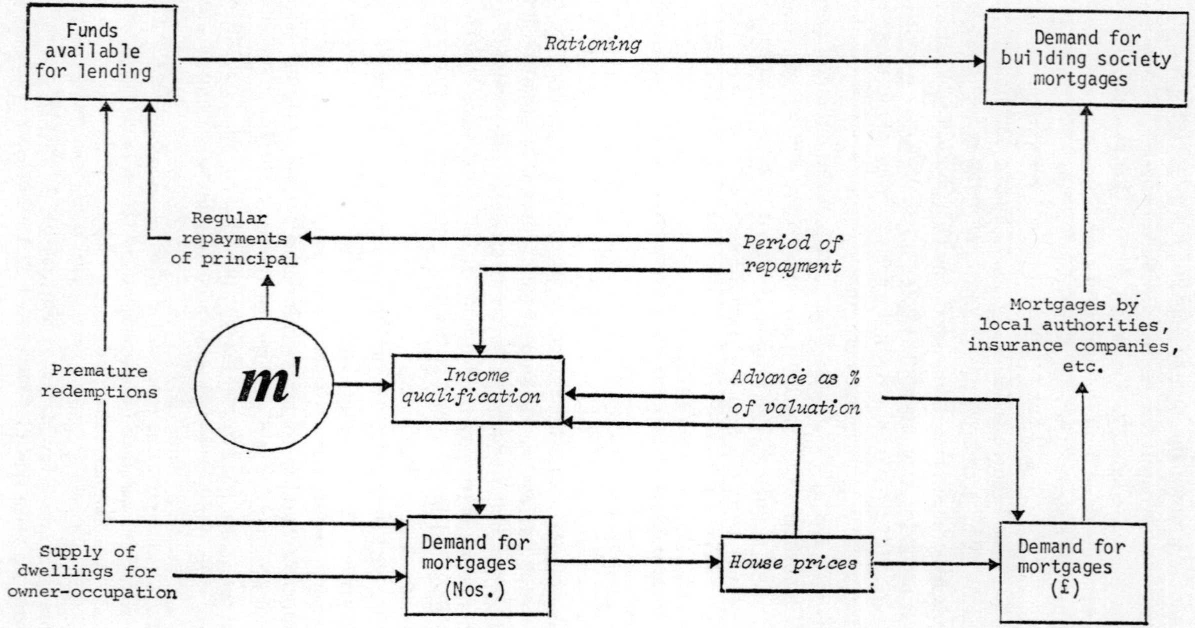

interest to the lending institution on the two sliding scales shown in Table 14.11, one for normal repayment (annuity) mortgages and one for mortgages associated with endowment assurance. The effect on the borrower is that his monthly repayments are calculated at a rate of interest equal to m' *less* the subsidy; with the current rate of 8% re-

Table 14.11   Rates of subsidy under the option mortgage scheme

Normal rate of interest	Rate of subsidy	
	Repayment mortgage	Endowment mortgage
6% to 7%	2%	$1\frac{3}{4}$%
Over 7% up to $7\frac{7}{8}$%	$2\frac{1}{8}$%	2%
Over $7\frac{7}{8}$% up to $8\frac{3}{4}$%	$2\frac{1}{2}$%	$2\frac{1}{4}$%
Over $8\frac{3}{4}$% up to $9\frac{5}{8}$%	$2\frac{3}{4}$%	$2\frac{1}{2}$%
Over $9\frac{5}{8}$%	3%	$2\frac{3}{4}$%

Note: When the normal rate of interest is below 6%, a flat rate of 4% is charged on option repayment mortgages ($4\frac{1}{4}$% on option endowment mortgages). Thus no subsidy is payable when the normal rate of interest is 4% or lower.

payments are calculated at $5\frac{1}{2}$%. With an option mortgage at this rate a weekly income of £20 will support a loan of £3225 over twenty-five years, compared with a loan of £2562 with normal repayments. When a borrower chooses an option mortgage, he forfeits all tax relief on mortgage interest; he may switch over to a tax relief mortgage after four years. Existing borrowers were allowed to switch over to an option mortgage when the scheme came into force, but since then borrowers may switch from a tax relief to an option mortgage only when they reach retirement age or in cases of hardship.

So far the option mortgage scheme has not proved particularly popular with building society mortgages. In 1970 nearly £100 million (5·1% of total advances) was advanced by building societies on option mortgages, and about one-third of this was for advances above the normal amount under the option indemnity scheme. Local authorities are thought to have advanced a higher proportion of option mortgages.

The effects of this scheme on building societies occur in three main directions. (1) The reduction of monthly repayments will increase the number of eligible potential applicants for a mortgage at any given m' over 4%. (2) The government subsidy goes entirely to the payment of interest, and for equivalent terms of mortgage a larger proportion of the borrower's regular repayment goes to reduce mortgage principal on an option mortgage than on a conventional mortgage. Borrowers will increase their equity in the house more quickly, and building societies will benefit from an increased flow of funds available for re-lending out of regular repayments. (3) The average size of advance is likely to be driven up yet further: not only will 100% mortgages have this effect, but the increase in the numbers of eligible applicants is likely to increase the upward pressure on house prices.

FURTHER READING

E. J. Cleary, *The Building Society Movement* (London: Elek, 1970).

PART D

Other Financial Institutions

15 Insurance Companies and Pension Funds

In this chapter we are considering a group of bodies with overlapping functions. Insurance companies are active in both life assurance and non-life (general) insurance, and they also operate the pension schemes of many companies. The remainder of the pension schemes are operated by independent pension funds. There are also several other types of body in this same general field, and it is convenient to consider them all together in one chapter.

1. STRUCTURE

A *Types of business*

All insurance business consists of a spreading of risks; risks are spread in two directions: (1) over time and (2) between persons and organisations. In statutory terms insurance business is divided into two broad classes: (1) long-term and (2) general. Long-term business has an emphasis on the spreading of risks over time, whereas general business is mainly concerned with the spreading of risks between persons and organisations. The division between the two broad classes is based on the ability of the insurer to cancel the contract, except that all life business is treated as long-term even if it is a contract for only one year (temporary or term assurance). With general business both the insurer and the insured have an option whether or not to renew the contract after a period (usually one year), and the insurer can alter the terms at renewal, whereas with long-term business renewal on the same terms is automatic for a period of years. It is for this reason that permanent health insurance counts as long-term business if the insurer cannot cancel the contract for a minimum period of five years.

Within long-term business the major part consists of life assurance,[1] the operation of which depends on the laws of mortality. Although the term conjures up a picture of business consisting of payments on the death of the person covered, this is only a small part of total life business; as we shall see, a large part of life business offers a channel for saving which is not greatly different from the business of a unit trust. Life assurance is split into two branches—ordinary and industrial. The industrial branch consists of life assurance in which the premiums are payable at intervals of less than two months and are collected by agents who call at the home of the policyholder; it is sometimes called 'home service' assurance. In the ordinary branch premiums are normally paid annually or quarterly by cheque or banker's order. The distinction is thus based on the frequency and method of payment of premiums, although the differences can be somewhat blurred in practice. The laws governing industrial life assurance are a little different from those governing ordinary life assurance, and companies and societies transacting industrial business come under some measure of government supervision through the Chief Registrar of Friendly Societies in his capacity as Industrial Assurance Commissioner. This supervision does not extend to control over the investment of funds.

In addition to the two branches of life assurance long-term business includes permanent health insurance, to which we have already referred, and capital redemption business. The latter consists of two main types of policy. The first is an annuity certain—an annuity for a fixed period of years whether the annuitant dies or not. The second is a sinking fund policy for the amortisation of debts, providing a lump sum to repay the debt on maturity. As Table 15.1 shows, permanent health insurance and capital redemption business are very small in relation to life assurance, and we shall not need to refer to them again.

The types of risk insured in the general branch are so diverse that grouping them is a matter of statistical convenience rather than of principle. There are five statutory classes laid down by the Department of Trade and Industry: (1) marine, aviation and transport, (2) motor vehicle, (3) pecuniary loss, (4) personal accident and (5) property. The last three of these classes are grouped together under 'fire and accident (non-motor)' in Table 15.4.

1. In this country it is customary to use the term 'assurance' for life business and the term 'insurance' for non-life business. This distinction is not adhered to rigidly, and it is not followed at all in the United States.

We have already mentioned the distinction between long-term and general business in terms of the ability of the insurer to cancel the contract. There is one further distinction between life (including capital redemption but excluding permanent health insurance) and general business. In life business the claim is fixed and certain; bonuses may have been added to the liability on with-profits policies, but at any one time a life office can compute exactly what its liability will be if a claim results. In general business, on the other hand, the insurance company can only guess at its liability if a claim results on a particular policy. If a house is insured for fire and storm, the damage may be total or it may be only superficial; in motor insurance the amount of the claim will depend on the cost of repairs; in liability insurance the amount of the claim may well depend on the award of a court in a case heard some years after the event. The amount of the claim is both variable in amount and ascertainable only some time after the event.

We do not need to consider pension business separately from the classification which we have just given. It is only a specialised form of life assurance. As such it forms a large part of the ordinary branch business of insurance companies carrying on life assurance business, and it is also carried on by independent pension funds, whose premiums and funds are not included in Table 15.1.

Table 15.1   Types of insurance business, 1970

£ million

Type of business		Premiums	Funds
Long-term			
Ordinary branch life assurance		1,538	12,080
Industrial branch life assurance		300	2,400
Capital redemption		7	40
Permanent health insurance		7	20
	Total	1,852	14,540
General		2,769	3,437

Source: estimates based on statistics of British Insurance Association, Life Offices' Association, Associated Scottish Life Offices and Industrial Life Offices Association, with allowance for non-members.

Note: The estimates cover the worldwide business of U.K. companies and of Lloyd's and the U.K. business of companies incorporated overseas.

B. *Types of organisation*

The operation of insurance companies and pension funds is a field in which consistent and complete coverage is very difficult to attain. Many of the statistics are produced by the associations of insurance companies, and cover only their members; the membership usually accounts for at least 90% by value of the business. The summarising of published accounts by the Department of Trade and Industry provides a complete coverage but is usually many years in arrears; the latest figures published at the time of writing relate to 1967. Very often figures for premiums are compiled on different bases by different organisations, and comparable figures can be estimated only roughly. Table 15.2 shows the best estimates which we can make of the

Table 15.2   Organisations conducting insurance and pensions business in the U.K., 1970

£ million

	Long-term		General	
	Premiums	Funds	Premiums	Funds
U.K. companies	1,730	13,500	2,205	2,600
Overseas companies	77	550	38	44
Lloyd's	–	–	526	793
Collecting societies	45	489	–	–
Pension funds	1,400	7,800	–	–
Total	3,252	22,340	2,769	3,437

Source: as for Table 15.1.
Notes: (1) The worldwide business of U.K. companies and Lloyd's is included, but only the U.K. business of companies incorporated overseas.
          (2) The premiums for Lloyd's are an estimate of the figure net of terminal reinsurance (see text).

premiums and funds for long-term and general business of the main types of organisation carrying on insurance business. It includes estimates for non-members of the associations; these are not carried into later tables.

The most important group in both long-term and general business is that of companies registered in the United Kingdom. Most of them are proprietary organisations, but bodies organised on a mutual basis account for around 25% of long-term business and about 10%

of general business. Altogether there are about 350 independent U.K. insurance companies. In round figures 40 of them are composites (carrying on both long-term and general business), about 50 do only long-term business and 260 do only general business. The composites dominate the field in terms of size, the dozen or so largest accounting for over 60% of long-term premium income and 85% of general premiums.

Companies registered overseas are much more important in long-term business than in general. In life assurance seven Canadian and three Australian companies account for about 99% of the life business in the United Kingdom carried on by non-British companies. The table also includes the premiums and funds relating to the overseas business of U.K. companies. Table 15.4 shows that about 65% of the premiums for fire, accident and motor business come from overseas, with about 28% coming from the U.S.A. alone. Although marine, aviation and transport business cannot be estimated geographically, it is generally reckoned that a similar proportion of premiums comes from overseas. The general business of Lloyd's is also dominated by the overseas element; about 75% of all premiums is estimated to come from overseas, and business in U.S. and Canadian dollars is known to be about 50% of the total. In long-term business the proportion of premiums coming from overseas is much smaller—just under 12% in 1970; three countries (Australia, Canada and the Republic of South Africa) accounted for 70% of the overseas premiums.

We shall be looking at the organisation of Lloyd's shortly. It is a market for insurance and not an organisation itself conducting insurance business. The underwriters are unincorporated, each personally responsible for his share of the liabilities of the syndicate of which he is a member.

The collecting societies are registered as friendly societies, and they are really those friendly societies which carry on life assurance. Although they do a tiny amount of ordinary branch business, they are important only in industrial life assurance. Even in this, however, they are completely overshadowed by the fifteen companies which have an industrial branch; the industrial assurance funds of these companies are around five times as large as those of the collecting societies. The number of collecting societies has declined from 100 in 1956 to 71 in 1970, and of these the eight largest receive about 99% of total premiums.

The last type of organisation listed consists of pension funds. Pension business is conducted both by life offices (as companies carrying on life assurance business are usually called) and by independent pension funds, which are set up by companies, nationalised industries and local authorities for their employees and placed under the control of a group of trustees. These independent pension funds control assets which make them most important financial institutions in their own right. The complex field of occupational pension schemes was last surveyed by the Government Actuary in 1967.[2] The results of this and earlier surveys showed that the number of pension schemes had risen from 37,500 in 1956 to 65,000 in 1967, each employer often having several schemes for different groups of his employees. Of the schemes active in 1967 it was estimated that around 90% by number were insured with life offices, all of the very small schemes but less than 50% of the very large schemes. The membership of pension schemes was estimated to have grown from about 8 million in 1956 to 12·2 million in 1967; this represented only just over 50% of the total employed population, but a more relevant fact is that the employers who had schemes accounted for over 90% of the total employed population. The estimated 11·4 million employees who were not members of schemes could therefore be split into 1·5 million whose employers had no schemes and just under 10 million who were not members of their employers' schemes for a variety of reasons—because they were too young, because they had not served long enough with the employer to qualify for the scheme or because their type of employment was ineligible.

Table 15.3 sets out what information is available about the distribution of contributions and funds between the different forms of scheme. We are concerned in this book only with those schemes which are funded, that is, which have funds equivalent to the actuarial liability invested in income producing assets; unfunded schemes have no assets and cannot be counted as financial institutions. The two last lines of the table show rough estimates of the contributions to notionally funded and unfunded schemes. The bulk of the pension arrangements in the central government sector do not figure in the table at all: pension schemes for the civil service and the armed forces are not only unfunded but also non-contributory. The estimates in the first two lines of the table show that the independent pension funds (uninsured funded schemes) account for around 60% of both contributions and funds of funded pension schemes.

On the fringes of the insurance fields are several types of body not

2. *Occupational Pension Schemes: Third Survey by the Government Actuary* (H.M.S.O., 1968).

listed in Table 15.2. The most important of these are friendly societies (other than the collecting societies mentioned above) and trade unions, which provide sickness, death, superannuation and other benefits to their members which are often similar to those provided by insurance companies.[3]

Table 15.3   Contributions and funds of pension schemes, 1967

£ million

Type of scheme	Contributions	Fund
Insured with life offices	328	4,000
Uninsured funded	533	6,000
Notionally funded public sector	350	–
Unfunded private sector	54	–
Total	1,265	10,000

Sources: (1) Government Actuary; (2) Inland Revenue; (3) Life Offices' Association; (4) author's estimates.

C   *Lloyd's*

Table 15.2 shows that in 1970 about 19% of the general insurance premiums received by British insurance organisations went to Lloyd's. Lloyd's is a unique organisation, and the Corporation of Lloyd's does not itself undertake insurance business. The risks are underwritten by unincorporated underwriters, each of whom is individually responsible with his own private wealth for his share of the risks insured. The Corporation of Lloyd's has three functions: (1) it provides the premises on which insurance business is undertaken; (2) through an elected Committee of twelve members it lays down the rules for the conduct of business; (3) it provides certain collective services, notably the centralised signing of policies and a centralised accounting system. Lloyd's is thus a market for insurance, on which individual members of Lloyd's compete for business.

The second function, that of laying down the rules of business, is the most important. Each new member of Lloyd's has to be elected by a

3. In *Insurance Business: Statistics September 1964 to August 1966* (H.M.S.O., 1969) the Board of Trade (now Department of Trade and Industry) provides an exhaustive survey of the many different types of organisation conducting insurance business, including bodies like friendly societies and trade unions.

ballot of existing members. Until recently membership was restricted to males of British nationality, but women and foreign nationals are now admitted. The rules laid down by the Corporation require that British members should be able to show evidence of a personal fortune in easily realisable assets of at least £50,000 (£75,000 for foreign nationals), and that a sum of at least £15,000 should be placed on deposit with the Corporation. All premiums must be paid into a Premium Trust Fund, and new members must make a substantial initial deposit to the Premium Trust Fund of their syndicate in addition to the deposit with the Corporation. These Premium Trust Funds operate under trust deeds approved by the Board of Trade and the Committee of Lloyd's. Out of the Trust Funds claims are paid, and ascertained profits are distributed to members. The business of each syndicate is subject to an annual audit, and the independent auditors may require higher proportions of reserves against each class of business than the minima laid down by the Committee. A further safe-guard is that members are required to negotiate with other members a guarantee policy for the amount by which their non-marine premiums exceed the deposit lodged with the Corporation. In addition there is a Central Fund, financed by a levy on premiums, out of which are paid any claims on which members default.

As members are unincorporated, they pay full income tax and surtax on all profits, but there is a concession by which profits may be ac-cumulated as reserves in a Special Reserve Fund without attracting surtax. There are thus three kinds of fund in which members' money is accumulated: the deposits with the Corporation, Premium Trust Funds and the Special Reserve Funds. The assets which may be held in these funds are laid down by the Committee. Until 1969 deposits had to contain 50% gilt-edged, but they may now be entirely in equities. A recent development is the formation by several unit trust managers of special unit trusts as collective pools for all the funds of syndicates. The rules as to proportions of certain types of asset are unaltered, but the unit trust can economise on assets held solely for liquidity pur-poses.

There are some 6300 individual underwriting members of Lloyd's ('names', as they are called), organised into about 270 syndicates, of which nearly one-half are concerned with marine insurance. The premises provided by the Corporation consist of one very large room, in which the syndicates are represented by underwriting agents. These agents sit in 'boxes' (rather like church pews) on the floor of the underwriting room, and accept business on behalf of the syndicates.

The agents are the only active participants in the market; for most of the 'names' Lloyd's underwriting is more akin to holding a portfolio of stocks and shares.

Insurance may be placed at Lloyd's only through the medium of about 250 firms of Lloyd's brokers. Representatives of the brokers operate in the underwriting room, and approach underwriting agents in turn with their business. When he has accepted business, the underwriting agent initials a 'slip' bearing brief particulars of the risk. It is customary for risks to be shared among a number of syndicates, each being responsible for a stated proportion of the total risk.

Lloyd's brokers are thus an integral part of the operation of this market for insurance. Although they act as agents of the insured in securing the lowest premium for his risk, they have other functions. They are often themselves underwriters, and they act as underwriting agents for syndicates. Balances with brokers, representing premiums that have not yet been passed on, are a considerable proportion of the assets of syndicates, and there is a perpetual effort on the part of syndicates to secure the more speedy passing on of premiums. Many of the larger broking firms are subsidiary companies of merchant banks.

One feature of Lloyd's is the three-year accounting system, in which each year's insurance account is kept open for three years and profits are not ascertained until the end of the third year. This system avoids the arbitrary estimation of unearned premiums and unpaid claims which is a feature of annual accounting. At the end of the three-year period outstanding claims are reinsured into an open account. This has the effect of inflating the reported premium income of Lloyd's as against that of companies carrying on general business because the premiums for this terminal reinsurance are counted as part of the premium income of the open account. We can make some sort of estimate of Lloyd's premium income on a basis comparable with that of companies by using an estimate of the Committee on Invisible Exports in its 1967 *Report* that the net overseas premium income of Lloyd's was £216 million in 1965. As the estimate assumed that overseas premiums were 75% of total net premium income, we can place the total net premiums at £288 million, just over 71% of the reported figure of £404 million. The estimate of Lloyd's premium income for 1970 in Table 15.2 is estimated by taking 71% of the reported figure of £739 million. Unfortunately we cannot spread this estimate over types of business in Table 15.4.

2. GENERAL INSURANCE

A. *Operation*

The business of general insurance is a service rather than financial intermediation. Policies for general insurance are not financial claims in the way that most life assurance policies are. General insurance business builds up funds, but these are nowhere near so large as the funds created by life assurance. As we have seen, the largest insurance companies do both sorts of business. For the most part they segregate the assets applicable to either sort of business, but several composite companies operate with pooled assets. Because the principles of general insurance are a useful introduction to the principles of life assurance, it is convenient to deal with it first.[4]

The essence of general insurance is the collective pooling of risks arising from fortuitous occurrences. The probability of the occurrence of events insured against can usually be assessed with reasonable certainty from past records, but the essence of insurance is that nobody can predict which of many persons or bodies at risk is likely to suffer during a particular period; if this prediction could be made, the risk would be uninsurable. For insurance to be worthwhile, the premium must be small in relation to the potential loss. Although it is quite possible to operate general insurance by waiting until the end of a period and then assessing a contribution from all members of the group at risk sufficient to pay the losses of those who have actually suffered, with an allowance for the expenses of administration, the premium is usually assessed at the beginning of the period and paid in advance.

Insurance companies and the underwriters of Lloyd's are professional risk-takers. They set their premiums on the basis of their past experience (if any) of the risks involved so that the total of premium shall cover all claims and the expenses of administration, as well as yielding an adequate profit. Policies in the general branch rarely run for longer than one year, and with some types (e.g. holiday insurance) the period is much shorter. There is no guarantee of renewal on the same terms, or indeed on any terms. Such short-term contracts do not create the large funds of invested assets which are characteristic of life assurance,

4. Readers will find a useful treatment in G. Clayton and W. T. Osborn, *Insurance Company Investment: Principles and Policy* (London: George Allen & Unwin, 1965) pp. 37–43.

but nevertheless the invested funds play a vital part in the operation of general insurance. As a rule of thumb it is usually reckoned that the fund must be 40% of annual premiums, net of both reinsurance and commission. This proportion is arrived at on the assumption of a steady inflow of premiums, so that at any one time the unexpired proportion of annual premium is equal to one-half. If we allow expenses at 20% of total premiums, the fund needs to be 40%. This is the minimum fund against unexpired risks (unearned premiums, outstanding claims and claims incurred but not reported), and in practice insurers hold additional reserves beyond these 'technical' reserves. The investment income from these general insurance funds is often enough to turn an underwriting loss into an overall profit.

The purpose of the assets held against the fund is primarily to provide cover for likely claims, but in addition the Companies Act, 1967, imposes two further requirements on companies carrying on general insurance business: (1) the paid-up share capital shall be not less than £100,000 and (2) free assets (which equal capital *plus* reserves) shall be not less than the amounts on the following sliding scale:

General premium income	Free assets
Up to £250,000	£50,000
£250,000 up to £2·5 million	20% of general premium income
Over £2·5 million	20% on first £2·5 million of general premium income and 10% on excess.

The second requirement imposes what is known as a 'solvency margin', and is equivalent to what we have called a minimum reserve ratio. The 1967 Act tightened the requirements so that they are now approximately double what they were under earlier legislation. This was because of the failures of several insurance companies in the period up to 1967.

Table 15.4 shows the net premium income of Lloyd's and U.K. companies in 1970 according to types of business and for U.K. companies geographically. No attempt has been made to secure comparability between the figures for Lloyd's and U.K. companies or between marine, aviation and transport and other classes of business of companies. Since the first line for U.K. companies combines three of the five statutory classes, it is clear that motor insurance is now the largest class of business. We have already commented on the geographical sources of premiums, two-thirds of U.K. company premiums and 75% of Lloyd's premiums coming from overseas. The contribution made by both com-

Table 15.4   Net premiums by type of general insurance business, 1970

£ million

| Type of business | U.K. companies | | | | Lloyd's |
	U.K.	U.S.A.	Rest of the world	Total	
Fire & accident (non-motor)	436	325	415	1,176	346
Motor	219	197	267	683	39
Marine, aviation & transport	...	...	...	225	354
Total	...	...	...	2,084	739

Sources: (1) British Insurance Association; (2) Lloyd's.

Notes: (1) All figures are net of reinsurance; those for the marine, aviation and transport business of U.K. companies and for all Lloyd's business are also net of commission (estimated at 15-20%).
   (2) Figures for Lloyd's are inflated by terminal reinsurance (see text).
   (3) Lloyd's motor business overseas is included with fire and accident.

panies and Lloyd's and insurance companies to invisible exports is considerable; for 1970 the Committee on Invisible Exports estimated that the total earned by insurance was £246 million (as against £90 million by banking), two-fifths being contributed by insurance companies, two-fifths by Lloyd's and one-fifth by insurance brokers.

The accounting arrangements for general insurance are complicated. There is a separate revenue account for each class of business conducted, with transfers to and from a combined profit and loss account for the company. The revenue account for marine, aviation and transport is on a three-year basis similar to that of Lloyd's, but the other revenue accounts are on an annual basis. Because the latest figures available are for 1968 and because it is impossible to secure comparability between marine, aviation and transport and the other accounts and between insurance companies and Lloyd's, there is little point in giving a table.

In the combined revenue accounts of insurance companies for all classes of general business except marine, aviation and transport commission was just under 17% of total premiums and management expenses were just over 17%. These figures illustrate the great importance of brokers and other agents in general insurance business; their importance in marine, aviation and transport business and for Lloyd's is even greater than for the classes of business for which we have figures. Insurance brokers are specialist advisers. They act as an agent of the insured in finding him the best policy for his needs, but they receive their commission from the insurer with whom they place the business; this is not an altogether happy situation. The commission is a remuneration, not only for securing the business, but also for carrying out many of the administrative tasks like processing claims and renewing policies on behalf of the insurer. Commission is paid each time a policy is renewed.

B. *Trends*

Over recent years there have been certain trends in general insurance business which serve to illustrate important points about its method of operation. General insurance has suffered from the effects of inflation along with all other activities, but over and above this there has been a rise in the cost of claims. With life assurance, as we pointed out earlier, the cost of an individual claim is known in advance, and the insurer has to worry only about the probability of the event insured against (death or the attaining of a certain age); with general insurance the probability that the event insured against will occur and the cost of the claim when it is made are two separate elements in the calculation. In some fields the probability of occurrence has increased and elsewhere it has diminished, but almost everywhere the cost of claims has risen, usually at a rate faster than inflation.

The British Insurance Association regularly produces estimates which show the effects of this process in certain fields. Estimated fire damage in the United Kingdom rose from £82·3 million in 1966 to £120·4 million in 1969; it was £110·9 million in 1970. Insurance company crime losses rose from £16·7 million in 1966 to £20·6 million in 1970. While the ratios of the number of claims on motor policies and of accidents on the roads involving personal injuries to the number of vehicles are on a downward trend, the cost of claims (total value of claims divided by the number of claims) rose by 60·3% from 1961 to 1970.

This phenomenon is due to three groups of causes: (1) the effects of increasing urbanisation, (2) modern technology and (3) sociological causes. Increasing urbanisation results in the concentration of risks of fire and storm damage, so that each claim is for a larger sum, and modern technology leads to larger factories and to processes which have a greater fire risk. In marine, aviation and transport insurance super-tankers of up to 500,000 tons and jumbo-jets are much more expensive than smaller craft; the jumbo-jets also carry far more passengers, so that personal accident claims arising out of a crash are much greater. The present increase in crime can be attributed to sociological causes.

The experience of insurers dealing with employers' liability and public liability illustrates other facets of this process. Many cases depend on court judgements, but the value of claims settled in other cases will be affected by the level of court awards. The awards of judges tend to increase stepwise; each judge follows his colleagues up to a point when one of them feels that a new level should be established, after which all fall into line again. The legal advisers of the claimant often urge delay in order to secure a higher award, and the insurance company is liable for interest from the date of the claim. One large company in this field finds that only 50% of claims by number are settled within one year; the average time between claim and settlement is eighteen months by number of claims and two years by value of claim. In this situation the estimating of the value of outstanding claims is extremely difficult.

Motor insurance is a good example of the effects of the extension of insurance to a mass market, caused in this case by the legal requirement for third-party insurance for all drivers. For weekly-paid workers the payment of premiums annually presents problems, and some insurers now make provision for quarterly or even monthly instalments. During the 1960s there was an outbreak of attempts to cut the price of motor insurance to meet the demands of poorer motorists; the result is well known—the failure of many of the companies providing cut-price insurance.

The insurance companies have reacted to this situation in several ways. In the first place they have increased premiums wherever they were able to do so. They have also become more selective in their premium rates, relying on better statistical information to sort out the good risks from the bad; this move soon runs into the difficulty that the segregation of risks increases administrative expenses. Lastly they have tightened up their business procedures. In particular they have become much stricter in applying the principle of 'averaging', by which an insured person who has economised on premiums by failing to state the full value of the premises or article insured receives only the appropriate proportion of his claim.

3. LIFE ASSURANCE

A. *Principles*

We have seen that in general insurance the contract is for a limited period, usually a year, and that the premium is, in principle at least, reassessed each time the policy comes up for renewal. There is no logical reason why life assurance should not be conducted on the same basis. The life office (as companies and societies carrying on life assurance are called) would assess the risk on each policy each year, and fix the premium accordingly. Clearly the premium would rise each year since the risk of dying increases with each year of age. This is an obvious disadvantage, but it is instructive to see in more detail how the scheme would work.

In order to assess the risk the life office uses mortality tables which summarise the mortality experience of a population. For policies in the industrial branch the life office will probably find the mortality experience of the general population sufficiently close, but for ordinary branch policies, the average value of which is considerably higher than for industrial branch policies, the office will rely on the results of a continuous statistical investigation of the actual mortality experience of those people who have taken out ordinary branch policies with all life offices in the past. In either case the mortality experience is summarised in a mortality table, which shows for each year of age the number of people who are likely to die out of a population of 100,000 persons of that age. We can get some idea of what a mortality table looks like by giving the average mortality in age groups of men according to the mortality of assured lives.

Age Group	Mortality per 100,000
10–34	85
35–44	170
45–54	533
55–64	1,498
65–74	3,992
75–84	10,088
85 and over	21,802

By the time the age group 85 and over is reached, the chances of a man's dying in any particular year are as high as 1 in 5. Of course, these figures are only averages, and the mortality table will show a picture of mortality increasing with each year. These are male figures, and it is these which are of most interest because relatively few women take out life policies. Female mortality is very much lower than male at all ages. In two age groups, 15–24 and 55–64, female mortality is little more than 50% of male mortality; for other age groups it lies between 60% and 75%, and approaches 90% in the 85 and over age group.

If life premiums were assessed annually on this table, a sum assured (sum payable on death) of £100 could be secured for a premium of about 10p at age 20, whereas the same sum assured would require a premium of about £10 at age 80. Beyond the age of 80 the premium would rise very fast each year, until at the age of 104 the premium would be equal to the sum assured. Clearly life assurance would be very attractive to the young, and there would come a time in each man's life when he would consider it no longer worth paying the premium. There is, in fact, one specialised form of life assurance conducted on this basis. This is group life assurance, which is used particularly by employers to provide life cover for their employees. Because a group of persons is involved, with some people withdrawing on retirement or death and new young persons entering each year, there is no necessary tendency for the premium to increase year by year. Term (or temporary) assurance, of which group life assurance forms a part, can be seen as the theoretical link between general insurance, with its annual renewal of the policy, and life assurance.

It is the basis of all other life assurance, however, that a level premium should be assessed when the policy is taken out, and that this premium should apply throughout the currency of the policy. The same principle applies when a single premium is paid to provide life cover for the years to come. The level annual premium is not just the average of the annual premiums which would be payable on the basis of annual reassessment, but is much lower. This is because a fund is created in the earlier years of a policy, and this fund earns interest, which is applied to the reduction of premiums. We can see how this works by considering the 'profiles' of three of the main types of policy —whole life, endowment and annuities. To do this we consider the progress of a group of identical policies all taken out at the same time.

We can begin with whole life assurance, which is the basic form of life assurance, providing for a lump sum payment only on death. The profile is illustrated in Figure 15.1, which shows the progress of a group of 965,000 policies, each for £1, taken out at the age of 40, on certain assumptions about the rate of interest and mortality.[5]

Figure 15.1 Whole life assurance

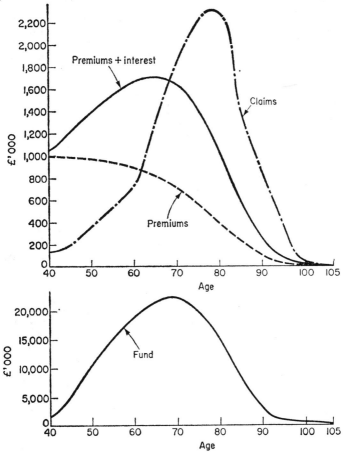

Progress of a fund comprising 965,000 whole life assurances effected at age 40. Premium: £1 per annum. Sum assured £63,339. Interest: 4% per annum, income tax and expenses ignored. Mortality: A1949–52 ultimate.

There are three periods in the progress of this fund. (1) Up to the

5. 965,000 is the number of survivors at age 40 of a population which numbered 1 million at age 10.

Figure 15.2 Endowment assurance

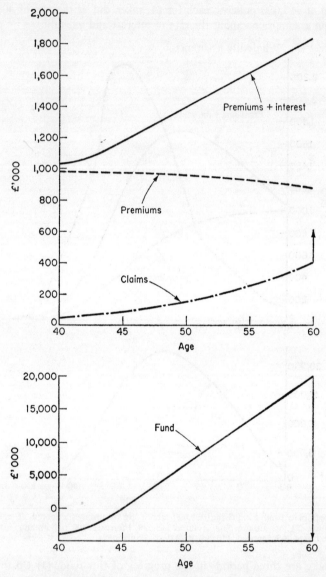

Progress of a fund comprising 965,000 whole life assurances effected at age 40, for a term of 20 years. Premium: £1 per annum. Sum assured: £28,843. Interest: 4% per annum, income tax and expenses ignored. Mortality: A1949–52 ultimate.

age of 59 premiums in each year exceed the value of claims paid out on death. It will be noticed that the amount of premiums received declines each year because policy-holders who have died drop out of the population. The excess of premiums over claims is invested in a

Figure 15.3   Annuities

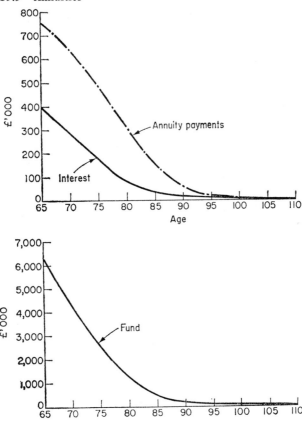

Progress of a fund comprising 781,000 annuities purchased at age 65. Purchase money invested: £6,664,100. Interest: 6% per annum, income tax and expenses ignored. Mortality: male lives of a(55) table for annuitants.

fund, which is assumed to earn interest at 4%. The total income of the **fund** thus consists of both premiums and interest, and the excess of income over claims in each year is available for ploughing back to earn further interest. During this period the fund rises all the time, as is shown in the lower half of the diagram. (2) From 60 to 67 the value of claims exceeds premiums but is still less than total income. The fund thus continues to grow, although at a decreasing pace. (3) At age 68 the value of claims exceeds total income for the first time. In order to pay the claims, some of the assets of the fund must be realised, and thereafter the fund declines, until finally at age 104, when the last death takes place, the fund is totally exhausted.

The same basic principles are at work with the other types of policy, although the profiles are quite different. Figure 15.2 illustrates the progress of a group of twenty-year endowment policies with the same assumptions as to mortality and interest rates as for whole life assurance. With an endowment policy payment is made either on maturity, in this case after twenty years, or on prior death. The curves of premiums and claims exhibit the same patterns as in Figure 15.1, but their slopes are gentle because the period is limited. The amount of interest earned rises consistently so as more than to offset the drop in premiums as some policyholders die, and the result is that the fund grows steadily, until it is all distributed on maturity at the end of the twentieth year. An endowment policy thus fulfils two functions: it provides life cover over its term (in this case only about 45% as much for each £1 of premium as with whole life assurance), and it acts as a means of saving. Endowment policies are used for three main purposes: (1) to save for retirement, (2) to amortise loans, as with house purchase when the proceeds on maturity are used to pay off the mortgage, and (3) to provide for expenses foreseen for a future period, such as school fees. It is useful to regard the premium for an endowment policy as divided into two parts—a relatively small part which purchases life cover and a larger part, which provides the savings element. We shall see later that with equity-linked assurance the two elements of the premium are explicitly separated.

The third main class of policy is an annuity, in which a lump sum is paid for the right to receive a stated income each year until death. The fund is created immediately from the purchase monies, and it is gradually dissipated in annual payments. The progress of a group of annuities is illustrated in Figure 15.3. In this example the purchase price of a £1 annuity is about £8.55. Annuity payments, interest (which represents total income for an annuity because there are no annual premiums) and the fund all decline steadily. It will be noticed that the mortality assumptions are different in this case, the last of the annuitants not dying until the age of 109 as against 104 for the assured lives. This illustrates another feature of life assurance. It is obviously in the interest of other policyholders and the life office that 'impaired lives', people with an illness or disability carrying an above average risk of early mortality, should be excluded from a life assurance fund, either whole life or endowment, or that at least they should pay higher premiums. For life assurance above a certain value life offices either insist on a medical examination or seek evidence from the proposer's doctor. With annuities the situation is reversed: people in poor health regard an annuity as a bad investment because the consideration is calculated on the basis of the average mortality of annuitants.

We can now see how pension schemes fit into the general picture of life assurance. The object of a pension scheme is to enable an employee, aided by contributions from his employer, to save during the period of employment enough to provide an income during the years of retirement. One obvious way in which this can be done is by a combination of two of the types of life assurance which we have considered, an endowment policy and an annuity. During employment contributions from the employee and the employer are used to pay premiums on an endowment policy, which matures on retirement. Although there is usually a guaranteed annuity option written into the policy, the employee is often free to invest some or all of the maturing proceeds in the best bargain he can find among immediate annuities offered by life offices at that time. Some pension schemes operated by life offices work on this principle, but a commoner method, applicable to both insured and independently-funded pension schemes, is that of the deferred annuity. The calculations of the actuary aim at building up a fund on retirement which will be sufficient to pay the annuity stated. With a deferred annuity there is no life cover, and this has to be provided separately.

The fourth main type of life assurance, which has grown fast in recent years, is temporary or term assurance. This has two major forms. The first is the group life assurance associated with pension schemes operated on the deferred annuity principle, which we mentioned above. The other is a policy which assures the repayment of the principal outstanding on a loan if the debtor should die before its maturity. The benefit to be received on death thus declines as the principal of the loan is gradually repaid. The difference between temporary assurance and endowment assurance, both of which are of limited terms, is that there is no payment to the policyholder of temporary assurance if he survives the stated period.

We have now dealt with the four basic types of policy. Life assurance polices are most flexible instruments, and these four types can be combined in many ways to serve different purposes. We have also examined the nature of the first three basic types by following the progress of groups of policies over their currency. This is a very artificial way of illustrating the operation of life assurance because in practice, of course, a life fund consists of different types of policy taken out in different years. The problem of a declining fund overall has arisen only in special circumstances in recent years because new business has almost always been to a greater value than claims paid: not only has life assurance become more widespread, but inflation has ensured a rising unit value of policies. We adopted this expedient of isolating groups of policies taken out at the same time only because it enables us to show the basic principles involved.

There is one further classification of assurance policies which must be mentioned, although we shall defer analysis until we deal with the question of valuation of the fund. Life policies of any type can be either 'with profits' or 'without profits'. In the latter case the sum paid out on maturity or at death is the sum assured of the policy when it was taken out; in the former case bonuses are added to the sum assured periodically during its currency or occasionally paid out in cash. The examples which we used in the profiles given above were all without-profits policies. The premiums on with-profits policies are higher ('loaded' in actuarial terminology) than on without-profits policies as an allowance for the bonuses that will be paid.

B. *Life funds and valuation*

The outlines of the various types of assurance policy given in the last section demonstrate the important role played by accumulated funds. These funds are invested in a variety of income-producing assets, and we shall look later at the general principles underlying the choice of assets. In this section our concern is with the size and value of the funds as an undifferentiated mass and the relationship of the fund to premiums on one hand and sums assured on the other. Because pension funds, both insured and independently-funded, are run on the same principles as life assurance, they too generate funds in exactly the same way, and we do not need to consider them separately.

We have already described how the fund is built up during the early years of a group of policies out of the excess of premiums and investment income over claims and expenses. This process is illustrated for the year 1970 in Table 15.5, which shows the revenue account of

British life assurance business. This table demonstrates the relative importance of investment income, which was more than 50% as large before tax as the flow of premiums. We shall be commenting on several of these figures in subsequent sections, but this is a convenient place at which to mention expenses and commission. For the ordinary branch

Table 15.5   Revenue account of long-term business, 1970

£ million

		Ordinary branch	Industrial branch
Income			
Premiums		1,381	298
Investment income (gross of tax)		746	165
Other income		41	3
	Total	2,170	466
Outgo			
Payments to policyholders			
Death claims		163	73
Maturities		259	103
Annuities (gross of tax)		199	–
Surrenders and refunds		241	70
Other		68	–
	Total	930	246
Management expenses		163 }	108
Commission		80 }	
U.K. taxation		95	23
Transfer to shareholders		21	5
Miscellaneous		–	2
	Total	1,289	384
Net addition to funds		880	83

Source: Life Offices' Association, Associated Scottish Life Offices and Industrial Life Offices Association.

these represented 17·6% of premiums (about one-third of which was commission), but for the industrial branch, with its expensive force of door-to-door agents, they were as high as 36%.

Life assurance can be very long-term business. Many whole life policies are held for forty, fifty or more years, and the term of an endowment policy is often thirty or more years. The premiums are fixed from the outset on actuarial calculations which assume future rates of mortality and an average rate of interest to be earned over the whole period of the policy. It is only prudent that these calculations should be checked periodically with up-to-date information to ensure that the fund has sufficient assets to cover its liabilities on policies. In Britain every life fund has to be valued at least every three years; with the advent of computers annual valuations are becoming more common.

An actuarial valuation is based on the method of discounting future income and expenditure back to the present. This is a method of valuation which originated with life assurance, but which is becoming commonplace in many other economic contexts. On the basis of a stated mortality table the actuary plots the receipts of premiums and the payments of claims for each future year, and then discounts each annual stream back to the present, using a rate of discount equal to the rate of interest which the fund's assets are expected to earn on average. Obviously both the choice of mortality table and the rate of interest are a matter of judgement, but actuarial calculations are inherently conservative, although with the rise of interest rates over the past fifteen or twenty years actuaries have begun to make some allowance for this in their calculations. There is one further element of conservatism. In the case of with-profits policies allowance must be made for future bonuses. Although specific allowance is sometimes made by estimating future bonuses (the 'bonus reserve' method of valuation), actuaries more often use the 'net premium' method, which makes a rough and ready allowance by using a lower rate of interest than would otherwise be necessary.

A life fund has a surplus if the value of the fund as built up from the excess of income over outgo is greater than the present value of future liabilities as determined by the actuarial valuation. Because of the improvement in mortality, higher interest rates and higher income earned from holdings of ordinary shares and properties, in recent years there has always been a surplus arising on valuation. The value of the surplus is determined by a calculation in the form: surplus = valuation − fund. The surplus is then available partly for distribution to policyholders (after allowing 5–10% for distribution to shareholders in the case of proprietary companies) and partly for adding to reserves. Only with-profits policies participate in the distribution.

There are three basic methods of distributing surplus to policyholders: in the form of cash, as a reduction in premium or as an addition to the value of the policy. The first two methods are not greatly used in this country, and the general method is the addition to the value of the policy, or reversionary bonus as it is usually called. This can be thought of as the free distribution of a premium sufficient to purchase an additional amount of assurance equal to the value of the reversionary bonus. The bonus may be declared either as a simple reversionary bonus, calculated on the original sum assured, or a compound reversionary bonus, calculated on the original sum assured *plus* any bonuses already declared. When the bonus is paid out in cash, the amount is considerably lower than the reversionary bonus declared because it has to be paid immediately. It can be seen that the reversionary bonus has quite a different effect on the operation of the life fund from the other two forms, since it represents an addition to net liabilities.

The surplus which we have just discussed is in the nature of a 'revenue' surplus, since it arises from an estimated excess of future income over future outgoings. There is also a kind of surplus which we may call a 'capital' surplus. The value of the fund is balanced by the values of the various assets of the life fund as recorded in the balance sheet. These assets are recorded basically at the cost of acquisition, although insurance companies in Britain have fairly complete freedom to write down or write up the value of various items in the balance sheet. Over recent years the increased holdings of ordinary shares and properties have ensured that the total of market values is nearly always in excess of the total of book values, and companies, spurred on by the competition from unit trusts, have begun to regard part of this capital surplus as available for distribution to the holders of with-profits policies. When a reversionary bonus of this type is declared, it is necessary to write up the balance sheet values of certain assets in order to balance out the increase in liabilities. Part of the capital surplus is often distributed as a 'terminal bonus' on those policies that become claims on death or maturity during the next year.

Until recently the main ways in which life offices competed were by declaring higher bonuses on with-profits policies and by setting competitively low levels of premium for all types of policy. The situation has been transformed over the past few years, however, by the introduction of equity-linked assurance. We shall look in more detail at the various forms of this type of assurance when we deal with unit trusts; here we are concerned only with the effect on life offices. Already in a very short space of time equity-linked assurance has became a major part of life assurance. In 1970 no less than 24% of the new yearly premiums obtained by life offices and 93% of the single premiums were for linked policies.

Equity-linked policies differ from conventional endowment policies in two main ways. (1) We mentioned above that it was possible to make a notional separation of the premium for an endowment policy into an element providing life cover and a savings element; this is done explicitly with an equity-linked policy. (2) The savings element of the premium is invested in a separate fund, usually composed entirely of equities or properties, run on unit trust principles. The fund may be notional, in which case it acts only as the *numéraire* in which the value of the units purchased with the savings element of the premium is expressed. The value of the policy is expressed in terms of the units in this actual or notional fund. The liability of the office therefore depends at all times on the market value of the assets in the fund, and the policyholder receives on maturity the value of the units which the savings element of his premiums has purchased. This procedure represents a method of determining and distributing surplus automatically. Reversionary bonuses, once declared, become a liability of the life office, and actuaries are therefore conservative in their recommendations. With equity-linked policies the function of the actuary is limited to the elements of mortality and expenses, and the investment risk is passed to the shoulders of the policyholder. If stock exchange or property prices are high when his policy matures, he will probably do better with an equity-linked policy than with a conventional one; if prices happen to be low, he will probably do worse. The money liability of the life offices is restricted to whatever money guarantee may be written into the policy.

C. *Life policies as a financial claim*

In their function as financial intermediaries insurance companies and pension funds hold a wide variety of financial assets and properties and issue policies as liabilities. (In the case of pension funds the individual member does not usually receive a formal policy.) Between them they are by far the largest outlet for personal savings. We have already examined the various types of policy, and in this section we look at the characteristics of life policies as financial claims.

A life assurance policy is a claim to a future payment of either a lump sum or an income. The valuation of a life policy is exactly analogous to the valuation of the fund, since a fund is no more than a group of policies. Thus the value of a policy is the present value of a lump sum or a future stream of income *less* the value of future premiums, the date of payment being determined by the maturity date or by reference to a mortality table. As with other financial claims there are methods of withdrawing from the obligation to contribute further premiums and of realising immediately the present value of the policy. The four methods of achieving these ends are: (1) the policy may be surrendered for cash, (2) it may be 'assigned' on the open market, (3) a loan may be raised with the policy as security and (4) it may be converted into a 'free' or 'paid-up' policy.

It is convenient to consider the last of these methods first. With a paid-up policy the policyholder ceases to pay premiums, but keeps the policy in force. Unless the cessation of premiums is provided for in the terms of the policy, this entails a reduction in the sum assured. The value of a paid-up policy is calculated on the assumption that there will be no further premiums, but that the assets representing the 'reserve' (or share of the fund) held against the policy will continue to earn interest. A paid-up policy value is thus a reduced sum assured. If a with-profits policy is involved, it may cease to benefit from bonuses declared after its conversion into a paid-up policy.

The other methods all involve an immediate realisation of the present value of the policy, and thus entail discounting the sum assured and future premiums back to the present. In the case of a surrender it is the life office which pays over the present value, whereas with an open market assignment (which is equivalent to a sale) it is a third party. Open market sales are possible only for policies of high value, and are conducted at specialised auctions; the price realised approximates the surrender value which would be paid by the life office but may well be higher. If the policyholder does not wish to lose the future benefits under the policy, he may obtain immediate cash by using the policy as collateral for a loan. Most insurance companies grant loans for 90% of the surrender value of a policy almost on demand, and many bank overdrafts and other loans are secured by life policies. At the end of 1970 the amount advanced by life offices on the security of their own policies was £194 million.

Since a surrender value is calculated on the basis of the present value of a policy, it is theoretically equal to the 'valuation reserve' (the amount held in the fund for this particular policy), but there are good reasons why no life office will pay out the full value of the reserve. In looking at the role of brokers and agents in general insurance business, we saw that commission was paid each time the policy was renewed, and that a large part of this commission was payment for administrative services. Life policies are long-term contracts, and the administrative work is nearly always carried out by the life office itself. Commissions are important, but they are paid for the introduction of new business, that is on the taking out of a policy. They are normally calculated as a percentage (1½–2% is common) of the sum assured. On the examples which we gave earlier commission calculated at 1½% would have taken 95p out of the first £1 premium on the whole life assurance and 40p out of the first £1 premium on the endowment assurances. In addition to commission there are heavy expenses associated with drawing up and signing the policy, and all of these come in the first year. If a policy is surrendered in the first few years, it has to bear all these initial expenses, and the surrender value is reduced accordingly. Not all policies may be surrendered or used as security for a loan. In particular policies associated with pensions schemes may not be surrendered or pledged.

Table 15.6 illustrates typical relationships between valuation reserve, surrender value and paid-up policy value for a forty-year endowment policy for £1000. The loan value can be taken as 90% of the surrender value throughout.

Table 15.6   Values of a non-profit endowment policy for £1,000
£

Years in force	Valuation reserve	Surrender value	Paid-up policy value
1	13	–	–
2	25	14	50
5	67	49	160
10	146	123	340
20	349	315	617
30	619	575	808

Assumptions: (1) Age at entry 25; (2) term of assurance 40 years; (3) mortality A 1949–52 ultimate; (4) rate of interest 3½%.

There are obvious reasons why life assurance and pension funds should be the most important channel for personal saving. With-profits endowment policies, which are perhaps the main form of assurance policy of recent years, provide life cover and a share in the rising income from equity holdings; pension schemes have become widespread over recent years. Even without tax advantages these forms of saving would be very important, but in fact they enjoy very considerable tax advantages. These are of four kinds: (1) a relief from income tax for premiums and contributions to pension funds; (2) a complete relief from income tax and corporation tax on investment income of independent pension funds and that part of a life fund devoted to pensions schemes, and a reduced rate of tax (currently 37·5%) for the other investment income of life funds; (3) estate duty concessions for life policies; (4) until the 1969 Budget a complete relief on interest paid on loans, whether secured by policies or otherwise. These add up to a considerable cheapening of the cost of life assurance and pension provision. We cannot follow all the different forms of tax relief through, but we shall develop the most important points.

The relief from income tax is at the standard rate on 40% of that part of premiums which does not exceed one-seventh of the sum assured and which does not exceed one-sixth of a person's gross income. With a standard rate of income tax of 38·75% this amounts to 15½% of the premium. Since the 1968 Budget policies must have a minimum life of ten years to qualify for full tax relief. With contributions to pension schemes assessed as such there is complete relief, but some contributions to policy-operated pension schemes are assessed as life assurance premiums and are given life assurance relief.

It is the tax relief on premiums which forms the basis of several savings schemes linking life assurance with the purchase of unit trust units and with house purchase. In the case of unit trusts between 4% and 14% of total payments goes to provide life cover (varying with the age at which the holder begins his payments); thus with the tax relief, which is reckoned on the total payment to the unit trust and not just on the cost of life cover, an assurance-linked unit trust scheme effectively provides life cover for nothing and still makes the purchase of units cheaper than it otherwise would be. The same principle applies to the building society savings schemes associated with life policies.

With the house purchase scheme there is tax relief on the endowment policy the proceeds of which will repay the loan, either from the insurance company itself or from a building society, on its maturity, and there is further tax relief on the interest paid on the loan. Until the 1969 Finance Act restricted interest relief to payments in connexion with housing, a combined endowment policy and loan arrangement was used in a number of ingenious schemes for the purchase of ordinary shares.

The important point to notice is that life policies have become in very many cases vehicles for carrying out some financial action which, if it were not for the tax advantages, could equally well have been performed without the intervention of life assurance. The taking out of life policies is more and more linked with such actions as house purchase, the provision of school fees, the purchase of unit trust units or ordinary shares and the straightforward avoidance of tax. In many of these cases the provision of life cover is regarded by the policyholder as an incidental, although it may be a valuable incidental.

D. *Structure of life funds*

In this section we shall begin to look at the structure of British life assurance, and to see what types of policy are the most important. We shall also try to estimate the origin of the different types of business in terms of the reasons for which policies were taken out. To do this we shall have to rely mainly on our own investigations and estimates, because the statistics available give some breakdown by types of policy for sums assured and for yearly premiums, although this is insufficient for our purposes, but none at all for the fund. It is the fund which is our main interest, since the fund is invested in real property and financial claims and hence represents the contribution of life offices and pension funds as financial intermediaries.

Table 15.7 gives a detailed breakdown of the different types of business conducted by British life offices at home and overseas and by Commonwealth companies in Britain. The figures are grossed up from an investigation of the valuation returns of twenty-four of the largest life offices. The figures cannot lay claim to any great accuracy, and they are best regarded as indications of orders of magnitude. The table gives estimates for the value of each major class of business in terms of the yearly premiums payable, the actuarial liability (equivalent to the fund) and sums assured. Policies or annuities purchased with a single premium have no figure in the first column under yearly premiums, but are included under the fund and sums assured figures. Since annuities yield an annual income but no lump sum, the equivalent to sums assured is the annual annuities payable. We cannot comment on all these figures, but we shall aim to bring out the most important points.

The most striking figure in the table is the total value of the U.K. annuity fund, which is just under 60% of the total ordinary branch fund for U.K. business. It is immediately apparent that pension business accounts for nearly two-thirds of the total annuity fund. Not all pension business is conducted on the basis of annuities; it can also be operated through endowment policies, the maturity proceeds from which are used to buy immediate annuities. The endowment policies provide death cover, but when schemes are operated through deferred annuities, group life assurance is usually purchased separately; this will appear in the table under term assurances. It can be estimated very roughly that the total fund associated with all three types of pension

Table 15.7   Structure of U.K. ordinary branch business, 1968

£ million

Type of policy	Yearly premiums (1)	Actuarial liability (2)	Sums assured/ *annuities* p.a. (3)	(2) / (1) (4)
With-profits assurances				
Whole life	42	261	1,720	*6.3*
Endowment	319	2,092	7,167	*6.6*
Term	8	16	1,135	*2.1*
Other	4	14	89	*3.8*
Total	372	2,384	10,111	*6.4*
Without-profits assurances				
Whole life	38	202	1,338	*5.3*
Endowment	96	797	2,439	*8.3*
Term	52	116	11,564	*2.2*
Other	14	53	3,387	*3.9*
Total	200	1,168	18,728	*5.8*
Annuities				
Immediate	–	1,684	*176*	...
Deferred	253	3,242	*1,190*	*12.8*
Total	253	4,926	*1,366*	...
Overall total	825	8,478	{ 28,839 / *1,366* }	*10.3*

Source: author's estimates.

policy (annuities, endowment and term) in 1968 was around £4400 million, without taking into account pension schemes operated overseas. This figure represented about 50% of the total ordinary branch fund in respect of U.K. business; premiums were over 40% of all U.K. ordinary branch premiums and sums assured about 25% of all U.K.

ordinary branch sums assured. (The figures in the last line of Table 15.8 give the percentages in relation to the total ordinary branch fund, including overseas business.)

In the last section we referred to the fact that life policies were often vehicles for other financial transactions, which would have been carried out without the intervention of life assurance if it were not for the tax advantages. The most important of these is house purchase, into

Table 15.8   Changes in the structure of ordinary branch business, 1952–68

Percentages

	Yearly premiums			Fund		
	1952	1960	1968	1952	1960	1968
Assurances in U.K.						
With profits	40.8	35.3	38.0	42.1	31.5	25.4
Without profits	27.9	27.0	20.4	20.1	21.3	12.4
Annuities in U.K.	21.0	25.1	25.8	30.8	37.6	52.4
Overseas business	10.3	12.6	15.7	7.0	9.6	9.8
Total	100.0	100.0	100.0	100.0	100.0	100.0
U.K. pensions business	*25.2*	*38.9*	*36.1*	*16.6*	*37.1*	*45.8*

Source: author's estimates.

Note: The estimates for the proportion of U.K. pensions business are subject to wide margins of error.

which life policies enter in two different ways. The most obvious is when a life office lends a proportion of the purchase price of the house and secures the loan by the issue of an endowment policy; about 15% of building society mortgages are also associated with endowment policies. Again very roughly we can estimate the fund involved at about £735 million in 1968, or around 9% of the total ordinary branch fund for U.K. business. The second way is when a term assurance is taken out to secure the payment of the outstanding debt on building society mortgage if the borrower should die before it has been repaid completely. The total sums assured on this type of term policy are probably of the order of £1500–£2000 million, but the fund associated with such policies is very small indeed, probably only £10–20 million.

The last column of Table 15.7 shows the ratio of the actuarial liability to the yearly premiums. Since the actuarial liability is equivalent to the fund, this can be referred to as a fund/premiums ratio. It is a most important ratio because it measures the extent to which personal saving in the form of life assurance results in the supply of fresh money to the capital market. A low fund/premiums ratio implies that a large proportion of each year's premiums is absorbed in claims and expenses and never gets through to the capital market. If we consider policies of different types but similar in all other respects (age at taking out, level of premium, mortality and interest rate assumptions), then deferred annuities and endowment policies make the greatest contribution to the fund, followed by whole life; term assurance makes only a very small contribution to the fund because of the short period involved. The fund/premiums ratio is higher for with-profits policies than for without-profits policies.

The overall fund/premiums ratio is the result of a number of different factors, of which five are the most important: (1) the proportions in which various types of policy figure in total business, (2) the average term for which each policy has been in force, (3) the proportion of with-profits polices, (4) the extent to which actual mortality has differed from that assumed in the calculation of premiums and (5) the extent to which the actual investment income earned has been greater or less than the rate of interest assumed in the calculation of premiums. The fund/premiums ratio of around 9 (or around 8 if single premiums are included) for the United Kingdom is one of the highest in the world, and compares with a ratio of about 5 for the United States, where term assurance and without-profits policies form a much greater part of the total. This average fund/premiums ratio for the United Kingdom implies that year by year the increase in the total life fund is equivalent to around two-thirds of total household saving in the form of life assurance premiums (including single premiums). Looked at from this technical point of view, British life offices are extremely efficient in converting personal saving into funds for the capital market.

E. *Growth of life funds*

Over the period 1952–70 the total life funds of insurance companies (worldwide funds of British companies and U.K. funds of overseas companies) have grown 4·6 times from £2982 million to £13,584 million. Within this total ordinary branch funds have grown 5·5 times from £2030 million to £11,223 million and industrial branch funds 2·5 times from £962 million to £2361 million. Independent pension funds have shown an even faster rate of growth from around £900 million in 1952 to around £7800 million in 1970, a rate of growth of over 8·6 times.

The major factor in the growth of life funds of both insurance companies and pension funds over this period has undoubtedly been the extension of occupational pension schemes. Uninsured funds grew more than 7 times in the period 1952–68, and rough estimates suggest that the growth in funds of insured schemes has been from about £7–800 million in 1952 to about £4400 million in 1968, or 5½ to 6 times. On these figures for the insured schemes just about one-half of the growth of ordinary branch funds has been associated with pension schemes.

We have already examined the structure of U.K. ordinary branch business for 1968. Table 15.8 covers all ordinary branch funds, but compares the structures for 1952, 1960 and 1968. Here again the dominant feature is the tremendous increase in the relative importance of pension business. Whole life assurance, both with and without profits, shows the greatest decline in relative importance, whereas those types of business which make a greater contribution to the fund for any given premium flow have grown: endowment assurances and pension annuities together have increased from 53·3% of the total fund in 1952 to 65·8% in 1968. The major changes in the structure of the fund have thus been of a character to increase the fund/premiums ratio, the only main offsetting factor being the increase in the proportion of the fund accounted for by overseas business, which has a lower fund/premiums ratio than U.K. business.

The actual figures for the fund/premiums ratio bear this out. In terms of yearly premiums the ratio has risen from around 7·5 in 1952 to about 9 in 1968; in terms of total premiums it has risen from about 7·25 to around 8. The ratio between the annual increase in the fund and total premiums has also risen from between 50% and 55% in the early years of the period to around 66% in the later years.

One feature of the changed structure of assurance business is brought out by the widening gap between the fund/premiums ratio in terms of yearly premiums and that in terms of total premiums. In the early years of the period single premiums accounted for only about 3·5% of total premiums; over the years 1964–68 single premiums were some 10–15% of total premiums. In part at least the increased relative importance of single premium business reflects the use of life assurance in various schemes for estate duty avoidance and in recent years the popularity of property bonds.

Although we have seen that the changes in structure of total business were such as to favour an increase in the fund/premiums ratio, these changes in structure are not the whole explanation. The other main factors have been high and rising interest rates, fairly steady increases in the earnings from ordinary shares and properties and further improvements in mortality, all resulting in rising bonuses on with-profits policies.

4. INVESTMENT POLICY

A. *Types of asset held*

In this section we are concerned with the proportions in which various types of asset are distributed in the balance sheets of insurance companies and pension funds at the present time. Table 15.9 shows estimates of the market values of the various types of invested asset held by insurance companies (U.K. business only) and pension funds at the end of 1966 and 1970.[6]

There are some notable differences between the asset proportions of insurance companies and those of pension funds. (1) Pension funds hold considerably higher proportions of ordinary shares than insurance companies. This is because nearly all pensions business is in real terms (pensions based largely on final salaries), whereas many of the liabilities of life offices are in money terms—sums assured and bonuses already declared. (2) Both insurance companies and pension funds hold large proportions of assets under the heading of loans and mortgages. In the case of insurance companies nearly half of these are house purchase loans. For pension funds a large part consists of loans to parent bodies; the heading would be even larger if loans of local authority pension funds to their parent authorities had not been classified under local authority securities, thus swelling that heading. (3) Insurance companies hold a larger proportion of preference shares because they need franked income for that part of their business which is subject to corporation tax; pension funds pay no tax. (4) Insurance companies hold a much higher proportion of overseas company securities; like investment trust companies they have borrowed dollars for investing in U.S. securi-

---

6. The method of calculation of the market values for insurance companies is described in J. Revell, *The Wealth of the Nation* (Cambridge: Cambridge University Press, 1967) pp. 212–17. Since 1962 the publication of actual transaction figures has made the estimation more exact.

ties. (5) The interest of pension funds in properties (a heading which covers freeholds, leases and ground rents) is more recent than that of insurance companies, but the proportion has risen fast.

When comparing distributions of investments at market value as between one date and another it is as well to take note of the move-

Table 15.9   Investment of insurance companies (U.K. business) and pension funds, market values, December 1966 and 1970

Percentages

	Insurance companies		Pension funds	
	1966	1970	1966	1970
British government stocks	16.3	13.9	18.4	12.3
U.K. local authority securities	4.0	3.1	11.0	7.7
U.K. debentures	13.8	11.2	14.6	13.9
U.K. preference shares	3.1	1.4	1.3	.5
U.K. ordinary shares	27.3	31.1	41.0	51.6
Overseas government stocks	1.1	.8	.9	.5
Overseas company securities	6.1	4.4	1.0	1.0
Loans & mortgages	15.9	16.1	7.1	3.8
Properties	12.5	17.9	4.7	8.8
Total	100.0	100.0	100.0	100.0
£ million	11,427	15,059	5,479	7,255

Sources: author's estimates.

Note: The estimates for 1970 are only rough.

ments of share prices and interest rates, because these can alter the proportions considerably. The F.T./Actuaries index of industrial ordinary shares stood at 98 in December 1966 as against 139 in December 1970. The yield on long-dated British government stocks was 6·78% in December 1966 and 9·82% in December 1970, implying a drop in price of around 30% between the two dates.

The business of pension funds is reasonably homogeneous, but with insurance companies we can usefully consider the different types of investment held by long-term and general funds and in respect of overseas business. Table 15.10 gives such an analysis, but unfortunately it has to be in terms of book values. The fourth column of this table is the book value equivalent of the market value distribution shown for the same date in Table 15.9. It is easy to see that it is the dominant overseas element in general business which leads to the large holding of overseas government stocks. The general funds hold lower proportions of British government securities, loans and mortgages and properties than the long-term funds; in the case of properties those held by the general funds are often the head office and branch offices of the insurance company as a whole. The proportion of properties is also lower in the assets held against overseas business (nearly all of them physical assets located in the countries concerned and financial claims issued in the countries concerned) than in the U.K.

Table 15.10   Investments of insurance companies (worldwide business), December 1970, book values

Percentages

	Total	Funds		Business	
		Long-term	General	U.K.	Overseas
U.K. public sector securities	14.6	15.8	8.2	17.4	–
Overseas government stocks	5.8	3.4	18.6	1.0	30.5
.Debentures & preference	19.0	18.5	21.9	20.8	10.0
Ordinary shares	28.6	27.5	34.4	28.3	30.0
Loans & mortgages	19.6	21.4	9.7	18.7	24.1
Properties	12.4	13.4	7.2	13.8	5.3
Total	100.0	100.0	100.0	100.0	100.0
£ million	*15,533*	*13,070*	*2,463*	*12,989*	*2,544*

Sources: (1) British Insurance Association;   (2) *Financial Statistics,* January, 1972, Table 71; (3) author's estimates.

The maturity distributions of British government stocks are shown in Table 15.11, this time with two different methods of valuation employed, insurance companies and local authority pension funds at nominal value and the remaining pension funds at market value. For any given portfolio of bonds a market valuation distribution will minimise the proportion of long-dated as against a nominal valuation. Despite this caveat the general picture is quite clear: none of the distribution has less than 65% in the two classes of over fifteen years and undated, and the highest proportion (at nominal value) is over 93%. Some of the medium-dated and short-dated stocks are holdings of what were once long-dated securities in the life funds, but a large proportion will be holdings of the general funds. We have no comparable in-

Table 15.11   Maturity distributions of British government stocks
               held by insurance companies and pension funds,
               December 1970

Percentages

Years to redemption	Insurance companies	Pension funds		
		Private sector	Local authority	Other public sector
	NV	*MV*	*NV*	*MV*
Up to 5	2.4	8.5	˙1.6	6.3
Over 5 and up to 15	12.1	22.0	5.2	28.6
Over 15	67.4	63.2	77.6˙	60.3
Undated	18.1	6.2	15.6	4.8
Total	100.0	100.0	100.0	100.0

Source: *Financial Statistics*, January 1972, Tables 71 & 73-5.

formation for the maturity distributions of debentures and mortgages,
but it is safe to say that the average maturity will be much shorter
than for the gilt-edged, since the original periods to redemption are
rarely longer than twenty years.

B. *Investment Policy*

The liabilities of life offices and pension funds are very long term. In
whole life assurance a term of fifty years is common, and for endowment policies the figure is often thirty-five to forty years. Pension funds
generally have a liability from the time that an employee enters the
scheme until his death (or that of his widow) as a pensioner. It might
be thought that this situation could be met by a policy of matching as
operated by secondary banks, in which assets and liabilities are
matched term for term for term and by currency. A moment's thought
will show that the investment problem of a life fund is quite different
from that of a secondary bank. The bank has an obligation to redeem
a liability at its face value at some future date, and the margin between interest received and interest paid is available to meet expenses
and to contribute to current profits. A life fund, however, receives
premiums or contributions year by year, and has to invest both these
and the interest received on existing assets at the rate of interest current at the time of receipt. The eventual liability is much greater than
the sum of premiums or contributions, and the life fund will be able
to meet it only if the assumptions about future mortality, expenses and

interest are fulfilled.

Models have been developed which apply the general principle of matching to life funds. They tend to be complex, and they are followed even less closely in practice than the corresponding model for secondary banks. The models set a norm, departure from which entails some degree of risk, but they do no more. Life offices can take comfort from the fact that interest rate changes affect both sides of their balance sheets equally: a rise in interest rates lowers the capital value of their assets but also reduces the value of their liabilities through the use of a higher rate of discount. Like all other investors life funds and pension funds aim to maximise the expected return on their assets, subject to the need for diversifying the portfolio to reduce risk. Apart from certain tax considerations life funds are indifferent as between income and capital appreciation, especially now that terminal bonuses enable growth in values to be credited on a conservative basis to policy values. Pension fund valuations also take into account growth in values. Life funds and pension funds differ from most other investors in the constraints which the essentially long-term nature of their liabilities imposes on their maximising behaviour. Long-term liabilities must be broadly matched by long-term assets, and the figures which we have given for the maturities of gilt-edged show that life funds and pension funds are fully conscious of this consideration.

'Maximisation of expected return' is not a very precise phrase, but it is not one which we can usefully go on to explore in a few simple models, as in the theory of the firm. Here we are more concerned with the constraints on maximisation and how investment decisions are taken in practice. We can deal only in generalisations, but we must emphasise the great diversity among life offices and pension funds in their investment practices and procedures. To begin with each fund has a different mixture of liabilities in terms of type of policy and maturity. Broadly speaking the greater the proportion of with-profits policies in a life office's funds the greater the freedom it has in its investment policies, because reversionary bonuses are not a contractual liability until they are declared. On the assets side funds differ in their existing structures, and they may be inhibited from moving too rapidly towards an entirely new structure even if all the arguments of expected return point in this direction. Investment managers and the boards of directors and trustees to which they are accountable will differ in their views of future interest rates at any one time, and there will be different degrees of conservatism in their general philosophy.

As between insurance companies and pension funds there is one immediate difference to consider—that of taxation. Pension funds are 'gross funds', that is they pay neither income tax nor capital gains tax. Insurance companies, however, are subject to three different tax régimes. On most of their pension business insurance companies pay no tax at all on income or capital gains, and on other life business they are taxed at special rates on profits used or reserved for the benefit of the policyholders—37·5% on net investment income and 30% on capital gains. Profits on general insurance business are subject to corporation tax. Insurance companies and pension funds also differ, as we pointed out in the previous section, in the proportions of their liabilities which are in real terms and in money terms. Both taxation and this last consideration will lead them to choose different types and combinations of investments.

The formulation of the general principle of investment in terms of maximising expected return implies that considerations of the balance of the portfolio as between different types of asset are only of secondary importance. It seems that very few if any life funds start out with a target balance sheet in mind, but balance sheet proportions do often play some part in investment decisions. We have already seen that conservatism may demand that changes from the last balance sheet should not be too drastic, and there may be reluctance to allow the holdings of certain assets, particularly British government stocks, to fall below a certain percentage of the balance sheet total. These inhibitions will certainly not apply in all funds, but there are two balance sheet constraints which are probably of fairly general application. The first relates to investment in properties. In many big offices property investment is the function of a specialist department. Organisational efficiency often demands that this department should be given a quota of funds to spend independently of the investment department, but the nature of property investment, with the long period between commitment of finance and its calling, dictates that this should be a fairly long-term quota, more akin to a balance sheet proportion. The second balance sheet constraint is more important; it relates to the proportion of equities to be held.

Since the last war insurance companies and pension funds have greatly increased the proportions of ordinary shares in their portfolios: at book values the proportion for insurance companies has gone up from 17·2% of the balance sheet total in 1957 to 28·6% in 1970 and from 16·6% to 31·1% in terms of market values. The rising dividend income and capital values have offset the effects of inflation, and inflation has also caused life funds to take on other investments with an equity element, notably direct investment in properties and property leases with frequent rent revisions. Because of the fluctations of both price and yield to which equities are subject, most life funds and pension funds impose some kind of upper limit on the equity proportion of their balance sheet. What this limit is will depend on a number of factors, of which the extent of liabilities in real terms and the proportion of with-profits assurances on which future bonuses must be maximised are probably the most important.

As with all types of financial institution the investment problems of insurance companies and pension funds depend to a great extent on the nature of the cash flow. The general characteristic of the cash flow is its regularity. This means that life offices and pension funds have little need for liquidity; nearly all payments can be foreseen far enough ahead to be met out of the cash flow. General insurance business requires more liquid resources, but the regular nature of the cash flow allows these to be still relatively small. This regular cash flow also forces life funds to find a permanent home for the incoming money without delay.

Although the major characteristic of the cash flow is its regularity, there are some unpredictable elements in both inflow and outgo. On the inflow side the major unpredictable item is new business, particularly for single premium assurances and immediate annuities. An office which has a large proportion of single premium and immediate annuity business has a ready means of adding to its cash flow at fairly short notice by quoting more attractive rates for this business; as most of the policies are for fairly large sums and negotiated through brokers, the response is quite rapid. Maturities of existing assets also swell the cash flow. A further way of adding to the cash flow is borrowing, but, while some offices and pension funds borrow whenever investment conditions justify it, others refuse as a matter of policy to borrow at all. On the outgo side unpredictable elements are surrenders of life policies and refunds of pension contributions to employees leaving the firm. Regularity of cash flow does not mean that it is equal every month or quarter, or that its size can be predicted exactly.

Once the size of the cash flow has been determined (in practice this will be continuous adjustment of an estimate as unpredictable elements come up), the problem is one of deciding on the types of asset to be bought. In theory all decisions should be taken by comparing the expected returns on all kinds of investment opportunities and choosing the best up to the limit of available resources. In practice, however, there are some constraints, and the actual investment procedure of life funds and pension funds has something of a sequential nature. In logical order the events are: (1) the honouring of lending commitments and payments for assets undertaken some time before, (2) the inspection of investment opportunities brought specially to the notice of the life fund managers, and finally (3) a search for outlets for remaining funds.

The first step is necessarily the honouring of past commitments. These are particularly associated with property investments, where the lag between undertaking a commitment to provide mortgage finance or to develop properties on the office's own account and actual payment is often long and where the timing of the calls is unpredictable. An office, can, of course, cover these commitments by buying a dated bond or certificate of deposit when they are undertaken, but some offices prefer to leave them uncovered.

Life offices and pension funds receive a constant stream of investment opportunities from different sources. Policyholders approach life offices on occasion for a loan on the security of their policies, and these are usually a contractual right. Less imperative is a request for a house purchase loan associated with the taking out of an endowment policy. Other opportunities come from clients of an insurance company for whom it manages a pension scheme or undertakes general insurance; these may require either mortgage finance or the taking up of debentures. Both life offices and pension funds receive special offers from merchant banks and stockbrokers of lines of stock, usually at advantageous prices, and are asked to underwrite new issues. Lastly there are rights issues on ordinary shares already held by the fund, through which life funds have obtained many of their equities in recent years, both by exercising their own rights and by acquiring the rights of other holders.

These special opportunities have to stand comparison on yield grounds with opportunities available on the open market, but there is often an element of goodwill involved. Refusal to take up an opportunity offered by a merchant bank or stockbroker may result in the drying up of future opportunities from this source, and other insurance business may be lost if clients do not receive some measure of preferential treatment.

Although life funds are never completely out of the equity market, and the official statistics of their purchases and sales of ordinary shares show that they are always trimming and adjusting their portfolios, each office will be more or less enthusiastic at different times about the current state of the equity market as compared with the markets for alternative assets. We suggested above that many offices would have a target for the total holdings of ordinary shares, but this is a long-term figure, and does not prevent them from holding off from the market for several months at a time.

Having honoured their past commitments, particularly in the field of properties, and reviewed their special opportunities, life funds are now free to search on the open market, for either equities or bonds. Many of the larger funds have their own research departments, and all funds receive investment analysis from stockbrokers and merchant banks. We have suggested that life funds will enter on this search with a general idea of how much they want to invest in equities over the period, and this leaves the decisions to be concentrated on a residual amount of bonds.

For life funds all bonds are effective substitutes for each other, and the choice between debentures, local authority securities and British government stocks is based on relative yields. This means in practice that debentures will be preferred to local authority securities, and the latter to gilt-edged, as long as two conditions are fulfilled: (1) debentures must fulfil rule-of-thumb criteria of eligibility for inclusion in the portfolio and (2) both debentures and local authority securities must show acceptable yield differentials as compared with gilt-edged. Until recently many investment managers had fixed ideas of the acceptable differentials between the three main classes of bond, but ideas are now more fluid. The actual decision between the classes of bond nearly always depends on the availablility of debentures, because life offices and pension funds obtain most of their holdings from new issues, and they will generally take a large proportion of new issues of debentures which match up to their criteria of eligibility and show a yield differential which is acceptable at the time.

All this seems to leave British government stocks as the final residual use for available funds after other investment opportunities have been exploited. This is true to a great extent, but as we pointed out in Chapter 3, British government stocks have special attractions which are denied to other forms of bond; sometimes it is these attractions which will determine the issue.

FURTHER READING

G. Clayton & W. T. Osborn, *Insurance Company Investment: Principles and Policy* (London: Allen & Unwin, 1965).

G. Clayton, *British Insurance* (London: Elek, 1970).

J. H. Dunning, *Insurance in the Economy*, Institute of Economic Affairs Occasional Paper 34 (1971).

G. L. Melville, 'The unit-linked approach to life insurance', *Journal of the Institute of Actuaries*, Vol. 96, Part III (1970).
*

16 Investment Trust Companies and Unit Trusts

1. COMMON FEATURES AND DIFFERENCES

The main feature which the various bodies to be examined in this chapter have in common is that the major type of financial claim which they issue is formally almost identical with the major assets which they hold. In this they are distinguished from other financial institutions, which have a sharp differentiation between the nature of the claims which they issue and the assets which they hold. Investment trust companies, unit trusts and the other similar bodies have portfolios which consist very largely of ordinary shares, and the main claims which they issue are equity claims on a proportionate part of the portfolio. Thus they are means whereby investors can obtain a share in a portfolio very much larger and more diversified than their individual portfolios could be. They are in essence the pooling of the portfolios of a number of different economic units.

The purposes which this pooling of portfolios fulfils are twofold: (1) it enables holdings to be diversified and risks to be reduced and (2) it secures professional management. Because the expenses of purchase of securities decline with the size of the purchase, it is possible for a large portfolio to have a much wider spread of assets than a small one. The diversification of assets naturally reduces risks, and the risks for the holder of a proportionate share in the diversified portfolio are those of the portfolio as a whole. Professional management of individual portfolios can be secured by using the services of a bank trustee department, a stockbroker or a portfolio management company, but by now it has become uneconomic to provide individual attention to portfolios of less than about £50,000. In many instances these two purposes are of equal importance, but sometimes one or the other predominates. When an investment trust company or unit trust is specialised in the type of assets which it holds—specialising in overseas shares, the shares of a particular industry or commodity shares, for example—the reduction of risks is partly lost, and the major purpose of indirect holding of shares of these types may well be the securing of professional and expert knowledge of the particular market concerned. Many investment trust company shares are held by large institutions. Their own portfolios are large enough to provide adequate diversification; they may wish to obtain the advantages of professional management in a specialised market, but often it is one of the other advantages of investment trust shares to which we shall refer later which is the main motive.

Under the laws of the United Kingdom the only two forms which a pooled portfolio can take are the investment trust company and the unit trust, and we must now consider the differences between them. (1) Although the titles of both forms contain the word 'trust', only a unit trust is a trust at law. An investment trust company is an investment-holding company, incorporated under the Companies Acts and having the same type of capital structure as an industrial or commercial company. It is for this reason that the term 'investment trust company' is gradually replacing the older 'investment trust'; these are alternative names for the same type of institution, and they can be used interchangeably. (2) The managers of a unit trust are obliged to buy back units whenever their holders wish to withdraw. The prices at which they buy back units and the prices at which they sell units are based on an official formula which keeps the prices of units in line with the value of the underlying assets. If the holder of an investment trust share or debenture wishes to sell his security, he must do so on the stock exchange, since under English and Scots law there is an absolute prohibition against the buying back of their own securities by companies. (3) Investment trust companies are empowered to do two things which are prohibited to unit trusts—to raise long-term debt and to refrain from distributing part of the income received. They can also issue several types of share—preference shares and different classes of ordinary share. For these reasons the stock exchange price of an ordinary share in an investment trust departs, often by a large margin, from the price calculated from the underlying net assets; only by a coincidence would the two prices be identical.

The differences between an investment trust company and a unit trust are summarised in the American terminology. Unit trusts are open-ended in that the fund expands and contracts as new unit-holders come along or existing unit-holders withdraw; it is this expansion and contraction of the fund which keeps the price of the unit in line with the price calculated from the total value of the underlying assets. (Unit trusts are known as mutual funds in the U.S.A.) An investment trust company is closed-ended in that it can expand only by issuing new share or loan capital and by retaining part of its income in the same way as any other company and contract only by redeeming past borrowing or by distributing reserves.

It is only under our legal system and that of some Commonwealth countries with similar systems of company law that this sharp differentiation between the methods of working of closed-ended and open-ended funds need obtain. Under other legal systems an investment company may have amounts of authorised but unissued share capital, which it can issue to new holders; it can also buy back shares from holders who wish to withdraw. This mechanism for 'making a market' in the shares of the investment company keeps the share price in line with the value of the underlying net assets. Even under English law such a system would be possible if the body making the market were legally independent from the investment trust—a bank or other financial institution. One investment trust company has an issue of capital loan stock which can be redeemed at a discount of 10% of the net asset value on the holder's request; this is done through a subsidiary dealing company.

2. INVESTMENT TRUST COMPANIES

A. *Description and history*

We have already defined an investment trust as an investment-holding company, but many bodies which are not investment trusts would come within this wide definition. Fortunately, however, we can give a precise definition because the granting of tax privileges and of a quotation on the stock exchange as an investment trust depend on recognition by the Inland Revenue, which requires the fulfilling of certain specific conditions. The requirements for investment trust status are laid down by statute, and are as follows. (1) It must not be a 'closed company', which broadly means that it must not be owned by a group of people fewer than five in number. (2) Its income must be derived wholly or mainly from shares or securities, and no single holding (other than of securities of another investment trust) may amount at the date of purchase to more than 15% of total investments. (3) Some of its share or loan capital must be quoted on a stock exchange in the United Kingdom. (4) The company's memorandum or articles of association must prohibit the distribution as dividends of any profits arising from the realisation of investments. (5) The company must not retain more than 15% of the income which it derives from shares and securities.

The main tax privilege which recognition as an investment trust brings with it is in relation to capital gains taxation, and here the distinction is between an investment-dealing company and an investment-holding company. Most financial institutions which are not granted specific exemption from taxation pay corporation tax on their profits arising from the realisation of securities; effectively they are classed as investment-dealing institutions. Before the 1972 Budget both investment trust companies and unit trusts were taxed on capital gains at the same rate as persons (30%), and there were provisions for enabling holders of shares and units to claim credit against their capital gains tax liability for any tax already paid by the investment trust company or unit trust. Since the 1972 Budget both types of institution pay tax on capital gains at 15%, and there is a 15% credit for holders against their personal tax liabilities.

The first investment trust of which there is any record was the Foreign and Colonial Government Trust formed in 1868. Between then and 1875 a total of sixteen trusts were formed to hold securities on behalf of certificate holders. In 1879 one of the trusts failed to meet its interest payment, and the ensuing litigation brought a judgement from the Master of the Rolls that these trusts contravened The Companies Act, 1862, and that they were illegal under the Lotteries Acts. Although this judgement was upset on appeal, most of the trusts had already taken steps to become incorporated as companies. This episode in legal history explains why investment trusts retain their name although they are all investment companies.

Although the Scots cannot claim credit for this particular financial innovation, several of the first sixteen trusts were formed by Robert Fleming of Dundee, a name which is now found in that of a London merchant bank specialising in portfolio management. At the time of the formation of the earliest trusts the main outlet for private money was in opening up the west of the United States, and the wealthy jute manufacturers of Dundee and many other wealthy individuals in Britain provided the finance through investment trusts for the American railways and organisations like Wells Fargo, the staple ingredients of so many western films. Up to 1914 the overseas component of investment trust portfolios was of the order of 85–90%. The investment trust managements were providing not only a means of spreading the risks but also expert knowledge of this inherently risky market. During both world wars the overseas holdings of investment trusts were mobilised to further the military effort, and then built up again afterwards. The overseas component has never reached the overwhelming dominance of the turn of the century: in 1933 it was about 55% after having been 67% in 1923; in 1957 it was 41% after a record low figure of 21% in 1949, but by 1971 it was down again to 29%.

Not all investment trusts began with the sole purpose of holding shares and securities. Many had portfolios consisting of a mixture of properties and financial assets. Many were formed because their original line of business could no longer be continued. Thus some were originally plantation companies, and one, Cable Trust (formerly Cable and Wireless), was formed by applying the compensation money on nationalisation to the purchase of a financial portfolio instead of distributing it to the shareholders.

As we have indicated above, the majority of the shareholders of the early investment trusts were wealthy persons, and during their history investment trusts have generally been considered as vehicles to enable persons, wealthy and not so wealthy, to diversify their portfolios. However, by 1963 a survey showed that investment trusts did not have a much greater percentage of persons among their shareholders than the general run of companies: persons (including executors and trustees) were registered holders of 54·8% of investment trust shares by value, as compared with 48·6% of the quoted ordinary shares of all companies.[1] Financial institutions held almost exactly the same percentage of investment trust shares as of the shares of all companies; insurance companies held 12·2% by value of investment trust shares, and other investment trusts held 3·3%.

Since the definition of an investment trust company is so precise, there ought to be no difficulty in defining the total population. Unfortunately very few of the available statistics cover the entire population of all those investment trust companies one or more of whose securities are quoted on a stock exchange in the United Kingdom. We shall be using two separate sets of statistics as our source material. In dealing with capital structure and associated points we shall use information and statistics provided in its annual booklet on investment companies by a firm of London stockbrokers, L. Messel & Co.[2] This booklet gave information on 263 companies in 1971, including all investment trust companies with total assets of £500,000 or more as

1. J. Revell and J. Moyle, *The Owners of Quoted Ordinary shares: A Survey for 1963* (London: Chapman & Hall, 1966) Table V.4.

2. Permission to quote these statistics and to compile our own statistics from the information provided by this firm is gratefully acknowledged.

well as eight investment companies which did not have investment trust status. (These have been excluded from our tables wherever possible.) For details of investments we shall use the Bank of England statistics, which cover some 240 investment trust companies, excluding some quoted companies on the grounds that they were too small but including a few others none of whose securities was quoted.

The size distribution of the investment trust companies listed in the Messel annual booklet for 1971 is shown in Table 16.1 It will be

Table 16.1   Investment trust companies and management groups by size of total assets, 1971

Size of total assets	Investment trust companies			Management groups		
	Com-panies	Total assets		Groups	Total assets	
£ *million*	*Nos.*	£ *million*	%	*Nos.*	£ *million*	%
Over 100	4	409	*9.3*	15	2,134	*48.6*
50-100	13	958	*21.8*	15	1,050	*23.9*
25-50	41	1,477	*33.6*	19	734	*16.7*
10-25	63	982	*22.4*	21	298	*6.8*
5-10	52	370	*8.4*	10	84	*1.9*
1-5	74	189	*4.3*	33	89	*2.0*
½-1	10	7	*.2*	6	4	*.1*
Total	257	4,393	*100.0*	119	4,393	*100.0*

Source: compiled from information provided by L. Messel & Co.

noted that the degree of concentration among a few large bodies is not so extreme as among other types of financial institution. Over recent years there have been many mergers of investment trust companies for a variety of reasons. One reason has been the desire to widen the market for investment trust shares; this has led to amalgamations of investment trusts within the same group. Investment trusts with a high market status have also used their position to buy the assets and earnings of other investment trusts cheaply. In more recent years some investment trusts have used mergers to augment their portfolios in certain directions, notably to acquire dollar portfolios by the issue of sterling securities to finance the merger and to acquire assets which yield franked income. (The significance of these two types of merger will be apparent from the discussion on dollar portfolios and taxation below.)

Many investment trust companies are under common management.

The management functions necessary in an investment trust are four in number: (1) the taking of investment decisions, (2) the actual buying and selling of securities, (3) the registration of the holders of the shares and debentures of the company and the payment of interest and dividends and (4) the functions carried out by a company secretary. All of these can be contracted out to specialists. Investment management can be undertaken by a specialist company or by a bank; buying and selling of securities can be facilitated by using the services of a bank nominee company; registration can be done by a bank or other specialist registrar; secretarial services can be obtained from an accountant or solicitor. Literally all that an investment trust company needs by way of personnel is a board of directors. In practice many of these different functions are contracted out, but often the whole management is contracted out to a single management company. When we come to deal with unit trusts, we shall find that the relationship between the management company and the trust is fixed and defined by law; the management company is inevitably the body which takes the initiative in setting up the trust. With investment trusts there may not be a separate management company at all, and the relationship between a management company and the investment trusts which it manages is much more variable—ranging from a situation comparable with that of unit trusts to management companies which perform only some of the management functions. Table 16.1 also gives a size distribution of these groups of investment trusts under common management. There is obviously a greater degree of concentration than among individual companies, but it is still not so great as we have found among most other types of financial institution.

The most easily recognisable among the management companies are those of the merchant banks. Of the investment trusts covered by the Messel statistics in 1971 about 27% by number and about 20% by value of total assets were managed by twenty merchant banks. In these cases it is fairly safe to assume that the investment trust was set up by the merchant bank. The remaining management companies are either specialised investment trust management companies, occasionally also managing unit trusts, or else professional firms—accountants or solicitors.

The management expenses of investment trusts are low. The Association of Investment Trust Companies suggests that the ratios of expenses to total assets range from around 0·25% for medium-sized investment trusts to 0.10% for the larger ones.

B. *Capital structure*

Because in law investment trusts are companies, they can issue all the different types of capital—ordinary shares, preference shares and debentures or loan stocks. As with any other company, preference shares and debentures are rewarded with a fixed rate of interest, which must be paid before any of the profits are available for distribution as dividends on the ordinary shares; preference shares and debentures are therefore known as 'prior charges'. In the event of liquidation of the company the holders of the preference shares and debentures must be paid out in full, and the residue is available for the owners of the equity, the holders of the ordinary shares. We can thus write

equity assets = total assets − prior charges.

The most important consequences of this ability of investment trusts to raise part of their capital in fixed-interest form is the possibility which it offers of 'gearing'. Gearing may be defined formally as the ratio of prior charges to total financing (which equals total assets). Gearing is only another way of looking at the borrowing ratio, to which we referred in Chapter 4.[3]

Table 16.2 illustrates the effect of gearing by showing the ordinary share dividends which could be paid at different levels of profit by two companies, one low-geared (1 : 6) and the other high-geared (5 : 6). In the case of the low-geared company the quadrupling of profit from £25,000 to £100,000 would enable the investment trust to increase the distribution to the owners of the equity by a shade under 5 times (from £19,000 to £94,000); even with this relatively low level of gearing the owners of the equity have benefited considerably at a time of rising profits. In the case of the high-geared company the benefit to the owners of the equity is even greater with rising profits, since a doubling of profits from £50,000 to £100,000 has raised the ordinary share dividend three times (from £20,000 to £70,000). The converse is, of course, true at a time of falling profits. The danger of high gearing is illustrated for Company B at the profit level of £25,000, when it cannot meet the whole dividend due on the preference shares. (In practice it would draw on accumulated reserves to do so.) High gearing is thus dangerous for companies with fluctuating profits.

The importance of gearing for investment trusts lies in the fact that the bulk of the investments consists of ordinary shares, the income from which is likely to be on a rising trend. The holding of investment

3. See p. 101.

trust shares rather than the direct holding of the ordinary shares of industrial and commercial companies enables the investor to magnify the rise in income and capital value by a factor related to the level of gearing in the investment trust. If the dividends from the shares in the

Table 16.2   The effect of gearing on ordinary share dividends

£ thousand

Capital		Dividends at different levels of profit		
Type	Nominal value	25	50	100
Company A (low-geared)				
6% preference shares	100	6	6	6
Ordinary shares	500	19	44	94
Company B (high-geared)				
6% preference shares	500	25	30	30
Ordinary shares	100	–	20	70

investment trust portfolio fall, the investor's income will fall by a similarly magnified amount unless the investment trust maintains its dividend out of accumulated reserves. It follows from what we have said that the benefit of gearing is lost to the extent that the investment trust holds fixed-interest securities in its portfolio: the real measure of gearing is the ratio of prior charges to total assets in the form of ordinary shares.

So far we have valued prior charges at nominal value, which takes no account of the effect on profits of different interest rates payable on the prior charges. If we substitute the same nominal value of 3% preference shares for the 6% preference shown in Table 16.2, the raising of profits from £25,000 to £100,000 would increase ordinary share dividends from £22,000 to £97,000 in Company A and from £12,500 to £87,500 in Company B. This factor can be taken care of by valuing prior charges at market value, as is done in court schemes for the winding-up of investment trust companies, or at some approximation to it. On this basis the overall gearing of the companies in the Messel population has declined from 41·2% in 1953 to 11·7% in 1970, reflecting mainly the considerable rise in interest rates over this period (causing market values of bonds and preference shares to drop below their nominal values).

Until the last few years the capital structure of all investment trusts was similar, consisting of an orthodox mixture of ordinary shares, preference shares and debentures, all in sterling. Since about 1965 several innovations have appeared. These consist, firstly, of the raising of loans in dollars and, secondly, of the introduction of new types of ordinary share and debenture.

The need for dollar loans arose from the fact that since the last war portfolio investment in the securities of hard currency countries has been permitted only out of currency provided by the sale of such securities. These 'investment dollars', as they are called, command a premium over the official exchange rate because the supply is limited, and the raising of a dollar loan is a way of avoiding the payment of the premium. More recently there has also been a rule that 25% of the proceeds of the sale of hard currency securities has to be surrendered to the authorities. It is because of this rule that usually only 75% of the investment currency premium is counted in computing total assets.

The dollar loans have been of two sorts. The earlier loans were negotiated for periods of around five years at interest rates which varied during the currency of the loan, often with movements in the rate for three-months euro-dollars. The more recent dollar loans have mostly been of the 'back-to-back' variety. By this method an investment trust borrows dollars, more often at a fixed rate of interest, from a U.S. corporation which has a subsidiary in the United Kingdom; this subsidiary then borrows an equal amount in sterling from the investment trust company. Since the investment trust company is making a loan in order to secure another loan, this is not a method of raising new capital, but it has enabled investment trust companies to switch their portfolios in the U.S.A. without surrendering 25% of the proceeds of each sale. 112 investment trust companies had £137 million of dollar loans outstanding at the middle of 1971, of which £34 million consisted of back-to-back loans. Dollar loans of both varieties have also been raised by other types of financial institution, especially insurance companies. As we indicated above some investment trusts have augmented their dollar portfolios by taking over other investment trust companies which already had a sizeable dollar portfolio.

Two features of the stock market over recent years have determined the popularity of a new form of loan capital for investment trust companies—the convertible debenture. The high level of interest rates has made fixed-interest loans expensive, and the fact that the ordinary shares of investment trusts have stood at a considerable discount on the value of the equity assets has made it difficult to raise new equity capital by rights issues or otherwise because the equity of existing shareholders would have been 'diluted' in the process. The solution has been to issue debenture stocks which carry a right to convert into ordinary shares near the asset value at the date of issue. One of the attractions of convertibles to the companies issuing them has been the lower coupon made possible by the existence of conversion rights. More recently investment trust companies have begun to issue debentures with warrants attached, giving holders the right to subscribe for equity capital in the future at a price stipulated in advance.

The next two innovations in capital were probably motivated in part by a desire on the part of investment trust managements to meet the growing competition from unit trusts, particularly for the larger personal holdings. They are especially designed to meet the needs of persons with different tax problems.

The first innovation, which was introduced in 1965, was the formation of new investment trusts with a split capital structure. The ordinary shares are split into two classes—income shares and capital shares. The split capital investment trust usually has a fixed life, during which all or most of the income is distributed to the holders of the income shares, and the capital shares receive no income. At the end of the fixed term the income shares are repaid at par or at a pre-determined price, and the whole of the surplus assets are distributed to the holders of the capital shares. These trusts may or may not have debenture stocks repayable on or before the final liquidation date, but in any case there is a large element of gearing in the structure of these split-capital investment trusts, since the capital shares receive the ultimate benefit from the assets bought with the money subscribed by the income shareholders. The capital shares are attractive to persons in high tax brackets who are prepared to wait for several years before receiving their return entirely in the form of capital gain, and the income shares to those who wish to maximise income, perhaps during retirement. By the middle of 1971 there were twenty split-capital investment trusts.

The innovation of 'B' shares, or non-dividend shares, appeared in 1967. These shares carry equal rights with the ordinary shares in the investment trust (which are sometimes renamed 'A' ordinary shares), but instead of receiving dividends they are given scrip issues. In one type of 'B' share the amount of the scrip issue is based on a net asset value equal to the gross dividend; in a second type the amount of the scrip issue is based on a value in ordinary shares equal to the gross dividend. This scrip issue is not subject to income tax or surtax because there is no option to receive a cash dividend instead. 'B' shares may be converted by the holder into ordinary shares at any time. Effectively the 'B' shares provide a means for the automatic re-investment of dividends without their having suffered income tax or surtax. By the middle of 1971 there were sixteen investment trust companies which had issued 'B' shares. In the majority of cases these represented 15–17% of the total equity capital, but in one investment trust company the proportion was as high as 50%.

The automatic reinvestment of dividends is one of the facilities which many unit trusts provide for their holders, and the 'B' shares can be seen as a move to enable investment trust companies to compete more effectively with unit trusts. In the latter half of 1969 the largest investment trust company, Alliance, introduced a variant of automatic reinvestment which does not have the tax advantages of 'B' shares. Under this scheme a third party, the Royal Bank of Scotland, will buy new shares in the market to the value of the net dividend to which the holder opting for the scheme is entitled. This, of course, provides no new capital for the trust, since the shares bought must have been sold by an existing holder. Two other investment trust companies provide similar facilities.

C. *Prices of investment trust shares*

In considering the differences between investment trust companies and unit trusts we pointed out that there would normally be a difference between the market value of the ordinary shares of an investment trust and the value of the underlying assets attributable to the holders of those shares. This arises because investment trust companies are closed-ended funds, so that their shares are subject in their own right to supply and demand on the stock exchange. In this section we look more closely at this point.

Table 16.3 shows the average discount over the period 1953–70 of the ordinary share capital of a group of around 200 investment companies studied by L. Messel & Co. The discount is computed by first calculating the ratio

$$\frac{\text{market value of ordinary share capital} \times 100}{\text{market value of equity assets}}.$$

The discount is 100 *minus* this percentage. It must be remembered that these are average figures, and that the shares of individual investment trust companies may be standing at a premium while most investment trust shares are at a discount. The table shows a decline in the discount from nearly 30% which obtained at the beginning of the period to a level of between 14% and 17%, which has prevailed in most of the years since 1959, with signs of a further narrowing at the end of the period. The discount was at its lowest level in 1962, and it was from the middle of April to the middle of June of that year that the shares of the twenty largest investment trusts collectively stood at a premium, which reached 7·5% in May 1962.

Table 16.3   Average discount of investment trust company ordinary
              shares, 1953–70

Percentages

Year	Discount	Year	Discount	Year	Discount
1953	29.7	1959	16.8	1965	16.8
1954	29.6	1960	14.2	1966	14.6
1955	31.0	1961	14.4	1967	16.3
1956	31.1	1962	8.9	1968	13.4
1957	26.3	1963	10.1	1969	16.1
1958	22.2	1964	13.2	1970	11.6

Source: L. Messel & Co.

There are three major factors which determine the extent of the discount or premium for investment trust shares in general and for any particular shares. The first two affect both the numerator and denominator of the ratio market valuation/equity assets, while the third affects only the numerator. (1) General movements of share prices are reflected in the prices of investment trust ordinary shares. (2) Each investment trust company has a limited portfolio of securities, and the portfolios of some of them are specialised in certain directions. The price movements of the securities in the portfolio have an independent influence on the prices of the investment trust ordinary shares. (3) Gearing, as we saw above, magnifies the effect of any movement in share prices generally or of the securities in the particular portfolio. If share prices are rising or are expected to rise, gearing will operate to lessen the discount or to increase the premium, and conversely if share prices are falling or are expected to fall.

There are several other factors of a less fundamental nature which also have an influence on the prices of investment trust shares. The first is that for many years the market in shares of smaller investment trust companies has generally been a narrow one. The effect of this is that prices quoted are often nominal, and that the spread between jobbers' bid and offer prices is wider than with shares which are regularly traded. Then again investment trust companies differ somewhat in the extent to which they retain income, and this can have a marginal effect on the prices of their shares. Lastly investment trust companies differ in the capital gains tax which they have already paid on switches in their portfolio and the capital gains tax which would be payable on a winding-up. We shall look at this factor in more detail in the next section.

Table 16.3 shows that the general experience of investment trust companies since the early 1950s is of a substantial discount on their shares, and this has made it difficult to raise new equity capital without harming the interests of existing shareholders. We have already noted some of the means whereby investment trusts have got round this particular difficulty. The persistent discount has made the smaller investment trust companies very vulnerable to take-over bids. The only sure way in which the discount could be severely narrowed or abolished would be for arrangements to be made for an independent body to stand ready to buy and sell the ordinary shares in the investment trust company at a price near to net assets value.

It must be remembered that the discount is a negative feature only to a holder who is worried about the re-sale value of his holding. When investment trust shares are held as a small part of a large portfolio, whether personal or institutional, the holder does not have to worry about this feature since he has plenty of other holdings to sell if need be. To an institution, such as an insurance company, investment trust shares represent a cheap way of buying an interest in an equity portfolio, with gearing operating to increase the dividend income more rapidly than with a direct holding at times of rising dividends and with dollar loans providing a means of acquiring an interest in an overseas portfolio immune or partly immune from the 25% surrender rule and the investment currency premium.

D. Taxation

The introduction of corporation tax in 1965 in place of the old income tax and profits tax on company profits made great changes in the incidence of taxation on investment trust companies, and it has taken them several years to make the changes in their portfolios and capital structures necessary to minimise the effects of the new tax system. Investment trust companies are taxed according to exactly the same principles as other companies except that they pay corporation tax at a reduced rate (15%) on their capital gains.

All the income received by an investment trust from the securities in its portfolio and from incidental activities is divided into two classes —'franked income' and 'unfranked income'. The purpose of the distinction is to avoid double taxation of company profits. Franked income is that received in dividends on preference and ordinary shares paid by companies whose profits have already been liable to U.K. corporation tax; the receiving company does not pay corporation tax on receipts of franked income. Debenture interest received from companies which pay U.K. corporation tax is unfranked income because the paying company is able to deduct debenture interest from its profits before the liability to corporation tax is computed. Similarly all overseas income and income from government or local authority stocks is unfranked because the paying bodies are not liable to U.K. corporation tax. An investment trust company thus pays corporation tax (currently at 40%) on the following sum:

U.K. unfranked income + overseas income − foreign withholding taxes paid − management expenses − debenture interest.

The income from incidental activities referred to above all counts as unfranked income, and comes from two main sources—underwriting commission and dealing profits. As with all other financial institutions which hold large portfolios of ordinary shares, investment trust companies are included in the underwriting lists of various issuing houses. The commissions which they receive are useful additions to investment income, but are in all cases relatively very small. For some investment trust companies profits of investment-dealing subsidiaries form a significant part of total income.

Nearly all the U.K. income which an investment trust company receives is net of income tax at the standard rate of 38·75%, and, like all other companies, it is required to deduct income tax at the standard rate from dividends which it pays on its preference and ordinary share capital. It can recover the income tax deducted from its franked investment income only as an offset against the income tax deducted from its own dividends. If the franked income is less than the dividends, the company has to pay over to the Inland Revenue the income tax on the difference.

This limitation of the offset of income tax deducted from its own dividends to the amount of income tax due on its franked income sets boundaries in several directions for the portfolio policy of an investment trust company. The ideal situation is that the franked income should exactly cover the dividends payable, and there are heavy tax penalties on investment trust companies which do not have sufficient franked income to cover their dividends. When corporation tax was first introduced in 1965, many investment trust companies found themselves short of franked income. There was undoubtedly some rearrangement of portfolios, but there were at least two other ways in which many investment trust companies coped with the situation. The first was to raise new loan capital. Even with high interest rates this might well be a profitable exercise because of the tax saving. The second way was to merge with another investment trust company which had plenty of franked income. This need for franked income to cover the dividend obviously limits the proportions of a portfolio which can profitably be in overseas securities, debentures and gilt-edged.

This does not exhaust the complications of taxation because all holders of investment trust shares must reckon with the certainty that over a long enough period the trust will realise all its present holdings and will thus be liable to corporation tax at 15% on all the capital gains resulting. Many investment trusts and unit trusts report their potential liability to tax on unrealised capital gains, and this must be taken into account in reckoning the present value of a holding of shares or units. The actual calculation is difficult because assumptions must be made about the dates on which the capital gains will be realised, and the tax liability must then be discounted back to the present.

E. *Other investment companies*

The definition of an investment trust company is a precise one, but there are many companies which derive most of their income from holdings of financial claims without falling within this restrictive definition. Among companies some of whose securities have a stock exchange quotation the investment-holding and investment-dealing companies will mostly be found in the Financial Trusts section of the *Stock Exchange Official Year Book*. A survey in 1963 estimated their total holdings of quoted ordinary shares at £90 million.[4]

Our discussion so far has been concerned mainly with investment trust companies some of whose securities have a stock exchange quotation, but there is a large population of unquoted investment trust companies. These range from investment trusts, often managed by merchant banks, which are as large as the quoted ones, to small family invest-

4. Revell and Moyle, *The Owners of Quoted Ordinary Shares*, Table IV.4.

ment trusts. The same survey estimated the holdings of the larger unquoted investment trusts in quoted ordinary shares of U.K. companies as £190 million in 1963. Since then the tax privileges have been withdrawn from unquoted investment trusts, and most of them will have acquired a stock exchange quotation. At the other end of the scale the small unquoted investment trusts were estimated to hold £240 million of quoted ordinary shares in 1963. Many of these small investment trust companies were vehicles for the holdings of a single family. By transferring their personal holdings of shares to a company persons were able to claim earned income relief on a salary which they paid themselves for managing the portfolio. The advent of corporation tax reduced the advantages of this method of incorporating personal holdings, and many of the companies have probably been dissolved, their portfolios often having been transferred to unit trusts.

3. AUTHORISED UNIT TRUSTS

A. *Trustees and management companies*

The powers of the Department of Trade and Industry (formerly Board of Trade) to authorise unit trust schemes come from the Prevention of Fraud (Investments) Act, 1958. This act lays it down that nobody may deal in securities without a licence from the D.T.I., but there is a specific exemption for the managers and trustees of 'authorised unit trust schemes'. The Act does not prohibit the formation of unauthorised unit trusts, but they are not allowed to distribute circulars containing an invitation to subscribe for units without special permission. Since advertisement plays such a large part in the operation of unit trusts, this limits the unauthorised trusts to special situations where advertising is not necessary.

The conditions imposed by the D.T.I. for authorisation of a unit trust can be summarised under four headings. (1) The management company and the trustee must be independent of each other. (2) Both must be companies incorporated in the United Kingdom with a place of business in Great Britain. (3) The company acting as trustee must have an issued capital of not less than £500,000, at least £250,000 of which must be paid up, or at least four-fifths of its capital must be owned by a company which fulfils this condition. (4) The trust deed must provide to the satisfaction of the Department for the matters specified in the First Schedule to the Act. Since the D.T.I. goes beyond the matters specified in that Schedule in laying down conditions for authorisation, we do not need to enquire what these matters are. Instead we shall refer to the points when we come to examine the operation of unit trusts.

There are thus three bodies concerned in a unit trust scheme—the trustee, the management company and the beneficial owners of the trust fund, the unitholders. The trust deed specifies in detail the rights and duties of each of the three parties. Unlike an investment trust company, a unit trust is a trust in law.

The requirements for being a trustee are such that only large financial institutions could fulfil them. In fact, at the end of 1969, deposit banks were trustees of 85% of all unit trusts and insurance companies of 11%; the remaining 4% was accounted for by merchant banks, an investment trust and the Royal Bank of Canada.[5] The corporate trustee has three functions in relation to the unit trust: (1) to hold all the investments and cash of the trust fund, (2) to maintain a register of unitholders and (3) to check that the actions of the management company, in particular those relating to the buying and selling of securities in the fund, are in accordance with the trust deed. Most trustees content themselves with checking that the manager is keeping within any provisions of the trust deed relating to the type of investments to be included in the portfolio. In earlier days it was customary for duplicate registers of unitholders to be maintained by the manager and the trustee, but nowadays the trustee usually fulfils his legal duty of maintaining the register by entrusting the work to an agent under his supervision; this agent is often the manager. In the last resort the trustee has the right to dismiss the management company and to appoint another in its place if the trustee holds that it is in the interests of the unitholders to do so. In effect, the trustee is the unitholders' watchdog.

The functions of the management company are to initiate the unit trust and to conduct all the day-to-day business connected with running it, including the investment decisions. In many cases some of their functions are contracted out to other bodies. Many of the management companies are under common ownership, and it is convenient to consider the group of management companies, or management group. Table 16.4 shows the size distribution of the seventy-five management groups according to the value of the funds of the unit trusts which they manage.

The ownership of unit trust management companies is a field which

5. These figures and most of the other statistics in this section have been compiled by the author from the *Unit Trust Year Book 1972*. Grateful acknowledgement is made to the publishers, Fundex Ltd., for permission to do so.

brings many different types of financial institution together, as is shown in Table 16.5. The largest single category is 'other', the companies which are independent of any other type of financial institution. They account for nearly 65% by value of all the trust funds, but this is largely because three of the four companies with total funds under their management of £100 million or more come into this category. The various types of financial institution were drawn into unit trust man-

Table 16.4   Unit trust management groups by size of funds, December
            1971

Size of total funds £ million	Groups Nos.	Total funds		Trusts Nos.	Accounts '000
		£ million	Percentages		
Over 100	4	1,103	55.5	76	1,229
50–100	6	416	20.9	59	431
25–50	6	221	11.1	16	293
10–25	8	138	6.9	39	181
1–10·	33	'99	5.0	63	79
Under 1	18	12	.6	24	9
Total	75	1,989	100.0	277·	2,222

Source: compiled from *Unit Trust Year Book 1972*.

agement for several reasons—the deposit banks and trustee savings banks because of their extensive branch networks, merchant banks because of their previous specialisation in portfolio management and the insurance companies because of the growth of assurance-linked units.

Table 16.6 shows the size distribution of the unit trusts authorised by the D.T.I. It is interesting to see how the number of trusts and the value of total funds have been built up over the years since the first unit trust was formed in Britain in 1931. From that date until 1939 altogether ninety-eight unit trusts were formed, and at the outbreak of war the total value of the funds was around £80 million. During the war and until 1953 the formation of new trusts and the promotion of existing ones was prohibited: the total value of funds in 1957 was only £60 million. The first post-war unit trust was formed in October 1957 and, when the first statistics were published at the end of 1959, there were forty-seven unit trusts in existence with funds of about £200 million.

Table 16.5   Ownership of unit trust management groups, December 1971

Ownership	Groups Nos.	£ million				Total funds
		Size groups				
		Over 100	10-100	1-10	Under 1	
Deposit banks	4	150	89	2	–	241
Trustee savings banks	1	–	25	–	–	25
Merchant banks	15	–	294	16	3	313
Insurance companies	12	–	28	19	3	50
Joint merchant bank-insurance company	5	–	13	10	–	23
Investment trust management	9	–	16	21	2	39
Stockbrokers	5	–	10	7	1	18
Other	24	953	301	23	3	1,280
Total	75	1,103	775	99	12	1,989

Source: compiled from *Unit Trust Year Book 1972.*

Note: The groups shown under 'stockbrokers' are closely associated with but not necessarily owned by a firm of stockbrokers.

Table 16.6   Unit trusts by size of funds, December 1971

Size of total funds £ million	Trusts Nos.	Total funds	
		£ million	Percentages
Over 100	1	167	8.5
20-100	25	901	45.7
10-20	25	362	18.4
5-10	37	261	13.2
1-5	105	247	12.5
Under 1	71	32	1.6
Total	264	1,970	100.0

Source: compiled from *Unit Trust Year Book 1972.*

Note: 10 trusts which are not actively promoted and 3 trusts the value of which is not reported by the managers are omitted from the table.

The statistics referred to in the preceding paragraph are published by the Association of Unit Trust Managers. Most management groups are members, although several of the largest groups did not become members until very recently. The association has the usual objects of representing the collective views of its members in negotiations with the government and other bodies, but it also lays down standards of conduct and vets all advertisements issued by member groups to ensure that they present a fair view of the advantages and risks inherent in ordinary share investment.

There is a fair degree of differentiation among unit trusts. The most important division is between those which aim at maximum capital growth, those which aim at maximum income and the middle-of-the-road trusts. Table 16.7 shows some other types of specialisation. Among

Table 16.7   Specialised unit trusts, 1971

	Trusts Nos.	Total funds £ million
Specialized portfolios		
Investment trusts	9	182
Financial institutions	14	246
Commodity and mineral shares	9	49
Overseas	11	36
Specialized by type of holder		
Charities and pension funds	18	79
Large personal holdings	22	165

Source: compiled from *Unit Trust Year Book 1972*.

those specialising by the nature of the portfolio trusts holding shares in financial institutions, either investment trust companies alone or banks, insurance companies and investment trusts, are the biggest group. The commodity and mineral shares are high-yielding, largely because there is a considerable degree of risk. The two main types of specialisation by holder are the 'exempt' funds catering for charities and pension funds and those intended for large personal holdings. Charities and pension funds are 'gross funds', exempt from all income and capital gains tax, but they have no means of reclaiming any capital gains tax which has been paid by a unit trust. By limiting their membership to holders exempt from capital gains tax the unit trusts themselves are granted exemption. The trusts catering for large personal holdings have initial subscriptions of at least £1000, levy initial charges of around 1% instead of the more usual 3·75% or 5% and often restrict dealing in units to one day a week or month. The trusts included in the table are only those which are completely specialised in a particular direction; many other trusts have a partial specialisation.

Many unit trusts offer various ancillary services, the most important of which are: (1) a savings scheme for regular monthly investment in units, (2) a life assurance scheme whereby the purchase of units is linked to the payment of monthly or quarterly premiums on a life policy, (3) a share exchange scheme whereby the manager will take over approved shares from the unitholder's personal portfolio (usually giving the unitholder the benefit of the fact that the manager acquires the securities without payment of a stockbroker's commission) and (4) a personal loan scheme. Some trusts offer an automatic withdrawal plan, under which sufficient units are sold each year to bring the trust's distribution up to a stated level, perhaps 5%. This sale involves a liability to capital gains tax, but the annual realisations of capital gains in this way, after allowing for the credit of 15% for capital gains taxed on the trust, are quite likely to come under the £50 minimum level for liability to the tax. Many trusts provide facilities for automatic re-investment of income distributions.

Unit trusts differ from each other in several other ways, particularly in the level of their charges and the minimum sizes of subscription for units, but we shall consider these after we have looked at the operation of unit trusts in the next section.

B. *Operation*

The essence of a unit trust is that there shall always be a direct relation between the value of a unit and the total value of the fund. At any one time a unit trust fund is divided between a number of unitholders in proportion to the value of the units for which each has subscribed. When new money is subscribed to the fund, the fund must expand by exactly that amount so that the value of the new units shall be equal to the value of existing units. When existing holders withdraw, they must be paid an amount for each unit which is exactly equal to the value of each unit held by continuing holders, and the fund must contract by that amount. In this section we look at the mechanism by which the value of units is kept in line with the value of the underlying assets.

The operation starts with the valuation of the securities in the fund (the capital property) and of the income received by the trustee as dividends on the securities (income property). For nearly all trusts this valuation is carried out daily, but a handful of trusts make a special point of keeping charges to the minimum and value weekly or monthly. Unlike valuations of portfolios in most other circumstances, this is not done from the *Stock Exchange Daily List*, but by the official broker to the trust (who must be approved by the trustee) approaching a jobber in the stock exchange and obtaining prices from him. This is because two prices are required for each security—the lowest market dealing offer price and the highest market dealing bid price.[6]

Once the offer and bid prices of the underlying securities have been ascertained, the D.T.I. requirements, as incorporated into the trust deed, provide a rigid formula for the maximum permitted offer price of a unit and the minimum permitted bid price of a unit. As an example we may show the calculation for a unit trust with 10 million units in issue. The official broker had ascertained that the offer prices of the securities in the fund had come to £5 million on the previous day, making the value of securities for each unit exactly 50p, and the calculation of the offer price proceeds on the lines shown opposite.[7]

It will be seen that the expenses and duties payable on the purchase of the securities and the value of the income property have been added to the value of the securities in the fund to give the appropriation price. This is the price which the manager must pay to the trustee for the creation of a new unit; the difference between this and the maximum permitted offer price is retained by the manager. The manager thus receives by way of immediate revenue on the creation of a unit his initial service charge and the benefit of the rounding up (maximum 1% or 1·25p, whichever is smaller), which is permitted by D.T.I. requirements to avoid dealing in awkward amounts. The object of the

6. The terms 'offer' (or 'offered') and 'bid' apply from the point of view of the jobber or unit trust manager. Thus an offer price is the price at which a jobber or a unit trust manager will sell, and a bid price is the price at which either of them will buy. The spread between offer and bid prices is the jobber's or manager's 'turn'.

7. The examples of the calculation of offer and bid prices are adapted by permission from those given by the Association of Unit Trust Managers in *Directory of Unit Trusts, 1970*. Fuller calculations are given in O. P. Stutchbury, *The Management of Unit Trusts* (London: Thomas Skinner, 1964), which contains far more detail of unit trust operations than we have space for here. The discussion which follows is largely based on Mr Stutchbury's exposition.

calculation is to compute exactly the cost of creating a new unit so that equity between existing and new unitholders is maintained.

Offer price calculation

	p	
Value of securities per unit	50·000	
+ Stamp duty (1% *ad valorem*)	·500	
+ Brokerage and contract stamp	·625	
+ Instrument duty (0·25% *ad valorem*)	·125	
	51·250	
+ Income property (£20,000)	·200	
Appropriation price	51·450	
+ Initial service charge (5%)	2·573	
	54·023	
+ Rounding up (1% = 0·540p)	·477	
Maximum permitted offer price per unit	54·500	54½p

When it comes to calculating the minimum permitted bid price, the stamp duty (payable by the purchaser of a security), the instrument duty and the initial service charge do not apply. We assume that the bid prices of the securities in the fund amounted to £4·9 million, giving a value of securities per unit of 49p.

Bid price calculation

	p	
Value of securities per unit	49·000	
+ Income property (£20,000)	·200	
	49·200	
− Brokerage and contract stamp	·615	
Expropriation price	48·585	
− Rounding down (1% = 0.486p)	·085	
Minimum permitted bid price per unit	48·500	48½p

The expropriation price is the amount received from the trustee when a unit is cancelled, the manager receiving the benefit of the rounding down.

The spread between the maximum permitted offer price and the minimum permitted bid price, calculated on the offer price of 54½p, is 6p or 11·01%, made up as follows:

	Percentages
Initial service charge	4·72
Buying expenses of securities and duties	2·29
Selling expenses of securities	1·13
Rounding	1·03
Jobber's turn on securities	1·84
	11·01

But this is the maximum spread permissible, whereas the usual spread between unit trust offer and bid prices is around 5·25%.

Before we see what determines the manager's decision on the level at which he will actually pitch the offer and bid prices between the maximum and minimum permitted by the D.T.I. formula, we must look at some extra inescapable expenses which the manager has to meet on different transactions. It is customary for most unit trust management groups to pay stockbrokers, bankers and professional men a commission of 1·25% for the introduction of business. Only a proportion of business is gained in this way, so that commission is not payable on every sale of new units. The second item of cost is stamp duty payable by the manager on the transactions in units (as distinct from the stamp duty payable on the transactions in securities, which enters into the calculations above). The sale of newly-created units attracts no stamp duty, but there is a 1% *ad valorem* stamp duty payable by the manager when he repurchases units from unitholders; this is recoverable if the units are cancelled within two months. If the repurchased units are sold again within two months, then a fixed stamp duty of 50p (or 1% *ad valorem* if it happens to be less) is payable; if the units are sold again after two months, the full 1% *ad valorem* is payable. The effect of these inescapable expenses is that the profit margin on the resale of repurchased units is reduced by commission and two lots of stamp duty: on an average bargain size of £100 the expenses amount to 2·75%. When repurchased units are sold again, none of the expenses and duties on the buying and selling of securities which enter into the D.T.I. calculation is incurred, and so the profit is the full spread of 11% *less* the inescapable expenses of 2·75%, which equals 8·25%.

We have already seen that the revenue to the manager on the sale of newly-created units is the initial service charge together with the rounding up, which may be anything from zero to 1%. In our example the initial service charge is 5%, so that the total revenue is at a minimum of 5%. Out of this the manager may have to pay a commission of 1·25%, giving him a minimum net profit of 3.75%. As we shall see, many trusts have initial service charges of 3·25% and 3·75%; on these the minimum net revenue on newly-created units will be respectively 2·0% and 2·5%. All these figures are considerably less than the net revenue of 8·25% which the manager would make on selling repurchased units if he took full advantage of the spread permitted by the D.T.I.; competition ensures that managers do not make such relatively large profits on resales. The observed average spread of 5·25% would result if a trust with an initial service charge of 3·75% were to aim to make the same profit on resales as on the sales of newly-created units (2·50 + 2·75 (inescapable expenses) = 5·25). Thus in practice it is the profit on resales which largely dictates the extent of the spread. A trust which is newly established or one which is making a special selling effort can afford to quote a narrower spread because sales of repurchased units represent a small proportion of total sales. At a time when share markets are unsettled the spread is bound to widen because jobbers will be quoting a wider spread on the securities of the fund.

Having decided on the extent of the spread which he will permit himself, the manager still has to fix the actual offer and bid prices at some point within the permitted range. To the nearest new penny a spread of 5·25% in our example is 3p. The manager thus has to choose between the two extremes of setting the offer price at the permitted maximum of 54½p (with a bid price of 51½p) and of setting the bid price at the permitted minimum of 48½p (with an offer price of 51½p). It is fairly clear what he will do. His profit on the sales of units is a fixed percentage of the value of the unit, and he will maximise his profits when the fund is expanding by setting the offer price close to the permitted maximum. This is a position which is in the interest of the existing unitholders since it maximises their receipts if they have to sell their units. When the fund is contracting, however, this position cannot be maintained because the trustee pays the manager just over 48½p for each unit which he cancels. He is actually losing money on each unit cancelled unless he changes the basis of his pricing so that the bid price is at the permitted minimum of 48½p. This change is, of course, contrary to the interests of the existing unitholders, because they receive less for their units when they sell them, but the manager has no option but to make it. In the process he may well also widen his spread.

C. *Charges and minimum transactions*

The managers receive their remuneration from two service charges which they are permitted to levy. The first is the initial service charge, which we have already met. It is known in the jargon as 'front-end loading', and is intended to recoup for the manager the various costs entailed in procuring and processing a new holding—commission for the introduction of new business, advertising, the initial entry in the register of unitholders and the issue of a certificate to the unitholder. It is levied as a flat percentage on the value of the unit. The second is the annual management charge, which covers such recurring expenses as the fees of the trustee, the cost of making semi-annual or quarterly income distributions and the general expenses of maintaining the management company's organisation. This again is levied as a flat percentage charge calculated on the capital value of the fund. In most cases it is paid out of the income property, but even if it is paid out of the capital property, it is an allowable expense against the gross income of the trust for corporation tax purposes.

The maximum level at which these two charges may be set according to D.T.I. requirements is 13·25% calculated over a twenty-year life of the trust; the D.T.I. will not approve initial service charges of more than 5%. The two most popular combinations which come up to or close to the permitted maximum are an initial service charge of 5% with an annual management charge of 0·375% and an initial service charge of 3·25% with an annual management charge of 0·5%.

For the small investor there is a factor which effectively reduces the cost of unit trusts. Since the minimum subscription to a unit trust is far below the minimum size of bargain on the stock exchange which a stockbroker would handle, the small investor who saves a small amount regularly secures the benefit of what is known as 'pound-cost averaging'. This arises because the same amount of money buys more units when the price is low than when the price is high, with the result that the average cost of units bought over a period is always less than the average of their prices. For example, a person who buys units to the value of £10 at the end of each of three consecutive months at prices of 50p, 40p and 25p would receive 85 units altogether (20 + 25 + 40) at an average cost per unit of just over 35p; the average of the three prices works out at just over 38p.

All trusts prescribe a minimum number of units which may be purchased when the holding is being acquired for the first time. This generally takes the form: 'Minimum initial purchase *x* units, thereafter in multiples of *y* units'. Sometimes the minimum is laid down in terms of a money sum instead of in units. Each management group appears to have its own policy on this point, and a wide variety of combinations is found. Perhaps the commonest minima are 100 or 200 units for an initial purchase (probably between £25 and £100), units thereafter being purchased in multiples of 10 or 20.

D. *Selling*

The economics of unit trust operation are such that there is a compelling need for the manager always to seek expansion of the fund. The factors which dictate an emphasis on selling as one of the primary functions of a unit trust management company are four in number. (1) The remuneration of the manager, both initial service charges and annual management charges, is calculated as a percentage of the value of the fund; his total profits rise with the value of the fund. Good management of the portfolio will raise this total value above the average, but expansion of the fund is a surer way of achieving a larger total value, and provides insurance against the effects of a drop in stock exchange prices. (2) Successful management of a portfolio is easier when its total size is expanding because it is always easier to alter the emphasis of a portfolio by directing new investments in the required direction than to switch the underlying securities, with a subsequent liability to capital gains tax. (3) Initial service charges are payable only on the sale of units, both newly-created units and repurchased units. If the manager is not achieving sales, his remuneration is restricted to the annual management charge. (4) We have seen that it is in the interests of existing unitholders that a fund should continue to expand so that the manager may maintain his offer price at or near to the permitted maximum, thus keeping the bid price as high as possible.

The initial service charge is identical in form to a commission on the value of a transaction, by which stockbrokers and other financial agents are remunerated, but unit trust managers are unique in having the annual management charge determined as a fixed percentage of the value of a fund invested almost entirely in ordinary shares. This and the other factors mentioned above mean that the categorical imperative for a unit trust manager is to achieve the highest volume of profitable sales. He does this subject to one constraint. As in all other spheres of finance, the administrative costs of a unit trust manager vary very closely with the *number of unitholders*, and do not depend on the *value* of the fund. The constraint is therefore that the manager must aim to keep the average size of holding on his register as high as possible consistent with selling units. The average size of holding at the end of 1971 was £858.

The various methods of selling which are available to unit trust managers may be summarised under the following headings: (1) sales through agents, (2) advertising, (3) the use of existing sales outlets, such as bank branches, (4) regular savings schemes and (5) direct sales. Each management group uses these methods or some of them in varying proportions.

No statistics of the sales of units achieved by different methods are available, but it is likely that sales through agents account for a high proportion. There is a standard rate commission payable, 1·25%. Commission is paid to the following: banks, stockbrokers, solicitors, accountants, insurance brokers, secretaries (members of the Chartered Institute of Secretaries and Administrators), actuaries and certain people who are wholly engaged in giving investment advice to the public.

Of the various kinds of agent, stockbrokers have a special place. For some years stockbrokers saw unit trusts as competitors, but over recent years they have regarded them as the answer to an awkward problem. As costs of specialised manpower and of office space in London have risen fast over recent years, stockbrokers have had to face losing money on small bargains and on managing the portfolios of their less wealthy clients. Increasingly they have encouraged these clients to invest in unit trusts and to transfer their individual portfolios into unit trusts. The various share exchange schemes operated by managers, under which the managers will accept suitable securities from individual portfolios in place of a cash subscription for units, have greatly facilitated this process.

Unit trust managers have a means of rewarding stockbrokers for the favour of new business in addition to the granting of commission: this is the placing of buying orders for securities on a reciprocal basis. Although there does not appear to have been any competitive raising of commission rates between managers, the same cannot be said of reciprocal purchasing orders. At one time reciprocal orders were generally granted to the value of the business introduced, but recently some groups have given reciprocal orders to a multiple of two or even more times the new business.

The second most important method of selling is advertising. Most of the advertising is in the press, especially in national newspapers and magazines, but unit trust groups have used other media, including commercial television. Until fairly recently most advertisements were for 'block offers', in which a stated number of units was offered at a price fixed for one week ahead. This was a means of securing the maximum response from very expensive advertising, but it is rarely used now, even when new unit trusts are being launched.

In the last few years various other groups of financial intermediaries have joined in the selling of units in order to exploit their existing sales outlets. The most important of these have been the deposit banks, who have formed their own management companies. They have been followed by the trustee savings banks. The other large branch network is that of sub-post offices throughout the country, and many groups have sought to use this widespread outlet. So far the Post Office has refused permission for unit sales, although one group has been permitted to promote assurance-linked bonds in this way.

Regular savings schemes and the automatic reinvestment of distributions have the attraction to the manager of continuing sales of units resulting automatically from one initial decision. On the whole regular savings schemes and automatic reinvestment facilities have not been stressed unduly in advertising, but the advent of assurance-linked schemes has, of course, meant that an increasing proportion of sales is achieved by monthly or quarterly subscriptions with automatic reinvestment.

The introduction of assurance-linked schemes also opened up a completely new method of selling, that of employing staff to sell direct to the public. D.T.I. regulations forbid canvassing for the sale of units, but assurance-linked unit trust schemes are life assurance, and the prohibition does not apply. Because of the heavy expenses of training and maintaining a field sales force, only one or two of the larger groups have so far entered into direct sales to the public.

The last point that we shall mention here is not a sales method but a method of avoiding resales. As we saw earlier, many management groups operate personal loan schemes, often in association with a finance house. Sometimes these limit the expenditure financed out of the loan to a particular purpose, but whatever the restriction placed on them these loan schemes have one thing in common: they make it less likely that a unitholder will sell his units in order to finance expenditure, offering him instead a loan with the units as collateral.

4. ASSURANCE-LINKED UNIT TRUST SCHEMES

We have already seen that many unit trusts have schemes under which units may be purchased under a life assurance contract. In this section we look at these schemes in detail, and we do so in a wider context—that of all schemes under which life contracts are connected with a fund comprised exclusively of ordinary shares or of properties. We may talk of assurance-linked unit trust schemes to indicate those schemes which are connected with authorised unit trusts, but to cover the wider field we must speak of 'equity-linked life assurance'.

In many ways the development of these schemes is the most significant development for unit trusts of recent years, and it is of almost equal importance for life offices. For unit trust managers the simple device of associating units in unit trusts with a life assurance contract has many advantages. (1) Since technically the whole of the payment for units purchased under an assurance scheme counts as a premium for life assurance, unit trust managers can escape from the detailed requirements of the D.T.I. when they operate through a life office. They are governed only by regulations for selling life assurance, which permit direct selling to the public and stipulate no maximum rates of expenses. (2) An assurance scheme is a way of reducing the cost of units to the public since the cost of life cover is never so much as the 15·5% income tax relief allowable on the whole of the payment. To the standard-rate taxpayer this means not only that his money buys more units than under a conventional unit trust purchase, but that life cover is thrown in for nothing. (3) The assurance schemes provide a regular cash flow for the unit trust manager, combining the advantages of a regular savings scheme with those of automatic re-investment of distributions.

Although the first scheme of this type was launched by a life office as long ago as 1957, it was the unit trust management companies which made the running when the idea caught on in the early 1960s. The success of these schemes represented a challenge to the life offices, whose conventional with-profits endowment policies no longer satisfied that section of the public which wanted the greater protection against inflation offered by a fund invested entirely in ordinary shares. During 1967 and 1968 most of the old-established life offices produced equity-linked assurance policies, operating either on their own or in association with unit trust management companies.

All equity-linked assurance schemes must have a life office connected with them, but the relationship of the life office to the scheme takes several forms. As we have seen, some unit trust management groups are owned by insurance companies, either alone or in association with a merchant bank, and life offices have made links with independent unit trust management groups to run these schemes. In other cases unit trust managers formed their own subsidiary life offices. However, an authorised unit trust is not essential to the scheme. Many life offices operate with internal funds of equities, and at least one has no separate fund but ties the value of the units to a notional fund invested in the component shares of a share price index.

When life assurance is linked with a unit trust scheme (whether it is an authorised unit trust or an internal fund), all the usual features of a life policy are present. The policy has a surrender value (which may not apply for the first two or three years), a paid-up policy value, a death benefit and a maturity value, and there is generally provision for a loan to be made against the policy. The essential difference between an equity-linked life policy and a conventional policy is that in the former the value of all these benefits is linked to the value at the particular time of a portfolio of ordinary shares instead of being built up by the accumulation of premiums, investment income and reversionary bonuses. It is thus quite possible for the value of the benefit to be less than the total of premiums paid if it falls for payment at a time when stock exchange prices are depressed. Most schemes have some sort of guarantee against this eventuality, and there are several schemes which are in effect hybrids between conventional policies and equity-linked ones. There is generally a choice between receiving a cash sum or the units themselves. In Chapter 15 we described unit-linked assurance as a means of distributing surplus alternative to reversionary bonuses, in which the investment risk was transferred from the life office to the policyholder. We also gave some statistics of premiums to these schemes.[8]

The majority of the linked policies operate, with only slight modifications, one essentially simple scheme. In this the sum assured is equated to the total of premiums payable; a proportion of the monthly, quarterly or annual premium depending on age (usually between 5% and 14%) is used to purchase life cover, and the remainder is invested in units. A variant is that the proportion invested in units increases over the duration of the policy. The death benefit is the bid value of the units already allocated together with a cash sum equal to the value of unpaid premiums; the guarantee is of a minimum sum equal to the sum assured, which is the same as total premiums payable. In this

8. See pp. 425–6.

✳

scheme the guarantee is a 'money back' one. There is usually a similar guarantee of a maturity value not less than the sum assured. The mortality risk is thus of a diminishing sum (unpaid premiums) during the currency of the policy, and can be covered by decreasing term assurance. There is a slight additional risk arising from the fact that at any point the bid value of the units already allocated may be lower than the premiums paid to date.

With this scheme it is general for the income received from the units to be reinvested automatically for the benefit of the policy-holders. In a few cases, however, the income is retained by the life office, which either reduces its premiums to allow for this or declares reversionary bonuses. In the other schemes which we shall now describe the retention of income by the life office is more common.

The remaining schemes are all associated with an endowment or whole-life policy, and there is therefore a basic sum assured secured by the policy. The death benefit consists normally of this basic sum assured together with the bid value of any units allocated. The most common variant is a non-profit endowment policy with extra premiums to provide for the purchase of units, which form a separate profit element. At least two further schemes are written as conventional whole-life policies, with premiums ceasing at age sixty-five. Two others are hybrids, consisting of with-profits endowment policies and a normal unit purchase scheme, half and half.

All the schemes which we have described so far involve the regular payment of premiums over a period, but there are several types of scheme in which the life policy is purchased with a single premium. They are usually called 'bonds'. The bond method of unit trust purchase is obviously suitable for any kind of transaction in which the purchase money is invested in a fund. It has been used to secure the advantages of life assurance for a single purchase of units in an authorised unit trust, but there are two special types of bond which account for most of the sales—property bonds, in which the fund is a portfolio of directly-owned properties, and schemes in which the purchase money is invested, after deduction for life cover, in the shares of one or a number of building societies. We dealt with building society bonds briefly in Chapter 14,[9] and we must now examine property bonds.

During 1970 and 1971 property bonds were sold aggressively by a number of life offices, several of which specialised in this field. Occasionally multi-premium policies were included under the term 'bond'.

9. See p. 371.

By the end of 1971 the total value of assets held against the contracts of which the premiums were invested in properties probably totalled around £200 million. The operators in this field formed a voluntary code of conduct, but a committee under Sir Hilary Scott is at present sitting on the whole question of property bonds and equity-linked life assurance. Among the questions being considered is the level of commission to agents, since many of the new operators paid rates of commission higher than those previously agreed among members of the Life Offices' Association and the Associated Scottish Life Offices.

Funds invested in properties pose certain problems which are absent from conventional unit trusts. For stock exchange securities held by a unit trust there is no difficulty in obtaining daily prices from a wide and independent market, but the valuation of properties is a matter of professional appraisal. This makes the valuation of the unit subject to judgement. Stock exchange securities can always be sold if a conventional unit trust is contracting, but the full value of properties can seldom be realised in a hurry. The property bond funds cope with this problem in two ways: (1) they hold sufficient liquid assets to meet normal withdrawals and (2) they impose a period of notice of up to six months before withdrawal. The purpose of the Hilary Scott Committee is to examine the existing framework of statutory regulation of life assurance in general to see whether it needs strengthening to meet the special features of property bonds and equity-linked assurance.

5. UNAUTHORISED UNIT TRUSTS

A. *Domestic*

One of the major groups of unauthorised unit trusts consists of the thirteen property trusts, statistics of which are summarised regularly by the Bank of England. They are unauthorised because the Prevention of Fraud (Investments) Act, 1958, limits the authorisation of unit trusts to those which hold securities. The thirteen funds cater exclusively for tax-exempt bodies, pension funds and charities, and are thus themselves exempt from all taxes on income and capital gains. The only handicap imposed by their unauthorised status is that they may not advertise for subscribers, but they are permitted to send circulars to selected pension funds and charities after requesting D.T.I. permission. Between March 1966 and December 1971 these funds sold units to a total value of £197 million and spent £148 million on purchasing properties, which were often leased back to their former owners.[10]

The next group of three unauthorised unit trusts has the peculiarity that each of them was set up by statute. These are the Local Authorities' Mutual Investment Trust (for local authority pension and general funds), the Charities Official Investment Fund (for any charitable fund) and the Central Board of Finance of the Church of England (for the funds of church bodies). The principle of pooling funds on the unit trust principle is also adopted by many other religious, charitable and educational bodies. It is common to have separate investment funds (for long-term investments) and deposit funds.

The last group of unauthorised unit trusts consists of the completely unofficial investment clubs, in which groups of like-minded people join to agree on a common investment policy for money which they subscribe. Nobody knows how many of these clubs there are, but there are about 500 clubs affiliated to the National Association of Investment Clubs.

B. *International*

Like most other types of financial institution investment trust companies and unit trusts have an international dimension. This is provided by the overseas or 'offshore' funds, which have been set up by banks and investment company management groups of many countries. They are, however, more truly international than the overseas offshoots of many other types of financial institution because they are invariably incorporated outside the country of origin of their managers, and they cater for investors in a number of different countries. They are international in the same sense that the euro-currency market is.

These overseas funds are incorporated in a tax haven. The British-managed ones are necessarily unauthorised because the writ of the D.T.I. does not run there. There are very many tax havens dotted around the world. Inside the sterling area the best known are the Isle of Man, the Channel Islands, Bermuda, the Bahamas and Grand Cayman; outside the sterling area Switzerland, Luxembourg, Curaçao and Panama are the most popular. The features which are desired in a tax haven are not only that taxation on income and inheritance shall be non-existent or minimal, but also that there shall be complete privacy for investment

10. An article in the September 1969 *Bank of England Quarterly Bulletin* gave more details of these property unit trusts. The regular statistics are to be found in the Statistical Annex to the *Bulletin*.

transactions and that the authorities of the haven shall positively welcome such business. Political stability is the last of the many features that must be present before an island or country can operate as a tax haven.

The attractiveness of the overseas funds operated from these tax havens varies according to the country of residence of the investor. The tax advantages of overseas funds are not very great for United Kingdom residents, since they must pay tax at full rates on all income remitted; they also have to pay capital gains tax when they realise their holding, but at least this liability is postponed, and the fund itself does not have to pay capital gains tax on profits arising out of switching. It is the other advantages which are attractive: funds which can invest in dollar securities without incurring the investment currency premium or the 25% surrender rule and which can avoid government restrictions, legal or voluntary, on the areas in which they should invest. In a fund denominated in sterling the U.K. investor can secure these advantages without difficulty because the funds can raise dollar loans; if the fund is denominated in dollars or another hard currency, the U.K. investors must obtain the dollars through the investment currency pool and surrender 25% of the proceeds when they realise their holdings.

At the end of 1969 there were about 375 of these overseas funds. The total disclosed assets of 152 of these funds came to $4506 million (about £1890 million); allowing for the assets of those which did not disclose, it is safe to say that the minimum total assets were £2000 million and probably more. The funds are denominated in a variety of currencies, with the U.S. dollar predominating. The total assets of those trusts denominated in sterling came to over £50 million.[11]

The operation of these funds is a truly international business, with banks and management groups in many countries participating. From the British side nearly all the merchant banks which manage investment trusts and unit trusts have overseas funds, and the larger independent unit trust management groups also have funds. The total value of funds controlled by U.K. institutions was more than £400 million at the end of 1969—not far short of 30% of the total value of domestic unit trusts. The method of operation of these funds depends on the company law of the country of incorporation. Most of them are open-ended, but in certain countries only closed-ended funds are permitted. Where

11. The estimates in this paragraph have been made by the author, with the kind permission of the publishers, from a survey of offshore funds produced by Intervestment Management Ltd.

the latter form of organisation is chosen, there is usually a purchasing company which stands ready to buy shares in the fund at or near asset value, thus preventing the emergence of a discount.

6. INVESTMENT POLICY

Table 16.8 shows the assets held by investment trusts and authorised unit trusts in December 1971. In both cases ordinary shares account for around 90% of total assets, the only difference being that investment trusts have a much larger proportion in the ordinary shares of overseas companies. All the other items are of negligible importance.

Table 16.9 is designed to show the nature of the cash flow of investment trust companies and to demonstrate the part that revaluations of assets play in the growth of the total value of assets. It is unfortunate that the figures do not distinguish between undistributed income, revaluations and capital gains tax paid, but the figure for new capital raised by new issues of share and loan capital or in exchange for the shares of investment trusts not previously included in the statistics is a fairly clear one. Over the four years investment trust companies gained some £383 million in new resources, a much lower figure than the £619 million of net sales by unit trusts. The cash flow of investment trust companies is irregular, since new resources can be acquired only by issuing new capital, which is done at infrequent intervals, or out of undistributed income. Except when it has issued new capital, an investment trust's investment problem is largely limited to switching its existing portfolio.

The cash flow of unit trusts is rather more regular than that of investment trust companies. A fairly large, well-established trust can count on a continuous flow of sales, although the level of sales from month to month is likely to be uneven. To the extent that sales are linked to savings schemes and to assurance-linked contracts there will be a steady element in the cash flow, more like that of a life office. For all unit trusts, however, there are discontinuous elements. These are introduced by advertising campaigns for a limited period of time, but the major factor is the behaviour of repurchases. Table 16.10 shows the cash flow of unit trusts over the period 1960–71 in such a way that the figures of sales and repurchases can be linked to movements in stock exchange prices (through revaluations).

One generalisation about the levels of sales seems possible: a drop in stock exchange prices (as shown by negative revaluations) halts the progress of sales. In 1969 and 1970 revaluations were negative for

Table 16.8　Assets of investment trust companies and authorised unit trusts, December 1971, market values

	£ million		Percentages	
	Investment trust companies	Unit trusts	Investment trust companies	Unit trusts
Net current assets				
Short-term assets	158	95	2.7	5.0
less Short-term borrowing	−58	−40	−1.0	−2.1
Total	100	55	1.7	2.9
Investments in U.K.				
British government stocks	105	32	1.8	1.7
Debentures	133	29	2.3	1.5
Preference shares	90	24	1.6	1.3
Ordinary shares	3,644	1,597	63.3	83.6
Other	43	−	.7	−
Total	4,015	1,681	69.7	88.0
Investments overseas				
Ordinary shares	1,545	164	26.8	8.6
Other	99	10	1.7	.5
Total	1,644	173	28.5	9.1
U.S.A.	*1,107*	*74*		
Canada	*123*	*9*		
Sterling area	*224*	*40*		
Other countries	*190*	*51*		
Total assets	5,758	1,910	100.0	100.0

Source: *Bank of England Quarterly Bulletin,* March 1972, Tables 17 and 18.

Table 16.9   Cash flow of investment trust companies, 1968–71

£ million

	1968	1969	1970	1971
Investment trust companies				
New capital & acquisitions	+ 167	+ 54	+ 25	+ 137
Adjustments	– 5	–	– 31	– 2
Revaluations, undistributed income, etc.	+ 1,408	– 735	– 427	+ 1,154
Assets at end of year	*5,583*	*4,902*	*4,469*	*5,758*

Sources: *Bank of England Quarterly Bulletin* (e.g. March 1972, p.155).

Table 16.10   Cash flow of unit trusts, 1960–71

£ million

Year	End-year total funds	Revaluations	Gross sales	Repurchases	Net sales	Repurchases as % of	
						average sales	*gross sales*
1960	201	– 12	27	13	14	*6.7*	*49.7*
1961	237	+ 28	22	14	7	*6.3*	*65.9*
1962	273	+ 2	45	11	34	*4.4*	*24.6*
1963	371	+ 39	77	18	60	*5.5*	*23.0*
1964	429	– 19	100	23	77	*5.5*	*22.7*
1965	522	+ 34	81	22	59	*4.6*	*27.0*
1966	582	– 46	130	24	105	*4.3*	*18.7*
1967	854	+ 188	127	43	84	*6.0*	*33.7*
1968	1,482	+ 370	329	70	258	*6.0*	*21.4*
1969	1,412	– 257	263	77	186	*5.4*	*29.1*
1970	1,398	– 112	171	73	98	*5.3*	*42.9*
1971	1,991	+ 517	204	127	77	*7.6.*	*62.4*

Source: Association of Unit Trust Managers.

two years running, and the level of sales in the second year was little over 50% of the peak reached in 1968.

The levels of repurchases are more complex. We must remember (1) that a very large part of unit sales is to older persons, either before or after retirement, and (2) that most of the units held at the present time have been bought little more than five years ago. One would therefore expect a rising absolute level of repurchases as these older people reached retiring age or died. Up to about 1970 one could have explained the whole behaviour of repurchases in these terms. The extraordinarily high level in 1971, however, calls for further explanation. Tentatively we may assume that many holders who wish to sell will not do so when stock exchange prices are depressed, especially if the sale would be at a price lower than the cost of the units; they therefore wait until the stock exchange recovers somewhat before making their sales. Unit trust managers can take some comfort from this behaviour, because it means that a time of low unit prices, when their remuneration has dropped, is not necessarily made worse by a higher level of repurchases. Some part of the rise in repurchases over recent years may have been caused by a greater sophistication of unitholders, who tend to change their holdings more frequently.

Whatever the discontinuities in their cash flow, unit trust managers nearly always have some new money to invest. Their investment problem is a continuous one.

When it comes to the choice of types of securities and of individual securities, neither investment trusts nor unit trusts have many constraints. The one major constraint which faces both types of institution is that imposed by tax considerations. We have already examined the tax position of investment trusts in detail, and we have seen that one of the major considerations of investment policy is that they should have enough franked income to cover their dividends. This consideration places a limit on the proportion of their portfolio which can usefully be in the form of securities which yield unfranked income—gilt-edged, U.K. debentures and overseas securities. Since the advent of corporation tax in 1965 the proportion of investment trust assets held in overseas securities has gone down somewhat, and investment trusts have taken various other measures to secure their overseas portfolios against the effects of the investment currency rules and to obtain sufficient franked income.

Unit trusts are subject to exactly the same tax regulations as investment trusts. They must pay corporation tax on the total of their unfranked income *less* management expenses, but they have no interest on long-term borrowing to act as an offset to unfranked income along with the management expenses. Since they must distribute all their net income, the constraint imposed by tax considerations is that unfranked income should not be larger than management expenses. Certain of the specialised trusts must obviously ignore this constraint unless they are to change their nature, but for unit trusts as a whole this consideration imposes a lower limit on overseas securities and other sources of unfranked income than is the case with investment trusts.

FUTHER READING

O. P. Stutchbury, *The Management of Unit Trusts* (London: Thomas Skinner, 1964).

H. Burton & D. C. Corner, *Investment and Unit Trusts in Britain and America* (London: Elek, 1970).

C. O. Merriman, *Mutual Funds and Unit Trusts* (London: Pitman, 1965).

F. H. Klopstock, 'Foreign demand for United States equities—the role of offshore mutual funds', *Federal Reserve Bank of New York Monthly Review* (July 1970).

17 Special Investment Agencies

1. GENERAL

Special investment agencies are created to fill gaps in the capital market. These gaps are of several sorts—arising from the smallness of the borrowing bodies or the particular industry in which they operate and a more general gap consisting of lack of facilities for a particular type of finance. The agencies fill these gaps in two main ways: (1) they use their names to borrow on the capital market and then pass on the funds to the deficit units which are unable to borrow in their own names or (2) they pool the risks of certain types of lending and thus enable existing institutions to participate in a form of finance which they are reluctant to undertake without such assistance.

We are concerned in this chapter with a handful of bodies, although these are far from being the sole agencies helping to fill the particular gaps in the capital market. All the agencies which we shall examine are private sector bodies, but alongside them there exist many public sector lending institutions with similar objects. The best-known of these are the National Research Development Corporation (N.R.D.C.), the Film Finance Corporation, the Colonial Development Corporation and the Public Works Loans Board (P.W.L.B.). The last named might be considered a bit outside the range of special investment agencies, since it is the normal channel for government loans to local authorities, but it is included to show the difficulty of drawing the line with public sector bodies. The Treasury and many government departments make loans and grants to various parts of the private sector, and it would be artificial to look only at those which happen to have a separate lending organisation. We have already made the point that the central government is by far the largest financial institution, but it is outside the scope of this book to examine the working of government in its role as a financial intermediary.

In addition to the handful of special investment agencies there are many private sector lending bodies which have very similar functions. They do not qualify for the title of special investment agencies because they are normal companies with a normal range of shareholders, whereas the special investment agencies are usually created by a number of existing financial institutions, often on the prompting of the government or the Bank of England, to perform a service which is thought to be in the national interest.

The tables in this chapter are all drawn from the published accounts of the various agencies, but they are shown in a standardised and abbreviated form. The only departure from normal accounting practice is that bank overdrafts are shown as a form of financing instead of as current liabilities. This is justified by the fact that many of the agencies derive a large part of their funds for lending from the banking system.

2. FINANCE CORPORATION FOR INDUSTRY

Finance Corporation for Industry Ltd. (F.C.I.) was formed in 1945 to fill the gap created by the fact that banks would not in those days grant term loans; the gap was that between the working capital provided by the banking system and the long-term capital provided by the capital market. F.C.I. was intended to be of assistance to larger companies, and the minimum size of loan is £200,000; it thus has a small number of large loans. Its terms of reference provide that the purposes for which the loans are required shall be (in some undefined sense) in the 'national interest' and that it can lend only if finance cannot be obtained on reasonable terms from any other source.

The shareholders of F.C.I. provide a good example of the way in which many of the special investment agencies are formed by a collective pooling of capital resources from a number of different financial institutions. 40% of the capital is held by insurance companies, 30% by investment trust companies and the remaining 30% by the Bank of England. The shares are not quoted, and transfers of shares are restricted so that the proportions held by the different types of institution shall be maintained.

Table 17.1 shows clearly the method of operation adopted by F.C.I. Nearly all the funds for lending are furnished by the London and Scottish clearing banks. The large element of uncalled capital acts as additional security for the loans, because the shareholders can be called upon to furnish the additional capital at any time. F.C.I. is permitted to borrow up to four times its authorised capital. Because the funds for lending are provided by banks, it is normal for the interest rate on loans to vary with base rate (formerly Bank rate) throughout the term of the loan. Loans vary in length according to the needs of the borrower, but they are all intended for cases in which normal bank overdrafts are inadequate or inappropriate and in which permanent capital is not the answer. In many cases F.C.I. takes an option to subscribe for or to

Table 17.1   Balance sheet of Finance Corporation for Industry Ltd.,
31 March 1971

£ thousand

Assets		
Loans and investment		70,235
Net current assets		1,216
	Total	71,451
Financing		
Issued share capital		7,500
(Share capital uncalled £17.5m.)		
Reserves		6,661
Bank advances		57,291
	Total	71,451.

convert part of the loan into an equity stake in the borrowing company.

The particular gap which F.C.I. was designed to fill has largely been closed by the recent willingness of the deposit banks to engage in term loans, just as the earlier move of secondary banks into term loans removed part of the market for F.C.I. It is most unlikely that F.C.I. will find itself without customers, however, because there will always be worthwhile projects which cannot find funds on reasonable terms from the normal sources. The heavy involvement of F.C.I. in the financing of the steel industry during the period when it had been returned to private hands but was faced with a threat of re-nationalisation is an example of the sort of situation which could well recur.

3. INDUSTRIAL AND COMMERCIAL FINANCE CORPORATION

Industrial and Commercial Finance Corporation Ltd. (I.C.F.C.) was formed at the same time as F.C.I., again with the Bank of England as prime mover and a major shareholder, but this time with the London and Scottish clearing banks as the other shareholders. I.C.F.C. is complementary to F.C.I., because it is designed to provide finance for the small and medium-sized company.

The gap which I.C.F.C. was intended to fill has become the most famous of all the gaps in the capital market—the 'Macmillan gap', named after the Macmillan Committee on Finance and Industry, which reported in 1931. The Committee's Report[1] described the gap as follows:

'It has been represented to us that great difficulty is experienced by the smaller and medium-sized businesses in raising the capital which they may from time to time require, even when the security offered is perfectly sound. To provide adequate machinery for raising long-dated capital in amounts not sufficiently large for a public issue, i.e. amounts ranging from small sums up to say £200,000 or more, always presents difficulties. The expense of a public issue is too great in proportion to the capital raised, and therefore it is difficult to interest the ordinary investor by the usual method ...'

The background to this situation is the growth pattern of business. Small firms are usually private companies, which are restricted to fifty shareholders, which cannot solicit subscriptions to their capital from the general public and which impose restrictions on the transfer of their shares. The initial capital is usually subscribed by a sole founder or by a small group of businessmen and their families. While the company remains small, it relies heavily on retained profits, and bank overdrafts are the only source of external funds. It is when these sources become insufficient as the company grows that the gap arises— a gap between what can be provided by the sources used so far and the minimum economic size of issue on the capital market.

Originally I.C.F.C. provided facilities of between £5000 and £200,000; more recently the upper limit for an initial investment has gone up to £300,000 and up to a total of £500,000 for an existing customer. The average size of loans and investments has remained roughly stable at around £60,000 since 1951, so that in real terms I.C.F.C. has steadily lowered the average size of its facilities outstanding. At 31 March 1971 roughly two-thirds of its customers had facilities outstanding below £50,000 and 22% had facilities outstanding below £10,000; only 7% of outstanding balances were over £200,000.

1. *Report of the Committee on Finance and Industry*, Cmd. 3897, 1931, para. 404.

Recently a government committee surveyed the whole field of small firms, and its report, known as the Bolton Report,[2] came to the conclusion that the Macmillan gap had largely been closed. It saw I.C.F.C. as the most important factor, but pointed out that other financial institutions had greatly improved the facilities which they offered to small and medium-sized firms. (1) Finance houses now offered term loans and instalment credit in relatively small sums. (2) Leasing and factoring had developed, although in both cases the really small firms were not adequately catered for. (3) Deposit banks had begun to offer term loans for the smaller firms. (4) A number of venture capital subsidiaries had been formed by deposit and secondary banks.

Table 17.2   Consolidated balance sheet of Industrial and Commercial Finance Corporation Ltd., 31 March 1971

£ thousand

Assets		
Investments & financial facilities		
Quoted investments *(MV £28.8m.)*		17,311
Other		127,201
Freehold and leasehold property		3,160
Plant and equipment		7,285
Ships under charter		22,957
Net current assets		25,723
	Total	203,637
Financing		
Issued share capital		40,000
Reserves		19,167
Debenture stocks		94,633
Bank advances & short-term loans		28,018
Other		21,819
	Total	203,637

Table 17.2 shows that the method of operation of I.C.F.C. is quite different from that of F.C.I. Instead of relying largely on bank finance with a large slice of uncalled capital as additional security, I.C.F.C. borrows on debentures and at short term, thus using its name to secure

2. *Small Firms: Report of the Committee of Inquiry on Small Firms*, Cmnd. 4811, 1971.

finance for passing on to small firms. The extent of short-term finance shown in the 1971 accounts is probably temporary, arising out of the widening gap between short and medium interest rates. The short-term borrowing was covered by a $25 million euro-dollar credit arranged with a consortium of banks.

Table 17.3 shows the nature of the facilities provided by I.C.F.C. More than 50% consists of loans, the rate of interest on which is fixed

Table 17.3   Financial facilities provided by IFC outstanding at 31 March 1971

	£ thousand	Percentages
Loans	91,626	51.5
Preference shares	11,023	6.2
Ordinary shares	34,274	19.2
Property, plant & equipment on lease	10,445	5.9
Post-delivery finance for shipbuilding	7,589	4.3
Ships under charter	22,957	12.9
Total	177,914	100.0

for the duration of the loan. The next largest item, at just under 20% of the total, is ordinary shares, which arise from the practice of often seeking an equity stake in the company to which a loan is being made. I.C.F.C. is like F.C.I. in not seeking to control any of the companies to which it lends; only in exceptional circumstances does it place a nominee on the board of directors. I.C.F.C. is itself an issuing house, and in many cases it nurses its customers up to the point at which they can seek a stock exchange quotation; it then often sells its own holding of ordinary shares in the company.

The remaining items in the table illustrate the wide range of facilities offered by I.C.F.C. One of the methods by which it provides finance is through a sale-and-leaseback agreement for freehold and leasehold properties and by the leasing of plant and equipment. The last item in the table, ships under charter, is a similar leasing operation for ships which is carried out by a subsidiary company, Ship Mortgage Finance Company Ltd. Under the heading of ships a wide range of other craft is included—dredgers, floating platforms and hovercraft. The post-delivery finance for shipbuilding is another function of the same company, which in 1963 was appointed agent for the Ministry of Transport in connexion with the official shipbuilding credit scheme.

I.C.F.C. has a number of other activities designed to help small and medium-sized companies, not all of which show up in the balance sheet; it describes itself as a 'finance service organisation'. It has a subsidiary, Technical Development Capital Ltd., which provides support for technical innovation, and another subsidiary, Industrial Mergers Ltd., which gives assistance to small companies whose growth can be assisted by a suitable merger with another company. Among the services which it provides are management consultancy and computer bureaux. In order to maintain contact with small firms it has a regional network of eighteen branch offices.

Table 17.4   Balance sheet of Estate Duties Investment Trust Ltd., 31 March 1971

£ thousand

Assets		
Investments		
Quoted *(MV £1.9m.)*		361
Unquoted		8,556
Net current assets		− *267*
	Total	8,649
Financing		
Issued share capital		6,655
Reserves		1,494
Debenture stock		500
	Total	8,649

A further special investment agency, Estate Duties Investment Trust Ltd. (always referred to as EDITH), is managed but not owned by I.C.F.C. Its balance sheet is shown in Table 17.4, but this gives no idea of its special function. The background to the operation of EDITH is the fact that the ordinary shares of many small companies are held by the founder and his immediate family and that these shares are the major part of the founder's estate. When he dies, there is a liability to estate duty, which can often be met only by selling up the company. EDITH exists to take over a sufficiently large minority interest in small companies to ensure their continuity when the major shareholder dies; its holding is liquidated to provide the funds for payment of estate duty.

4. AGRICULTURAL LOANS

Two bodies were set up in 1928 to provide loans for agriculture. These
are the Agricultural Mortgage Corporation Ltd. (A.M.C.) for England
and Wales and its Scottish counterpart, Scottish Agricultural Securities
Corporation Ltd. (S.A.S.C.). The shareholders of A.M.C. are the Bank
of England and the London clearing banks; the Scottish clearing banks

Table 17.5   Balance sheets of Agricultural Mortgage Corporation Ltd.,
             and Scottish Agricultural Securities Corporation Ltd.,
             31 March 1971

£ thousand

	AMC	SASC
Assets		
Loans	170,344	10,072
Quoted investments *(MV £9.8m. + £0.7m.)*	12,212	954
Net current assets	− 283	103
Other assets	251	10
Total	182,524	11,139
Financing		
Issued share capital	750	125
Reserves	1,970	304
Debenture stocks and short-term bonds	152,541	10,000
Government loans	11,270	710
Bank advances	15,994	—
Total	182,524	11,139

are the shareholders in S.A.S.C. There are three government nominees
on the board of A.M.C. and a Treasury nominee on the board of S.A.S.C.
Both bodies are able to lend on the first mortgage of agricultural land
and for farm improvement. Only owners of land are eligible, although a
large proportion of loans is for the purchase of an agricultural holding.

Both bodies raise their funds by way of debenture issues, which
have a status on the stock exchange akin to that of local authority debt.
A.M.C. has followed the logic of this status by issuing short-term bonds
similar to local authority negotiable bonds. The debentures are secured
on the mortgage assets. There is also a guarantee fund invested in

British government securities, the money for which came from a government loan.

Both bodies offer a range of types of loan. (1) Long-term loans for ten to forty years include provision for repayment of capital during the period of the loan. Loans may be repaid on an annuity basis (as with normal building society mortgages), in association with an endowment policy or by equal instalments of capital, with interest on the out-

Table 17.6   Consolidated balance sheet of Commonwealth Development Finance Co. Ltd., 31 March 1971

£ thousand

Assets		
Investments		
Loans and debentures		20,938
Shares		5,457
Net current assets		1,459
Other assets		1,017
	Total	28,871
Financing		
Issued share capital		7,329
(Share capital uncalled £19m.)		
Reserves		2,261
Debenture stocks		13,500
Bank advances & short-term loans		5,585
Other		196
	Total	28,871

standing balance. The rate of interest is normally fixed for the full period of the loan, but recently a new facility was offered of having up to 50% of the loan at a variable rate of interest, assessed half-yearly. (2) Eight to ten year 'straight' loans, with repayment of capital on maturity. Up to 50% of one of these loans can be at a variable interest rate. (As from 1 June 1972 up to 50% of ten to forty year borrowing can be on a 'straight loan' basis, and the variable rate option has been extended to the whole of the loan.)

5. COMMONWEALTH DEVELOPMENT FINANCE COMPANY

Commonwealth Development Finance Company Ltd. (C.D.F.C.) was formed in 1953 to invest in business enterprises in the Commonwealth; subject to certain limitations it is prepared to invest in countries outside the Commonwealth. It becomes a minority shareholder in the companies to which it lends, either immediately or by way of conversion rights or share options. Its customers are both companies indigenous to the Commonwealth countries and British companies wishing to undertake business in those countries. Its 160 shareholders include the Bank of England, British industrial companies and financial institutions and the central banks of Commonwealth countries.

C.D.F.C. is another one of the special investment agencies with a large element of uncalled capital. Table 17.6 shows that the greater part of the funds for lending is provided by the raising of debentures. Bank advances, at call, represented just over £5 million of the £5·6 million shown for bank advances and short-term loans.

Index

Bold face references indicate main treatment of the subject